2nd Workshop for NLP Open Source Software (NLP-OSS 2020)

Online
19 November 2020

ISBN: 978-1-7138-2000-0

Printed from e-media with permission by:

Curran Associates, Inc.
57 Morehouse Lane
Red Hook, NY 12571

Some format issues inherent in the e-media version may also appear in this print version.

Printed with permission by Curran Associates, Inc. (2021)

For permission requests, please contact the Association for Computational Linguistics
at the address below.

Association for Computational Linguistics
209 N. Eighth Street
Stroudsburg, Pennsylvania 18360

Phone: 1-570-476-8006
Fax: 1-570-476-0860

acl@aclweb.org

Additional copies of this publication are available from:

Curran Associates, Inc.
57 Morehouse Lane
Red Hook, NY 12571 USA
Phone: 845-758-0400
Fax: 845-758-2633
Email: curran@proceedings.com
Web: www.proceedings.com

2nd Workshop for NLP Open Source Software (NLP-OSS 2020)

Online
19 November 2020

EMNLP 2020

**The Second Workshop for
NLP Open Source Software (NLP-OSS)**

Proceedings of the Workshop

November 19, 2020
(Online)

Introduction

With great scientific breakthrough comes solid engineering and open communities. The Natural Language Processing (NLP) community has benefited greatly from the open culture in sharing knowledge, data, and software. The primary objective of this workshop is to further the sharing of insights on the engineering and community aspects of creating, developing, and maintaining NLP open source software (OSS), which we seldom talk about in scientific publications. Our secondary goal is to promote synergies between different open source projects and encourage cross-software collaborations and comparisons.

We refer to Natural Language Processing OSS as an umbrella term that not only covers traditional syntactic, semantic, phonetic, and pragmatic applications; we extend the definition to include task-specific applications (e.g., machine translation, information retrieval, question-answering systems), low-level string processing that contains valid linguistic information (e.g. Unicode creation for new languages, language-based character set definitions) and machine learning/artificial intelligence frameworks with functionalities focusing on text applications.

In the earlier days of NLP, linguistic software was often monolithic and the learning curve to install, use, and extend the tools was steep and frustrating. More often than not, NLP OSS developers/users interact in siloed communities within the ecologies of their respective projects. In addition to the engineering aspects of NLP software, the open source movement has brought a community aspect that we often overlook in building impactful NLP technologies.

An example of precious OSS knowledge comes from SpaCy developer Montani (2017), who shared her thoughts and challenges of maintaining commercial NLP-OSS, such as handling open issues on the issue tracker, model release and packaging strategy and monetizing NLP OSS for sustainability.[1]

More recently, the Transformers library created by Hugging Face, has gathered much interest from the community by open sourcing implementations to use pretrained weights of BERT-like models, in a clean and well-organized structure. The interoperability of various pretrained models trained with different tools in one library enables quick benchmarking across the models, as well as developing best practices for reading/saving serialized interoperable.[2]

We hope that the NLP-OSS workshop becomes the intellectual forum to collate various open source knowledge beyond the scientific contribution, announce new software/features, promote the open source culture and best practices that go beyond the conferences.

---

[1] https://ines.io/blog/spacy-commercial-open-source-nlp
[2] models.https://github.com/huggingface/transformers

Organizers:

Lucy Park, NAVER Corp.
Masato Hagiwara, Octanove Labs LLC
Dmitrijs Milajevs, KPMG LLP
Nelson Liu, Stanford University
Geeticka Chauhan, Massachusetts Institute of Technology
Liling Tan, Rakuten Institute of Technology

Program Committee:

Aline Paes, Universidade Federal Fluminense
Amandalynne Paullada, University of Washington
Amittai Axelrod, DiDi Chuxing (Los Angeles)
Anca Dumitrache, FD Mediagroep
Arwen Twinkle Griffioen, Zendesk Inc.
Carolina Scarton, University of Sheffield
Chris Hokamp, AYLIEN
Christian Federmann, Microsoft Research
Dan Simonson, BlackBoiler, LLC
Daniel Braun, TU Muchen
Dave Howcroft, Heriot-Watt University
David Przybilla, Idio
Delip Rao, AI Foundation
Denny Britz, Prediction Machines
Ehsan Khoddammohammadi, Elsiever
Eleftherios Avramidis, German Research Center for Artificial Intelligence
Elijah Rippeth, MITRE Corporation
Emiel van Miltenburg, Vrije Universiteit Amsterdam
Emily Dinan, Facebook AI
Eric Schles, New York University & Sema4
Fabio Kepler, Unbabel
Francis Bond, Nanyang Technological University
Fred Blain, University of Sheffield
Gerard Dupont, Airbus
Ian Soboroff, NIST
Ignatius Ezeani, Lancaster Uni
Ines Montani, Explosion AI
James Bradbury, Google
Joel Nothman, University of Sydney
Karin Sim Smith, Lingo24
Kevin Cohen, University of Colorado Boulder
KhengHui Yeo, Institute for Infocomm Research
Laura Martinus, Explore AI

Madison May, Indico Data Solutions
Marcel Bollmann, University of Copenhagen
Marcos Zampieri, University of Wolverhampton
Mary Ellen Foster, University of Glasgow
Marzieh Fadaee, University of Amsterdam
Matthew Honnibal, Explosion AI
Micah Shlain, Allen Institute for Artificial Intelligence
Michael Wayne Goodman, Nanyang Technological University
Mohd Sanad Zaki Rizvi, Microsoft Research India
Moshe Wasserblat, Intel
Muthu Kumar Chandrasekaran, NUS, SG
Nahid Alam, Ople Inc
Paul P Liang, Carnegie Mellon University
Philipp Koehn, Johns Hopkins University
Sandya Mannarswamy , Independent Researcher
Shamil Chollampatt, Rakuten Institute of Technology
Sharat Chikkerur, Microsoft
Shilpa Suresh, Singapore Managment University
Shubhanshu Mishra, Twitter
Steve DeNeefe, SDL Research Labs
Steve Sloto, AWS AI
Steven Bethard, University of Arizona
Steven Bird, Charles Darwin University
Sung Kim, NAVER Corp.
Svitlana Vakulenko, University of Amsterdam
Tareq Al-Moslmi, University of Bergen
Thomas Kober, Rasa Technologies GmbH
Tilahun Abedissa, Addis Ababa University
Tommaso Teofili, Roma Tre University & Red Hat
Tommi A Pirinen, University of Hamburg
Varun Kumar, Amazon Alexa
Vlad Niculae, Instituto de Telecomunicações
Yves Peirsman, NLP Town

Invited Speaker:

Chip Huyen, Stanford & Snorkel AI
Spencer Kelly, Freelance Developer
Thomas Wolf, Huggingface

Invited Talks

Principles of Good Machine Learning Systems Design
Chip Huyen, Stanford & Snorkel AI

On Typing: Historical and Potential Interactions in Word-processing
Spencer Kelly, Freelance Developer

An Introduction to Transfer Learning in NLP and HuggingFace
Thomas Wolf, Huggingface

Principles of Good Machine Learning Systems Design

Chip Huyen
Stanford & Snorkel AI

Abstract

This talk covers what it means to operationalize Machine Learning (ML) models. It starts by analyzing the difference between ML in research vs. in production, ML systems vs. traditional software, as well as myths about ML production.

It then goes over the principles of good ML systems design and introduces an iterative framework for ML systems design, from scoping the project, data management, model development, deployment, maintenance, to business analysis. It covers the differences between DataOps, ML Engineering, MLOps, and data science, and where each fits into the framework.

The talk ends with a survey of the ML production ecosystem, the economics of open source, and open-core businesses.

Biography

Chip Huyen is an engineer who develops tools and best practices for machine learning production. She's currently with Snorkel A and she'll be teaching Machine Learning Systems Design at Stanford. Previously, she was with Netflix, NVIDIA, Primer. She's also the author of four best-selling Vietnamese books.

On Typing: Historical and Potential Interactions in Word-processing

Spencer Kelly
Freelance Developer

Abstract

People love typing, in a surprising and universal way. In this talk we look at the development of word-processing, and the design-decisions in this historic interface. Can NLP contribute to word-processing, without making it worse? What would a text-centered computer really look like? We look at the history of punctuation, keyboards, and markup languages. We look at Wikipedia, text-editors, and data structures - with the goal of authoring usable data in text.

Biography

Spencer is the author of compromise - a small natural language processing library for the browser. He is a web developer, and maintainer of open-source libraries. His background is in the semantic web and Wikipedia. Today his work focuses on creating infographics. His open-source work is funded by freelance web development. He is from Toronto, Canada.

An Introduction to Transfer Learning in NLP and HuggingFace

Thomas Wolf
Huggingface

Abstract

In this talk I'll start by introducing the recent breakthroughs in NLP that resulted from the combination of Transfer Learning schemes and Transformer architectures. The second part of the talk will be dedicated to an introduction of the open-source tools released by HuggingFace, in particular our Transformers, Tokenizers and Datasets libraries and our models.

Biography

Thomas Wolf is co-founder and Chief Science Officer of HuggingFace. His team is on a mission to catalyze and democratize NLP research. Prior to HuggingFace, Thomas gained a Ph.D. in physics, and later a law degree. He worked as a physics researcher and a European Patent Attorney.

Table of Contents

Workshop Program

A Framework to Assist Chat Operators of Mental Healthcare Services

Thiago de Oliveira Madeira, Heder Soares Bernardino, Jairo Francisco de Souza,
Nathália Munck Machado, Bruno Marcos Pinheiro da Silva, Alexandre Vieira Pereira Pacelli
Universidade Federal de Juiz de Fora, Brazil
{madeira, heder, jairo.souza}@ice.ufjf.br
{muncknathalia, brunomarcospsilva, alexandrevpp}@gmail.com

Henrique Gomide
Universidade Federal de Viçosa, Brazil
henriquepgomide@gmail.com

Abstract

Conversational agents can be used to make diagnoses, classify mental states, promote health education, and provide emotional support. The benefits of adopting conversational agents include widespread access, increased treatment engagement, and improved patient relationships with the intervention. We propose here a framework to assist chat operators of mental healthcare services, instead of a fully automated conversational agent. This design eases the adverse effects of applying chatbots in mental healthcare. The proposed framework is capable of improving the quality and reducing the time of interactions via chat between a user and a chat operator. We also present a case study in the context of health promotion on reducing tobacco use. The proposed framework uses artificial intelligence, specifically natural language processing (NLP) techniques, to classify messages from chat users. A list of suggestions is offered to the chat operator, with topics to be discussed in the session. These suggestions were created based on service protocols and the classification of previous chat sessions. The operator can also edit the suggested messages. Data collected can be used in the future to improve the quality of the suggestions offered.

1 Introduction

Due to recent advances in Natural Language Processing (NLP), chatbots are being developed and used in different domains, such as customer support, voice assistant, and medicine. Particularly, chatbots are used in medicine to diagnose medical conditions based on patients' symptoms (Srivastava and Singh, 2020), to classify mental states (Patel et al., 2019), and to promote health education (Brixey et al., 2017).

Besides, chatbots have been developed for providing advice and education on mental health conditions. Pereira and Díaz (2019) reviewed the academic literature and found applications that targeted neurological disorders (e.g., insomnia, dementia, depression), well-being, addictions, sexually-transmitted-diseases, among others. The authors pointed out that the field is still in its youth and is more focused on developing rather than testing and assessing efficacy. They also suggested that chatbots are more likely to promote health and behavior change (e.g., Andersson and Cuijpers (2009)) if integrated with human support, which had been overlooked by studies included in their review.

However, physicians believe that actual chatbots cannot effectively care for all of the patients' needs (Palanica et al., 2019). Standard chatbots cannot display human emotion, and cannot provide detailed diagnosis and treatment due to their limitation in consider all of the factors of the patient (Palanica et al., 2019). Palanica et al. (2019) also stated that healthcare chatbots can be a risk to patients when the patients do not fully understand a diagnosis.

In this work, we describe an open-source framework for developing a chatbot with human support using well-known NLP libraries. Then, we showcase an application for promoting smoking cessation using the framework.

2 Related Work

In this section, we discuss the ethical implications of developing chatbots for mental health. We also present examples of applications of healthcare assistance, emphasizing their benefits and their distinct architectural designs. Lastly, we distinguish our proposed framework from the current literature showing why it can potentially be an improvement.

People diagnosed with a mental disorder are not always inclined to seek treatment (Corrigan

1

Proceedings of Second Workshop for NLP Open Source Software (NLP-OSS), pages 1–7
Virtual Conference, November 19, 2020. ©2020 Association for Computational Linguistics

et al., 2014). Bendig, Erb, Schulze-Thuesing, and Baumeister (2019) discuss the causes of this behavior, such as concerns about social opinion and negative attitudes towards drug-based treatment options, negative experiences with professional caregivers, lack of insight into their illness, and accessibility barriers like time or location (shift workers and rural communities). Chatbots are a potential solution as they can be available 24/7 over an internet connection (Cameron et al., 2018; Abd-Alrazaq et al., 2020).

It is indispensable to address ethical and social implications when applying Artificial Intelligence (AI) in healthcare (Fiske et al., 2019; Kretzschmar et al., 2019). The first thing to note is that regulations are often general and are one step behind AI's advances. Fiske et al. (2019) provided an analysis of the risks and benefits of implementing AI solutions to mental health from an ethical perspective. According to the authors, conversational agents can potentially stop working and incorporate human biases. Also, security is a high priority due to the nature of the information. Conversational agents users must be aware that they are not interacting with a human, but with an AI. Benefits include new opportunities for reaching patients (e.g., fear of stigmatization), increase treatment engagement, and improve patients' response (Fiske et al., 2019).

In addition to the ethical perspective, most healthcare conversational agents still have to be tested in randomized controlled trials. It can better determine how well the agents can assist a patient in the long run (Abd-Alrazaq et al., 2020). Research should also focus on providing better guidelines for chatbots development (Fiske et al., 2019).

Conversational agents are designed accordingly with their goals. They can have a specific task to accomplish. Symptoma (Martin et al., 2020) and Aquabot (Mujeeb et al., 2017) are examples of conversational agents for specific tasks. Symptoma differentiates more than 20,000 diseases, whereas Aquabot diagnoses Autism and Achluophobia (the fear of darkness).

On the other hand, there are non-specific task agents, such as Vik (Chaix et al., 2019) and Clara (Miner et al., 2020). The former helps patients diagnosed with breast cancer, their relatives, and friends with advice and reminders. The latter is used to share information, suggest behavior, and offer emotional support during the COVID-19 pandemic.

As this work aims to implement a conversational assistant and apply it to promote smoking cessation, it is suitable to examine the impacts of a chatbot acting in this environment. In a two-arm controlled trial, Perski et al. (2019) compared the standard version of the pro version of the Smokefree app against the standard version plus a chatbot. A total of 54,214 smokers participated in the study. After one month, researchers compared the groups for engagement (number of login sessions) and self-reported quit rates. They found that chatbot plus the standard version led to a 101% increase of engagement. However, quit rates did not differ statistically (Perski et al., 2019).

There are some examples of real-time messaging recommendations. In (TouchPal, 2008; Microsoft, 2010), keyboard applications recommend emojis based on the typed words. Gmail has a smart reply feature to suggest short responses to emails (Henderson et al., 2017). An example of a tool that supports humans in a conversation is SolutionChat (Lee et al., 2020). The framework proposed by the authors of SolutionChat can assist the moderators of a discussion group. It provides an environment where multiple users can discuss matters, express their thoughts, and vote for potential solutions. There is the presence of a human moderator to guide the debate. The moderators in charge of managing discussions are often overloaded. SolutionChat can offer suggestions to moderators and ends up promoting time-saving and even quality improvement to the discussion. According to the authors, their work is the first moderator assistance system for online chat conversation to combine summarization and real-time messaging suggestions.

Moreover, to the best of our knowledge, SolutionChat is the framework that comes closest to our proposal. Both can read messages and assist a human operator as suggesting intents. The difference between the frameworks lies in their objectives. SolutionChat's authors designed it for management purposes. It aims to identify discussion stages and featured opinions in a structured discussion. Our proposed framework aims to answer questions and offer information in the form of a *Question and Answer* approach. Also, a human is present here to confirm the suggestions. Consequently, this supervision can be used to provide implicit feedback. Healthcare is an area where the adoption of a fully automated chatbot is delicate. The presence of a human guiding the conversation is desirable.

To overcome the risks of deploying a fully automated chatbot and benefit from the NLP techniques' advantages, we propose a conversational agent that assists human operators. The framework can classify users' utterances and provides content suggestions.

3 General Architecture

A framework to provide support to an operator of an assistance chat in the healthcare field is proposed here. Instead of being a fully automated chatbot, the proposal provides support for the chat operators. The main benefits of using the proposal are improving the quality of the conversation and reducing its time. When chat operators are supplanted (which is a latent tendency for our case study), the framework assists their training, giving them suggestions for the conversation in practice. More details are in Section 4. This section describes the general architecture, which considers the benefits of advances in NLP and overcomes the opposing sides of applying chatbots in healthcare.

In the proposed framework, the user's intent is identified when a message is sent to the chat operator. When a user sends multiple messages, they are gathered together into a single one. As a result, one intent is predicted for this new merged message. Next, a set of potential answers related to that predicted intent is selected and displayed to a chat operator. The operator then selects and edits the message. Subsequently, the operator sends the answer to the user. Data generated during the framework's execution is collected to improve the quality of the classification and suggestions. Figure 1 presents the proposed framework.

3.1 Intents and Suggestions

Users of chatting services may have many different intents. Chatbots must be aware of the users' intent to trigger a proper response. An architectural strategy to handle it is via a set of predefined intents defined by domain specialists. This set covers as much as possible queries that a chatbot may encounter (Srivastava and Prabhakar, 2020). It is worth mentioning that in addition to domain-specific queries, conversational agents are also susceptible to receive unexpected or unprompted messages [1]. An intent set covering greetings, ac-

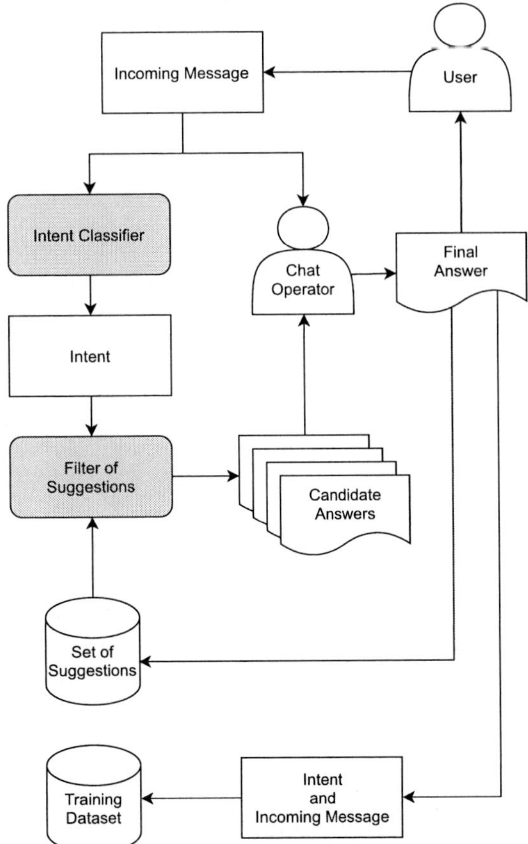

Figure 1: General Architecture

knowledgments, reactions, and off-topic chitchat can manage surprising situations.

Domain specialists should also anticipatedly design a set of suggestions for each intent previously established. The proposed framework has a filter component responsible for displaying suggestions related to the intent predicted by the classifier to the chat operator. However, the predicted intent may not adequately address the user's utterance. In this case, the framework has to handle a misclassification. The next section discusses the classification problems and also the training set used to fit the model.

3.2 Classification and Training Set

To classify a user's utterance's intent is the same to identify what the user is trying to accomplish with its interaction. An intent classifier is trained with dialogue utterances labeled with its intents. The classification consists of predicting the intent of a given user's utterance. It is a one-off problem, where each user's utterance is associated with a

---

[1] https://rasa.com/docs/rasa/
dialogue-elements/small-talk/

single intent (Schuurmans and Frasincar, 2019).

A chatbot may misclassify the intent of a user's utterance (Joigneau, 2018). To overcome this obstacle and enhance the accuracy of intent classifiers, Joigneau (2018) proposes methods to perform reclassifications. However, the proposed framework does not intend to substitute a human completely. Its main goal is to support a real-time conversation between a user and a chat operator. Therefore, each misclassified intent can be correctly labeled by the human operating the chat. We define it as a misclassification when the framework can not predict at least one intent with a probability of σ higher than a threshold σ_l. In Section 4, we describe a case study of our framework and how we handled the misclassification issue.

The data used for training the classifier consists of a corpus labeled with intents from the fixed set of predefined intents. Corpus's text can either be extracted from real conversations or manually crafted. Data augmentation can also be used to increase a corpus' size (Wei and Zou, 2019). The quality and size of the dataset can impact on the classifier's accuracy (Srivastava and Prabhakar, 2020).

3.3   Feedback Module

The framework includes a feedback module. The feedback occurs in two situations. In the first situation, there is implicit feedback. When the chat operator uses a suggestion from the framework, it means that the classifier correctly predicted the intent of the user's utterance. In this case, the framework uses the input data to improve the training dataset. The training dataset incorporates the pair of the user's utterance and the predicted intent.

In the second situation, the feedback is slighter more explicit. It occurs when the chat operator edits a suggested message. The proposed framework stores the new message in the set of suggestions and can recommend it in the future.

Each time the chat operator uses a suggestion without editing, the framework adds up an internal score for that suggestion. The higher the suggestion's score, the higher is the priority for the framework to display it to the chat operator.

4   Case Study: Viva sem Tabaco

Viva sem Tabaco (VST) is a web-based intervention for smoking cessation. The website's content was adapted from evidence-based guidelines for treating tobacco addiction (Gomide et al., 2016).

VST provides information, quizzes, personalized quit smoking plans, and a chat. In this platform's chat, the chat operator is a counselor. A counselor is responsible for identifying a user's concerns and answering appropriately. The counselors are undergraduate students of health courses, trained by the psychologists' team. Due to the healthcare area's delicateness, it is desirable that counselors are well trained and adequately follow the intervention's guidelines.

A team of psychologists guarantees the quality of the VST platform's content. They create the web site's content and train new counselors. The psychologists also composed a document containing instructions for the chat interactions, specifying how the counselors should assist a user looking for help on VST. According to this document, the counselor must identify the user's need and answer with appropriate content from the VST's website.

The current version of the open-source implementation of the proposed framework is available in the Python programming language[2]. We are incorporating the framework into VST to enhance the counselor's performance by (i) keeping the conversation focused and avoid ambiguities, and (ii) reducing the response time. We used spaCy and Rasa. The former is a free, open-source library for Natural Language Processing. We imported its pretrained word embedding for Portuguese. The latter is an open-source machine learning framework, developed to implement contextual AI assistants and chatbots. Rasa is used for generating models to classify intents of an utterance. Rasa uses SpaCy's word embeddings models to represent texts numerically.

4.1   Intents and Suggestions

Through the analysis of the document of chat assistance's instructions, we created a set of potential intents, which are listed in Table 1. The proposed framework classifies the user's utterances into one of these intents.

The team of psychologists also conceived a set of predetermined suggestions for each intent of Table 1. For each intent, the framework exhibits the set of suggestions associated with it to the counselor. So, the counselor can choose one of the suggestions and reply to the user's message. Alternatively, the message can be edited to fit the conversation bet-

---

[2] https://github.com/t-madeira/Chatbot_VsT-AeS

Greetings
Technical Issues
Chitchat
Acknowledgments
Farewell
TBD (To Be Determined)
Benefits of stopping and risks of smoking
Financial costs
Withdrawal and craving
Weight Gain
Anxiety and Depression
How to deal with withdrawal
Overcoming cravings
Medication
Ways to quit: gradual or cold-turkey
How to avoid relapses
Learning from previous quit attempts
Identifying slips and relapses
Most common relapses causes

Table 1: Intents defined to classify the user's utterances.

ter. Figure 2 is a representation of the counselor's perspective using the application.

4.2 Classification and Training

For the classification of the user's utterances, Rasa uses the Sklearn Intent Classifier. This classifier consists of an SVM optimized via grid search. The classifier returns probabilities σ associated with each intent, making it possible to rank the predicted intents. Due to the small size of the training data used in this case study, the classification process still has a place for improvement via feedback by gathering usage data.

In the ranking of classified intents, there can be at least one with a probability σ higher than a threshold σ_h. In this case, our implementation displays to the counselor the intents associated with the intent with the highest probability. We defined a misclassification when any predicted intent has a probability σ higher than a threshold σ_l. In this case, there is a fallback intent name TBD (to be determined). The counselor still receives suggestions but most likely has to handle the conversation by itself. When this situation occurs, the framework records the message sent by the user for future analysis.

Lastly, the highest intent's probability σ can be higher than σ_l but still lower than σ_h. That be-

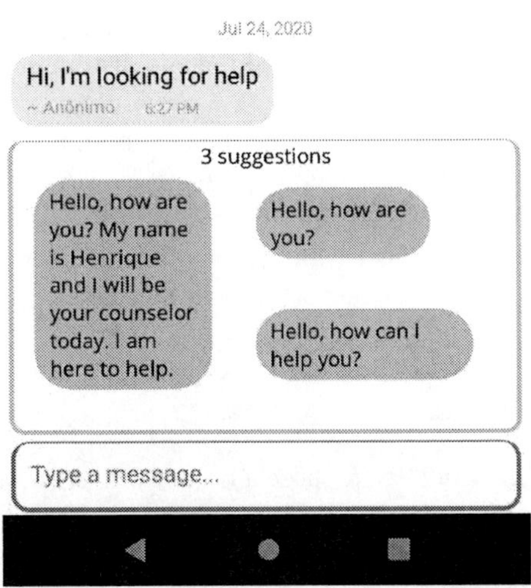

Figure 2: Counselor's view in the implemented application with examples of suggestions provided. In this illustration, the messages are answers for the intent "Greetings".

ing so, our implementation of the framework asks the counselor to solve the uncertainty and manually choose an intent from the top 3 intents of the probabilities ranking.

We used real-world conversations from the VST platform to train the classifying model. The training set consists of 373 interactions between users and counselors. We manually labeled each message presented in an interaction between a user and a counselor with a potential intent from Table 1. If it was a user's message, we labeled as trying to figure out what he or she intended to say or ask. If it was a counselor's message, we labeled as trying to figure out the user's intention that the counselor was trying to answer. We labeled 1100 messages from the 373 interactions.

4.3 Feedback

The framework can improve itself with data gathered from its usage. Each time a counselor sends a message to a user, the framework adds the intent predicted and the user's utterance to the training dataset. If the highest probability σ of an intent classification in the ranking is lower than the threshold σ_h, the counselor solves the uncertainty. In this case, the intent added to the training dataset is the one chosen by the counselor. Another exception is if the framework classifies the user's utterance as TBD. In this case, nothing is added to the training dataset, and the user's utterance is recorded for future analysis.

When the counselor edits a suggestion offered by the framework, the edited suggestion is added to the set of suggestions. As previously explained in Section 3.3, each time the chat operator uses a suggestion without editing, the framework adds up an internal score for it. The higher the suggestion's score, the higher is the priority for the framework to display it to the chat operator.

5 Concluding Remarks and Future Works

In this work, we propose a framework to assist chat operators of healthcare systems. The framework classifies the user's utterances into intents. It provides real-time suggestions to the chat operators of mental healthcare services.

The advantages of adopting the proposed framework include improving the quality and reducing the time of conversations between users and counselors. The conversation's quality is increased due to the assumption that the framework's suggestions reduce ambiguity and rambling in the chat operator's discourse. The conversation's time is reduced due to the real-time suggestions offered by the framework. The chat operator does not waste time overthinking or searching for appropriate content to answer the users. A fully automated approach would be faster, but removing the human from the framework would lead to the negative characteristics of conversational agents present in the literature. Users looking for mental assistance are often mentally weakened, and a human can handle unusual situations. However, through the feedback module and further evaluation, the framework may become fully automated in the future.

Future works include adopting the framework in other health-related domains, gathering and analyzing data of its usage. The framework can be easily adapted to be used in other domains, by adding new training data, sets of intents, and sets of suggestions. Reports from users and counselors can be collected in order to evaluate the framework's efficacy.

Acknowledgments

This study was financed in part by the Coordination of Superior Level Staff Improvement – Brazil (CAPES) – Finance Code 001. The authors also thank the financial support provided by FAPEMIG (APQ-00337-18), CNPq (312682/2018-2), and UFJF.

References

Alaa Ali Abd-Alrazaq, Asma Rababeh, Mohannad Alajlani, Bridgette M Bewick, and Mowafa Househ. 2020. Effectiveness and safety of using chatbots to improve mental health: Systematic review and meta-analysis. *Journal of Medical Internet Research*, 22(7):e16021.

Gerhard Andersson and Pim Cuijpers. 2009. Internet-based and other computerized psychological treatments for adult depression: A meta-analysis. *Cognitive Behaviour Therapy*, 38(4):196–205.

Eileen Bendig, Benjamin Erb, Lea Schulze-Thuesing, and Harald Baumeister. 2019. The next generation: chatbots in clinical psychology and psychotherapy to foster mental health–a scoping review. *Verhaltenstherapie*, pages 1–13.

Jacqueline Brixey, Rens Hoegen, Wei Lan, Joshua Rusow, Karan Singla, Xusen Yin, Ron Artstein, and Anton Leuski. 2017. Shihbot: A facebook chatbot for sexual health information on hiv/aids. In *Proceedings of the 18th Annual SIGdial Meeting on Discourse and Dialogue*, page 370–373. Association for Computational Linguistics.

Gillian Cameron, David Cameron, Gavin Megaw, Raymond Bond, Maurice Mulvenna, Siobhan O'Neill, Cherie Armour, and Michael McTear. 2018. Assessing the usability of a chatbot for mental health care. In *International Conference on Internet Science*, pages 121–132. Springer.

Benjamin Chaix, Jean-Emmanuel Bibault, Arthur Pienkowski, Guillaume Delamon, Arthur Guillemassé, Pierre Nectoux, and Benoît Brouard. 2019. When chatbots meet patients: one-year prospective study of conversations between patients with breast cancer and a chatbot. *JMIR cancer*, 5(1):e12856.

Patrick W Corrigan, Benjamin G Druss, and Deborah A Perlick. 2014. The impact of mental illness stigma on seeking and participating in mental health care. *Psychological Science in the Public Interest*, 15(2):37–70.

Amelia Fiske, Peter Henningsen, and Alena Buyx. 2019. Your robot therapist will see you now: ethical implications of embodied artificial intelligence in psychiatry, psychology, and psychotherapy. *Journal of medical Internet research*, 21(5):e13216.

H. P. Gomide, H. S. Bernardino, K. Richter, L. F. Martins, and T. M. Ronzani. 2016. Development of an open-source web-based intervention for brazilian smokers – viva sem tabaco. *BMC Medical Informatics and Decision Making*, 16:103.

Matthew Henderson, Rami Al-Rfou, Brian Strope, Yun-Hsuan Sung, László Lukács, Ruiqi Guo, Sanjiv Kumar, Balint Miklos, and Ray Kurzweil. 2017. Efficient natural language response suggestion for smart reply. *arXiv preprint arXiv:1705.00652*.

Axel Joigneau. 2018. Utterances classifier for chatbots' intents.

Kira Kretzschmar, Holly Tyroll, Gabriela Pavarini, Arianna Manzini, Ilina Singh, and NeurOx Young People's Advisory Group. 2019. Can your phone be your therapist? young people's ethical perspectives on the use of fully automated conversational agents (chatbots) in mental health support. *Biomedical Informatics Insights*, 11:1178222619829083.

Sung-Chul Lee, Jaeyoon Song, Eun-Young Ko, Seongho Park, Jihee Kim, and Juho Kim. 2020. Solutionchat: Real-time moderator support for chat-based structured discussion. In *Proceedings of the 2020 CHI Conference on Human Factors in Computing Systems*, pages 1–12.

Alistair Martin, Jama Nateqi, Stefanie Gruarin, Nicolas Munsch, Isselmou Abdarahmane, and Bernhard Knapp. 2020. An artificial intelligence-based first-line defence against covid-19: digitally screening citizens for risks via a chatbot. *bioRxiv*.

Microsoft. 2010. Microsoft swiftkey keyboard.

Adam S Miner, Liliana Laranjo, and A Baki Kocaballi. 2020. Chatbots in the fight against the covid-19 pandemic. *npj Digital Medicine*, 3(1):1–4.

Sana Mujeeb, Muhammad Hafeez Javed, and Tayyaba Arshad. 2017. Aquabot: a diagnostic chatbot for achluophobia and autism. *Int J Adv Comput Sci Appl*, 8.

Adam Palanica, Peter Flaschner, Anirudh Thommandram, Michael Li, and Yan Fossat. 2019. Physicians' perceptions of chatbots in health care: cross-sectional web-based survey. *Journal of medical Internet research*, 21(4):e12887.

Falguni Patel, Riya Thakore, Ishita Nandwani, and Santosh Kumar Bharti. 2019. Combating depression in students using an intelligent chatbot: A cognitive behavioral therapy. In *2019 IEEE 16th India Council International Conference (INDICON)*, page 1–4. IEEE.

Juanan Pereira and Óscar Díaz. 2019. Using health chatbots for behavior change: A mapping study. *Journal of Medical Systems*, 43(5):135.

Olga Perski, David Crane, Emma Beard, and Jamie Brown. 2019. Does the addition of a supportive chatbot promote user engagement with a smoking cessation app? an experimental study. *Digital health*, 5:2055207619880676.

Jetze Schuurmans and Flavius Frasincar. 2019. Intent classification for dialogue utterances. *IEEE Intelligent Systems*, 35(1):82–88.

Prakhar Srivastava and Nishant Singh. 2020. Automatized Medical Chatbot (Medibot). In *2020 International Conference on Power Electronics & IoT Applications in Renewable Energy and its Control (PARC)*, pages 351–354, Mathura, Uttar Pradesh, India. IEEE.

Saurabh Srivastava and TV Prabhakar. 2020. Intent sets: Architectural choices for building practical chatbots. In *Proceedings of the 2020 12th International Conference on Computer and Automation Engineering*, pages 194–199.

TouchPal. 2008. Touchpal keyboard.

Jason Wei and Kai Zou. 2019. Eda: Easy data augmentation techniques for boosting performance on text classification tasks. *arXiv preprint arXiv:1901.11196*.

ARBML: Democratizing Arabic Natural Language Processing Tools

Zaid Alyafeai
Dhahran, Saudi Arabia
g201080740@kfupm.edu.sa

Maged S. Al-Shaibani
Dhahran, Saudi Arabia
g201381710@kfupm.edu.sa

Abstract

Automating natural language understanding is a lifelong quest addressed for decades. With the help of advances in machine learning and particularly, deep learning, we are able to produce state of the art models that can imitate human interactions with languages. Unfortunately, these advances are controlled by the availability of language resources. Arabic advances in this field , although it has a great potential, are still limited. This is apparent in both research and development. In this paper, we showcase some NLP models we trained for Arabic. We also present our methodology and pipeline to build such models from data collection, data preprocessing, tokenization and model deployment. These tools help in the advancement of the field and provide a systematic approach for extending NLP tools to many languages.

1 Introduction

Arabic language is a widely used language. It is the sixth most spoken language in the world (Farghaly and Shaalan, 2009). It also has a noticeable influence on many other languages around the globe. Compared to English, Arabic is morphologically a very rich language (Habash, 2010) with relatively complex grammar and cursive script including the use of diacritics. Diacritics are special characters added to Arabic writing to replace the absence of short vowels. Moreover, Arabic has a variety of dialects that may greatly differ in style and grammar.

Arabic content on the web is vastly emerging with great diversity in style and subjects, written in many dialects. This opportunity opens doors for research to hone machine capabilities to automate language understanding and comprehension. However, Arabic inherent characteristics makes it difficult to resolve and require linguistic expertise.

Natural Language Processing is gaining a lot of attractions within the research community. The aim is to create machines that can replicate or exceed human language understanding. On another perspective, a lot of effort is invested to develop software applications to port research advances to industry. Another effort is also directed to facilitate researchers job by automating routine workflows, cleaning and preprocessing, for example. Some examples of this are huggingface, allennlp and flare. Most of these tools are designed to work for English or generalize the pipeline to work for other languages. Arabic, although it is not as popular as other languages tools, also has some contributions, but in the linguistics part only. Some promising examples are MADAMIRA (Pasha et al., 2014), FARASA (Abdelali et al., 2016), Adawat (Zerrouki, 2020) and CAMeL NLP (Obeid et al., 2020). These tools address a large spectrum of NLP tasks for Arabic like segmentation, part of speech tagging, named entity recognition, diacritizatoin and grammatical analysis. However, most of these tools are not using the recent advances in NLP. Unfortunately, in the Arabic community, open source contribution is not widely accepted. This is due to the copyrights restrictions made by authors as some of these tools are not licensed for commercial use. Although, the source code can be delivered on demand, this mechanism is still not development friendly with unclear methodology and processes to version control and collaboration.

In this paper, we introduce our contribution to the Arabic language open source community. We present a collection of models that can be utilized and improved to solve a wide variety of many Natural Language Processing tasks. Moreover, we introduce three libraries for scrapping, cleaning and tokenization. We also provide notebooks that can be easily used to replicate our experiments. We provide a flexible code design that can be implemented and extended to other languages.

Proceedings of Second Workshop for NLP Open Source Software (NLP-OSS), pages 8–13
Virtual Conference, November 19, 2020. ©2020 Association for Computational Linguistics

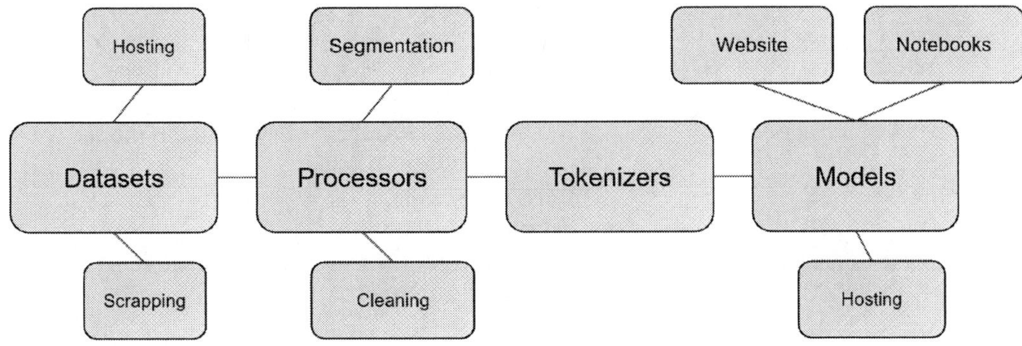

Figure 1: ARBML pipeline.

2 Design

We created ARBML in the hope of democratizing Arabic natural language processing by creating a set of demos as well as tools for making it easy to use for novice users, developers and researchers. We revise the NLP pipeline and make it suitable for Arabic as indicated in Figure 1. We provide datasets, preprocessors, tokenizers and models. Furthermore, we host notebooks that can replicate our experiments and help users to understand how to do each task. In the next few sections we explain our main tools.

2.1 Tnqeeb

This is a repository that hosts a collections of data gathered from multiple websites. This data is collected using scrapy, a well-known python scraping library. This implementation comes as a mature result after a sequence of scraping efforts using low level python libraries like *requests* and *beautifulsoup*. The current available data is a collected from three giant Arabic poetry websites: aldiwan, poetry encyclopedia, and poets gate. We plan to scrape as many sources as possible on a given topic, poetry, news, or blogs for instance. We then group, do initial processing, and de-duplicate these data into an individual repositories to be easy to work on.

2.2 Tnkeeh

Tnkeeh is a library that is responsible for preprocessing datasets. It has four main procedures

- Cleaning: this module is used for cleaning datasets by removing diacritics, extra spaces, remove English characters and remove

Tatweel - a character used for increasing the length of characters.

- Segmentation: we use FARASA (Abdelali et al., 2016) for segmenting texts into morphemes.

- Normalization: Arabic letters can appear in different forms due to different Unicode's representing the same characters. We created a dictionary to map the same representations to their fixed characters.

- Data Splitting: we use a set of of procedures to split different types of datasets depending on the tasks to train on. For instance, we can split datasets if they are for unsupervised, classifications or parallel tasks.

- Reading: this module reads the different modes of datasets into python variables.

2.3 Tkseem

Tkseem is a tokenization library that implements multiple tokenization algorithms optimized for Arabic. We provide six categories of tokenizers with a simple interface.

- Word Tokenizer: splits words based on white spaces.

- Character Tokenizer: splits characters depending on their position on text.

- Sentencepiece Tokenizer: A wrapper for the sentencepiece library (Kudo and Richardson, 2018).

Dataset	Description
Arabic Digits	70,000 images (28 x 28) (El-Sawy et al., 2016)
Arabic Letters	16,759 images (32 x 32) (El-Sawy et al., 2016)
Arabic Poems	146,604 poems scrapped from (Aldiwan, 2013)
Arabic Translation	100,000 parallel Arabic to English translation ported from OpenSubtitles
Product Reviews	1,648 reviews on products ported from (ElSahar and El-Beltagy, 2015)
Image Captions	30,000 Image paths with captions extracted and translated from (Lin et al., 2014)
Arabic Poem Meters	55,440 verses with their associated meters collected from (Aldiwan, 2013)
Arabic Fonts	516 images (100 x100) for two fonts

Table 1: Collected and preprocessed Datasets.

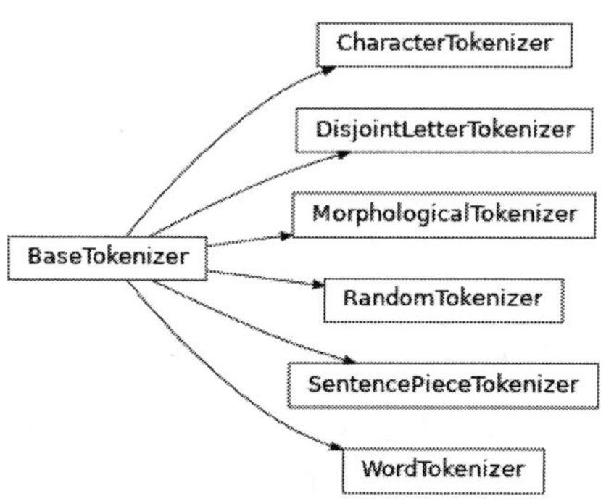

Figure 2: Base Tokenizer.

Function	Description
`tokenize`	Converts text to tokens
`encode`	Converts tokens to integers
`decode`	Converts integers to tokens
`detokenize`	Converts tokens back to text
`encode_sentences`	Encodes a set of sentences
`load_model`	Loads a saved model
`save_model`	Saves a given model
`encode_and_save`	Encodes and saves the model as numpy array

Table 2: Tokenizer functions.

- Morphological Tokenizer: splits words based on morphology. This was trained using Madamira (Pasha et al., 2014) on a large Arabic news corpus.

- Random Tokenizer: tokenizes text based on random splitting of words.

- Disjoint Letter Tokenizer: splits based on letters that are not connected in Arabic script writing.

All these tokenizers extend a common Base class Tokenizer (Figure 2) that implements the main functionalities like *encode*, *decode*, *tokenize*, and *detokenize* (Table 2). One useful function of these tokenizers is the ability to serialize them and load them on demand. This approach relaxes the time for training specially on large corpus. We also provide different methods for optimization like caching and memory-mapped files to speed up the tokenization process.

These tokenizers are evaluated on three NLP tasks: sentiment analysis, Arabic meter poetry classification and neural machine translation.

2.4 Models and Datasets

This main module is responsible for storing and serving different datasets and models. The main purpose is to give a real time experience for different models that are related to Arabic and NLP. The main strategy is highlighted in Figure 3. This procedure shows off our main approach for making the models easily accessible via different interfaces. We follow three main stages

- Preprocess Dataset: we collect and preprocess different datasets that are related to different tasks. Table 1 shows the main datasets that we collected. The datasets cover different areas like translation, sentiment analysis, poem classification, etc.

- Training: We train the model on the datasets

Model	Description
Arabic Diacritization	Simple RNN model ported from (Barqawi, 2017)
Arabic2English Translation	seq2seq with Attention
Arabic Poem Generation	CharRNN model with multinomial distribution
Arabic Words Embedding	N-Grams model ported from Aravec (Soliman et al., 2017)
Arabic Sentiment Classification	RNN with Bidirectional layer
Arabic Image Captioning	Encoder-Decoder architecture with attention
Arabic Word Similarity	Embedding layers using cosine similarity
Arabic Digits Classification	Basic RNN model with classification head
Arabic Speech Recognition	Basic signal processing and classification
Arabic Object Detection	SSD Object detection model
Arabic Poems Meter Classification	Bidirectional GRU from (Al-shaibani et al., 2020)
Arabic Font Classification	CNN

Table 3: Trained and deployed models.

using Keras with TensorFlow backend (Abadi et al., 2016). We used Keras because it is straight forward to convert the models using TensorFlow.js. We use Google Colab for training our models with proper documentations in a tutorial-like procedure. We make all the model available in this repository.

- Deployment: We make the models available in the browser using TensorFlow.js (Smilkov et al., 2019). TensorFlow.js is part of the TensorFlow ecosystem that supports training and inference of machine learning models in the browser. The main advantage is a device-agnostic approach that makes all the models available on any device that has a browser. Moreover, the models are light and can run offline. The main motive is to make the models easily accessible via a simple interface like the browser. This makes it easier for users to test different models in a few clicks.

We make all the datasets and models available on our GitHub : https://github.com/ARBML/ARBML. The procedure we follow makes it easier for developers to contribute to our project. Moreover, our strategy is language-agnostic and encourages extending it to other languages. In Table 4 we compare ARBML against other tools in the literature.

3   End-user Experience

ARBML provides a solid contribution from two main perspectives:

- Educational Perspective: People who wish to learn NLP will greatly benefit from ARBML.

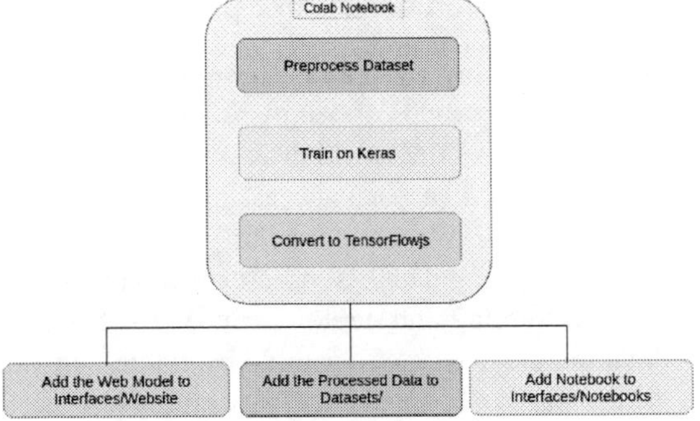

Figure 3: Models procedure.

ARBML provides various training models with different techniques for both, command line and web interfaces using Keras and TensorFlow.js. The pipeline from cleaning the dataset to model training and deployment is documented in details as Colab Notebooks. Additionally, users can test different models directly in the browser. For instance, we have a translation model where the users can enter a statement in Arabic and it will be translated in English.

- Development and Research: From development prospective a lot of tools like tnqeeb, tkseem and tnkheeh can be used in different projects related to NLP. Furthermore, developers can use our deployed models as prototype to test the possibility of implementing them in industry. Moreover researchers can use our pipeline to create new state-of-the-art models by using our models as a starting point.

Framework	Methodology	Models Availability	Datasets	Accessibility	Generalization	Programming Language	Web
Stanford CoreNLP (Manning et al., 2014)	Probabilistic models	N/A	N/A	The source code can be downloaded from the main website	Multilingual	Java	No
MADAMIRA (Pasha et al., 2014)	Morphological analysis developed with machine learning tools	Models are available via the API and the web interface	N/A	Source code is accessible by email for education uses only	Arabic	Java	Yes
FARASA (Abdelali et al., 2016)	Different Models built with machine learning	Binaries are available but the code used for training the models is not	N/A	Source code for the API is accessible by email with license for educational uses only	Arabic	Java	Yes
CAMeL NLP (Obeid et al., 2020)	Multitasks learning models	Models are available for download	Yes	Source code is open on GitHub	Arabic	Python	No
Adawat (Zerrouki, 2020)	General tools not necessarily built with machine learning	N/A	Yes	Source code is open on GitHub	Arabic	Python	Yes
ARBML	NLP tasks built with the recent advances in NLP field	Models are available on GitHub	Yes	Source code is available on GitHub along with the training notebooks	Generalizable	Python	Yes

Table 4: Comparing ARBML against other Arabic NLP tools.

4 Conclusion and future plans

Recently, many NLP tools have been developed but they only focus on English. In this work we showcased ARBML which is a set of tools that make Arabic NLP easily accessible through different interfaces. We target the NLP pipeline starting from scrapping datasets, preprocessing, tokenization to training and deployment. We focused on making the design of our tools language-agnostic and hence can be extended to many other languages, given we change the morphological aspects. We collected many datasets that can be easily used by researchers to develop new models. We also designed three libraries tnqeeb, tnkeeh and tkseem which can be easily utilized by developers to develop tools to support Arabic NLP. The tools utilize the morphological nature of Arabic to provide different functionalities that are unique for Arabic.

We plan to add many other models and make them easily accessible through the browser. Mainly, our next step is to tackle more advanced models like transformers (Vaswani et al., 2017). Furthermore, we want to apply different techniques like quantization and distillation to make the models available in the browser. Moreover, we would like to focus on light models like MobileBERT (Sun et al., 2020), retrain it for Arabic and make it readily usable in the browser.

5 Acknowledgements

ARBML is and open source project that will keep growing in the future. We would like to thank all developers who shared ideas, models and helped us address different issues.

References

Martín Abadi, Paul Barham, Jianmin Chen, Zhifeng Chen, Andy Davis, Jeffrey Dean, Matthieu Devin, Sanjay Ghemawat, Geoffrey Irving, Michael Isard, et al. 2016. Tensorflow: A system for large-scale machine learning. In *12th {USENIX} symposium on operating systems design and implementation ({OSDI} 16)*, pages 265–283.

Ahmed Abdelali, Kareem Darwish, Nadir Durrani, and Hamdy Mubarak. 2016. Farasa: A fast and furious segmenter for arabic. In *Proceedings of the 2016 conference of the North American chapter of the association for computational linguistics: Demonstrations*, pages 11–16.

Maged S Al-shaibani, Zaid Alyafeai, and Irfan Ahmad. 2020. Meter classification of arabic poems using deep bidirectional recurrent neural networks. *Pattern Recognition Letters*.

Aldiwan. 2013. Aldiwan.

Zerrouki Barqawi. 2017. Shakkala, arabic text vocalization.

Ahmed El-Sawy, EL-Bakry Hazem, and Mohamed Loey. 2016. Cnn for handwritten arabic digits recognition based on lenet-5. In *International conference on advanced intelligent systems and informatics*, pages 566–575. Springer.

Hady ElSahar and Samhaa R El-Beltagy. 2015. Building large arabic multi-domain resources for sentiment analysis. In *International Conference on Intelligent Text Processing and Computational Linguistics*, pages 23–34. Springer.

Ali Farghaly and Khaled Shaalan. 2009. Arabic natural language processing: Challenges and solutions. *ACM Transactions on Asian Language Information Processing (TALIP)*, 8(4):1–22.

Nizar Y Habash. 2010. Introduction to arabic natural language processing. *Synthesis Lectures on Human Language Technologies*, 3(1):1–187.

Taku Kudo and John Richardson. 2018. Sentencepiece: A simple and language independent subword tokenizer and detokenizer for neural text processing. *arXiv preprint arXiv:1808.06226*.

Tsung-Yi Lin, Michael Maire, Serge Belongie, James Hays, Pietro Perona, Deva Ramanan, Piotr Dollár, and C Lawrence Zitnick. 2014. Microsoft coco: Common objects in context. In *European conference on computer vision*, pages 740–755. Springer.

Christopher D Manning, Mihai Surdeanu, John Bauer, Jenny Rose Finkel, Steven Bethard, and David Mc-Closky. 2014. The stanford corenlp natural language processing toolkit. In *Proceedings of 52nd annual meeting of the association for computational linguistics: system demonstrations*, pages 55–60.

Ossama Obeid, Nasser Zalmout, Salam Khalifa, Dima Taji, Mai Oudah, Bashar Alhafni, Go Inoue, Fadhl Eryani, Alexander Erdmann, and Nizar Habash. 2020. Camel tools: An open source python toolkit for arabic natural language processing. In *Proceedings of The 12th Language Resources and Evaluation Conference*, pages 7022–7032.

Arfath Pasha, Mohamed Al-Badrashiny, Mona T Diab, Ahmed El Kholy, Ramy Eskander, Nizar Habash, Manoj Pooleery, Owen Rambow, and Ryan Roth. 2014. Madamira: A fast, comprehensive tool for morphological analysis and disambiguation of arabic. In *Lrec*, volume 14, pages 1094–1101.

Daniel Smilkov, Nikhil Thorat, Yannick Assogba, Ann Yuan, Nick Kreeger, Ping Yu, Kangyi Zhang, Shanqing Cai, Eric Nielsen, David Soergel, et al. 2019. Tensorflow. js: Machine learning for the web and beyond. *arXiv preprint arXiv:1901.05350*.

Abu Bakr Soliman, Kareem Eissa, and Samhaa R El-Beltagy. 2017. Aravec: A set of arabic word embedding models for use in arabic nlp. *Procedia Computer Science*, 117:256–265.

Zhiqing Sun, Hongkun Yu, Xiaodan Song, Renjie Liu, Yiming Yang, and Denny Zhou. 2020. Mobilebert: a compact task-agnostic bert for resource-limited devices. *arXiv preprint arXiv:2004.02984*.

Ashish Vaswani, Noam Shazeer, Niki Parmar, Jakob Uszkoreit, Llion Jones, Aidan N Gomez, Łukasz Kaiser, and Illia Polosukhin. 2017. Attention is all you need. In *Advances in neural information processing systems*, pages 5998–6008.

Taha Zerrouki. 2020. Towards an open platform for arabic language processing.

CLEVR Parser: A Graph Parser Library for Geometric Learning on Language Grounded Image Scenes

Raeid Saqur[1,2]
[1]University of Toronto Computer Science
[2]Vector Institute for Artificial Intelligence
raeidsaqur@cs.toronto.edu

Ameet Deshpande
Department of Computer Science
Princeton University
asd@cs.princeton.edu

Abstract

The CLEVR dataset has been used extensively in language grounded visual reasoning in Machine Learning (ML) and Natural Language Processing (NLP) domains. We present a **graph parser library** for CLEVR, that provides functionalities for object-centric attributes and relationships extraction, and construction of structural graph representations for dual modalities. Structural order-invariant representations enable geometric learning and can aid in downstream tasks like language grounding to vision, robotics, compositionality, interpretability, and computational grammar construction. We provide three extensible main components – **parser, embedder, and visualizer** that can be tailored to suit specific learning setups. We also provide out-of-the-box functionality for seamless integration with popular deep graph neural network (GNN) libraries. Additionally, we discuss downstream usage and applications of the library, and how it accelerates research for the NLP research community[1].

1 Introduction

The CLEVR dataset (Johnson et al., 2017a) is a modern 3D incarnation of historically significant shapes-based datasets like SHRDLU (Winograd, 1970), used for demonstrating AI efficacy on language understanding (Ontanon, 2018; Winograd, 1980; Hudson and Manning, 2018). Although originally aimed at the visual question answering (VQA) problem (Santoro et al., 2017; Hu et al., 2018), its versatility has seen its use in diverse ML domains, including extensions to physics simulation engines for language augmented hierarchical reinforcement learning (Jiang et al., 2019) and causal reasoning (Yi et al., 2019).

---

[1]Code is available at - https://github.com/raeidsaqur/clevr-parser

(a) Question on image (Figure 2): 'Is the color of the *metal block* that is *right* of the *yellow rubber object* the same as the *large metal cylinder*?'

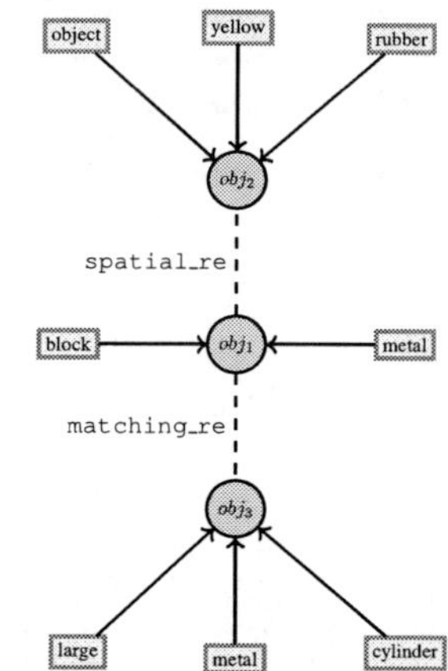

(b) Image (Figure 2) scene graph parsed representation

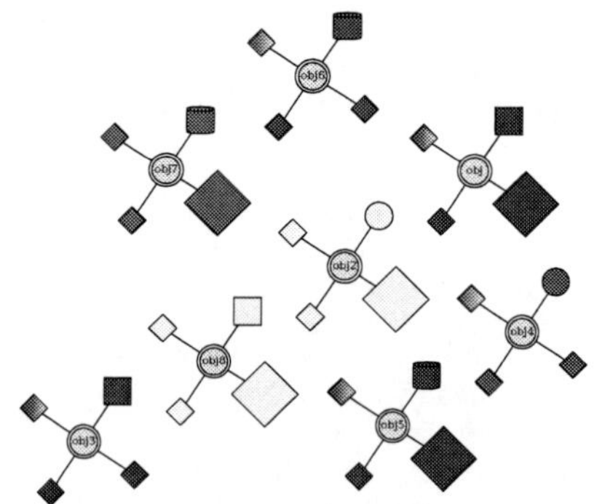

Figure 1: A question about a CLEVR image visualized as multimodal parsed graphs

Parallelly, research interest in geometric learning and GNN (Kipf and Welling, 2016; Schlichtkrull et al., 2018; Hamilton et al., 2017) based techniques have seen a dramatic surge in recent deep learning zeitgeist. In this focused paper, we present a library that allows easy integration and application of geometric representation learning on CLEVR dataset

Proceedings of Second Workshop for NLP Open Source Software (NLP-OSS), pages 14–19
Virtual Conference, November 19, 2020. ©2020 Association for Computational Linguistics

tasks - enabling the NLP research community to apply GNN based techniques to their research (see 4).

The library has three main (extensible) components: 1. **Parser**: allows extraction of graph structured relationships among objects of the environment – both for textual questions, and semantic image scene graphs, 2. **Embedder**: allows generation of latent embeddings using any models or desired backend of choice (like PyTorch[2]), 3. **Visualizer**: provides tools for visualizing structural graphs and latent embeddings.

2 Background

CLEVR Environment The dataset consists of images with rendered 3D objects of various shapes, colors, materials, and sizes, along with corresponding image scene graphs containing visual semantic information. Templated question generation on the images allows the creation of complex questions that test various aspects of scene understanding. The original dataset contains $\approx$1M questions generated from $\approx$100k questions with 90 question template families that can be broadly categorized into five question types: count, exist, numerical comparison, attribute comparison, and query.

Figure 2: A CLEVR image

The dataset also comes with a defined domain-specific-language (DSL) function library $\mathcal{F}$, containing primitive functions that can be composed together to answer questions on CLEVR images (Johnson et al., 2017b). We delegate further details of this dataset to (Johnson et al., 2017a) and the appendix A.

3 CLEVR-PARSER

Here we describe each of the main library components in detail.

---

[2]https://pytorch.org/

3.1 Parser

Text The parser takes a language utterance, which can be a question, caption or command, that is valid in the CLEVR environment, and outputs a structural graph representation – G_s, capturing object attributes, spatial relationships (`spatial_re`), and attribute similarity based matching predicates (`matching_re`) in the textual input. This is implemented by adding a CLEVR object entity recognizer (NER) in the NLP parse pipeline as depicted by Figure 3. Note that the NER is permutationally equivariant to the object attributes – i.e. a 'large red rubber ball' will be detected as an object by any of these spans: 'red large rubber ball', 'large ball', 'ball' etc.

Figure 3: Entity visualization

Images The parser takes image scene graphs as input and outputs a structural graph – G_t. The synthesized image scenes accompanying the original dataset can be used as input. Alternatively, parsed image scenes generated using any modern semantic image segmentation method (for e.g. 'Mask-RCNN' (He et al., 2017)) can also be used as input (Yi et al., 2018). A visualized example of a parsed image is shown in figure 4a. For the ease of reproducibility, we also include a curated dataset '1obj' with parsed image scenes using Mask-RCNN semantic segmentation (AppendixA).

While we provide a concrete implementation using the SpaCy[3] NLP library, any other library like the Stanford Parser[4], or NLTK[5] could be used in its place. The output of the parser from a question and image is depicted in Figure 1.

3.2 Embedder

The embedder provides 'word-embedding' (Mikolov et al., 2017) based representation of input text utterances and image scenes using a pre-trained language model (LM). The end-user can instantiate the embedder with a preferred LM, which could be a simple one-hot representation of the CLEVR environment vocabulary, or a large transformer based SotA LMs like BERT, GPT-2, XLNet (Peters et al., 2018; Devlin et al.,

---

[3]https://spacy.io/
[4]https://nlp.stanford.edu/software/lex-parser.shtml
[5]https://www.nltk.org/

2018; Radford et al., 2019; Yang et al., 2019). The embedder uses the parser (see section 3.1) generated graphs $\mathcal{G}_s, \mathcal{G}_t$ – where graph $\mathcal{G}_s$ and $\mathcal{G}_t$ are defined as generic graph $\mathcal{G} = (\mathcal{V}, \mathcal{E}, \mathcal{A})$, where $\mathcal{V}$ is the set of nodes $\{1,2,..\}$, $\mathcal{E}$ is the set of edges, and $\mathcal{A}$ is the adjacency matrix – and returns $\mathcal{X}$, E, the feature matrices of the nodes and edges respectively:

$$\mathcal{X}_s, A_s, E_s \leftarrow \text{EMBED}(S)$$
$$\mathcal{X}_t, A_t, E_t \leftarrow \text{EMBED}(T), \tag{1}$$

The output signature of the embedder is a tuple: $(\mathcal{X}, A, E)$, which matches the fundamental data-structure of popular geometric learning libraries like PyTorch Geometric (Fey and Lenssen, 2019), thus allowing seamless integration. We show a concrete implementation of this use case using **PyTorch Geometric** (Fey and Lenssen, 2019) and Pytorch in 3.3.2.

3.3 Visualizer

We provide multiple visualization tools for analyzing images, text, and latent embeddings.

3.3.1 Visualizing Structural Graphs

This visualizer sub-component enables visualization of the multimodal structural graph outputs – G_s, G_t – by the parser (see 3.1) using `Graphviz` and `matplotlib`.

Visualizing Images Image graphs (G_t) can have a large number of objects and attributes. For ease of viewing, attributes like size, shape (e.g. cylinder), color (e.g. yellow), and material (e.g. metallic) are displayed as nodes of the graph (Figure 4a). We explain elements of Figure 4a to describe the **legend** in greater detail. The double circles represent the objects, and the adjacent nodes are their attributes. The *shape* is depicted using the actual shape (e.g. the cyan cylinder – $obj2$), and the other attributes are depicted as diamonds. The *size* of one of the diamonds depicts if the object is small or large, e.g. the large cyan diamond attached to $obj2$ means that it is large. The *color* of all the attribute nodes depicts the color of the object (e.g. the cyan color of $obj2$). The presence of a gradient in the remaining diamond depicts the *material* of the object. For example, the gradient in the diamond attached to $obj4$ means that it is *metallic*, and the solid fill for $obj2$ means that it is *rubber*. While this legend is a little lengthy, we found that it makes visualiza-tion easier, but the user can choose to revert to the simpler setting of using text to depict the attributes.

Visualizing Text Text corresponding to an image is a partially observable subset of objects, their relationships, and attributes. The dependency graph of the text is visualized just like the images, with only the observable information being depicted (Figure 4b).

Composing image and text We also provide an option to view an image and the text in the same graph. By connecting corresponding object nodes from the image and text, we create a bipartite graph that allows us to visualize all the information that an image-text pair contains (Figure 4c). Additional examples from the visualizer are presented in appendix A.4.

3.3.2 Visualizer - Embeddings

We also provide a visualizer to analyze the embeddings produced by using methods in section 3.2. We use t-SNE (Maaten and Hinton, 2008), which is a method used to visualize high-dimensional data on 2 or 3 dimensions. We also offer clustering support to allow grouping of similar embeddings together. Both image (Frome et al., 2013) and word embeddings (Mikolov et al., 2013) from learned models have the nice property of capturing semantic information, and our visualizers capture this semantic similarity information in the form of clusters.

Figure 5 plots the embeddings for questions drawn from two different distributions *train* and *test*, which represent semantically different sequences, and they separate out into distinct clusters.

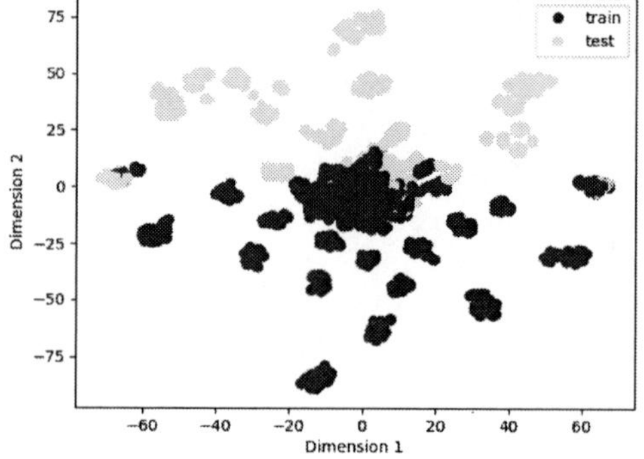

Figure 5: Questions from two different distributions which form separate clusters

Similarly, Figure 6 analyzes embeddings drawn from 7 different templates. Questions that corre-

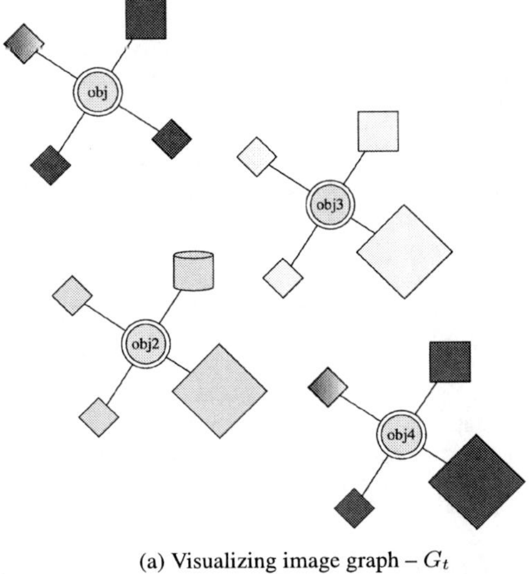

(a) Visualizing image graph – G_t

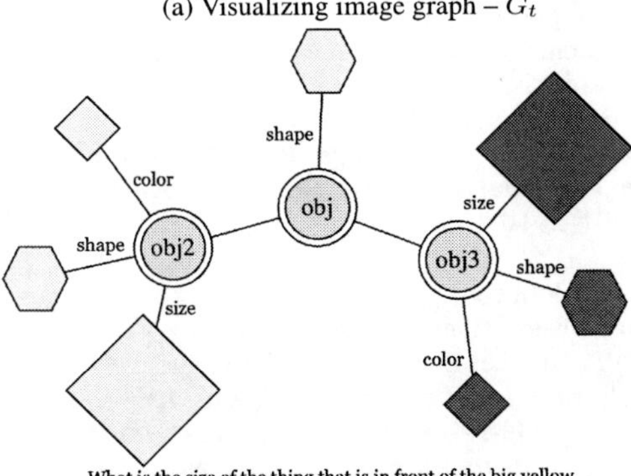

(b) Visualizing text graph – G_s

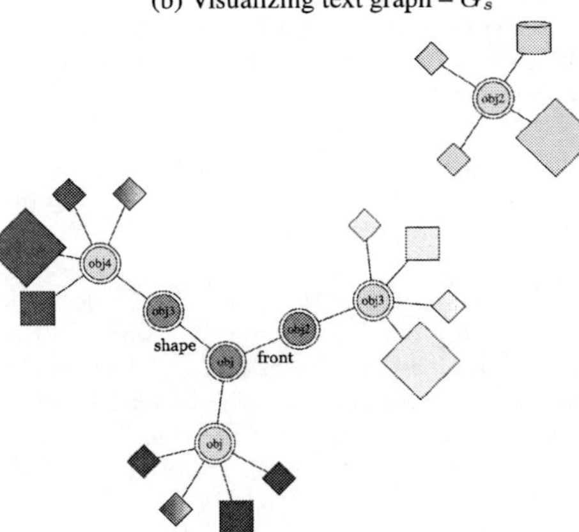

(c) Visualizing joint (image and text) graph – G_u for the above two figures

Figure 4: Visualizing G_s, G_t, G_u

spond to the same templates form tight clusters while being far away from other questions.

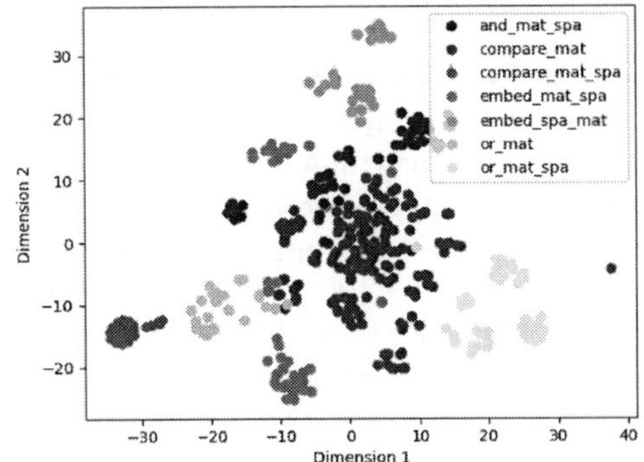

Figure 6: Questions from 7 different templates forming tight clusters

4 Related Work and Applications

Some lines of work attempt to generate scene graphs for images. The Visual Genome library (Krishna et al., 2017), in a real-world image setting, is a collection of annotated images (from Flickr, COCO) and corresponding knowledge graph associations. The work of (Schuster et al., 2015) and the corresponding library which is a part of the Stanford NLP library[6], allows scene graph generation from text (image caption) as input.

Our work is orthogonal to these in that our target dataset is synthetic, which allows full control over the generation of images, questions, and ground truth semantic program chains. Thus, coalesced with our library's functionalities, it allows end-to-end (e2e) control over experimenting on every modular aspect of research hypotheses (see 4.1). Further, our work premises on providing multimodal representations – including ground-truth paired graph (joint graph $G_u \leftarrow (G_s, G_t)$) – which has interesting downstream research applications.

4.1 Usages and Applications

Applications of language grounding in ML/NLP research are quite broad. To avoid sounding overly grandiose, we exemplify possible applications citing work that pertains to the CLEVR dataset.

Recent work by (Bahdanau et al., 2019) has shown lack of distributional robustness and compositional generalization (Fodor et al., 1988) in NLP. Permutation equivariance within local linguistic component groups has been shown to help with language compositionality (Gordon et al., 2020). Graph-based representations are intrinsically or-

---

[6]https://nlp.stanford.edu/software/scenegraph-parser.shtml

17

der invariant – thus, may help with language compositionality research. Language augmented reward mechanisms are a dense topic in concurrent (human-in-the-loop) reinforcement learning (Knox and Stone, 2012; Griffith et al., 2013), robotics (Knox et al., 2013; Kuhlmann et al., 2004), long-horizon, hierarchical POMDP problems in general (Kaplan et al., 2017) – like command completion in physics simulators (Jiang et al., 2019). Other applications could be in program synthesis and interpretability (Mascharka et al., 2018), causal reasoning (Yao, 2010), and general visually grounded language understanding (Yu et al., 2016).

In general, we expect and hope that any existing line or domain of work in NLP using the CLEVR dataset (hundreds, based on citations), will benefit from having graph-based representational learning aided by our proposed library.

References

Dzmitry Bahdanau, Harm de Vries, Timothy J O'Donnell, Shikhar Murty, Philippe Beaudoin, Yoshua Bengio, and Aaron Courville. 2019. Closure: Assessing systematic generalization of clevr models. *arXiv preprint arXiv:1912.05783*.

Jacob Devlin, Ming-Wei Chang, Kenton Lee, and Kristina Toutanova. 2018. Bert: Pre-training of deep bidirectional transformers for language understanding. *arXiv preprint arXiv:1810.04805*.

Matthias Fey and Jan Eric Lenssen. 2019. Fast graph representation learning with pytorch geometric. *arXiv preprint arXiv:1903.02428*.

Jerry A Fodor, Zenon W Pylyshyn, et al. 1988. Connectionism and cognitive architecture: A critical analysis. *Cognition*, 28(1-2):3–71.

Andrea Frome, Greg S Corrado, Jon Shlens, Samy Bengio, Jeff Dean, Marc'Aurelio Ranzato, and Tomas Mikolov. 2013. Devise: A deep visual-semantic embedding model. In *Advances in neural information processing systems*, pages 2121–2129.

Jonathan Gordon, David Lopez-Paz, Marco Baroni, and Diane Bouchacourt. 2020. Permutation equivariant models for compositional generalization in language. In *International Conference on Learning Representations*.

Shane Griffith, Kaushik Subramanian, Jonathan Scholz, Charles L Isbell, and Andrea L Thomaz. 2013. Policy shaping: Integrating human feedback with reinforcement learning. In *Advances in neural information processing systems*, pages 2625–2633.

William L Hamilton, Rex Ying, and Jure Leskovec. 2017. Representation learning on graphs: Methods and applications. *arXiv preprint arXiv:1709.05584*.

Kaiming He, Georgia Gkioxari, Piotr Dollár, and Ross Girshick. 2017. Mask r-cnn. In *Proceedings of the IEEE international conference on computer vision*, pages 2961–2969.

Han Hu, Jiayuan Gu, Zheng Zhang, Jifeng Dai, and Yichen Wei. 2018. Relation Networks for Object Detection. Technical report.

Drew A. Hudson and Christopher D. Manning. 2018. Compositional attention networks for machine reasoning. Technical report.

Yiding Jiang, Shixiang Shane Gu, Kevin P Murphy, and Chelsea Finn. 2019. Language as an abstraction for hierarchical deep reinforcement learning. In *Advances in Neural Information Processing Systems*, pages 9414–9426.

Justin Johnson, Bharath Hariharan, Laurens van der Maaten, Li Fei-Fei, C Lawrence Zitnick, and Ross Girshick. 2017a. Clevr: A diagnostic dataset for compositional language and elementary visual reasoning. In *Proceedings of the IEEE Conference on Computer Vision and Pattern Recognition*, pages 2901–2910.

Justin Johnson, Bharath Hariharan, Laurens Van Der Maaten, Judy Hoffman, Li Fei-Fei, C Lawrence Zitnick, and Ross Girshick. 2017b. Inferring and executing programs for visual reasoning. In *Proceedings of the IEEE International Conference on Computer Vision*, pages 2989–2998.

Russell Kaplan, Christopher Sauer, and Alexander Sosa. 2017. Beating atari with natural language guided reinforcement learning. *arXiv preprint arXiv:1704.05539*.

Thomas N Kipf and Max Welling. 2016. Semi-supervised classification with graph convolutional networks. *arXiv preprint arXiv:1609.02907*.

W Bradley Knox and Peter Stone. 2012. Reinforcement learning from simultaneous human and mdp reward. In *Proceedings of the 11th International Conference on Autonomous Agents and Multiagent Systems-Volume 1*, pages 475–482. International Foundation for Autonomous Agents and Multiagent Systems.

W Bradley Knox, Peter Stone, and Cynthia Breazeal. 2013. Training a robot via human feedback: A case study. In *International Conference on Social Robotics*, pages 460–470. Springer.

Ranjay Krishna, Yuke Zhu, Oliver Groth, Justin Johnson, Kenji Hata, Joshua Kravitz, Stephanie Chen, Yannis Kalantidis, Li-Jia Li, David A Shamma, et al. 2017. Visual genome: Connecting language and vision using crowdsourced dense image annotations. *International Journal of Computer Vision*, 123(1):32–73.

Gregory Kuhlmann, Peter Stone, Raymond Mooney, and Jude Shavlik. 2004. Guiding a reinforcement learner with natural language advice: Initial results in robocup soccer. In *The AAAI-2004 workshop on supervisory control of learning and adaptive systems*. San Jose, CA.

Laurens van der Maaten and Geoffrey Hinton. 2008. Visualizing data using t-sne. *Journal of machine learning research*, 9(Nov):2579–2605.

David Mascharka, Philip Tran, Ryan Soklaski, and Arjun Majumdar. 2018. Transparency by design: Closing the gap between performance and interpretability in visual reasoning. In *Proceedings of the IEEE conference on computer vision and pattern recognition*, pages 4942–4950.

Tomas Mikolov, Edouard Grave, Piotr Bojanowski, Christian Puhrsch, and Armand Joulin. 2017. Advances in pre-training distributed word representations. *arXiv preprint arXiv:1712.09405*.

Tomas Mikolov, Ilya Sutskever, Kai Chen, Greg S Corrado, and Jeff Dean. 2013. Distributed representations of words and phrases and their compositionality. In *Advances in neural information processing systems*, pages 3111–3119.

Santiago Ontanon. 2018. Shrdlu: A game prototype inspired by winograd's natural language understanding work. In *Fourteenth Artificial Intelligence and Interactive Digital Entertainment Conference*.

Matthew E Peters, Mark Neumann, Mohit Iyyer, Matt Gardner, Christopher Clark, Kenton Lee, and Luke Zettlemoyer. 2018. Deep contextualized word representations. *arXiv preprint arXiv:1802.05365*.

Alec Radford, Jeffrey Wu, Rewon Child, David Luan, Dario Amodei, and Ilya Sutskever. 2019. Language models are unsupervised multitask learners. *OpenAI Blog*, 1(8):9.

Adam Santoro, David Raposo, David G.T. Barrett, Mateusz Malinowski, Razvan Pascanu, Peter Battaglia, and Timothy Lillicrap. 2017. A simple neural network module for relational reasoning. *Advances in Neural Information Processing Systems*, 2017-Decem(Nips):4968–4977.

Michael Schlichtkrull, Thomas N Kipf, Peter Bloem, Rianne Van Den Berg, Ivan Titov, and Max Welling. 2018. Modeling relational data with graph convolutional networks. In *European Semantic Web Conference*, pages 593–607. Springer.

Sebastian Schuster, Ranjay Krishna, Angel Chang, Li Fei-Fei, and Christopher D Manning. 2015. Generating semantically precise scene graphs from textual descriptions for improved image retrieval. In *Proceedings of the fourth workshop on vision and language*, pages 70–80.

Terry Winograd. 1970. Shrdlu.

Terry Winograd. 1980. What does it mean to understand language? *Cognitive science*, 4(3):209–241.

Zhilin Yang, Zihang Dai, Yiming Yang, Jaime Carbonell, Russ R Salakhutdinov, and Quoc V Le. 2019. Xlnet: Generalized autoregressive pretraining for language understanding. In *Advances in neural information processing systems*, pages 5754–5764.

Shuiying Yao. 2010. Stage/individual-level predicates, topics and indefinite subjects. In *Proceedings of the 24th Pacific Asia Conference on Language, Information and Computation*, pages 573–582, Tohoku University, Sendai, Japan. Institute of Digital Enhancement of Cognitive Processing, Waseda University.

Kexin Yi, Chuang Gan, Yunzhu Li, Pushmeet Kohli, Jiajun Wu, Antonio Torralba, and Joshua B Tenenbaum. 2019. Clevrer: Collision events for video representation and reasoning. *arXiv preprint arXiv:1910.01442*.

Kexin Yi, Antonio Torralba, Jiajun Wu, Pushmeet Kohli, Chuang Gan, and Joshua B. Tenenbaum. 2018. Neural-symbolic VQA: Disentangling reasoning from vision and language understanding. *Advances in Neural Information Processing Systems*, 2018-Decem(NeurIPS):1031–1042.

Yanchao Yu, Arash Eshghi, and Oliver Lemon. 2016. Training an adaptive dialogue policy for interactive learning of visually grounded word meanings. In *Proceedings of the 17th Annual Meeting of the Special Interest Group on Discourse and Dialogue*, pages 339–349, Los Angeles. Association for Computational Linguistics.

End-to-end NLP Pipelines in Rust

Guillaume Becquin
guillaume.becquin@gmail.com

Abstract

The recent progress in natural language processing research has been supported by the development of a rich open source ecosystem in Python. Libraries allowing NLP practitioners but also non-specialists to leverage state-of-the-art models have been instrumental in the democratization of this technology. The maturity of the open-source NLP ecosystem however varies between languages. This work proposes a new open-source library aimed at bringing state-of-the-art NLP to Rust. Rust is a systems programming language for which the foundations required to build machine learning applications are available but still lacks ready-to-use, end-to-end NLP libraries. The proposed library, rust-bert, implements modern language models and ready-to-use pipelines (for example translation or summarization). This allows further development by the Rust community from both NLP experts and non-specialists. It is hoped that this library will accelerate the development of the NLP ecosystem in Rust. The library is under active development and available at https://github.com/guillaume-be/rust-bert.

1 Introduction

Natural language processing (NLP) has undergone a rapid transformation over the last few years. Modern architectures based on the Transformers (Vaswani et al., 2017), leveraging efficiently the large amount of data available for unsupervised pre-training, have enabled significant progress for a variety of tasks including sentiment analysis, question answering, summarization or translation. These research efforts have been accompanied by the development of a rich Python ecosystem enabling a democratization of these technologies for both practitioners and users, from tokenization to deep learning architectures. The Transformers library (Wolf et al., 2019) is an example of a library proposing APIs at various levels to either promote further development of NLP or their integration in higher level applications.

The adoption of these technologies in other programming languages has unfortunately not been as fast, for example in Rust. Rust (Klabnik and Nichols, 2018) is a promising modern static, strongly typed language that offers execution speeds similar to C. Its built-in memory safety design makes it an attractive alternative to C++ for the development of productive machine learning systems. Rust does not include a garbage collector but instead relies on strict ownership rules for the variables, dropping them when going out of scope. Its modern implementation of the strings data model that complies with UTF-8 standards is especially relevant to NLP applications. Finally, Rust includes a powerful utility called *cargo* to manage external dependencies. This allows the development of open-source ecosystems, similar to Python's *PyPI (Python Packaging Authority, 2000)* or Java's *Maven (Miller et al., 2010)*.

Rust is a modern programming language for which the foundations of a machine learning ecosystem are still being built. A number of initiatives including array manipulation (rust-ndarray Team, 2011), low-level CUDA libraries and deep learning framework bindings for Tensorflow (Tensorflow Project, 2016) or Torch (Mazare, 2019) are now maturing. However, there is still a lack of end-to-end, ready to use libraries leveraging state-of-the-art NLP models. The proposed library aims at filling this gap and exposes both Transformers-based architectures to NLP practitioners in Rust and pipelines that are ready for integration in Rust-based back-ends. The proposed library, *rust-bert*, is available at https://github.com/guillaume-be/rust-bert or https://crates.io/crates/rust-bert and is shared under Apache 2.0 license.

Proceedings of Second Workshop for NLP Open Source Software (NLP-OSS), pages 20–25
Virtual Conference, November 19, 2020. ©2020 Association for Computational Linguistics

2 Related Work

This work leverages the rich open-source resources available in Python. Especially relevant is the Transformers library (Wolf et al., 2019), of which large sections of the proposed Rust library were ported from. The model architectures and layers naming have been aligned with the Transformers implementation, and Rust-compatible pre-trained weights are available in Hugging Face's Model Hub (Hugging Face, 2019). The general API for the high-level and ready-to-use pipelines has been strongly inspired by the SpaCy library (Honnibal and Montani, 2017).

A number of specialized libraries have been developed for Rust, including high performance tokenizers ((Hugging Face, 2020) or (Becquin, 2020)) and language detection libraries (Potapov, 2016).

3 Architecture Design

The library exposes three main features:

- Language models implementation, covering state-of-the-art architectures including for example BERT (Devlin et al., 2019) or GPT2 (Radford et al., 2019).

- Ready-to-use pipelines, combining these models with pre-and post-processing routines.

- Utilities to load external resources, including a converter from PyTorch (Paszke et al., 2019) pickled model files to a C-array format.

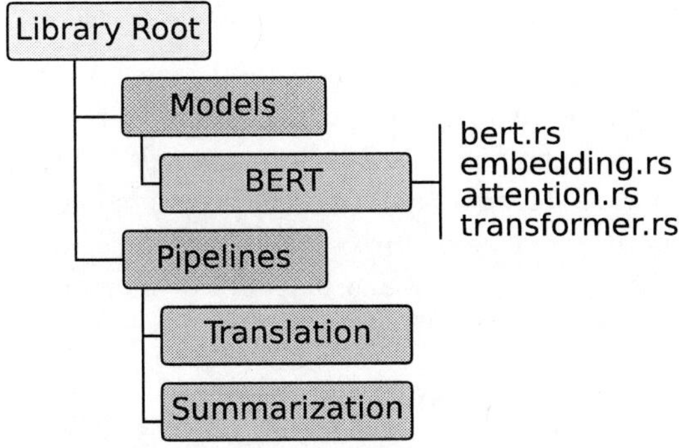

Figure 1: High-level library structure.

The language models and the pipelines are separated in different modules. Within the models, a sub-module is defined for each model (for example, BERT) with individual files for the major model components (for example, its attention mechanism). This promotes readability and modularity of the code base (Figure 1).

An important design aspect of the library is related to the choice of abstractions. Rust does not implement the concept of classes and inheritance in a similar way to Python. Rather, data is arranged in *structs* that may implement associated methods in an *impl* block or shared behaviour via *traits*. As opposed to Python, layers do not inherit from a shared *nn.Module* because Rust requires a strict definition of the names and types of the inputs and outputs (those may differ significantly from model to model). As a consequence the registration of the model parameters in the variable store is done manually:

```
1  pub struct ModelA {
2      dense: nn::Linear
3  }
4  impl ModelA {
5      pub fn new(p: &VarStore) -> Self {
6          // manual varstore registration
7      }
8      pub fn forward(&self,
9                  arg1: Tensor,
10                 arg2: bool)
11         -> OutputType {
12         // forward pass
13     }
14 }
```

While the model architectures have been generally ported from the Python Transformers' library, the proposed work is innovative in its handling of shared behavior. Models and configurations share capabilities using *Traits*. This includes for example the possibility for a model to be used as a conditional text generator by implementing the *LanguageGenerator* trait. A given model implements the trait by providing model-specific methods (e.g. *prepare_inputs* or *reorder_cache*). The complex text generation post-processing steps (beam search, sampling, non-repetition rules...) and the generation routine can then be readily leveraged by this model.

```
1  trait PrivateLanguageGenerator {
2      fn prepare_inputs() {}
3      fn reorder_cache() {}
4      fn top_k_top_p_filtering() {...}
5      fn generate_beam_search() {...}
6  }
7  pub trait LanguageGenerator:
8      PrivateLanguageGenerator
9  {
10     fn generate() {...}
11 }
12
13 impl PrivateLanguageGenerator
14     for ModelA {
15         fn prepare_inputs() {...}
16         fn reorder_cache() {...}
17     }
18 impl LanguageGenerator for ModelA {}
```

Shared behavior is also required for the ready-to-use pipelines that implement logic valid for a wide range of language models. Here the mechanism instead relies on *Enums* wrapping specific models in a shared abstraction. A given pipeline takes a Model Enum, a Tokenizer Enum and a Configuration Enum as inputs. The pipeline calls generic functions that are implemented by the enum (for example a forward pass). Each variant of the enum defines how the forward method is implemented. Note that this allows defining a common interface to models expecting a different set of inputs.

```
1  pub enum ClassifierModel {
2    BERT(BertModel),
3    XLNet(XLNetModel)
4  }
5  impl ClassifierModel{
6    pub fn forward(x, y) {
7      match *self {
8        BERT(mdl)=>{mdl.forward(x)},
9        XLNet(mdl)=>{mdl.forward(x, y)}
10     }
11   }
12 }
13 pub struct Classifier {
14   pub model: ClassifierModel
15 }
16 impl Classifier{
17   pub fn predict(text: &str) {
18     self.model.forward(x, y)
19   }
20 }
```

This pattern is similar to dependency injection (while the traits are closer to inheritance) and has benefits of a greater flexibility in the interface for model loading and forward methods and reduced coupling between the model and the pipelines.

4 Capabilities Overview

The library exposes an API at two different levels: the language models themselves, allowing to build NLP pipelines from scratch, and end-to-end pipelines that can readily be integrated in higher level applications.

A rust implementation for a wide range of language models has been implemented, including BERT (Devlin et al., 2019), DistilBERT (Sanh et al., 2019), RoBERTa (Liu et al., 2019), GPT (Radford, 2018), GPT2 (Radford et al., 2019), AL-BERT (Lan et al., 2019), BART (Lewis et al., 2020), Marian (Junczys-Dowmunt et al., 2018), XLM-RoBERTa (Conneau et al., 2020) and T5 (Raffel et al., 2019). For each of these models, pre-trained weights have been converted to a C-array format and are hosted alongside the Python version on Hugging Face's model hub (Hugging Face, 2019).

A large user base of NLP technologies also benefits from the availability of state of the art, end-to-end pipelines requiring little to no familiarity with NLP to be integrated in higher level applications. To answer these needs of the Rust community, the following capabilities have been implemented:

- Translation between 8 language pairs using either Marian (Junczys-Dowmunt et al., 2018) or T5 (Raffel et al., 2019) models.

- Summarization using a BART (Lewis et al., 2020) model trained on the CNN / Daily Mail summarization dataset (See et al., 2017).

- Conversational model using DialoGPT (Zhang et al., 2020).

- Question Answering using a DistilBERT (Sanh et al., 2019) model trained on the SQuAD dataset (Rajpurkar et al., 2016).

- Sentiment Analysis using a DistilBERT model trained on the SST-2 dataset (Socher et al., 2013)

- Named Entity Recognition for English, German, Spanish and Dutch trained on CoNLL03 (Tjong Kim Sang and De Meulder, 2003) and CoNLL02 (Tjong Kim Sang, 2002) datasets

These pipelines can be created and used in a few lines of code without prior knowledge in NLP.

```
1  let model = TranslationModel::
2    new(translation_config)?;
3  let input = ["Hello, world!"];
4  model.translate(&input);
```

While the implementation of the language models is a prerequisite, the availability of powerful end-to-end pipelines is key to a broader adoption of NLP technology in Rust. These pipelines can easily be integrated with server back-ends running Rust with queuing and batching of incoming requests (Walsh, 2020).

5 Benchmarks

This library was developed with the primary goal of making state of the art NLP capabilities available to the Rust community rather than speeding up inference. Nevertheless, Rust is a high performance language with execution speeds matching C or C++. Efficient predictions using NLP systems has become a key subject of research and engineering development over the past few months. Several methods have been investigated to improve the

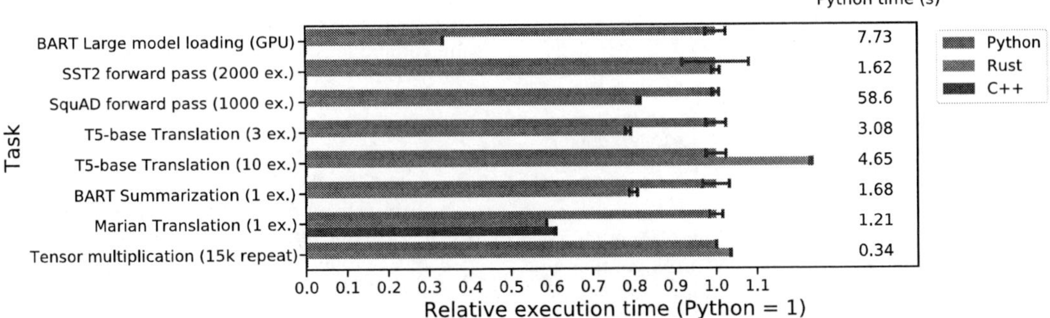

Figure 2: Rust-Python benchmark results.

model predictions performance, including for example pruning, quantization and Huffman Coding ((Han et al., 2016), (Shen et al., 2020)), distillation (Sanh et al., 2019), graph optimizations and layer fusing (Nvidia, 2020) or optimized runtimes such as ONNX (Bai et al., 2019). The high performance of the state of the art models usually comes with a significant computational cost.

It should be noted that the proposed library is based on bindings (Mazare, 2019) to LibTorch (Paszke et al., 2019), and therefore limited benefits can be expected from the tensor operations. These are executed in the CUDA layer that is effectively shared with the Python-based models. The following investigates if these high performance features of the language translate into benefits for the proposed NLP pipelines.

Benchmarks between Python and Rust are shown in Figure 2 using a Turing RTX2070 GPU with a AMD 2700X CPU. For all experiments the average time relative to Python is reported with the standard deviation. For all prediction tasks, the Transformers (Wolf et al., 2019) library (v3.2.0) is used as a reference. All experiments are run for 10 iterations, with various number of samples (provided in brackets). For reference, the Python absolute execution time per iteration is provided.

The loading benchmarks represent the average time required to load models into the GPU buffer. Significant benefits can be observed for Rust. This is probably caused by the simpler serialization format based on C-arrays for Rust, and may be advantageous for event-driven applications loading models on a per-request basis (short warm-up time).

The forward pass results vary between applications. As expected, pipelines with very simple pre- and post-processing steps offer virtually identical performance (for example sentiment analysis).

Significant benefits can be observed for question answering, coming entirely from the tokenization process (At the time this document was prepared, the Transformers' (Wolf et al., 2019) question answering pipeline did not leverage Rust-based tokenizers yet). The performance of pipelines involving complex post-processing steps (text generation with sampling and beam search) can show significant benefits. Marian-based translation models (Tiedemann and Thottingal, 2020) exhibit a 40% speedup (in line with the native C++ implementation (Junczys-Dowmunt et al., 2018)). The T5 implementation is faster for small effective batch sizes (with a beam size of 6) but slower for larger batches, indicating optimization potential remains. In general it was observed that the actual model forward pass (tensor operations) is comparable albeit slightly slower in Rust than in Python. A last experiment (large matrix multiplication) shows the Rust LibTorch bindings seem to be 1 to 2% slower than the PyTorch equivalent.

6   Conclusion

Rust is a promising language for the development of NLP systems. Its concurrency capabilities, memory safety features and modern strings data model make it a good alternative to C++ for production systems. While evolving quickly, the Rust NLP open-source ecosystem still lags behind Python rich set of libraries. Complementing the availability of high performance tokenizers, *rust-bert* makes state-of-the-art language models and end-to-end NLP pipelines available to the Rust community.

7   Acknowledgments

The list of contributors to the *rust-bert* project is available on the project repository.

References

Junjie Bai, Fang Lu, Ke Zhang, et al. 2019. Onnx: Open neural network exchange. https://github.com/onnx/onnx.

Guillaume Becquin. 2020. rust-tokenizers. https://github.com/guillaume-be/rust-tokenizers.

Alexis Conneau, Kartikay Khandelwal, Naman Goyal, Vishrav Chaudhary, Guillaume Wenzek, Francisco Guzmán, Edouard Grave, Myle Ott, Luke Zettlemoyer, and Veselin Stoyanov. 2020. Unsupervised cross-lingual representation learning at scale. In *Proceedings of the 58th Annual Meeting of the Association for Computational Linguistics*, pages 8440–8451, Online. Association for Computational Linguistics.

Jacob Devlin, Ming-Wei Chang, Kenton Lee, and Kristina Toutanova. 2019. BERT: Pre-training of deep bidirectional transformers for language understanding. In *Proceedings of the 2019 Conference of the North American Chapter of the Association for Computational Linguistics: Human Language Technologies, Volume 1 (Long and Short Papers)*, pages 4171–4186, Minneapolis, Minnesota. Association for Computational Linguistics.

Song Han, Huizi Mao, and William J. Dally. 2016. Deep compression: Compressing deep neural network with pruning, trained quantization and huffman coding. *CoRR*, abs/1510.00149.

Matthew Honnibal and Ines Montani. 2017. spaCy 2: Natural language understanding with Bloom embeddings, convolutional neural networks and incremental parsing. To appear.

Hugging Face. 2019. Hugging face model hub.

Hugging Face. 2020. tokenizers. https://github.com/huggingface/tokenizers.

Marcin Junczys-Dowmunt, Roman Grundkiewicz, Tomasz Dwojak, Hieu Hoang, Kenneth Heafield, Tom Neckermann, Frank Seide, Ulrich Germann, Alham Fikri Aji, Nikolay Bogoychev, André F. T. Martins, and Alexandra Birch. 2018. Marian: Fast neural machine translation in C++. In *Proceedings of ACL 2018, System Demonstrations*, pages 116–121, Melbourne, Australia. Association for Computational Linguistics.

Steve Klabnik and Carol Nichols. 2018. *The Rust Programming Language*. No Starch Press, USA.

Zhenzhong Lan, Mingda Chen, Sebastian Goodman, Kevin Gimpel, Piyush Sharma, and Radu Soricut. 2019. Albert: A lite bert for self-supervised learning of language representations.

Mike Lewis, Yinhan Liu, Naman Goyal, Marjan Ghazvininejad, Abdelrahman Mohamed, Omer Levy, Veselin Stoyanov, and Luke Zettlemoyer.

2020. BART: Denoising sequence-to-sequence pre-training for natural language generation, translation, and comprehension. In *Proceedings of the 58th Annual Meeting of the Association for Computational Linguistics*, pages 7871–7880, Online. Association for Computational Linguistics.

Yinhan Liu, Myle Ott, Naman Goyal, Jingfei Du, Mandar Joshi, Danqi Chen, Omer Levy, Mike Lewis, Luke Zettlemoyer, and Veselin Stoyanov. 2019. Roberta: A robustly optimized BERT pretraining approach. *CoRR*, abs/1907.11692.

Laurent Mazare. 2019. tch-rs. https://github.com/LaurentMazare/tch-rs.

Frederic P Miller, Agnes F Vandome, and John McBrewster. 2010. *Apache Maven*. Alpha Press.

Nvidia. 2020. Optimizing the performance of tensorrt.

Adam Paszke, Sam Gross, Francisco Massa, Adam Lerer, James Bradbury, Gregory Chanan, Trevor Killeen, Zeming Lin, Natalia Gimelshein, Luca Antiga, Alban Desmaison, Andreas Kopf, Edward Yang, Zachary DeVito, Martin Raison, Alykhan Tejani, Sasank Chilamkurthy, Benoit Steiner, Lu Fang, Junjie Bai, and Soumith Chintala. 2019. Pytorch: An imperative style, high-performance deep learning library. In H. Wallach, H. Larochelle, A. Beygelzimer, F. d'Alché-Buc, E. Fox, and R. Garnett, editors, *Advances in Neural Information Processing Systems 32*, pages 8024–8035. Curran Associates, Inc.

Sergey Potapov. 2016. whatlang-rs. https://github.com/greyblake/whatlang-rs.

Python Packaging Authority. 2000. Python package index (pypi).

Alec Radford. 2018. Improving language understanding by generative pre-training.

Alec Radford, Jeff Wu, Rewon Child, David Luan, Dario Amodei, and Ilya Sutskever. 2019. Language models are unsupervised multitask learners.

Colin Raffel, Noam Shazeer, Adam Roberts, Katherine Lee, Sharan Narang, Michael Matena, Yanqi Zhou, Wei Li, and Peter J. Liu. 2019. Exploring the limits of transfer learning with a unified text-to-text transformer. *arXiv e-prints*.

Pranav Rajpurkar, Jian Zhang, Konstantin Lopyrev, and Percy Liang. 2016. SQuAD: 100,000+ questions for machine comprehension of text. In *Proceedings of the 2016 Conference on Empirical Methods in Natural Language Processing*, pages 2383–2392, Austin, Texas. Association for Computational Linguistics.

rust-ndarray Team. 2011. rust-ndarray. https://github.com/rust-ndarray/ndarray.

Victor Sanh, Lysandre Debut, Julien Chaumond, and Thomas Wolf. 2019. Distilbert, a distilled version of bert: smaller, faster, cheaper and lighter. *ArXiv*, abs/1910.01108.

Abigail See, Peter J. Liu, and Christopher D. Manning. 2017. Get to the point: Summarization with pointer-generator networks. In *Proceedings of the 55th Annual Meeting of the Association for Computational Linguistics (Volume 1: Long Papers)*, pages 1073–1083, Vancouver, Canada. Association for Computational Linguistics.

Sheng Shen, Zhen Dong, Jiayu Ye, Linjian Ma, Zhewei Yao, Amir Gholami, Michael W. Mahoney, and Kurt Keutzer. 2020. Q-bert: Hessian based ultra low precision quantization of bert. In *AAAI*.

Richard Socher, Alex Perelygin, Jean Wu, Jason Chuang, Christopher D Manning, Andrew Ng, and Christopher Potts. 2013. Recursive deep models for semantic compositionality over a sentiment treebank. In *Proceedings of the 2013 conference on empirical methods in natural language processing*, pages 1631–1642.

Tensorflow Project. 2016. Tensorflow rust. `https://github.com/tensorflow/rust`.

Jörg Tiedemann and Santhosh Thottingal. 2020. OPUS-MT — Building open translation services for the World. In *Proceedings of the 22nd Annual Conferenec of the European Association for Machine Translation (EAMT)*, Lisbon, Portugal.

Erik F. Tjong Kim Sang. 2002. Introduction to the CoNLL-2002 shared task: Language-independent named entity recognition. In *COLING-02: The 6th Conference on Natural Language Learning 2002 (CoNLL-2002)*.

Erik F. Tjong Kim Sang and Fien De Meulder. 2003. Introduction to the CoNLL-2003 shared task: Language-independent named entity recognition. In *Proceedings of the Seventh Conference on Natural Language Learning at HLT-NAACL 2003*, pages 142–147.

Ashish Vaswani, Noam Shazeer, Niki Parmar, Jakob Uszkoreit, Llion Jones, Aidan N Gomez, Ł ukasz Kaiser, and Illia Polosukhin. 2017. Attention is all you need. In I. Guyon, U. V. Luxburg, S. Bengio, H. Wallach, R. Fergus, S. Vishwanathan, and R. Garnett, editors, *Advances in Neural Information Processing Systems 30*, pages 5998–6008. Curran Associates, Inc.

Evan Pete Walsh. 2020. rust-dl-server. `https://github.com/epwalsh/rust-dl-webserver`.

Thomas Wolf, Lysandre Debut, Victor Sanh, Julien Chaumond, Clement Delangue, Anthony Moi, Pierric Cistac, Tim Rault, R'emi Louf, Morgan Funtowicz, and Jamie Brew. 2019. Huggingface's transformers: State-of-the-art natural language processing. *ArXiv*, abs/1910.03771.

Yizhe Zhang, Siqi Sun, Michel Galley, Yen-Chun Chen, Chris Brockett, Xiang Gao, Jianfeng Gao, Jingjing Liu, and Bill Dolan. 2020. DIALOGPT : Large-scale generative pre-training for conversational response generation. In *Proceedings of the 58th Annual Meeting of the Association for Computational Linguistics: System Demonstrations*, pages 270–278, Online. Association for Computational Linguistics.

Fair Embedding Engine: A Library for Analyzing and Mitigating Gender Bias in Word Embeddings

Vaibhav Kumar[*]   **Tenzin Singhay Bhotia**[*]   **Vaibhav Kumar**[*]
Delhi Technological University
Delhi, India
{kumar.vaibhav1o1, tenzinbhotia0, vaibhavk992}@gmail.com

Abstract

Non-contextual word embedding models have been shown to inherit human-like stereotypical biases of gender, race and religion from the training corpora. To counter this issue, a large body of research has emerged which aims to mitigate these biases while keeping the syntactic and semantic utility of embeddings intact. This paper describes Fair Embedding Engine (FEE), a library for analysing and mitigating gender bias in word embeddings. FEE combines various state of the art techniques for quantifying, visualising and mitigating gender bias in word embeddings under a standard abstraction. FEE will aid practitioners in fast track analysis of existing debiasing methods on their embedding models. Further, it will allow rapid prototyping of new methods by evaluating their performance on a suite of standard metrics.

1 Introduction

Non-contextual word embedding models such as Word2Vec (Mikolov et al., 2013b,a), GloVe (Pennington et al., 2014) and FastText (Bojanowski et al., 2017) have been established as the cornerstone of modern natural language processing (NLP) techniques. The ease of usage followed by performance improvements (Turian et al., 2010) have made word embeddings pervasive across various NLP tasks. However, as with most things, the gains come at a cost, word embeddings also pose the risk of introducing unwanted stereotypical biases in the downstream tasks. Bolukbasi et al. (2016a) showed that a Word2Vec model trained on the Google news corpus, when evaluated for the analogy *man:computer programmer :: woman:?* results to the answer *homemaker*, reflecting the stereotypical biases towards woman. Further, Zhao

et al. (2018a) showed that models operating on biased word embeddings can leverage stereotypical cues in downstream tasks like co-reference resolution as heuristics to make thier final predictions.

Addressing the issues of unwanted biases in learned word representations, recent years have seen a surge in the development of word embedding debiasing procedures. The fundamental aim of a debiasing procedure is to mitigate stereotypical biases while introducing minimal semantic offset, hence maintaining the usability of embeddings. Based upon the mode of operation, the debiasing methods can be classified into two categories: First, post-processing methods, which operate upon pre-trained word vectors (Bolukbasi et al., 2016a; Kaneko and Bollegala, 2019; Yang and Feng, 2020). Second, learning based methods, which involve re-training the word embedding models by either making changes to the training data or to the training objective. (Zhao et al., 2018b; Lu et al., 2018; Bordia and Bowman, 2019). Along with the development of debiasing procedures, numerous metrics to evaluate the efficacy of each debiasing procedure have also been proposed (Zhao et al., 2018b; Bolukbasi et al., 2016a; Kumar et al., 2020). Although the domain has largely benefited from the contributions of different researchers, the domain still lacks open source software projects that unify such diverse but fundamentally similar methods in an organized and standard manner. Therefore, the domain has a high barrier for newcomers to overcome, and the domain experts may still need to put in extra effort of building and maintaining their own codebases.

To solve this problem, we introduce Fair Embedding Engine (FEE), a library which combines state of the art techniques for debiasing, quantifying and visualizing gender bias in non-contextual word embeddings for the English language. The goal of FEE is to serve as a unified framework towards the

---

[*]Authors have contributed equally.

Proceedings of Second Workshop for NLP Open Source Software (NLP-OSS), pages 26–31
Virtual Conference, November 19, 2020. ©2020 Association for Computational Linguistics

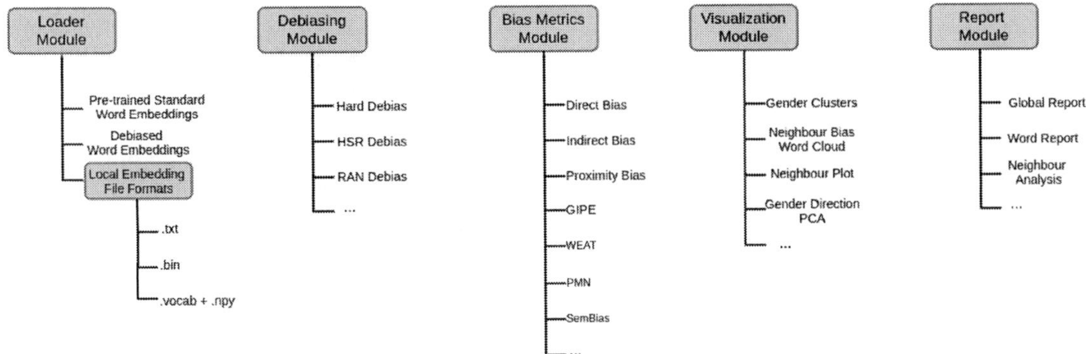

Figure 1: An inventory of implemented methods under four major modules that constitute FEE. Out of the box, FEE provides a subset of the prominent methods in each the modules. Further, each module can be easily extended to incorporate latest methods.

analysis of biases in word embeddings and the efficient development of better debiasing and bias evaluation methods. Conforming to the common style of implementation in some existing research works (Bolukbasi et al., 2016b; Zhao et al., 2018b), we use Numpy (Oliphant, 2006; Van Der Walt et al., 2011) arrays to store word vectors while keeping an index mapping to the strings of corresponding words. Further, we use the PyTorch (Paszke et al., 2017) Autograd engine for gradient based optimization and Matplotlib (Hunter, 2007) for generating plots. FEE is made available at: `https://github.com/FEE-Fair-Embedding-Engine/FEE`.

2 Related Work

Since the study of stereotypical biases in NLP has received attention only in the recent years, the domain has not been a part of open source efforts that attempt to integrate diverse sets of independent methods. The only relevant open source software (OSS) that we came across during our investigation was Word Embedding Fairness Evaluation (WEFE) framework (Badilla et al., 2020). For a given collection of pre-trained word embedding and a set of fairness criteria, WEFE ranks the embeddings based on their performance on an encapsulation of the fairness metrics. In order to achieve this ranking over an otherwise disparate set of fairness metrics (WEAT (Caliskan et al., 2017a), RND (Garg et al., 2018), and RNSB (Sweeney and Najafian, 2019)) WEFE introduces an abstraction which generalizes over the metrics using a set of *target* (the intended social class for which fairness is to be evaluated) and *attribute* words (the traits over which bias might exist for the selected target words). Fur-

ther, (Badilla et al., 2020) conclude that while existing fairness metrics show a strong correlation when used for evaluating gender bias, only a weak correlation results when evaluating biases like religion and race.

Therefore, the focus of WEFE is limited to the evaluation of pre-trained word vectors on a suite of fairness metrics, lacking any support for debiasing methods. Further, only those evaluation metrics can be used which comply with the abstraction. FEE, on the other hand, provides holistic functionality by equipping a suite of evaluation and debiasing methods, along with a flexible design to assist researchers in developing new solutions.

FEE currently offers three debiasing methods as a part of its debiasing module: HardDebias (Bolukbasi et al., 2016b), HSRDebias (Yang and Feng, 2020), and RANDebias (Kumar et al., 2020). The bias metrics module consist of the following: SemBias (Zhao et al., 2018b), direct and indirect bias (Bolukbasi et al., 2016a), Gender-basied Illicit Proximity Estimate (GIPE) and Proximity bias (Kumar et al., 2020), Percent Male Neighbours (PMN) (Gonen and Goldberg, 2019) and Word Embedding Association Test (WEAT) (Caliskan et al., 2017b).

3 Fair Embedding Engine

The core functionality of FEE is governed by five modules, namely *Loader*, *Debias*, *Bias Metrics*, *Visualization*, and *Report*. Figure 1 illustrates the components for each module of FEE. In the following subsections, we delineate upon the implementation of each of the modules along with the motivation for their development.

3.1 Loader Module

Motivation: The foremost step in the analysis of word embeddings is to load them into the random access memory. However, different formats of local embedding files, and heterogeneous formats of pre-trained embedding sources may entail disparate forms of access, making the loading process non-trivial. The loader module abstracts this pre-processing step and provides a standardized object based access of word embeddings to its users.

Working: The workhorse of the loader module is its Word Embedding class, `WE`. Any version of a word embedding model can be considered as a unique instance of the `WE` class. It consists of a user accessible `loader()` method that either takes in an embedding name representing a pre-trained word embedding, or a local embedding file path as input and returns an initialized `WE` object. We integrate the well established Gensim (Řehůřek and Sojka, 2010) API in our loader module for providing access to several pre-trained embeddings. However, since FEE focuses on the bias domain, it also provides the functionality to either store the debiased counterparts of Gensim-loaded embeddings, or load an externally downloaded debiased embedding file. For flexibility, the loader module supports three prominent file formats i.e. `.txt`, `.bin`, and `.vocab` (words) + `.npy` (vectors). Once, a `WE` object is initialized with an embedding version via the `loader()` method, a user can obtain the vector representation for a word by calling its vector method, `v()` with that word as its argument. All the subsequent modules of FEE operate on the `WE` object for achieving their objectives.

3.2 Debiasing Module

Motivation: The domain of bias in word representations considers effective debiasing methods as one of their ultimate objectives. Much effort has been made in the recent years to develop good debiasing methods. However, most works flaunt the efficacy of their debiasing procedures by applying them to a limited number of pre-trained embeddings. We hope that future works try to experiment their new methods or the existing ones on different embeddings. However, such a task involves refactoring and modification of individually tailored prior works. The debiasing module of FEE re-implements these diverse algorithms and provides a standardized access to users while facilitating reproducible research.

Working: The debiasing module of FEE currently provides access to some of the proposed post-processing debiasing procedures in the past, as shown in Figure 1. Each debiasing method is represented by a unique class in the module. For instance, the Hard Debias methods proposed by Bolukbasi et al. (2016a) is assigned a class named, `HardDebias`. Since all debiasing methods are fundamentally applied to a word embedding, the class of each debiasing method is initialised by a `WE` object. Each debiasing class has a common method called `run()` that takes in a list of words as argument and runs the entire debiasing procedure on it. As the debiasing procedure operates upon the `WE` object, the engineering effort in dealing with different embedding formats is mitigated.

3.3 Bias Metrics Module

Motivation: Evaluation metrics provide the necessary quantitative support for comparing and contrasting between different debiasing methods. However, different research articles often show different results for the same metric despite having theoretically similar configurations. The bias metrics module of FEE is aimed at filling this gap, it provides a suite of bias metrics built on a common framework for facilitating reliable inference.

Working: The bias metrics module of FEE currently provides access to a number of evaluation metrics, as shown in Figure 1. Each evaluation metric is represented by a unique class in the module. Each metric class depends on some common utilities and consists of multiple methods that implement their unique evaluation procedure. Similar to the debiasing module, each metric class's instance is initialised by a `WE` object. The metrics either operate on a single word, pair of words or list of words. Each metric class has a common method called `compute()` that returns the final result by accepting different arguments corresponding to the type of metric. The unified design of bias metric module fosters a standardized access to any bias based evaluation metric and facilitates reproducible research.

3.4 Visualization Module

Motivation: Visualizations provide useful insights into the behaviour of a set of data points. Many prior debiasing methods (Bolukbasi et al., 2016a; Kumar et al., 2020) have strongly motivated their work by illustrating certain undesirable associations prevalent in standard word embeddings. Thus,

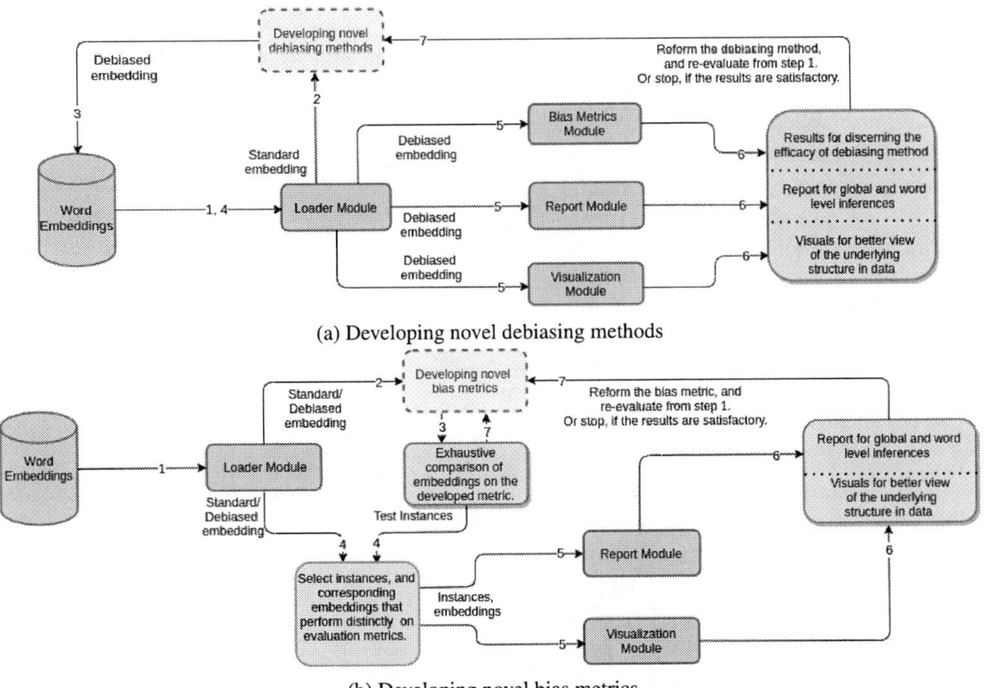

(a) Developing novel debiasing methods

(b) Developing novel bias metrics

Figure 2: FEE serves as a centralized resource for practitioners and researchers to develop novel debiasing methods and bias evaluation metrics. Figure (a) and (b) illustrate the possible workflow associated with each of the tasks respectively all made possible by the powerful abstraction provided by FEE.

through `FEE` we also provide off the shelf visualization capabilities that might help users to build reliable intuitions and uncover hidden biases in their models.

Working: In this module, we implement a separate class for each visualization type. Just like other modules, a visualization class object is initialized by `WE` object, and makes use of some common utilities. Each visualization class has a `run()` method that takes in a word list and other optional arguments for producing the final visualizations. Figure 1 illustrates some off the shelf visualization options provided by FEE.

3.5 Report Module

Motivation: The bias metrics and visualization modules incorporate a plethora of components which provide an exhaustive set of results. However, sometimes a specific combination of their components can provide the needed information succinctly. Accordingly, the report module aims to provide a descriptive summary of bias in word embeddings at the word and global level.

Working: The report module is comprised of two separate classes that are representative of a word and a global level report respectively. Both the classes operate on `WE` initialized embedding object and implement a common `generate()` method that creates a descriptive report. The `WordReport` class is useful for providing an abridged information about a single word vector in terms of bias. A call to the `generate()` method of `WordReport` utilizes the components of other modules and instantly reports the direct bias, proximity bias, neighbour analysis (`NeighboursAnalysis`), neighbour plot and a neighbour word cloud for a word. The `GlobalReport` class, in contrast creates a concise report at the entire embedding level. Unlike the word level, `GlobalReport` class does not make use of the other modules, since it achieves all the required content from the embedding object. The `generate()` method of `WordReport` provides the information about n most and least biased words in a word embedding space.

4 Developing new methods with FEE

Despite the development of a large number of debiasing methods, the issue of bias in word representations still persists (Gonen and Goldberg, 2019) making it an active area of research. We believe that the design and wide variety of tools provided by FEE can play a significant role in assisting practitioners and researchers to develop better debiasing and evaluation methods. Figure 2 portrays FEE assisted workflows which abstract the routing engineering tasks and allow users to invest more time on the intellectually demanding questions.

5 Conclusion and future work

In this paper, we described Fair Embedding Engine (FEE), a python library which provides central access to the state-of-the-art techniques for quantifying, mitigating and visualizing gender bias in non-contextual word embedding models. We believe that FEE will facilitate the development and testing of debiasing methods for word embeddings. Further, it will make it easier to visualize the existing bias present in word vectors. In future, we would like to expand the capabilities of FEE towards contextual word vectors and also provide support towards biases other than gender and language other than English. We also look forward to integrate OSS such as WEFE (Badilla et al., 2020) to enhance the bias evaluation capabilities of FEE.

References

Pablo Badilla, Felipe Bravo-Marquez, and Jorge Pérez. 2020. Wefe: The word embeddings fairness evaluation framework. In *Proceedings of the Twenty-Ninth International Joint Conference on Artificial Intelligence, IJCAI-20*, pages 430–436. International Joint Conferences on Artificial Intelligence Organization.

Piotr Bojanowski, Edouard Grave, Armand Joulin, and Tomas Mikolov. 2017. Enriching word vectors with subword information. *Transactions of the Association for Computational Linguistics*, 5:135–146.

Tolga Bolukbasi, Kai-Wei Chang, James Y Zou, Venkatesh Saligrama, and Adam T Kalai. 2016a. Man is to computer programmer as woman is to homemaker? debiasing word embeddings. In *Advances in neural information processing systems*, pages 4349–4357.

Tolga Bolukbasi, Kai-Wei Chang, James Y Zou, Venkatesh Saligrama, and Adam T Kalai. 2016b. Man is to computer programmer as woman is to homemaker? debiasing word embeddings. In *Advances in neural information processing systems*, pages 4349–4357.

Shikha Bordia and Samuel R. Bowman. 2019. Identifying and reducing gender bias in word-level language models. *CoRR*, abs/1904.03035.

Aylin Caliskan, Joanna J Bryson, and Arvind Narayanan. 2017a. Semantics derived automatically from language corpora contain human-like biases. *Science*, 356(6334):183–186.

Aylin Caliskan, Joanna J Bryson, and Arvind Narayanan. 2017b. Semantics derived automatically from language corpora contain human-like biases. *Science*, 356(6334):183–186.

Nikhil Garg, Londa Schiebinger, Dan Jurafsky, and James Zou. 2018. Word embeddings quantify 100 years of gender and ethnic stereotypes. *Proceedings of the National Academy of Sciences*, 115(16):E3635–E3644.

Hila Gonen and Yoav Goldberg. 2019. Lipstick on a pig: Debiasing methods cover up systematic gender biases in word embeddings but do not remove them. *Proceedings of the 2019 Conference of the North American Chapter of the Association for Computational Linguistics: Human Language Technologies, Volume 1 (Long and Short Papers)*, page 609–614.

J. D. Hunter. 2007. Matplotlib: A 2d graphics environment. *Computing in Science & Engineering*, 9(3):90–95.

Masahiro Kaneko and Danushka Bollegala. 2019. Gender-preserving debiasing for pre-trained word embeddings. *Proceedings of the 57th Annual Meeting of the Association for Computational Linguistics*, page 1641–1650.

Vaibhav Kumar, Tenzin Singhay Bhotia, Vaibhav Kumar, and Tanmoy Chakraborty. 2020. Nurse is closer to woman than surgeon? mitigating gender-biased proximities in word embeddings. *Transactions of the Association for Computational Linguistics*, 8:486–503.

Kaiji Lu, Piotr Mardziel, Fangjing Wu, Preetam Amancharla, and Anupam Datta. 2018. Gender bias in neural natural language processing. *arXiv preprint arXiv:1807.11714*.

Tomas Mikolov, Kai Chen, Greg Corrado, and Jeffrey Dean. 2013a. Efficient estimation of word representations in vector space. *1st International Conference on Learning Representations, ICLR 2013, Workshop Track Proceedings*, pages 1–12.

Tomas Mikolov, Ilya Sutskever, Kai Chen, Greg S Corrado, and Jeff Dean. 2013b. Distributed representations of words and phrases and their compositionality. In *Advances in neural information processing systems*, pages 3111–3119.

Travis E Oliphant. 2006. *A guide to NumPy*, volume 1. Trelgol Publishing USA.

Adam Paszke, Sam Gross, Soumith Chintala, Gregory Chanan, Edward Yang, Zachary DeVito, Zeming Lin, Alban Desmaison, Luca Antiga, and Adam Lerer. 2017. Automatic differentiation in pytorch.

Jeffrey Pennington, Richard Socher, and Christopher Manning. 2014. Glove: Global vectors for word representation. In *Proceedings of the 2014 conference on empirical methods in natural language processing (EMNLP)*, pages 1532–1543.

Radim Řehůřek and Petr Sojka. 2010. Software Framework for Topic Modelling with Large Corpora. In *Proceedings of the LREC 2010 Workshop on New Challenges for NLP Frameworks*, pages 45–50, Valletta, Malta. ELRA.

Chris Sweeney and Maryam Najafian. 2019. A transparent framework for evaluating unintended demographic bias in word embeddings. In *Proceedings of the 57th Annual Meeting of the Association for Computational Linguistics*, pages 1662–1667, Florence, Italy. Association for Computational Linguistics.

Joseph Turian, Lev-Arie Ratinov, and Yoshua Bengio. 2010. Word representations: A simple and general method for semi-supervised learning. In *Proceedings of the 48th Annual Meeting of the Association for Computational Linguistics*, pages 384–394, Uppsala, Sweden. Association for Computational Linguistics.

Stefan Van Der Walt, S Chris Colbert, and Gael Varoquaux. 2011. The numpy array: a structure for efficient numerical computation. *Computing in Science & Engineering*, 13(2):22.

Zekun Yang and Juan Feng. 2020. A causal inference method for reducing gender bias in word embedding relations. In *AAAI*, pages 9434–9441.

Jieyu Zhao, Tianlu Wang, Mark Yatskar, Vicente Ordonez, and Kai-Wei Chang. 2018a. Gender bias in coreference resolution: Evaluation and debiasing methods. *arXiv preprint arXiv:1804.06876*.

Jieyu Zhao, Yichao Zhou, Zeyu Li, Wei Wang, and Kai-Wei Chang. 2018b. Learning gender-neutral word embeddings. *Proceedings of the 2018 Conference on Empirical Methods in Natural Language Processing*, page 4847–4853.

Flexible retrieval with NMSLIB and FlexNeuART

Leonid Boytsov [*]
Pittsburgh, PA, USA
leo@boytsov.info

Eric Nyberg
Carnegie Mellon University
Pittsburgh, PA, USA
ehn@cs.cmu.edu

Abstract

Our objective is to introduce to the NLP community an existing k-NN search library NMSLIB, a new retrieval toolkit FlexNeuART, as well as their integration capabilities. NMSLIB, while being one the fastest k-NN search libraries, is quite generic and supports a variety of distance/similarity functions. Because the library relies on the distance-based structure-agnostic algorithms, it can be further extended by adding new distances. FlexNeuART is a modular, extendible and flexible toolkit for candidate generation in IR and QA applications, which supports mixing of classic and neural ranking signals. FlexNeuART can *efficiently* retrieve *mixed* dense and sparse representations (with weights learned from training data), which is achieved by extending NMSLIB. In that, other retrieval systems work with purely sparse representations (e.g., Lucene), purely dense representations (e.g., FAISS and Annoy), or only perform mixing at the re-ranking stage.

1 Introduction

Although there has been substantial progress on machine reading tasks using neural models such as BERT (Devlin et al., 2018), these approaches have practical limitations for open-domain challenges, which typically require (1) a retrieval and (2) a re-scoring/re-ranking step to restrict the number of candidate documents. Otherwise, the application of state-of-the-art machine reading models to large document collections would be impractical even with recent efficiency improvements (Khattab and Zaharia, 2020).

The first retrieval stage is commonly referred to as the *candidate generation* (i.e., we generate candidates for re-scoring). Until about 2019, the candidate generation would exclusively rely on a traditional search engine such as Lucene,[1] which indexes occurrences of individual terms, their lemmas or stems (Manning et al., 2010). In that, there are several recent papers where promising results were achieved by generating dense embeddings and using a k-NN search library to retrieve them (Lee et al., 2019; Karpukhin et al., 2020; Xiong et al., 2020). However, these studies typically have at least one of the following flaws: (1) they compare against a weak baseline such as untuned BM25 or (2) they rely on exact k-NN search, thus, totally ignoring practical efficiency-effectiveness and scalability trade-offs related to using k-NN search, see, e.g., §3.3 in Boytsov (2018). FlexNeuART implements some of the most effective non-neural ranking signals: It produced best non-neural runs in the TREC 2019 deep learning challenge (Craswell et al., 2020) and would be a good tool to verify these results.

Furthermore, there is evidence that when dense representations perform well, even better results may be obtained by combining them with traditional sparse-vector models (Seo et al., 2019; Gysel et al., 2018; Karpukhin et al., 2020; Kuzi et al., 2020). It is not straightforward to incorporate

---

[*]Work done primarily while at CMU.

[1]https://lucene.apache.org/

Proceedings of Second Workshop for NLP Open Source Software (NLP-OSS), pages 32–43
Virtual Conference, November 19, 2020. ©2020 Association for Computational Linguistics

these representations into existing toolkits, but `FlexNeuART` supports dense and dense-sparse representations out of the box with the help of `NMSLIB` (Boytsov and Naidan, 2013a; Naidan et al., 2015a).[2] `NMSLIB` is an efficient library for k-NN search on CPU, which supports a wide range of similarity functions and data formats. `NMSLIB` is a commonly used library[3], which was recently adopted by Amazon.[4] Because `NMSLIB` algorithms are largely distance-agnostic, it is relatively easy to extend the library by adding new distances. In what follows we describe `NMSLIB`, `FlexNeuART`, and their integration in more detail. The code is publicly available:

- `https://github.com/oaqa/FlexNeuART`

- `https://github.com/nmslib/nmslib`

2 `NMSLIB`

Non-Metric Space Library (NMSLIB) is an efficient cross-platform similarity search library and a toolkit for evaluation of similarity search methods (Boytsov and Naidan, 2013a; Naidan et al., 2015a), which is the first commonly used library with a principled support for non-metric space searching.[5] `NMSLIB` is an extendible library, which means that is possible to add new search methods and distance functions. `NMSLIB` can be used directly in C++ and Python (via Python bindings). In addition, it is also possible to build a query server, which can be used from Java (or other languages supported by Apache Thrift[6]).

k-NN search is a conceptually simple procedure that consists in finding k data set elements that have highest similarity scores (or, alternatively, smallest distances) to another element called *query*. Despite its formulaic simplicity, k-NN search is a notoriously difficult problem, which is hard to do efficiently, i.e., faster than the brute-force scan of the data set, for high dimensional data and/or non-Euclidean distances. In particular, for some data sets exact search methods do not outperform the brute-force search in just a dozen of dimensions (see, e.g., a discussion in § 1 and § 2 of Boytsov 2018).

For sufficiently small data sets and simple similarities, e.g., L_2, the brute-force search can be a feasible solution, especially when the data set fits into a memory of an AI accelerator. In particular, the Facebook library for k-NN search `FAISS` (Johnson et al., 2017) supports the brute-force search on GPU [7]. However, GPU memory is quite limited compared to the main RAM. For example, the latest A100 GPU has only 40 GB of memory[8] while some commodity servers have 1+ TB of main RAM.

In addition, GPUs are designed primarily for dense-vector manipulations and have poor support for sparse vectors (Hong et al., 2018). When data is very sparse, as in the case of traditional text indices, it is possible to efficiently retrieve data using search toolkits such as Lucene. Yet, for less sparse sets, more complex similarities, and large dense-vector data sets we have to resort to *approximate* k-NN search, which does not have accuracy guarantees.

One particular efficient class of k-NN search methods relies on the construction of neighborhood graphs for data set points (see a recent survey by Shimomura et al. (2020) for a thorough description). Despite initial promising results were published nearly 30 years ago (Arya and Mount, 1993), this approach has only recently become popular due to good performance of `NMSLIB` and `KGraph` (Dong et al., 2011)[9].

Specifically, two successive ANN-Benchmarks challenges (Aumüller et al., 2019) were won first by our efficient implementation of the Navigable Small World (NSW) (Malkov et al., 2014) and then by the Hierarchical Navigable Small World (HNSW) contributed to `NMSLIB` by Yury Malkov (Malkov and Yashunin, 2018). HNSW performance was particularly impressive.

---

[2]`https://github.com/nmslib/nmslib`
[3]`https://pypistats.org/packages/nmslib`
[4]`https://amzn.to/3aDCMtC`
[5]`https://github.com/nmslib/nmslib`
[6]`https://thrift.apache.org/`

[7]`https://github.com/facebookresearch/faiss/wiki/Running-on-GPUs`
[8]`https://www.nvidia.com/en-us/data-center/a100/`
[9]`https://github.com/aaalgo/kgraph`

Unlike many other libraries for k-NN search, NMSLIB focuses on retrieval for generic similarities. The generality is achieved by relying largely on *distance-based* methods: NSW (Malkov et al., 2014), HNSW (Malkov and Yashunin, 2018), NAPP (Tellez et al., 2013; Boytsov et al., 2016), and an extension of the VP-tree (Boytsov and Naidan, 2013b; Boytsov and Nyberg, 2019b). Distance-based methods can only use values of the mutual data point distances, but cannot exploit the structure of the data, e.g., they have no direct access to vector elements or string characters. In addition, NMSLIB has a simple (no compression) implementation of a traditional inverted file, which can be used to carry out an *exact* maximum-inner product search on sparse vectors.

Graph-based retrieval algorithms have been shown to work efficiently for a variety of non-metric and non-symmetric distances (Boytsov and Nyberg, 2019a; Boytsov, 2018; Naidan et al., 2015b). This flexibility permits adding new distances/similarities with little effort (as we do not have to change the retrieval algorithms). However, this needs to be done in C++, which is one limitation. It is desirable to have an API where C++ code could call Python-implemented distances. NMSLIB supports only in-memory indices and with a single exception all indices are static, which is another (current) limitation of the library.

There is a number of data format and distances—a combination which we call a *space*—supported by NMSLIB. A detailed description can be found online[10]. Most importantly, the library supports L_p distances with the norm $\|x\|_p = \left(\sum_{i \in I} |x_i|^p\right)^{1/p}$, the cosine similarity, and the inner product similarity. For all of these, the data can be both fixed-size "dense" and variable-size "sparse" vectors. Sparse vectors can have an unlimited number of non-zero elements and their processing is less efficient compared to dense vectors. On Intel CPUs the processing is

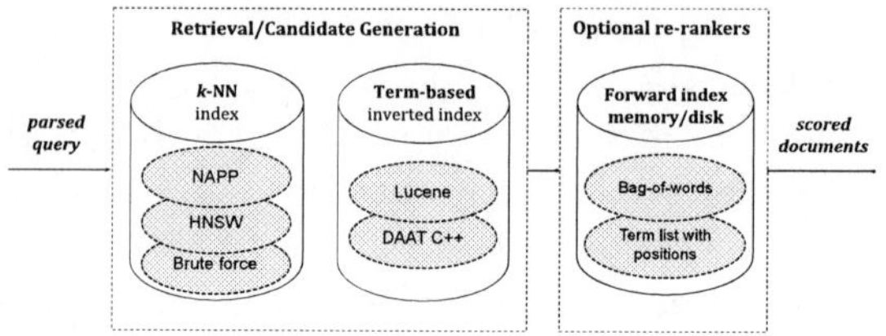

Figure 1: Retrieval Architecture and Workflow Overview

speed up using special SIMD operations. In addition, NMSLIB supports the Jaccard similarity, the Levenshtein distance (for ASCII strings), and the number of (more exotic) divergences (including the KL-divergence).

The library has substantial documentation and additional information can be found online[11].

3 FlexNeuART

3.1 Motivation

Flexible classic and NeurAl Retrieval Toolkit, or shortly FlexNeuART (intended pronunciation flex-noo-art) is a modular text retrieval toolkit, which incorporates some of the best classic, i.e., traditional, information retrieval (IR) signals and provides capabilities for integration with recent neural models. This toolkit supports all key stages of the retrieval pipeline, including indexing, generation of training data, training the models, candidate generation, and re-ranking.

FlexNeuART has been under active development for several years and has been used for our own projects, in particular, to investigate applicability of k-NN search for text retrieval (Boytsov et al., 2016). It was also used in recent TREC evaluations (Craswell et al., 2020) as well as to produce strong runs on the MS MARCO document leaderboard.[12] The toolkit is geared towards TREC evaluations: For broader acceptance we would clearly need to implement Python bindings and experimentation code at the Python level.

---

[10]https://github.com/nmslib/nmslib/blob/master/manual/spaces.md

[11]https://github.com/nmslib/nmslib/tree/master/manual

[12]https://microsoft.github.io/msmarco/#docranking

FlexNeuART was created to fulfill the following needs:

- *Shallow* integration with Lucene and state-of-the-art toolkits for k-NN search (i.e., the candidate generation component should be easy to change);

- Efficient retrieval and efficient re-ranking with basic relevance signals;

- An out-of-the-box support for multi-field document ranking;

- An ease of implementation and/or use of most traditional ranking signals;

- An out-of-the-box support for learning-to-rank (LETOR) and basic experimentation;

- A support for mixed dense-sparse retrieval and/or re-ranking.

Packages most similar to ours in retrieval and LETOR capabilities are Anserini (Yang et al., 2018), Terrier (Ounis et al., 2006), and OpenNIR (MacAvaney, 2020). Anserini and Terrier are Java packages, which were recently enhanced with Python bindings through Pyserini[13] and PyTerrier (Macdonald and Tonellotto, 2020). OpenNIR implements re-ranking code on top of Anserini. These packages are tightly integrated with specific retrieval toolkits, which makes implementation of re-ranking components difficult, as these components need to access retrieval engine internals—which are frequently undocumented—to retrieve stored documents, term statistics, etc. Replacing the core retrieval component becomes problematic as well. In contrast, our system decouples retrieval and re-ranking modules by keeping an *independent* forward index, which enables *plugable* LETOR and IR modules. In addition to this, OpenNIR and Pyserini do not provide API for fusion of relevance signals and none of the toolkits incorporates a lexical translation model (Berger et al., 2000), which can substantially boost accuracy for QA.

```
1 {
2   "DOCNO"  :  "0",
3   "text"  :  "nfl team represent super bowl 50",
4   "text_unlemm"  :  "nfl teams represented super bowl 50"
5 }
```

Figure 2: Sample input for question "Which NFL team represented the AFC at Super Bowl 50?"

3.2 System Design and Workflow

The FlexNeuART system—outlined in Figure 1—implements a classic multi-stage retrieval pipeline, where documents flow through a series of "funnels" that discard unpromising candidates using increasingly more complex and accurate ranking components. In that, FlexNeuART supports one intermediate and one final re-ranker (both are optional). The initial ranked set of documents is provided by the so-called *candidate generator* (also known as the *candidate provider*).

FlexNeuART is designed to work with plugable candidate generators and re-rankers. Out-of-the-box it supports Apache Lucene[14] and NMSLIB, which we describe in § 2. NMSLIB works as a standalone multi-threaded server implemented with Apache Thrift.[15] NMSLIB supports an efficient approximate (and in some cases exact) maximum inner-product search on sparse and sparse-dense representations. Sparse-dense retrieval is a recent addition.

Lucene full-text search algorithms rely on classic term-level inverted files, which are stored in compressed formats (so Lucene is quite space-efficient). NMSLIB (see § 2) supports the classic (uncompressed) inverted files with document-at-at-time (DAAT) processing, the brute-force search, the graph-based retrieval algorithms HNSW (Malkov and Yashunin, 2018) and NSW (Malkov et al., 2014), as well the pivoting algorithm NAPP (Tellez et al., 2013; Boytsov et al., 2016).

The indexing and querying pipelines ingest data (queries and documents) in the form of multi-field JSON entries, which are generated by external Java and/or Python

---

code. Each field can be *parsed* or *raw*. The parsed field contains *white-space* separated tokens while the raw field can keep arbitrary text, which is tokenized directly by re-ranking components. In particular, BERT models rely on their own tokenizers (Devlin et al., 2018).

The core system does not directly incorporate any text processing code, instead, we assume that an external pipeline does all the processing: parsing, tokenization, stopping, and possibly stemming/lemmatization to produce a string of white-space separated tokens. This relieves the indexing code from the need to do complicated parsing and offers extra flexibility in choosing parsing tools.

An example of a two-field input JSON entry for a SQuAD 1.1 (Rajpurkar et al., 2016) question is given in Fig. 2. Document and query entries contain at least two mandatory fields: `DOCNO` and `text`, which represent the document identifier and *indexable* text. Queries and documents may have additional optional fields. For example, HTML documents commonly have a `title` field. In Fig. 2, `text_unlemm` consists of lowercased original words, and `text` contains word lemmas. Stop words are removed from both fields. From our prior TREC experiments we learned that it is beneficial to combine scores obtained for the lemmatized (or stemmed) and the original text (Boytsov and Belova, 2011).

Retrieval requires a Lucene or an `NMSLIB` index, each of which can be created *independently*. To support re-ranking, we also need to create *forward* indices. There is one forward index for each data field. For parsed fields, it contains bag-of-word representations of documents (term IDs and frequencies) and (optionally) an ordered sequence of words. For raw fields, the index keeps unmodified text. A forward index is also required to create an `NMSLIB` index.

The `FlexNeuART` system has a configurable re-ranking module, which can combine results from several ranking components. A sample configuration file shown in Fig. 3

```
1  {"extractors": [
2    {"type": "TFIDFSimilarity",
3     "params": {
4      "indexFieldName": "text",
5      "queryFieldName": "text",
6      "similType": "bm25",
7      "k1": "1.2",
8      "b": "0.75"}
9    },
10   {"type": "avgWordEmbed",
11    "params": {
12     "indexFieldName": "text_unlemm",
13     "queryFieldName": "text_unlemm",
14     "queryEmbedFile": "embeds/starspace_unlemm.query",
15     "docEmbedFile": "embeds/starspace_unlemm.answer",
16     "useIDFWeight": "True",
17     "useL2Norm": "True",
18     "distType": "l2"}
19    }
20  ]}
```

Figure 3: Sample scoring configuration.

contains an array of scoring sub-modules whose parameters are specified via nested dictionaries (in curly brackets). Each description contains the mandatory parameters `type` and `params`. Scoring modules are feature *extractors*, each of which produces one or more numerical feature that can be used by a LETOR component to train a ranking model or to score a candidate document.

The special composite feature extractor reads the configuration file and for each description of the extractor it creates an instance of the feature extractor whose type is defined by `type`. The value of `params` can be arbitrary: parsing and interpreting parameters is delegated to the constructor of the extractor object.

A sample configuration in Fig. 3 defines a BM25 (Robertson, 2004) scorer with parameters $k_1 = 1.2$ and $b = 0.25$ for the index field `text` (and query field `text`) as well as the averaged embedding generator for the fields `text_unlemm`. The latter creates dense query and document representations using StarSpace embeddings (Wu et al., 2018). There are separate sets of embeddings for queries and documents. Word embeddings are weighted using IDFs and subsequently L_2 normalized. Finally, this extractor produces a single feature equal to the L_2 distance between averaged embeddings of the query and the document.

From the forward indices, we can export

```
 1  [
 2    {
 3      "experSubdir": "final_exper",
 4      "candProvAddConfParam" : "exper_desc/lucene.json",
 5      "extrType": "exper_desc/final_extr.json",
 6      "extrTypeInterm" : "exper_desc/interm_extr.json",
 7      "modelInterm" : "exper_desc/classic_ir.model",
 8      "candQty" : 2000,
 9      "testOnly": 0,
10      "runId" : "sample_run_id"
11    }
12  ]
```

Figure 4: Sample experimental configuration.

data to NMSLIB and create an index for k-NN search. This is supported only for inner-product similarities. As discussed in the following subsection § 3.3, there are two scenarios. In the first scenario we export one vector per feature extractor. In particular, we generate a sparse vector for BM25 and a dense vector for the averaged embeddings. Then, NMSLIB combines these representations on its own using adjustable weights, which can be tweaked after data is exported. In the second scenario–which is more efficient but less flexible—we create one composite vector per document/query, where individual component weights cannot be changed further after export.

3.3 Scoring Modules

Similarity scores between queries and documents are computed for a pair of query and a document field (typically these are the same fields).[16] Scores from various scorers are then combined into a single score by a learning-to-rank (LETOR) algorithm (Liu et al., 2009). FlexNeuART use the LETOR library RankLib from which we use two particularly effective learning algorithms: a coordinate ascent (Metzler and Croft, 2007) and LambdaMART (Burges, 2010). We have found a bug in RankLib implementation of the coordinate ascent: We, thus, use our own, bugfixed, version.

Coordinate ascent produces a linear model. It is most effective when the number of features and/or the number of examples is small. LambdaMART is a boosted tree

model, which, in our experience, is effective primarily when the number of features and training examples is quite large.

We provide basic experimentation support. An experiment is described via a JSON descriptor, which defines parameters of the candidate generating, re-ranking, and LETOR algorithms. Some experimentation parameters such as training and testing subsets can also be specified in the command line.

A sample descriptor is shown in Fig. 4. It uses an intermediate re-ranker which re-scores 2000 entries with the highest Lucene scores. A given number of highly scored entries can be further re-scored using the "final" re-ranker. Note that the experimental descriptor references feature-extractor JSONs rather than defining everything in a single configuration file.

Given an experimental descriptor, the training pipeline generates specified features, exports results to a special RankLib format and trains the model. Training of the LETOR model also requires a relevance file (a QREL file in the TREC NIST format), which lists known relevant documents. After training, the respective retrieval system is evaluated on another set of queries. The user can disable model training: This mode is used to tune BM25.

Based on our experience with TREC and community QA collections (Boytsov and Naidan, 2013b; Boytsov, 2018), we support the following scoring approaches:

- A proxy scorer that reads scores from one or more standalone scoring servers, which can be implemented in Python or any other language supported by Apache Thrift.[17] Our system implements neural proxy scorers for CEDR (MacAvaney et al., 2019) and MatchZoo (Fan et al., 2017). We have modified CEDR by providing a better parameterization of the training procedure, adding support for BERT large (Devlin et al., 2018) and multi-GPU training.

---

[16]There can be multiple scorers for each pair of fields.

[17]https://thrift.apache.org/

- The **TF×IDF** similarity BM25 (Robertson, 2004), where logarithms of inverse document term frequencies (IDFs) are multiplied by normalized and smoothed term counts in a document (TFs).

- Sequential dependence model (Metzler and Croft, 2005): our re-implementation is based on the one from `Anserini`.

- BM25-based proximity scorer, which treats ordered and unordered pairs of query terms as a single token. It is similar to the proximity scorer used in our prior work (Boytsov and Belova, 2011).

- **Cosine/L_2 distance** between averaged *word* embeddings. We first train word embeddings for the corpus, then construct a dense vector for a document (or query) by applying TF×IDF weighting to the individual word embeddings and summing them. Then we compare averaged embeddings using the cosine similarity (or L_2 distance).

- **IBM Model 1** is a lexical translation model trained using expectation maximization. We use Model 1 to compute an alignment log-probability between queries and answer documents. Using Model 1 allows us to reduce the vocabulary gap between queries and documents (Berger et al., 2000).

- A proxy query- and document embedder, that produces fixed-size dense vectors for queries and documents. The similarity is the inner product between query and document embeddings. This scorer operates as an Apache Thrift server.

- A BM25-based pseudo-relevance feedback model RM3. Unlike a common approach where RM3 is used for query-expansion, we use it in re-ranking mode (Diaz, 2015).

Although `FlexNeuART` supports complex scoring models, these can be computationally too expensive to be used directly for retrieval (Boytsov et al., 2016; Boytsov, 2018).

Instead we should stick to a simple vector-space model, where similarity is computed as the inner product between query and document vectors (Manning et al., 2010). The respective retrieval procedure is a maximum inner-product search (a form of k-NN search). For example both BM25 and the cosine similarity between query and document embeddings belong to this class of scorers.

Under the vector-space framework we need to (1) generate/read a set of field-specific vectors for queries and documents, (2) compute field-specific scores using the inner product between query and document vectors, and (3) aggregate the scores using a linear model. Alternatively, we can create *composite* queries and document vectors, where we concatenate field-specified vectors multiplied by field weights. Then, the overall similarity score is computed as the inner product between composite query and document vectors.

Our system supports both computation scenarios. To this end, all inner-product equivalent scorers should inherit from a specific abstract class and implement the functions to generate respective query and document vectors. This abstraction simplifies generation of sparse and sparse-dense query/document vectors, which can be subsequently indexed by `NMSLIB`.

4   Experiments

We carry out experiments with two objectives: (1) measuring effectiveness of implemented ranking models; (2) demonstrating the value of a well-tuned traditional IR system. We use two recently released MS MARCO collections (Craswell et al., 2020; Nguyen et al., 2016) and a community question answering (CQA) collection Yahoo Answers Manner (Surdeanu et al., 2011). Collection statistics is summarized in Table 1.

MS MARCO has a document and a passage re-ranking task where all queries can be answered using a short text snippet. There are three sets of queries in each task. In addition to one large query set with sparse judgments, there are two small evaluation

| | MS MARCO | | Yahoo Answers |
	documents	passages	
	general statistics		
# of documents	3.2M	8.8M	819.6K
# of doc. lemmas	476.7	30.6	20.1
# of query lemmas	3.2	3.5	11.9
	# of queries		
train/fusion	10K	20K	14.3K
train/modeling	357K	788.7K	100K
development	2500	20K	7034
test	2693	3000	3000
TREC 2019	100	100	
TREC 2020	100	100	
	BITEXT tokens		
# of QA pairs	43.9M	4M	572.8K
# of query tokens	2.7	2.8	12.6
# of doc. tokens	4.3	4.2	20
	BITEXT BERT word pieces		
# of QA pairs	50M	9.5M	572.8K
# of query tokens	6.1	2.8	42.3
# of doc. tokens	9.4	4.3	62.7

Table 1: Data set statistics

| candidate generator | MS MARCO documents | | MS MARCO passages | |
	TREC 2019	develop.	TREC 2019	develop.
BM25	0.647	0.443	0.707	0.452
Tuned system	0.693	0.472	0.739	0.480
Gain	7.08%	6.39%	4.57%	6.08%

Table 2: The effect of using a more effective candidate generator (evaluation metric is NDCG@10). BM25 is tuned for MS MARCO passages, but not documents.

sets from the TREC 2019/2020 deep learning track (Craswell et al., 2020). MS MARCO collections query sets were randomly split into training, development (to tune hyper parameters), and test sets.

Yahoo Answers Manner has a large number of paired question-answer pairs. We include it in our experiments, because Model 1 was shown to be effective for CQA data in the past (Jeon et al., 2005; Riezler et al., 2007; Surdeanu et al., 2011; Xue et al., 2008). It was randomly split into the training and evaluation sets.

Document text is processed using Spacy 2.2.3 (Honnibal and Montani, 2017) to extract tokens and lemmas. The frequently occurred tokens and lemmas are filtered out using Indri's list of stopwords (Strohman et al., 2005), which is expanded to include a few contractions such as "n't" and "'ll". Lemmas are indexed using Lucene 7.6. In the case of MS MARCO documents, entries come in the HTML format. We extract HTML body and title (and store/index them separately).

In additional to traditional tokenizers, we also use the BERT tokenizer from the HuggingFace Transformers library (Wolf et al., 2019). This tokenizer can split a single word into several sub-word pieces (Wu et al., 2016). The stopword list is not applied to BERT tokens.

Training Model 1, which is a translation model, requires a parallel corpus where queries are paired with respective relevant documents. The parallel corpus is also known as a *bitext*. In the case of MS MARCO collections documents are much longer than queries, which makes it impossible to compute translation probabilities using standard alignment tools (Och and Ney, 2003).[18] Hence, for each pair of query q and its relevant document d, we first split d into multiple short chunks $d_1, d_2, \ldots d_n$. Then, we replace the pair (q, d) with a set of pairs $\{(q, d_i)\}$.

We evaluate performance of several models and their combinations. Each model name is abbreviated as X (Y), where X is a type of the model (see §3.3 for details) and Y is a type of the text field. Specifically, we index original tokens, lemmas, as well as BERT tokens extracted from the main document text. For MS MARCO documents, which come in HTML format, we also extract tokens and lemmas from the title field.

First, we evaluate performance of the *tuned* BM25 (lemmas). Second, we evaluate fusion models that combine BM25 (lemmas) with BM25, proximity, and Model 1 scores (see §3.3) computed for various fields. Note that our fusion models are linear. Third, we evaluate collection-specific combinations of manually-selected models: Except for minor changes these are the fusion models that we used in our TREC 2019 and 2020 submissions.

All models were trained and/or tuned using training and development sets listed in

---

[18] https://github.com/moses-smt/mgiza/

	MS MARCO documents			MS MARCO passages			Yahoo Answers
	test	TREC 2019	TREC 2020	test	TREC 2019	TREC 2020	test
	MRR	NDCG@10	NDCG@10	MRR	NDCG@10	NDCG@10	NDCG@10
BM25 (lemmas)	0.270	0.544	0.524	0.256	0.522	0.516	0.152
BM25 (lemmas)+BM25 (BERT tokens)	0.283	0.528	0.537	0.270	0.518	0.525	0.159
BM25 (lemmas)+BM25 (tokens)	0.274	0.544	0.523	0.265	0.517	0.521	0.157
BM25 (lemmas)+BM25 (title tokens)	0.294	0.550	0.527				
BM25 (lemmas)+proximity (lemmas)	0.282	0.559	0.524	0.257	0.538	0.523	
BM25 (lemmas)+proximity (tokens)	0.284	0.560	0.531	0.265	0.534	0.524	
BM25 (lemmas)+Model1 (tokens)	0.283	0.548	0.535	0.274	0.522	0.567	0.160
BM25 (lemmas)+Model1 (BERT tokens)	0.284	0.557	0.525	0.271	0.517	0.509	0.175
best combination	0.310	0.565	0.542	0.290	0.558	0.560	

Table 3: Evaluation of various fusion models.

Table 1. For TREC 2019 and 2020 query sets (as well as for Yahoo Answers Manner), the evaluation metric is NDCG@10 (Järvelin and Kekäläinen, 2002), which the main metric in the TREC deep learning track (Craswell et al., 2020). For subsets of MS MARCO collections, we use the mean reciprocal rank (MRR) as suggested by Craswell et al. (2020).

From the experiments in Table 3, we can see that for all large query sets the fusion models outperform BM25 (lemmas). In particular, the best MS MARCO fusion models are 13-15% better than BM25 (lemmas). In the case of Yahoo Answers Manner, combining BM25 (lemmas) with Model 1 scores computed for BERT tokens also boost performance by about 15%. For small TREC 2019 and 2020 query sets the gains are marginal. However, our fusion models are still better than BM25 (lemmas) by 4-8%.

We further compare the accuracy of the BERT-based re-ranker (Nogueira and Cho, 2019) applied to the output of the tuned traditional IR system with the accuracy of the *same* BERT-based re-ranker applied to the output of Lucene (with a BM25 scorer). The BERT scorer is used to re-rank 150 documents: Further increasing the number of candidates degraded performance on the TREC 2019 test set.

By mistake we used the same BM25 parameters for both passages and documents. As a result, MS MARCO documents candidate generator was suboptimal (passage retrieval did use the properly tuned BM25 scorer). However, we refrained from correcting this error to illustrate how a good fusion model can produce a strong ranker via a combination of suboptimal weak rankers.

Indeed, as we can see from Table 2, there is a substantial 4.5-7% loss in accuracy by re-ranking the output of BM25 compared to re-ranking the output of the well-tuned traditional pipeline. This degradation occurs in all four experiments.

5 Conclusion and Future Work

We present to the NLP community an existing k-NN search library NMSLIB, a new retrieval toolkit FlexNeuART, as well as their integration capabilities, which enable efficient retrieval of sparse and sparse-dense document representations. FlexNeuART implements a variety of effective traditional relevance signals, which we plan to use for a fairer comparison with recent neural retrieval systems based on representing queries and documents via fixed-size dense vectors.

6 Acknowledgements

This work was done primarily while Leonid Boytsov was a PhD student at CMU where he was supported by the NSF grant #1618159. We thank Sean MacAvaney for making CEDR (MacAvaney et al., 2019) publicly available and Igor Brigadir for suggesting to experiment with indexing of BERT word pieces.

References

Sunil Arya and David M Mount. 1993. Approximate nearest neighbor queries in fixed dimensions. In *Proceedings of the fourth annual ACM-SIAM symposium on Discrete algorithms*, pages 271–280.

Martin Aumüller, Erik Bernhardsson, and Alexander Faithfull. 2019. ANN-benchmarks: A benchmarking tool for approximate nearest neighbor algorithms. *Information Systems*.

Adam L. Berger, Rich Caruana, David Cohn, Dayne Freitag, and Vibhu O. Mittal. 2000. Bridging the lexical chasm: statistical approaches to answer-finding. In *SIGIR 2000: Proceedings of the 23rd Annual International ACM SIGIR Conference on Research and Development in Information Retrieval, July 24-28, 2000, Athens, Greece*, pages 192–199.

Leonid Boytsov. 2018. *Efficient and Accurate Non-Metric k-NN Search with Applications to Text Matching*. Ph.D. thesis, Carnegie Mellon University.

Leonid Boytsov and Anna Belova. 2011. Evaluating learning-to-rank methods in the web track adhoc task. In *TREC*.

Leonid Boytsov and Bilegsaikhan Naidan. 2013a. Engineering efficient and effective non-metric space library. In *Proceedings of SISAP 2013*, pages 280–293. Springer.

Leonid Boytsov and Bilegsaikhan Naidan. 2013b. Learning to prune in metric and non-metric spaces. In *Advances in Neural Information Processing Systems*, pages 1574–1582.

Leonid Boytsov, David Novak, Yury Malkov, and Eric Nyberg. 2016. Off the beaten path: Let's replace term-based retrieval with k-NN search. In *Proceedings of CIKM 2016*, pages 1099–1108. ACM.

Leonid Boytsov and Eric Nyberg. 2019a. Accurate and fast retrieval for complex non-metric data via neighborhood graphs. In *International Conference on Similarity Search and Applications*, pages 128–142. Springer.

Leonid Boytsov and Eric Nyberg. 2019b. Pruning algorithms for low-dimensional non-metric k-nn search: A case study. In *Similarity Search and Applications*.

Christopher JC Burges. 2010. From RankNet to LambdaRank to LambdaMart: An overview. Microsoft Technical Report MSR-TR-2010-82.

Nick Craswell, Bhaskar Mitra, Emine Yilmaz, Daniel Campos, and Ellen M Voorhees. 2020. Overview of the trec 2019 deep learning track. *arXiv preprint arXiv:2003.07820*.

Jacob Devlin, Ming-Wei Chang, Kenton Lee, and Kristina Toutanova. 2018. Bert: Pretraining of deep bidirectional transformers for language understanding. *arXiv preprint arXiv:1810.04805*.

Fernando Diaz. 2015. Condensed list relevance models. In *Proceedings of the 2015 International Conference on The Theory of Information Retrieval*, pages 313–316.

Wei Dong, Charikar Moses, and Kai Li. 2011. Efficient k-nearest neighbor graph construction for generic similarity measures. In *Proceedings of the 20th international conference on World wide web*, pages 577–586.

Yixing Fan, Liang Pang, JianPeng Hou, Jiafeng Guo, Yanyan Lan, and Xueqi Cheng. 2017. Matchzoo: A toolkit for deep text matching. *arXiv preprint arXiv:1707.07270*.

Christophe Van Gysel, Maarten De Rijke, and Evangelos Kanoulas. 2018. Neural vector spaces for unsupervised information retrieval. *ACM Transactions on Information Systems (TOIS)*, 36(4):38.

Changwan Hong, Aravind Sukumaran-Rajam, Bortik Bandyopadhyay, Jinsung Kim, Süreyya Emre Kurt, Israt Nisa, Shivani Sabhlok, Ümit V Çatalyürek, Srinivasan Parthasarathy, and P Sadayappan. 2018. Efficient sparse-matrix multi-vector product on gpus. In *Proceedings of the 27th International Symposium on High-Performance Parallel and Distributed Computing*, pages 66–79.

Matthew Honnibal and Ines Montani. 2017. spaCy 2: Natural language understanding with Bloom embeddings, convolutional neural networks and incremental parsing. To appear.

Kalervo Järvelin and Jaana Kekäläinen. 2002. Cumulated gain-based evaluation of ir techniques. *ACM Transactions on Information Systems (TOIS)*, 20(4):422–446.

Jiwoon Jeon, W. Bruce Croft, and Joon Ho Lee. 2005. Finding similar questions in large question and answer archives. In *Proceedings of the 2005 ACM CIKM International Conference on Information and Knowledge Management, Bremen, Germany, October 31 - November 5, 2005*, pages 84–90.

Jeff Johnson, Matthijs Douze, and Hervé Jégou. 2017. Billion-scale similarity search with gpus. *arXiv preprint arXiv:1702.08734*.

Vladimir Karpukhin, Barlas Oğuz, Sewon Min, Ledell Wu, Sergey Edunov, Danqi Chen, and Wen-tau Yih. 2020. Dense passage retrieval for open-domain question answering. *arXiv preprint arXiv:2004.04906*.

Omar Khattab and Matei Zaharia. 2020. Colbert: Efficient and effective passage search via contextualized late interaction over bert. In *Proceedings of the 43rd International ACM SIGIR Conference on Research and Development in Information Retrieval*, SIGIR '20, page 39–48, New York, NY, USA. Association for Computing Machinery.

Saar Kuzi, Mingyang Zhang, Cheng Li, Michael Bendersky, and Marc Najork. 2020. Leveraging semantic and lexical matching to improve the recall of document retrieval systems: A hybrid approach. *arXiv preprint arXiv:2010.01195*.

Kenton Lee, Ming-Wei Chang, and Kristina Toutanova. 2019. Latent retrieval for weakly supervised open domain question answering. *arXiv preprint arXiv:1906.00300*.

Tie-Yan Liu et al. 2009. Learning to rank for information retrieval. *Foundations and Trends® in Information Retrieval*, 3(3):225–331.

Sean MacAvaney. 2020. OpenNIR: A complete neural ad-hoc ranking pipeline. In *WSDM 2020*.

Sean MacAvaney, Andrew Yates, Arman Cohan, and Nazli Goharian. 2019. Cedr: Contextualized embeddings for document ranking. In *Proceedings of the 42nd International ACM SIGIR Conference on Research and Development in Information Retrieval*, pages 1101–1104.

Craig Macdonald and Nicola Tonellotto. 2020. Declarative experimentation in information retrieval using pyterrier. *arXiv preprint arXiv:2007.14271*.

Yury Malkov, Alexander Ponomarenko, Andrey Logvinov, and Vladimir Krylov. 2014. Approximate nearest neighbor algorithm based on navigable small world graphs. *Information Systems*, 45:61–68.

Yury A Malkov and Dmitry A Yashunin. 2018. Efficient and robust approximate nearest neighbor search using hierarchical navigable small world graphs. *IEEE transactions on pattern analysis and machine intelligence*.

Christopher Manning, Prabhakar Raghavan, and Hinrich Schütze. 2010. Introduction to information retrieval. *Natural Language Engineering*, 16(1):100–103.

Donald Metzler and W Bruce Croft. 2005. A markov random field model for term dependencies. In *Proceedings of the 28th annual international ACM SIGIR conference on Research and development in information retrieval*, pages 472–479.

Donald Metzler and W. Bruce Croft. 2007. Linear feature-based models for information retrieval. *Inf. Retr.*, 10(3):257–274.

Bilegsaikhan Naidan, Leonid Boytsov, Yury Malkov, and David Novak. 2015a. Non-metric space library manual. *arXiv preprint arXiv:1508.05470*.

Bilegsaikhan Naidan, Leonid Boytsov, and Eric Nyberg. 2015b. Permutation search methods are efficient, yet faster search is possible. *Proceedings of the VLDB Endowment*, 8(12).

Tri Nguyen, Mir Rosenberg, Xia Song, Jianfeng Gao, Saurabh Tiwary, Rangan Majumder, and Li Deng. 2016. Ms marco: A human generated machine reading comprehension dataset.

Rodrigo Nogueira and Kyunghyun Cho. 2019. Passage re-ranking with bert. *arXiv preprint arXiv:1901.04085*.

Franz Josef Och and Hermann Ney. 2003. A systematic comparison of various statistical alignment models. *Computational Linguistics*, 29(1):19–51.

Iadh Ounis, Gianni Amati, Vassilis Plachouras, Ben He, Craig Macdonald, and Christina Lioma. 2006. Terrier: A high performance and scalable information retrieval platform. In *Proceedings of the OSIR Workshop*, pages 18–25.

Pranav Rajpurkar, Jian Zhang, Konstantin Lopyrev, and Percy Liang. 2016. Squad: $100,000+$ questions for machine comprehension of text. In *Proceedings of EMNLP 2016*, pages 2383–2392.

Stefan Riezler, Alexander Vasserman, Ioannis Tsochantaridis, Vibhu O. Mittal, and Yi Liu. 2007. Statistical machine translation for query expansion in answer retrieval. In *ACL 2007, Proceedings of the 45th Annual Meeting of the Association for Computational Linguistics*.

Stephen Robertson. 2004. Understanding inverse document frequency: on theoretical arguments for IDF. *Journal of Documentation*, 60(5):503–520.

Minjoon Seo, Jinhyuk Lee, Tom Kwiatkowski, Ankur P Parikh, Ali Farhadi, and Hannaneh Hajishirzi. 2019. Real-time open-domain question answering with dense-sparse phrase index. *arXiv preprint arXiv:1906.05807*.

Larissa C Shimomura, Rafael Seidi Oyamada, Marcos R Vieira, and Daniel S Kaster. 2020. A survey on graph-based methods for similarity searches in metric spaces. *Information Systems*, page 101507.

Trevor Strohman, Donald Metzler, Howard Turtle, and W Bruce Croft. 2005. Indri: A language-model based search engine for complex queries. http://ciir.cs.umass.edu/pubfiles/ir-407.pdf [Last Checked Apr 2017].

Mihai Surdeanu, Massimiliano Ciaramita, and Hugo Zaragoza. 2011. Learning to rank answers to non-factoid questions from web collections. *Computational Linguistics*, 37(2):351–383.

Eric Sadit Tellez, Edgar Chávez, and Gonzalo Navarro. 2013. Succinct nearest neighbor search. *Inf. Syst.*, 38(7):1019–1030.

Thomas Wolf, Lysandre Debut, Victor Sanh, Julien Chaumond, Clement Delangue, Anthony Moi, Pierric Cistac, Tim Rault, Rémi Louf, Morgan Funtowicz, Joe Davison, Sam Shleifer, Patrick von Platen, Clara Ma, Yacine Jernite, Julien Plu, Canwen Xu, Teven Le Scao, Sylvain Gugger, Mariama Drame, Quentin Lhoest, and Alexander M. Rush. 2019. Huggingface's transformers: State-of-the-art natural language processing. *ArXiv*, abs/1910.03771.

Ledell Yu Wu, Adam Fisch, Sumit Chopra, Keith Adams, Antoine Bordes, and Jason Weston. 2018. Starspace: Embed all the things! In *Proceedings of AAAI 2018*.

Yonghui Wu, Mike Schuster, Zhifeng Chen, Quoc V. Le, Mohammad Norouzi, Wolfgang Macherey, Maxim Krikun, Yuan Cao, Qin Gao, Klaus Macherey, Jeff Klingner, Apurva Shah, Melvin Johnson, Xiaobing Liu, Lukasz Kaiser, Stephan Gouws, Yoshikiyo Kato, Taku Kudo, Hideto Kazawa, Keith Stevens, George Kurian, Nishant Patil, Wei Wang, Cliff Young, Jason Smith, Jason Riesa, Alex Rudnick, Oriol Vinyals, Greg Corrado, Macduff Hughes, and Jeffrey Dean. 2016. Google's neural machine translation system: Bridging the gap between human and machine translation. *CoRR*, abs/1609.08144.

Lee Xiong, Chenyan Xiong, Ye Li, Kwok-Fung Tang, Jialin Liu, Paul Bennett, Junaid Ahmed, and Arnold Overwijk. 2020. Approximate nearest neighbor negative contrastive learning for dense text retrieval. *arXiv preprint arXiv:2007.00808*.

Xiaobing Xue, Jiwoon Jeon, and W. Bruce Croft. 2008. Retrieval models for question and answer archives. In *Proceedings of the 31st Annual International ACM SIGIR Conference on Research and Development in Information Retrieval, SIGIR 2008, Singapore, July 20-24, 2008*, pages 475–482.

Peilin Yang, Hui Fang, and Jimmy Lin. 2018. Anserini: Reproducible ranking baselines using Lucene. *J. Data and Information Quality*, 10(4):16:1–16:20.

fugashi, a Tool for Tokenizing Japanese in Python

Paul McCann

Cotonoha

howdy@cotonoha.io

Abstract

Recent years have seen an increase in the number of large-scale multilingual NLP projects. However, even in such projects, languages with special processing requirements are often excluded. One such language is Japanese. Japanese is written without spaces, tokenization is non-trivial, and while high quality open source tokenizers exist they can be hard to use and lack English documentation. This paper introduces fugashi, a MeCab wrapper for Python, and gives an introduction to tokenizing Japanese.

1 Introduction

Over the past several years there's been a welcome trend in NLP projects to be broadly multilingual. However, even when many languages are supported, there are a few that tend to be left out. One of these is Japanese. Japanese is written without spaces, and deciding where one word ends and another begins is not trivial. While highly accurate tokenizers are available, they can be hard to use, and English documentation is scarce. This is a short guide to tokenizing Japanese in Python that should be enough to get you started adding Japanese support to your application. [1]

This paper will begin with a tutorial on Japanese tokenization using fugashi, along with notes on issues to be aware of. Following that will be a discussion of the development of fugashi, closing with a brief overview of other Japanese tokenizers usable in Python.

---

[1] This paper was originally made available as a blog post. https://www.dampfkraft.com/nlp/how-to-tokenize-japanese.html

2 Preparation

First, you'll need to install fugashi and a tokenizer dictionary. For this tutorial we'll use fugashi with unidic-lite. You can install them with this command:

```
pip install fugashi[unidic-lite]
```

fugashi comes with a script so you can test it out at the command line. Type in some Japanese and the output will have one word per line, along with other information like part of speech. Refer to Table 1 for an example. [2]

3 Sample Code

Now we're ready to get started with converting plain Japanese text into a list of words in Python.

```python
import fugashi
# This is our sample text.
# "Fugashi" is a Japanese snack primarily made
# of gluten.
text = " 麸菓子は、麸を主材料とした日本の菓子。"

# The Tagger object holds state about the
# dictionary.
tagger = fugashi.Tagger()

words = [word.surface for word in tagger(text)]
print(*words)
# => 麸 菓子 は 、 麸 を 主材料 と した 日本
# の 菓子 。
```

This prints the original sentence with spaces inserted between words. In many cases, that's all you need, but fugashi provides a lot of other information, such as part of speech, lemmas, broad etymological category, pronunciation, and more. This information all comes from

---

[2] All examples in this text use fugashi v1.0.4 and unidic-lite v1.0.7.

Proceedings of Second Workshop for NLP Open Source Software (NLP-OSS), pages 44–51
Virtual Conference, November 19, 2020. ©2020 Association for Computational Linguistics

麩	フ	フ	麩	名詞-普通名詞-一般			0
菓子	カシ	カシ	菓子	名詞-普通名詞-一般			1
は	ワ	ハ	は	助詞-係助詞			
、			、	補助記号-読点			
麩	フ	フ	麩	名詞-普通名詞-一般			0
を	オ	ヲ	を	助詞-格助詞			
主材	シュザイ	シュザイ	主材	名詞-普通名詞-一般			0
料	リョー	リョウ	料	接尾辞-名詞的-一般			
と	ト	ト	と	助詞-格助詞			
し	シ	スル	為る	動詞-非自立可能	サ行変格	連用形-一般	0
た	タ	タ	た	助動詞	助動詞-タ	連体形-一般	
日本	ニッポン	ニッポン	日本	名詞-固有名詞-地名-国			3
の	ノ	ノ	の	助詞-格助詞			
菓子	カシ	カシ	菓子	名詞-普通名詞-一般			1
。			。	補助記号-句点			
EOS							

Table 1: Example output from fugashi on the command line. Each column is a different field from UniDic. This format can be customized; the format here is the default format distributed with UniDic 2.1.2. "EOS" means "End of Sentence", though MeCab does not perform sentence tokenization, and EOS is simply emitted at the end of any output.

UniDic (Den et al., 2008), a dictionary provided by the National Institute for Japanese Language and Linguistics (NINJAL).[3]

fugashi is a wrapper for MeCab (Kudo et al., 2004), a C++ Japanese tokenizer. MeCab is doing all the hard work here, but fugashi wraps it to make it more Pythonic, easier to install, and to clarify some common error cases.

You may wonder why part of speech and other information is included by default. In the classical NLP pipeline for languages like English, tokenization is a separate step before part of speech tagging. In Japanese, however, knowing part of speech is important in getting tokenization right, so they're conventionally solved as a joint task. This is why Japanese tokenizers are often referred to as "morphological analyzers" (形態素解析器 *keitaisokaisekiki*).

4 Notes on Japanese Tokenization

There are several things about Japanese tokenization that may be surprising if you're used to languages like English.

4.1 Lemmas May Not Resemble the Words in the Text at All

Here's how you get lemma information with fugashi:

```
import fugashi
tagger = fugashi.Tagger()
text = "..."

print("input:", text)
for word in tagger(text):
    # feature is a named tuple
    # holding all the Unidic info
    print(word.surface, word.feature.lemma,
        sep="\t")
```

For the output of the script refer to Table 2.

You can see that 用い has 用いる as a lemma, and that し has 為る and い has 居る, handling both inflection and orthographic variation. すでに is not inflected, but the lemma uses the kanji form 既に.

An important detail here is that while MeCab provides all this information in its output, it's returned as unstructured text data. Conventionally a user could use MeCab's output formatting language to get just the fields they need, or output all fields and parse the output to get the desired fields. fugashi provides wrappers for UniDic formatted data that handle the parsing and put it in named tuples for structured access, like `word.feature.lemma`.

These lemmas come from UniDic, which by convention uses the "dictionary form" of a word for lemmas. This is typically in kanji even if the word isn't usually written in kanji because the kanji form is considered less ambiguous. For example, この (*kono*, "this [thing]") has 此の (same pronunciation and meaning) as a lemma, even though normal

---

[3]Besides the version for modern written Japanese used here, there are also versions of UniDic for spoken Japanese and different historical varieties of the language, all available from the UniDic homepage. https://unidic.ninjal.ac.jp/

<table>
<tr><td>Input</td><td>麩 を 用い た 菓子 は 江戸 時代 から すでに 存在 し て い た 。</td></tr>
<tr><td>Lemmas</td><td>麩 を 用いる た 菓子 は エド 時代 から 既に 存在 為る て 居る た 。</td></tr>
<tr><td>Translation</td><td>Snacks using gluten already existed in the Edo Period.</td></tr>
<tr><td>Input</td><td>すもも も もも も もも の 内</td></tr>
<tr><td>Lemmas</td><td>李 も 桃 も 桃 の 内</td></tr>
<tr><td>Translation</td><td>Japanese plums and peaches are both kinds of peaches.</td></tr>
<tr><td>Input</td><td>彷徨う 陽射し</td></tr>
<tr><td>Lemmas</td><td>さ迷う 日差し</td></tr>
<tr><td>Translation</td><td>Wandering sunbeams.</td></tr>
</table>

Table 2: Input tokens and their associated lemmas. Lemmas may not bear any visual resemblance to the raw forms, which can look like an error to users unfamiliar with Japanese, and can be surprising even to Japanese speakers.

modern writing would never use that form. This is also true of 為る in the above example.

This can be surprising if you aren't familiar with Japanese, but it's not a problem. It is worth keeping in mind if your application ever shows lemmas to your user for any reason, though, as it may not be in a form they expect.

Another thing to keep in mind is that most lemmas in Japanese deal with orthographic rather than inflectional variation. This orthographic variation is called 表記ゆれ *hyoukiyure* and causes problems similar to spelling errors in English.

4.2 Verbs Will Often Be Multiple Tokens

Inflections of a verb will typically result in multiple tokens. This can also affect adjectives that inflect, like 赤い *akai* ("red"). You can see this in the verbs at the end of the previous example, or see Table 3.

This would be like if "looked" was tokenized into "look" and "ed" in English. This feels strange even to native Japanese speakers, but it's common to all modern tokenizers. The main reason for this is that verb inflections are extremely regular, so registering verb stems and verb parts separately in the dictionary makes dictionary maintenance easier and the tokenizer implementation simpler and faster. It also works better in the rare case an unknown verb shows up. (Verbs are a closed class in Japanese, which means new verbs aren't common.)

In the early 90s several tokenizers handled verb morphology directly, but that approach has been abandoned over time because of the advantages of the fine-grained approach (Kudo, 2018, pp. 21–22). Depending on your application needs you can use some simple rules based on part of speech to lump verb parts together or just discard non-stem parts as stop words.

4.3 The Tagger Object Has a Startup Cost

It's fast enough that you won't notice for one invocation, but creating the Tagger is a lot of work for the computer. When processing text in a loop it's important you re-use the Tagger rather than creating a new Tagger for each input.

Don't do this:

```
for text in texts:
    tagger = fugashi.Tagger()
    words = tagger(text)
```

Do this instead:

```
tagger = fugashi.Tagger()
for text in texts:
    words = tagger(text)
```

If you follow the second pattern MeCab shouldn't be a speed bottleneck for normal applications.

4.4 Always Note Your Tokenizer Details

If you publish a resource using tokenized Japanese text, always be careful to mention what tokenizer and what dictionary you used so your results can be replicated. Saying you used MeCab isn't enough information to reproduce your results, because there are many different dictionaries for MeCab that can give completely different results. Even if you specify the dictionary, it's critical that you specify the version too, since popular dictionaries like UniDic may be updated over time.[4]

---

[4] If for some reason you are unable to identify the version of your dictionary, at least report the number of entries it has, which can be used as a primitive checksum.

Raw Text	Tokenized Output	Translation
見た	見 | た	saw, looked
見ました	見 | まし | た	saw, looked (polite)
見なかった	見 | なかっ | た	did not see
受け渡した	受け渡し | た	handed over
遊べませんでした	遊べ | ませ | ん | でし | た	was unable to play (polite)
赤かった	赤かっ | た	red (past tense)

Table 3: Examples of tokenized verbs and adjectives resulting in multiple tokens. Using UniDic results in fine-grained tokenization, where some tokens are not words in any conventional sense. One class of adjectives resembles verbs and will also frequently result in multiple tokens when inflected.

5 Development Background

fugashi was originally developed as part of adding Japanese support to spaCy (Honnibal and Montani, 2017) due to lack of maintenance of the mecab-python3[5] library, but has since evolved to differentiate itself from that library in a few ways. The primary goal of fugashi is to make it as easy as possible to get fast Japanese tokenization while improving access to existing linguistic resources.

This section will introduce the important features of fugashi and touch on how they were implemented. These features are not unique in isolation, but bringing them together in one place is the distinguishing feature of fugashi.

5.1 Binary Wheels

"Wheels" are modern Python packages that can include platform-specific binary code.[6] Distributing wheels allows users to install compiled packages even without having a compiler or other necessary dependencies on their systems. fugashi provides wheels for Linux, OSX, and Windows, so that it can be installed with a single pip command.

Before wheels for MeCab were provided, a user had to install it from source or through a package manager. Some Linux distributions like Debian use code that differs from the most recent source, making consistent use of MeCab difficult. Compiling MeCab on Windows is also known to be challenging. Providing wheels allows for consistent versioning and easy installs across platforms. This is critical for integration in open-source projects where maintainers want to support Japanese but don't have the time to set up a special development environment to handle it.

fugashi was the first MeCab wrapper to provide binary wheels for all of Windows, Linux, and OSX. The code used to build fugashi wheels was later used to distribute wheels for mecab-python3.

5.2 Dictionary Packages

Use of MeCab requires a dictionary. Historically MeCab shipped with some dictionaries, but these have not been updated since 2013 (if not earlier). Installing dictionaries required manual configuration that could vary depending on how MeCab had been installed, which made integrating a dictionary in open-source Python packages difficult.

As part of supporting fugashi, the UniDic and IPAdic dictionaries have been packaged so that they can be installed directly via pip.[7] IPAdic is a dictionary that, while not updated since roughly 2007, remains popular for natural language applications for a variety of reasons such as compatibility with historical benchmarks. The previously introduced UniDic is maintained by NINJAL and is the official dictionary of Japanese Universal Dependencies (Asahara et al., 2018).

Because of size limitations on PyPI[8], UniDic is provided in two flavors: the full UniDic package, based on the latest version, requires an extra download step, but is otherwise simple to install and configure. unidic-lite is based on the 2.1.2 release of UniDic, which is the most recent release to fit under PyPI's file size limit

---

[5]https://github.com/SamuraiT/mecab-python3
[6]PEP 427 – The Wheel Binary Package Format 1.0 https://www.python.org/dev/peps/pep-0427/

[7]The PyPI package names are unidic, unidic-lite, and ipadic.
[8]PyPI is the Python Package Index, a service that hosts packages to be installed via pip. https://pypi.org/

of 60MB compressed. Both of these dictionaries have been modified slightly to avoid issues with the default distribution such as marking unusual punctuation as nouns or tokenizing any numbers into individual digits.[9]

Before fugashi was developed, mecab-python3 releases starting in 2018 included a bundled IPAdic. Leaving aside the issues with IPAdic being out of date, this approach is similar to Janome and makes the tokenizer easier to use, but has the downside that it makes it harder to use other dictionaries. In the case of mecab-python3 this also had the issue that it was a change from prior behavior without notice and caused some confusion. Following development of pip installable dictionaries for fugashi, the feature was backported to mecab-python3.

5.3 Structured Data

Another important feature of fugashi is providing access to structured data. UniDic in particular provides a wealth of linguistic information, such as pronunciation, lemma, etymological category, pitch accent, and even foreign spelling.[10] Traditionally this information would be presented in MeCab as a string and the application would parse it as necessary. By performing this parsing up-front and dealing with variations in dictionary format automatically, fugashi makes it more accessible for downstream applications.

This feature is common in tokenizers not based directly on MeCab, but fugashi was the first Python MeCab wrapper to include it, and is (to my knowledge) the only Python tokenizer providing structured access to all fields in UniDic.

5.4 A Pythonic Interface

Besides structured data, the changes fugashi makes to the MeCab API to make it more Pythonic are subtle but important. The most obvious example is that the `parseToNode` function, used to turn an input string into a Node object for each token, would normally return the head of a linked list. Navigating a linked list using member variables is unremarkable in C/C++ but distinctly odd in Python. In deference to the MeCab API mecab-python3 strictly maintains the old interface, while fugashi returns a Python list of nodes, allowing use in list comprehensions and other Pythonic idioms.

5.5 Detailed Error Messages

One other significant change is a creative workaround for failed initializations of the `Tagger` object. Issues like forgetting to install a dictionary are very common and show up as errrors at initialization, and are the most common cause of issues on mecab-python3's Github repository, but a bug in MeCab[11] causes error messages to be unavailable when MeCab is used as a library. The workaround involves passing the intialization arguments to a separate class and getting the error message for that. This convoluted process is invisible to the user. This particular feature doesn't affect the API and has been backported to mecab-python3.

The text of the error message used when initialization fails is also a departure from MeCab's default error messages, which are all one-line and often leave users confused. In contrast the fugashi (or mecab-python3) error message includes a link to a detailed FAQ in the README, debug information, and a note that issues need not be filed in English. This was inspired by similarly detailed error messages in spaCy.[12]

5.6 Speed

The difference in processing speed between tokenizers can be dramatic. In developing fugashi I created a simple benchmark that counts words in Natsume Souseki's *I Am a Cat* to make sure I wasn't unknowingly introducing performance issues. This is not reflective of all

---

[9]The MeCab documentation provides instructions on how to mitigate some of these issues, but doesn't distribute modified dictionaries. `https://taku910.github.io/mecab/unk.html`

[10]"Foreign spelling" refers to the spelling of loanwords in the original language. For example, a naive romanization of ポール would be *pooru*, but the UniDic lemma is ポール-Paul. Similarly パン *pan*, "bread", has the lemma パン-pao because it comes from the Portuguese. These spellings can optionally be used in cutlet, a romanization tool based on fugashi. `https://github.com/polm/cutlet`

[11]`https://github.com/taku910/mecab/issues/57`

[12]See the spaCy error code for examples of error messages written in a friendly style that include links to related issues or documentation. `https://github.com/explosion/spaCy/blob/master/spacy/errors.py`

Tokenizer	Time	Relative Time
mecab-python3	290	1.00
fugashi	294	1.01
natto-py	1173	4.04
kytea	2254	7.77
sudachipy	10103	34.83
janome	16496	56.88

Table 4: Processing time in milliseconds for a simple benchmark word count task. fugashi and mecab-python3 are roughly equivalent in speed, with other packages being slower.

real-world workloads, but it is a good task for getting a rough idea of tokenizer speed. See Table 4 for the results, which demonstrate that MeCab is very fast. The run times presented here are the average over ten runs. The source code for this benchmark is available online.[13]

6 Comparison with Other Tokenizers

There are a tremendous number of tokenizers for Japanese, and a comprehensive comparison is beyond the scope of this paper. This is a short overview of other tokenizers usable in Python.

Tokenizers usable in Python may be broadly grouped into three categories: MeCab wrappers, MeCab-like tokenizers, and other tokenizers.

6.1 MeCab Wrappers

Over the years there have been many MeCab wrappers for Python, though only a few are still maintained. The original MeCab code[14] includes a SWIG[15] wrapper which has been the basis of several tokenizers. The MeCab wrappers are the fastest Python tokenizers.

mecab-python3 is a MeCab wrapper based on the SWIG code included in the main MeCab repository, and is the oldest of the tokenizer packages mentioned here, with its first release in 2014. fugashi was initially developed in response to a lack of maintenance of mecab-python3, but since then I have taken over the project and maintain it in parallel

with fugashi. Several developments in fugashi are based on personal pain points with mecab-python3, and improvements to fugashi that don't affect the API, like pip-installable dictionary support, have been backported. Because mecab-python3 is widely used the main priority of maintenance is keeping the existing API stable for legacy applications, while fugashi is free to make the API more Pythonic for use in new applications.

The **mecab**[16] project on PyPI, formerly known as **mecab-python-windows**, is based on the same SWIG code as mecab-python3 and has basically the same API. It provided Windows wheels long before mecab-python3, but since mecab-python3 began offering Windows wheels the differences between the packages are relatively minor.

natto-py[17] is a MeCab wrapper that uses a cffi interface to avoid needing a compiler and has simplified some of the MeCab API to be more Pythonic. However, the cffi interface is slower than Cython or SWIG, and since a separate MeCab install with dictionary is required that still leaves the user responsible for getting configuration right.

6.2 MeCab-like Tokenizers

Some tokenizers more or less explicitly copy the design of MeCab while adding features or improving usability. These tokenizers all started life as Python projects, which greatly simplifies tooling, but comes at the expense of speed; they are much slower than the MeCab wrappers. This is still fast enough for small to medium sized corpora, but presents issues when processing larger amounts of text.

The main features that make a tokenizer MeCab-like are the use of an extensive dictionary with part of speech information, typically accessed via a double-array trie, and use of the Viterbi algorithm to find a minimum cost tokenization of a string.

Janome[18] is a pure Python tokenizer with a long history. It includes a slightly modified IPAdic with the addition of 令和 *Reiwa*, the current era name. Since everything necessary is included it's very easy to use, and

---

[13] https://github.com/polm/ja-tokenizer-benchmark

[14] https://github.com/taku910/mecab

[15] "Simplified Wrapper and Interface Generator". SWIG allows a developer to write an interface file for C/C++ code and generate wrappers in a variety of languages. http://www.swig.org/

[16] https://pypi.org/project/mecab/

[17] https://github.com/buruzaemon/natto-py

[18] https://github.com/mocobeta/janome

was an inspiration in the development of fugashi. However, since the implementation is in pure Python, it's much slower than MeCab; the Japanese FAQ says it's roughly ten times slower.[19] Because IPAdic is tightly integrated it's also not straightforward to use significantly different dictionaries, though there is experimental support for the IPAdic-based Neologd[20].

SudachiPy[21] is a Python port of the Java-based Sudachi tokenizer (Takaoka et al., 2018). It has a high-quality UniDic-like dictionary and multiple modes of segmentation, and has recently been used when creating gold corpora for NER datasets. I have contributed to the code base in the interest of improving performance, Cythonizing performance critical parts of the code, but unfortunately it is still significantly slower than MeCab. Like fugashi it distributes dictionaries as pip packages.

6.3 Other Tokenizers

Some tokenizers use a very different strategy than MeCab when tokenizing. The examples listed here all use a model to decide whether to treat each character boundary as a word boundary or not.

Nagisa[22] is a relatively new tokenizer implemented in Python and based on neural networks. It's easy to use, but at present is significantly slower than SudachiPy or Janome.

Juman++[23] is implemented in C++ and uses neural networks to determine word boundaries (Morita et al., 2015). It has an official Python wrapper, but requires the core tokenizer to be installed separately, making configuration difficult. Version 2 of the software has had release candidates released annually since roughly 2017, but it's unclear which version should be used now. I attempted to do a simple benchmark using the most recent v2 release candidate but it failed with an error.

KyTea[24] uses logistic regression or SVM to determine word boundaries (Neubig et al., 2011). It's implemented in C++, but it has a few Python wrappers. None of them distribute wheels, so it's necessary to install the C++ tokenizer on your own. It is slower than MeCab but faster than the MeCab-like tokenizers.

7   Summary

fugashi combines the speed of MeCab with the ease-of-use of more recent tokenizers, striking a balance that's widely useful. fugashi is not faster than existing tokenizers; it does not have a new or better dictionary; it does not have new features; it merely takes the best of the available resources, puts them together, and makes sure that everything works in a variety of environments with a minimum of effort. As noted in (Agirre et al., 2018), to document best practices is good, but to automate them is better. While it's hoped that newer tokenizers like SudachiPy will be able to catch up in performance soon, at present fugashi is a good choice for many applications.

The past year has seen many new developments in the world of Japanese tokenizers. For more information on current Japanese tokenizers in Python, refer to Konoha[25] or Toiro[26], which wrap multiple tokenizers and allow comparisons between them.

8   Acknowledgments

The author would like to thank all the contributors to fugashi, particularly Aki Ariga for providing Windows support.

References

Eneko Agirre, Oier López de Lacalle, and Aitor Soroa. 2018. The risk of sub-optimal use of open source NLP software: UKB is inadvertently state-of-the-art in knowledge-based WSD. In *Proceedings of Workshop for NLP Open Source Software (NLP-OSS)*, pages 29–33, Melbourne, Australia. Association for Computational Linguistics.

Masayuki Asahara, Hiroshi Kanayama, Takaaki Tanaka, Yusuke Miyao, Sumire Uematsu, Shinsuke Mori, Yuji Matsumoto, Mai Omura, and Yugo Murawaki. 2018. Universal dependencies version 2 for japanese. In *LREC*.

---

[19] https://mocobeta.github.io/janome/
[20] https://mocobeta.github.io/janome/#experimental-neologd-v0-3-3
[21] https://github.com/WorksApplications/SudachiPy
[22] https://github.com/taishi-i/nagisa
[23] http://nlp.ist.i.kyoto-u.ac.jp/EN/index.php?JUMAN++
[24] http://www.phontron.com/kytea/

[25] https://github.com/himkt/konoha
[26] https://github.com/taishi-i/toiro

Yasuharu Den, Junpei Nakamura, Toshinobu Ogiso, and Hideki Ogura. 2008. A proper approach to japanese morphological analysis: Dictionary, model, and evaluation. In *LREC*.

Matthew Honnibal and Ines Montani. 2017. spaCy 2: Natural language understanding with Bloom embeddings, convolutional neural networks and incremental parsing. To appear.

Taku Kudo. 2018. 形態素解析の理論と実装 *[Morphological Analysis: Theory and Implementation] (Japanese)*. 近代科学社.

Taku Kudo, Kaoru Yamamoto, and Y. Matsumoto. 2004. Applying conditional random fields to japanese morphological analysis. In *EMNLP*.

Hajime Morita, D. Kawahara, and S. Kurohashi. 2015. Morphological analysis for unsegmented languages using recurrent neural network language model. In *EMNLP*.

G. Neubig, Yosuke Nakata, and S. Mori. 2011. Pointwise prediction for robust, adaptable japanese morphological analysis. In *ACL*.

Kazuma Takaoka, Sorami Hisamoto, Noriko Kawahara, Miho Sakamoto, Yoshitaka Uchida, and Yuji Matsumoto. 2018. Sudachi: a Japanese tokenizer for business. In *Proceedings of the Eleventh International Conference on Language Resources and Evaluation (LREC 2018)*, Miyazaki, Japan. European Language Resources Association (ELRA).

Going Beyond T-SNE: Exposing `whatlies` in Text Embeddings

Vincent D. Warmerdam
Rasa
Schönhauser Allee 175
10119 Berlin
`v.warmerdam@rasa.com`

Thomas Kober
Rasa
Schönhauser Allee 175
10119 Berlin
`t.kober@rasa.com`

Rachael Tatman
Rasa
Schönhauser Allee 175
10119 Berlin
`r.tatman@rasa.com`

Abstract

We introduce `whatlies`, an open source toolkit for visually inspecting word and sentence embeddings. The project offers a unified and extensible API with current support for a range of popular embedding backends including spaCy, tfhub, huggingface transformers, gensim, fastText and BytePair embeddings. The package combines a domain specific language for vector arithmetic with visualisation tools that make exploring word embeddings more intuitive and concise. It offers support for many popular dimensionality reduction techniques as well as many interactive visualisations that can either be statically exported or shared via Jupyter notebooks. The project documentation is available from `https://rasahq.github.io/whatlies/`.

1 Introduction

The use of pre-trained word embeddings (Mikolov et al., 2013a; Pennington et al., 2014) or language model based sentence encoders (Peters et al., 2018; Devlin et al., 2019) has become a ubiquitous part of NLP pipelines and end-user applications in both industry and academia. At the same time, a growing body of work has established that pre-trained embeddings codify the underlying biases of the text corpora they were trained on (Bolukbasi et al., 2016; Garg et al., 2018; Brunet et al., 2019). Hence, practitioners need tools to help select which set of embeddings to use for a particular project, detect potential need for debiasing and evaluate the debiased embeddings. Simplified visualisations of the latent semantic space provide an accessible way to achieve this.

Therefore we created `whatlies`, a toolkit offering a programmatic interface that supports vector arithmetic on a set of embeddings and visualising the space after any operations have been carried out. For example, Figure 1 shows an example

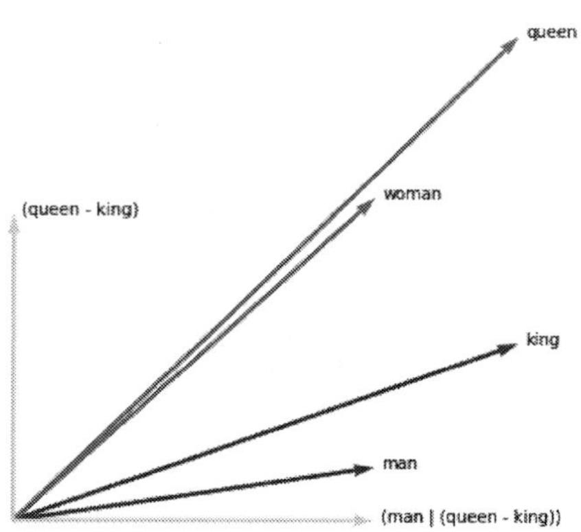

Figure 1: Projections of w_{king}, w_{queen}, w_{man}, $w_{\text{queen}} - w_{\text{king}}$ and w_{man} projected away from $w_{\text{queen}} - w_{\text{king}}$. Both the vector arithmetic and the visualisation were done using the `whatlies`. The support for arithmetic expressions is integral in `whatlies` because it leads to more meaningful visualisations and concise code.

of how representations for *queen, king, man,* and *woman* can be projected along the axes $v_{\text{queen}-\text{king}}$ and $v_{\text{man}|\text{queen}-\text{king}}$ in order to derive a visualisation of the space along the projections.

Perhaps the most widely known tool for visualising embeddings is the tensorflow projector[1] which offers 3D visualisations of any input embeddings. The visualisations are useful for understanding the emergence of clusters and the neighbourhood of certain words and the overall space. However, the projector is limited to dimensionality reduction as the sole preprocessing method. More recently, Molino et al. (2019) have introduced parallax which allows explicit selection of the axes on which to project a representation. This creates an additional level of flexibility as these axes can also be derived from arithmetic operations on the embeddings.

The major difference between the tensorflow pro-

---

[1] `https://projector.tensorflow.org/`

Proceedings of Second Workshop for NLP Open Source Software (NLP-OSS), pages 52–60
Virtual Conference, November 19, 2020. ©2020 Association for Computational Linguistics

jector, parallax and `whatlies` is that the first two provide a non-extensible browser-based interface, whereas `whatlies` provides a programmatic one. Therefore `whatlies` can be more easily extended to any specific practical need and cover individual use-cases. The goal of `whatlies` is to offer a set of tools that can be used from a Jupyter notebook with a range of visualisation capabilities that goes beyond the commonly used static T-SNE (van der Maaten and Hinton, 2008) plots. `whatlies` can be installed via `pip`, the code is available from `https://github.com/RasaHQ/whatlies`[2] and the documentation is hosted at `https://rasahq.github.io/whatlies/`.

2 What lies in `whatlies` — Usage and Examples

Embedding backends. The current version of `whatlies` supports word-level as well as sentence-level embeddings in any human language that is supported by the following libraries:

- BytePair embeddings (Sennrich et al., 2016) via the BPemb project (Heinzerling and Strube, 2018)

- fastText (Bojanowski et al., 2017)

- gensim (Řehůřek and Sojka, 2010)

- huggingface (Wolf et al., 2019)

- sense2vec (Trask et al., 2015); via spaCy

- spaCy[3]

- tfhub[4]

Embeddings are loaded via a unified API:

```
from whatlies.language import \
SpacyLanguage, FasttextLanguage, \
TFHubLanguage, HFTransformersLangauge

# spaCy
lang_sp = SpacyLanguage('en_core_web_md')
emb_king = lang_sp["king"]
emb_queen = lang_sp["queen"]

# fastText
ft = 'cc.en.300.bin'
lang_ft = FasttextLanguage(ft)
emb_ft = lang_ft['pizza']

# TF-Hub
tf_hub = 'https://tfhub.dev/google/'
```

---

[2]Community PRs are greatly appreciated ☺.
[3]`https://spacy.io/`
[4]`https://www.tensorflow.org/hub`

```
model = tf_hub + 'nnlm-en-dim50/2'
lang_tf = TFHubLanguage(model)
emb_tf = lang_tf['whatlies is awesome']

# Huggingface
bert = 'bert-base-cased'
lang_hf = HFTransformersLanguage(bert)
emb_hf = lang['whatlies rocks']
```

Retrieved embeddings are python objects that contain a vector and an associated named. It comes with extra utility methods attached that allow for easy arithmetic and visualisation.

The library is capable of retreiving embeddings for sentences too. In order to retrieve a sentence representation for word-level embeddings such as fastText, `whatlies` returns the summed representation of the individual word vectors. For pretrained encoders such as BERT (Devlin et al., 2019) or ConveRT (Henderson et al., 2019), `whatlies` uses its internal `[CLS]` token for representing a sentence.

Similarity Retrieval. The library also supports retrieving similar items on the basis of a number of commonly used distance/similarity metrics such as cosine or Euclidean distance:

```
from whatlies.language import \
SpacyLanguage

lang = SpacyLanguage('en_core_web_md')

lang.score_similar("man", n=5,
                   metric='cosine')
[ (Emb[man], 0.0),
 (Emb[woman], 0.2598254680633545),
 (Emb[guy], 0.29321062564849854),
 (Emb[boy], 0.2954298257827759),
 (Emb[he], 0.3168887495994568)]
# NB: Results are cosine _distances_
```

Vector Arithmetic. Support of arithmetic expressions on embeddings is integral in any `whatlies` functions. For example the code for creating Figure 1 from the Introduction highlights that it does not make a difference whether the plotting functionality is invoked on an embedding itself or on a representation derived from an arithmetic operation:

```
import matplotlib.pylab as plt
from whatlies import Embedding

man   = Embedding("man", [0.5, 0.1])
woman = Embedding("woman", [0.5, 0.6])
king  = Embedding("king", [0.7, 0.33])
queen = Embedding("queen", [0.7, 0.9])
man.plot(kind="arrow", color="blue")
woman.plot(kind="arrow", color="red")
king.plot(kind="arrow", color="blue")
queen.plot(kind="arrow", color="red")
```

```python
diff = (queen - king)
orth = (man | (queen - king))

diff.plot(color="pink",
          show_ops=True)
orth.plot(color="pink",
          show_ops=True)
# See Figure 1 for the result :)
```

This feature allows users to construct custom queries and use it e.g. in combination with the similarity retrieval functionality. For example, we can validate the widely circulated analogy of Mikolov et al. (2013b) on spaCy's medium English model in only 4 lines of code (including imports):

$$w_{\text{queen}} \approx w_{\text{king}} - w_{\text{man}} + w_{\text{woman}}$$

```python
from whatlies.language import \
SpacyLanguage

lang = SpacyLanguage('en_core_web_md')

> e = lang["king"] - lang["man"] + \
lang["woman"]
> lang.score_similar(e, n=5,
                     metric='cosine')
[(Emb[king], 0.19757413864135742),
 (Emb[queen], 0.2119154930114746),
 (Emb[prince], 0.35989218950271606),
 (Emb[princes], 0.37914562225341797),
 (Emb[kings], 0.37914562225341797)]
```

Excluding the query word *king*[5], the analogy returns the anticipated result: *queen*.

The library also allows the user to add/subtract embeddings but also project unto (via the > operator) or away from them (via the | operator). This means that the user is very flexible when it comes to retrieving embeddings.

Multilingual Support. whatlies supports any human language that is available from its current list of supported embedding backends. This allows us to check the royal analogy from above in languages other than English. The code snippet below shows the results for Spanish and Dutch, using pre-trained fastText embeddings[6].

```python
from whatlies.language import \
FasttextLanguage
es = FasttextLanguage("cc.es.300.bin")
nl = FasttextLanguage("cc.nl.300.bin")

emb_es = es["rey"] - es["hombre"] + \
es["mujer"]
emb_nl = nl["koning"] - nl["man"] + \
nl["vrouw"]
```

---

[5]As appears to be standard practice in word analogy evaluation (Levy and Goldberg, 2014).

[6]The embeddings are available from https://fasttext.cc/docs/en/crawl-vectors.html.

```python
es.score_similar(emb_es, n=5,
                 metric='cosine')
[(Emb[rey], 0.04499000310897827),
 (Emb[monarca], 0.24673408269882202),
 (Emb[Rey], 0.2799408435821533),
 (Emb[reina], 0.2993239760398865),
 (Emb[príncipe], 0.3025314211845398)]

nl.score_similar(emb_nl, n=5,
                 metric='cosine')

[(Emb[koning], 0.48337286710739136),
 (Emb[koningen], 0.5858825445175171),
 (Emb[koningin], 0.6115483045578003),
 (Emb[Koning], 0.6155656576156616),
 (Emb[kroonprins], 0.658723771572113)]
```

While for Spanish, the correct answer *reina* is only at rank 3 (excluding *rey* from the list), the second ranked *monarca* (female form of *monarch*) is getting close. For Dutch, the correct answer *koningin* is at rank 2, surpassed only by *koningen* (plural of *king*). Another interesting observation is that the cosine distances — even of the query words — vary wildly in the embeddings for the two languages.

Sets of Embeddings. In the previous examples we have typically only retrieved single embeddings. However, whatlies also supports the notion of an "Embedding Set", that can hold any number of embeddings:

```python
from whatlies.language import \
SpacyLanguage

lang = SpacyLanguage("en_core_web_lg")

words = ["prince", "princess", "nurse",
         "doctor", "man", "woman",
         "sentences also embed"]
# NB: 'sentences also embed' will be
#     represented as the mean of the
#     3 individual words. This behavior
#.    is driven by spaCy currently.

emb = lang[words]
```

It is often more useful to analyse a set of embeddings at once, rather than many individual ones. Therefore, any arithmetic operations that can be applied to single embeddings, can also be applied to all of the embeddings in a given set.

The emb variable in the previous code example represents an EmbeddingSet. These are collections of embeddings which can be simpler to analyse than many individual variables. Users can, for example, apply vector arithmetic to the entire EmbeddingSet.

```python
new_emb = emb | (emb['man'] - emb['woman'])
```

Visualisation Tools. Any visualisations in `whatlies` are most useful when performed on `EmbeddingSets`. They offer a variety of methods for plotting, such as the distance map in Figure 2:

```python
words = ['man', 'woman', 'king', 'queen',
         'red', 'green', 'yellow']
emb = lang[words]
emb.plot_distance(metric='cosine')
```

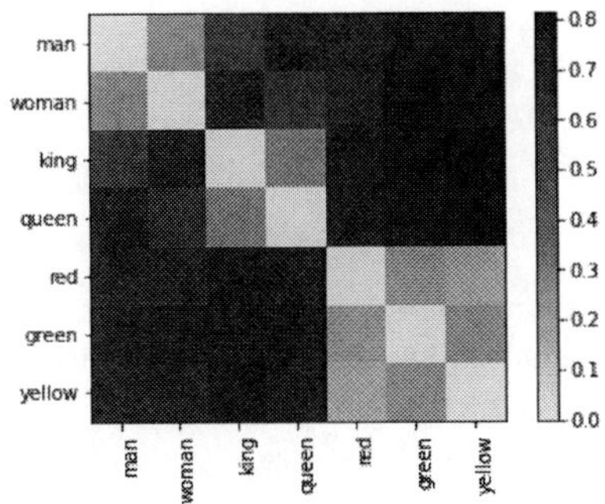

Figure 2: Pairwise distances for a set of words using cosine distance.

`whatlies` also offers interactive visualisations using "Altair" as a plotting backend[7]:

```python
emb.plot_interactive(x_axis="man",
                     y_axis="yellow",
                     show_axis_point=True)
```

The above code snippet projects every vector in the `EmbeddingSet` onto the vectors on the specified axes. This creates the values we can use for 2D visualisations. For example, given that *man* is on the x-axis the value for 'yellow' on that axis will be:

$$v(\text{yellow} \rightarrow \text{man}) = \frac{w_{\text{yellow}} \cdot w_{\text{man}}}{w_{\text{man}} \cdot w_{\text{man}}}$$

which results in Figure 3.

These plots are built on top of Altair (VanderPlas et al., 2018) and are fully interactive. It is possible to click and drag in order to navigate through the embedding space and zoom in and out. These plots can be hosted on a website but they can also be exported to `png`/`svg` for publication. It is furthermore possible to apply any vector arithmetic operations for these plots, resulting in Figure 4:

```python
e = emb["man"] - emb["woman"]
emb.plot_interactive(x_axis=e,
                     y_axis="yellow",
                     show_axis_point=True)
```

---

[7]Examples of the interactive visualisations can be seen on the project's github page: `https://github.com/RasaHQ/whatlies`

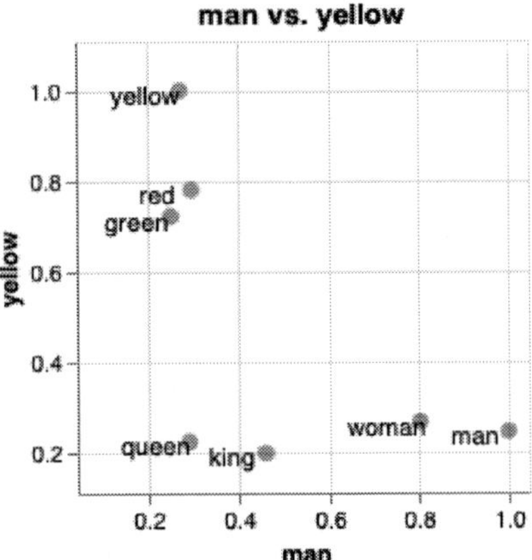

Figure 3: Plotting example terms along the axes *man* vs. *yellow*. Note how the title/axes automatically update.

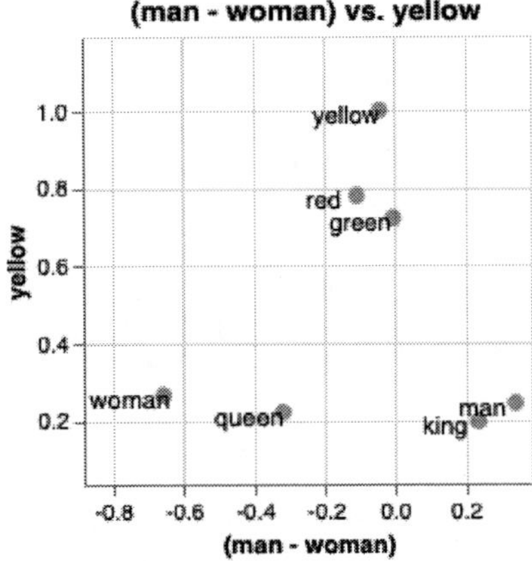

Figure 4: Plotting example terms along the transformed *man - woman* axis and the *yellow* axis.

Transformations. `whatlies` also supports several techniques for dimensionality reduction of `EmbeddingSets` prior to plotting. This is demonstrated in Figure 5 below.

```python
from whatlies.transformers import Pca
from whatlies.transformers import Umap

p1 = (emb
      .transform(Pca(2))
      .plot_interactive())
p2 = (emb
      .transform(Umap(2))
      .plot_interactive())
p1 | p2
```

Transformations in `whatlies` are slightly different than for example scikit-learn transformations because in addition to dimensionality reduction, the transformation can also add embeddings that represent each principal component to the

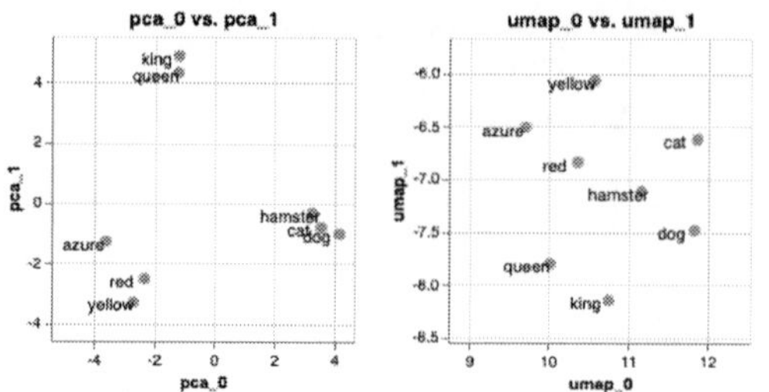

Figure 5: Demonstration of PCA and UMAP transformations.

`EmbeddingSet` object. As a result, they can be referred to as axes for creating visualisations as seen in Figure 5.

Scikit-Learn Integration. To facilitate quick exploration of different word embeddings we have also made our library compatible with scikit-learn (Pedregosa et al., 2011). The Rasa library uses numpy (Harris et al., 2020) to represent the numerical vectors associated to the input text. This means that it is possible to use the `whatlies` embedding backends as feature extractors in scikit-learn pipelines, as the code snippet below shows[8]:

```
from whatlies.language import \
BytePairLanguage
from sklearn.pipeline import Pipeline

pipe = Pipeline([
    ("embed", BytePairLanguage("en")),
    ("model", LogisticRegression())
])

X = [
    "i really like this post",
    "thanks for that comment",
    "i enjoy this friendly forum",
    "this is a bad post",
    "i dislike this article",
    "this is not well written"
]

y = np.array([1, 1, 1, 0, 0, 0])

pipe.fit(X, y).predict(X)
```

This feature enables fast exploration of many different word embedding algorithms.[9]

3   A Tale of two Use-cases

Visualising Bias. One use-case of `whatlies` is to gain insight into bias-related issues in an em-

---

[8]Note that this is an illustrative example and we do not recommend to train and test on the same data.

[9]At the moment, however, it is not yet possible to use the `whatlies` embeddings in conjunction with scikit-learn's grid search functionality.

bedding space. Because the library readily supports vector arithmetic it is possible to create an `EmbeddingSet` holding pairs of representations:

```
lang = SpacyLanguage("en_core_web_lg")

emb_of_pairs = EmbeddingSet(
    (lang["nurse"] - lang["doctor"]),
    (lang["nurse"] - lang["surgeon"]),
    (lang["woman"] - lang["man"]),
)
```

Subsequently, the new `EmbeddingSet` can be visualised as a distance map as in Figure 6, revealing a number of spurious correlations that suggest a gender bias in the embedding space.

```
emb_of_pairs.plot_distance(metric="cosine")
```

Visualising issues in the embedding space like this creates an effective way to communicate potential risks of using embeddings in production to non-technical stakeholders.

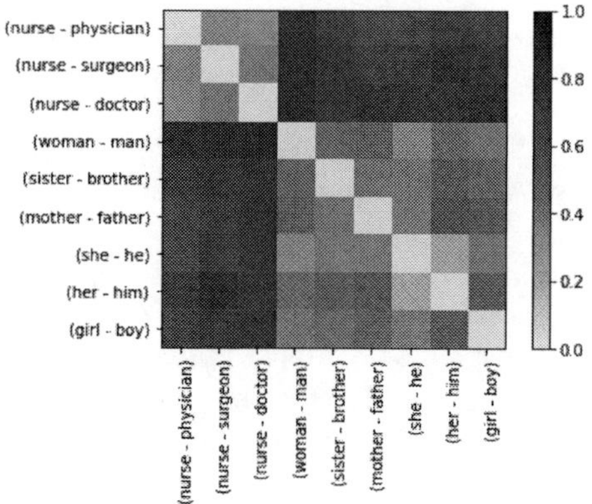

Figure 6: Distance map for visualising bias. If there was no bias then we would expect 'she-he' to have a distance near 1.0 compared to 'nurse-physician'. The figure shows this is not the case.

It is possible to apply the debiasing technique introduced by Bolukbasi et al. (2016) in order to approximately remove the direction corresponding to gender. The code snippet below achieves this by, again, using the arithmetic notation.

```
lang = SpacyLanguage("en_core_web_lg")

emb = lang[words]
axis = EmbeddingSet(
    (lang['man'] - lang['woman']),
    (lang['king'] - lang['queen']),
    (lang['father'] - lang['mother'])
).average()
emb_debias = emb | axis
```

Figure 7 shows the result of applying the debiasing technique, highlighting that some of the spurious correlations have indeed been removed.

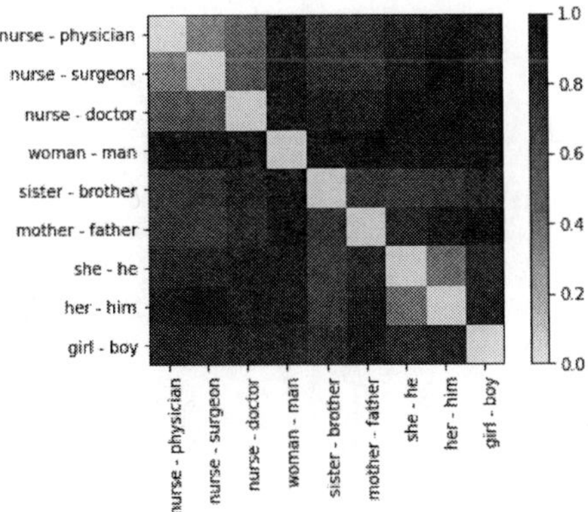

Figure 7: Distance map for visualising the embedding space after the debiasing technique of Bolukbasi et al. (2016) has been applied.

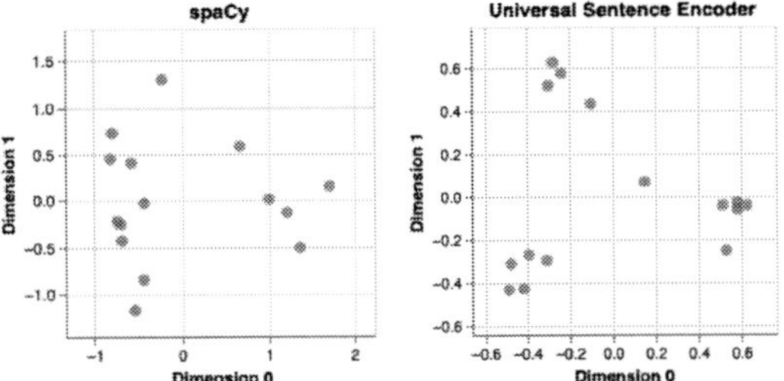

Figure 8: Side-by-side comparison of spaCy and Universal Sentence Encoder for embedding example sentences from 3 different intent classes. Universal Sentence Encoder embeds the sentences into relatively tight and coherent clusters, whereas class boundaries are more difficult to see with spaCy.

It is important to note though, that the above technique does not reliably remove all relevant bias in the embeddings and that bias is still measurably existing in the embedding space as Gonen and Goldberg (2019) have shown. This can be verified with `whatlies`, by plotting the neighbours of the biased and debiased space:

```
emb.score_similar("maid", n=7)

[(Emb[maid], 0.0),
 (Emb[maids], 0.18290925025939941),
 (Emb[housekeeper], 0.2200336456298828),
 (Emb[maidservant], 0.3770867586135864),
 (Emb[butler], 0.3822709918022156),
 (Emb[mistress], 0.3967094421386719),
 (Emb[servant], 0.40112364292144775)]


 emb_debias.score_similar("maid", n=7)

[(Emb[maid], 0.0),
 (Emb[maids], 0.18163418769836426),
 (Emb[housekeeper], 0.21881639957427979),
 (Emb[butler], 0.3642127513885498),
 (Emb[maidservant], 0.3768376111984253),
 (Emb[servant], 0.382546067237854),
 (Emb[mistress], 0.3955296277999878)]
```

As the output shows, the neighbourhoods of *maid* in the biased and debiased space are almost equivalent, with e.g. *mistress* still appearing relatively high-up the nearest neighbours list.

Comparing Embedding Backends. Another use-case for `whatlies` is for comparing different embeddings. For example, we wanted to analyse two different encoders for their ability to capture the intent of user utterances in a task-based dialogue system. We compared spaCy and the Universal Sentence Encoder for their ability to embed sentences from the same intent class close together in space. Figure 8 shows that the utterances encoded with the Universal Sentence Encoder form more coherent clusters.

Figure 9 highlights the same trend with a distance map, where for spaCy there is barely any similarity between the utterances, the coherent clusters from Figure 8 are well reflected in the distance map for the Universal Sentence Encoder.

The superiority of Universal Sentence Encoder in comparison to spaCy for this example is expected, though, as it is aimed at sentences, but it is certainly useful to have a tool — `whatlies` — at one's disposal with which it is possible to quickly validate this.

4   Roadmap

`whatlies` is in active development. While we cannot predict the contents of future community PRs, this is our current roadmap for future development:

- We want to make it easier for people to research bias in word embeddings. We will continue to investigate if there are visualisation techniques that can help spot issues and we aim to make any robust debiasing techniques available in `whatlies`.

- We would like to curate labelled sets of word lists for attempting to quantify the amount of bias in a given embedding space. Properly labelled word lists can be useful for algorithmic bias research but it might also help understand clusters. We plan to make any evaluation resources available via this package.

- One limit of using Altair as a visualisation library is that we cannot offer interactive visualisations with many thousands of data points.

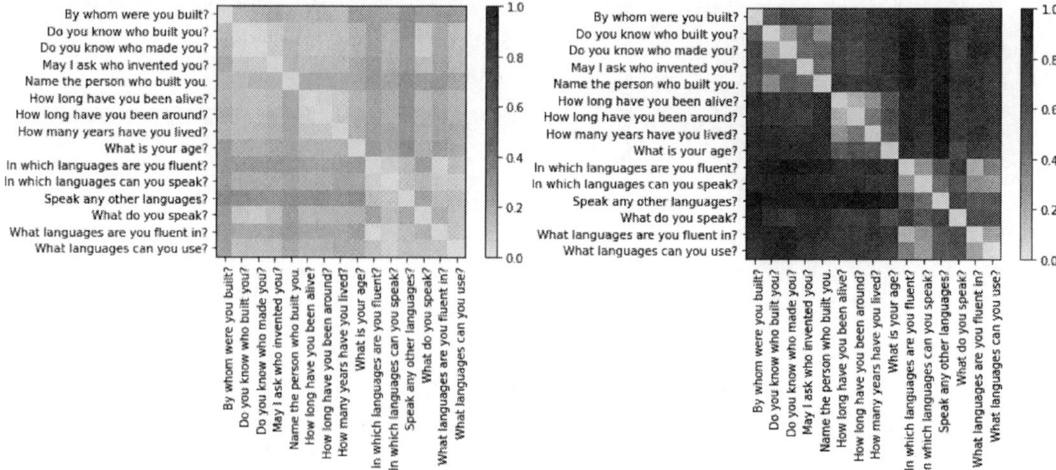

Figure 9: Side-by-side comparison of spaCy and Universal Sentence Encoder for embedding example sentences from 3 different intent classes. The distance map highlights the "clustery" behaviour of Universal Sentence Encoder, where class membership is nicely reflected in the intra-class distances. For spaCy on the other hand, there is less difference between intra-class vs. inter-class distances.

We might explore other visualisation tools for this library as well.

- Since we're supporting dynamic backends like BERT at the sentence level, we are aiming to also support these encoders at the word level, which requires us to specify an API for retrieving contextualised word representations within `whatlies`. We are currently exploring various ways for exposing this feature and are working with a notation that uses square brackets that can select an embedding from the context of the sentence that it resides in:

```
mod_name = "en_trf_robertabase_lg"
lang = SpacyLanguage(mod_name)
emb1 = lang['[bank] of the river']
emb2 = lang['money on the [bank]']
assert emb1.vector != emb2.vector
```

At the moment we only support spaCy backends with this notation but we plan to explore this further with other embedding backends.[10]

- A related issue is that not every vocabulary based back-end uses the same method of pooling word-embeddings to represent a sentence. Some take the sum, while others take the mean and others introduce yet another standard. Our goal for vocabulary based back-ends is to allow the user to control this manually for consistency.

5 Conclusion

We have introduced `whatlies`, a python library for inspecting word and sentence embeddings that is very flexible due to offering a programmable interface. We currently support a variety of embedding models, including fastText, spaCy, BERT, or the Universal Sentence Encoder. This paper has showcased its current use as well as plans for future development. The project is hosted at `https://github.com/RasaHQ/whatlies` and we are happy to receive community contributions that extend and improve the package.

Acknowledgements

Despite being only a few months old the project has started getting traction on github and has attracted the help of outside contributions. In particular we'd like to thank Masoud Kazemi for many contributions to the project.

We would furthermore like to thank Adam Lopez for many rounds of discussion that considerably improved the paper.

References

Piotr Bojanowski, Edouard Grave, Armand Joulin, and Tomas Mikolov. 2017. Enriching word vectors with subword information. *Transactions of the Association for Computational Linguistics*, 5:135–146.

---

[10]Ideally we also introduce the necessary notation for retrieving the contextualised embedding from a particular layer, e.g. `lang['bank'][2]` for obtaining the representation of *bank* from the second layer of the given language model.

Tolga Bolukbasi, Kai-Wei Chang, James Zou, Venkatesh Saligrama, and Adam Kalai. 2016. Man is to computer programmer as woman is to homemaker? debiasing word embeddings. In *Proceedings of the 30th International Conference on Neural Information Processing Systems*, NIPS'16, pages 4356–4364, USA. Curran Associates Inc.

Marc-Etienne Brunet, Colleen Alkalay-Houlihan, A. Anderson, and R. Zemel. 2019. Understanding the origins of bias in word embeddings. In *ICML*.

Jacob Devlin, Ming-Wei Chang, Kenton Lee, and Kristina Toutanova. 2019. BERT: Pre-training of deep bidirectional transformers for language understanding. In *Proceedings of the 2019 Conference of the North American Chapter of the Association for Computational Linguistics: Human Language Technologies, Volume 1 (Long and Short Papers)*, pages 4171–4186, Minneapolis, Minnesota. Association for Computational Linguistics.

Nikhil Garg, Londa Schiebinger, Dan Jurafsky, and James Zou. 2018. Word embeddings quantify 100 years of gender and ethnic stereotypes. *Proceedings of the National Academy of Sciences*, 115(16):E3635–E3644.

Hila Gonen and Yoav Goldberg. 2019. Lipstick on a pig: Debiasing methods cover up systematic gender biases in word embeddings but do not remove them. In *Proceedings of the 2019 Conference of the North American Chapter of the Association for Computational Linguistics: Human Language Technologies, Volume 1 (Long and Short Papers)*, pages 609–614, Minneapolis, Minnesota. Association for Computational Linguistics.

Charles R. Harris, K. Jarrod Millman, Stéfan J van der Walt, Ralf Gommers, Pauli Virtanen, David Cournapeau, Eric Wieser, Julian Taylor, Sebastian Berg, Nathaniel J. Smith, Robert Kern, Matti Picus, Stephan Hoyer, Marten H. van Kerkwijk, Matthew Brett, Allan Haldane, Jaime Fernández del Río, Mark Wiebe, Pearu Peterson, Pierre Gérard-Marchant, Kevin Sheppard, Tyler Reddy, Warren Weckesser, Hameer Abbasi, Christoph Gohlke, and Travis E. Oliphant. 2020. Array programming with NumPy. *Nature*, 585:357–362.

Benjamin Heinzerling and Michael Strube. 2018. BPEmb: Tokenization-free pre-trained subword embeddings in 275 languages. In *Proceedings of the Eleventh International Conference on Language Resources and Evaluation (LREC 2018)*, Miyazaki, Japan. European Language Resources Association (ELRA).

Matthew Henderson, Iñigo Casanueva, Nikola Mrkvsi'c, Pei hao Su, Tsung-Hsien, and Ivan Vulic. 2019. Convert: Efficient and accurate conversational representations from transformers. *ArXiv*, abs/1911.03688.

Omer Levy and Yoav Goldberg. 2014. Linguistic regularities in sparse and explicit word representations. In *Proceedings of the Eighteenth Conference on Computational Natural Language Learning*, pages 171–180, Ann Arbor, Michigan. Association for Computational Linguistics.

Laurens van der Maaten and Geoffrey Hinton. 2008. Visualizing data using t-SNE. *Journal of Machine Learning Research*, 9:2579–2605.

Tomas Mikolov, Ilya Sutskever, Kai Chen, Greg S Corrado, and Jeff Dean. 2013a. Distributed representations of words and phrases and their compositionality. In C.J.C. Burges, L. Bottou, M. Welling, Z. Ghahramani, and K.Q. Weinberger, editors, *Advances in Neural Information Processing Systems 26*, pages 3111–3119. Curran Associates, Inc.

Tomas Mikolov, Wen-tau Yih, and Geoffrey Zweig. 2013b. Linguistic regularities in continuous space word representations. In *Proceedings of the 2013 Conference of the North American Chapter of the Association for Computational Linguistics: Human Language Technologies*, pages 746–751, Atlanta, Georgia. Association for Computational Linguistics.

Piero Molino, Yang Wang, and Jiawei Zhang. 2019. Parallax: Visualizing and understanding the semantics of embedding spaces via algebraic formulae. In *Proceedings of the 57th Annual Meeting of the Association for Computational Linguistics: System Demonstrations*, pages 165–180, Florence, Italy. Association for Computational Linguistics.

Fabian Pedregosa, Gaël Varoquaux, Alexandre Gramfort, Vincent Michel, Bertrand Thirion, Olivier Grisel, Mathieu Blondel, Peter Prettenhofer, Ron Weiss, Vincent Dubourg, Jake Vanderplas, Alexandre Passos, David Cournapeau, Matthieu Brucher, Matthieu Perrot, and Édouard Duchesnay. 2011. Scikit-learn: Machine learning in python. *Journal of Machine Learning Research*, 12:2825–2830.

Jeffrey Pennington, Richard Socher, and Christopher Manning. 2014. Glove: Global vectors for word representation. In *Proceedings of the 2014 Conference on Empirical Methods in Natural Language Processing*, pages 1532–1543, Doha, Qatar. Association for Computational Linguistics.

Matthew Peters, Mark Neumann, Mohit Iyyer, Matt Gardner, Christopher Clark, Kenton Lee, and Luke Zettlemoyer. 2018. Deep contextualized word representations. In *Proceedings of the 2018 Conference of the North American Chapter of the Association for Computational Linguistics: Human Language Technologies, Volume 1 (Long Papers)*, pages 2227–2237. Association for Computational Linguistics.

Radim Řehůřek and Petr Sojka. 2010. Software Framework for Topic Modelling with Large Corpora. In *Proceedings of the LREC 2010 Workshop on New Challenges for NLP Frameworks*, pages 45–50, Valletta, Malta. ELRA.

Rico Sennrich, Barry Haddow, and Alexandra Birch. 2016. Neural machine translation of rare words with subword units. In *Proceedings of the 54th Annual Meeting of the Association for Computational Linguistics (Volume 1: Long Papers)*, pages 1715–1725, Berlin, Germany. Association for Computational Linguistics.

Andrew Trask, Phil Michalak, and John Liu. 2015. sense2vec - a fast and accurate method for word sense disambiguation in neural word embeddings. *ArXiv*, abs/1511.06388.

Jacob VanderPlas, Brian E. Granger, Jeffrey Heer, Dominik Moritz, Kanit Wongsuphasawat, Arvind Satyanarayan, Eitan Lees, Ilia Timofeev, Ben Welsh, and Scott Sievert. 2018. Altair: Interactive statistical visualizations for python. *Journal of Open Source Software*, 3(32):1057.

Thomas Wolf, Lysandre Debut, Victor Sanh, Julien Chaumond, Clement Delangue, Anthony Moi, Pierric Cistac, Tim Rault, R'emi Louf, Morgan Funtowicz, and Jamie Brew. 2019. Huggingface's transformers: State-of-the-art natural language processing. *ArXiv*, abs/1910.03771.

Howl: A Deployed, Open-Source Wake Word Detection System

Raphael Tang,[1]* Jaejun Lee,[1]* Afsaneh Razi,[2] Julia Cambre,[2] Ian Bicking,[2] Jofish Kaye,[2] and Jimmy Lin[1]

[1] David R. Cheriton School of Computer Science, University of Waterloo
[2] Mozilla

Abstract

We describe Howl, an open-source wake word detection toolkit with native support for open speech datasets such as Mozilla Common Voice (MCV) and Google Speech Commands (GSC). We report benchmark results of various models supported by our toolkit on GSC and our own freely available wake word detection dataset, built from MCV. One of our models is deployed in Firefox Voice, a plugin enabling speech interactivity for the Firefox web browser. Howl represents, to the best of our knowledge, the first fully productionized, open-source wake word detection toolkit with a web browser deployment target. Our codebase is at howl.ai.

1 Introduction

Wake word detection is the task of recognizing an utterance for activating a speech assistant, such as "Hey, Alexa" for the Amazon Echo. Given that such systems are meant to support fully automatic speech recognition, the task seems simple. However, it introduces a different set of challenges because these systems have to be always listening, computationally efficient, and, most of all, privacy respecting. Therefore, researchers treat it as a separate line of work, with most recent advancements driven by neural networks (Sainath and Parada, 2015; Tang and Lin, 2018).

Unfortunately, most existing toolkits are closed source and often specific to a target platform. Such design choices restrict the flexibility of the application and add unnecessary maintenance as the number of target domains increases. We argue that using JavaScript is a solution: unlike many languages and their runtimes, the JavaScript engine powers a wide range of modern user-facing applications ranging from mobile to desktop ones.

To this end, we have previously developed Honkling, a JavaScript-based keyword spotting system (Lee et al., 2019). Leveraging one of the lightest models available for the task from Tang and Lin (2018), Honkling efficiently detects the target commands with high precision. However, we notice that Honkling is still quite far from being a stable wake word detection system. This gap mainly arises from the model being trained as a speech commands classifier instead of a wake word detector; its high false alarm rate results from the limited number of negative samples in the training dataset (Warden, 2018).

In this paper, to achieve greater real-world impact, we close this gap in the Honkling ecosystem and present Howl, an open-source wake word detection toolkit with support for open datasets such as Mozilla Common Voice (MCV; Ardila et al., 2019) and the Google Speech Commands dataset (GSC; Warden, 2018). Howl is the first in-browser wake word detection system which powers a widely deployed consumer application, Firefox Voice.[1] By processing the audio in the browser and being completely open source, including the datasets and models, Howl is a privacy-respecting, non-eavesdropping toolkit that users can trust. With a false reject rate of 16% at five false alarms per hour of speech, our deployed model has enabled Firefox Voice to provide a completely hands-free experience to over 8,000 users in the 9 days since its launch in August 2020.[2]

2 Background and Related Work

Although mainstream voice technologies such as Siri and Alexa are driven by proprietary wake word detection systems, open toolkits like Porcupine and

---

* Equal contribution. Order decided by coin flip.

[1]`https://github.com/
mozilla-extensions/firefox-voice`
[2]`https://twitter.com/jofish/status/
1293017304423215104`

Proceedings of Second Workshop for NLP Open Source Software (NLP-OSS), pages 61–65
Virtual Conference, November 19, 2020. ©2020 Association for Computational Linguistics

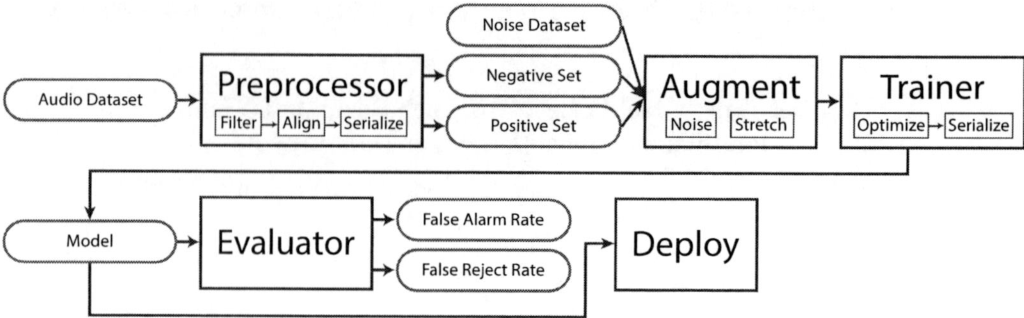

Figure 1: An illustration of Howl's end-to-end pipeline and its control flow. First, we preprocess the incoming audio dataset by filtering for the wake word vocabulary, aligning the speech, and saving the negative and positives examples to disk. Next, we introduce a noise dataset and augment the data on the fly at training time. Finally, we evaluate the optimized model and, if the results are satisfactory, export it for deployment.

Snowboy also exist. Such ecosystems provide an open-source modeling toolkit, some data, and deployment capabilities. Unfortunately, these ecosystems are still closed at heart; they keep their data, models, or deployment proprietary. As far as open-source ecosystems go, Precise[3] represents a step in the right direction, but its datasets are limited, and its deployment target is the Raspberry Pi.

We further make the distinction between wake word detection and speech commands classification toolkits such as Honk (Tang and Lin, 2017). These frameworks focus on classifying fixed-length audio as one of a few dozen keywords, with no evaluation on a sizable negative set, as required in wake word detection. While these trained models may be used in detection applications, they are not rigorously tested for such.

3   System Description

We present a high-level description of our toolkit and its goals (see Howl's architecture in Figure 1). For specific details, we refer users to our code repository, as linked in the abstract.

3.1   Requirements

Howl is written in Python 3.7+, with notable dependencies being PyTorch (Paszke et al., 2019) for model training, Librosa (McFee et al., 2015) for audio preprocessing, and the Montreal Forced Aligner (MFA; McAuliffe et al., 2017) for speech data alignment. We release Howl under the Mozilla

Public License v2, a file-level copyleft free license. For speedy model training, we recommend a CUDA-enabled graphics card with at least 4GB of VRAM; we used an Nvidia Titan RTX in all of our experiments. For resource-restricted users, we suggest exploring Google Colab[4] and other cloud-based solutions.

3.2   Components and Pipeline

Howl consists of the three following major components: audio preprocessing, data augmentation, and model training and evaluation. These components form a pipeline, in the written order, for producing deployable models from raw audio data.

Preprocessing. A wake word dataset must first be preprocessed from an annotated data source, which is defined as a collection of (audio, transcription) pairs, with predefined training, development, and test splits. Since Howl is a frame-level keyword spotting system, it relies on a forced aligner to provide word- or phone-based alignment. We choose MFA for its popularity and free license, and hence Howl structures the processed datasets to interface well with MFA.

Another preprocessing task is to parse the global configuration settings for the framework. Such settings include the learning rate, the dataset path, and model-specific hyperparameters. The toolkit reads in most of these settings as environment variables, which enable easy shell scripting.

Augmentation. For improved robustness and better model quality, we implement a set of popular

---

[3]https://github.com/MycroftAI/
mycroft-precise

[4]https://colab.research.google.com/

augmentation routines: time stretching, time shifting, synthetic noise addition, recorded noise mixing, SpecAugment (without time warping; Park et al., 2019), and vocal tract length perturbation (Jaitly and Hinton, 2013). These are readily extensible, so practitioners may easily add new augmentation modules.

Training and evaluation. Howl provides several off-the-shelf neural models, as well as training and evaluation routines using PyTorch for computing the loss gradient and the task-specific metrics, such as the false alarm rate and reject rate. These routines are also responsible for serializing the model and exporting it to our browser-side deployment.

Pipeline. Given these components, our pipeline, visually presented in Figure 1, is as follows: First, users produce a wake word detection dataset, either manually or from a data source like Common Voice and Google Speech Commands, setting the appropriate environment variables. This can be quickly accomplished using Common Voice, whose ample breadth and coverage of popular English words allow for a wide selection of custom wake words; for example, it has about a thousand occurrences of the word "next." In addition to a positive subset containing the vocabulary and wake word, this dataset ideally contains a sizable negative set, which is necessary for more robust models and a more accurate evaluation of the false positive rate.

Next, users (optionally) select which augmentation modules to use, and they train a model with the provided hyperparameters on the selected dataset, which is first processed into log-Mel frames with zero mean and unit variance, as is standard. This training process should take less than a few hours on a GPU-capable device for most use cases, including ours. Finally, users may run the model in the included command line interface demo or deploy it to the browser using Honkling, our in-browser keyword spotting (KWS) system, if the model is supported (Lee et al., 2019).

3.3 Data and Models

For the data sources, Howl works out of the box with Mozilla Common Voice, a general speech corpus, and Google Speech Commands, a commands recognition dataset. Users can quickly extend Howl to accept other speech corpora such as LibriSpeech (Panayotov et al., 2015) or the Hey Snips dataset (Coucke et al., 2019). Howl also accepts any folder that contains audio files and

Model	Dev/Test	# Par.
EdgeSpeechNet (Lin et al., 2018)	–/96.8	107K
res8 (Tang and Lin, 2018)	–/94.1	110K
RNN (de Andrade et al., 2018)	–/95.6	202K
DenseNet (Zeng and Xiao, 2019)	–/97.5	250K
Our res8	**97.6/97.8**	111K
Our LSTM	95.6/95.2	128K
Our LAS encoder	97.6/97.7	478K
Our MobileNetv2	97.3/97.3	2.3M

Table 1: Model accuracy (%) on Google Speech Commands with the number of parameters. res8 achieves the best accuracy considering the small model size.

interprets them as recorded noise for data augmentation, which covers popular noise datasets such as MUSAN (Snyder et al., 2015) and Microsoft SNSD (Reddy et al., 2019).

For modeling, Howl provides implementations of convolutional neural networks (CNNs) and recurrent neural networks (RNNs) for wake word detection. These models are from the existing literature, such as residual CNNs (Tang and Lin, 2018), a modified listen–attend–spell (LAS) encoder (Chan et al., 2015; Park et al., 2019), and MobileNetv2 (Sandler et al., 2018). Most of the models are lightweight since the end application requires efficient inference, though some are parameter heavy to establish a rough upper bound on the quality, as far as parameters go. Of particular focus is the lightweight res8 model (Tang and Lin, 2018), which is directly exportable to Honkling, the in-browser KWS system. For this reason, we choose it in our deployment to Firefox Voice.

4 Benchmark Results

To verify the correctness of our implementation, we first train and evaluate our models on the Google Speech Commands dataset, for which there exists many known results. Next, we curate a wake word detection datasets and report our resulting model quality. Training details are in the repository.

Commands recognition. Table 1 summarizes the metrics collected from Howl for the twelve-keyword recognition task from Speech Commands (v1), where we classify a one-second clip as one of "yes," "no," "up," "down," "left," "right," "on," "off," "stop," "go," unknown, or silence. We report average accuracy collected from fifty iterations. The results indicate that our implementations are com-

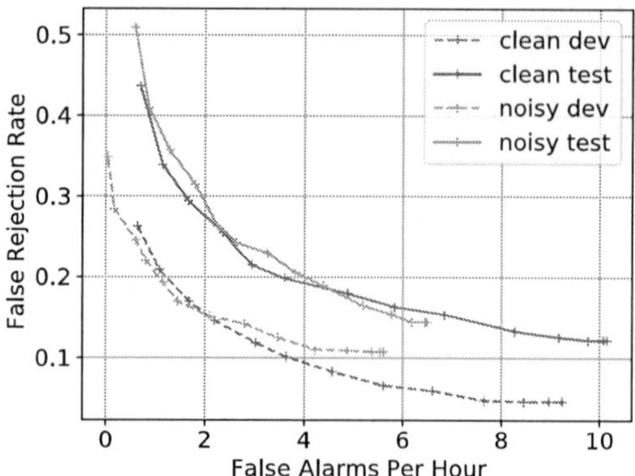

Figure 2: Receiver operating characteristic (ROC) curves for the wake word. The threshold ranges from 0.05 to 1.00 with a marker for every increment of 0.05.

petitive with the state of the art, with the `res8` model achieving the highest accuracy of 97.8% on the test set, despite having fewer parameters. Our other implemented models, the LSTM, LAS encoder, and MobileNetv2, compare favorably.

Wake word detection. For wake word detection, we target "hey, Firefox" for waking up Firefox Voice. From the single-word segment of MCV, we use 1,894 and 1,877 recordings of "hey" and "Firefox," respectively; from the MCV general speech corpus, we select all 1,037 recordings containing "hey," "fire," or "fox." We additionally collect 632 recordings of "hey, Firefox" from volunteers. For the negative set, we use about 10% of the entire MCV speech corpus. We choose the training, dev, and test splits to be 80%, 10%, and 10% of the resulting corpus, stratified by speaker IDs for the positive set. For robustness to noise, we use portions of MUSAN and SNSD as the noise dataset. We arrive at 31 hours of data for training and 3 hours each for dev and test.

For the model, we select `res8` (Tang and Lin, 2018) for its high quality on Speech Commands (see evaluation results above) and easy adaptability with our browser deployment target. We follow the pipeline mentioned in the previous section to train ten models with different seeds; details are not repeated, and hyperparameters can be found in the repository.

In Figure 2, we present the resulting receiver operating characteristic (ROC) curves generated from the averaged metrics. As we increase the threshold in increments of 0.05, we naturally observe lower false alarm rates at the expense of higher false re-

ject rates. From the figure, we find that, at a threshold of 0.8, Howl achieves five false alarms per hour of speech with an acceptable 16% false reject rate. Our negative set contains diverse adversarial examples that misrepresent real-world usage, e.g., many utterances of "Firefox," which are responsible for at least 90% of the false positives. Thus, combined with preliminary results from live testing the system ourselves, we comfortably choose the operating point at five false alarms per hour.

We finally note that the discrepancy between the dev and test curves is likely explained by differences in the data distribution, not hyperparameter fiddling, because there are only 76 and 54 clips in the positive dev and test sets, respectively.

5 Browser Deployment

To protect user security and privacy, wake word detection must be directly performed on the user's device. This setting introduces various technical challenges, as the available resources are often limited and may not be accessible. In the case of Firefox Voice, our target application, the platform is Firefox, where the major challenge is the limited support in machine learning frameworks.

However, our previous work demonstrates the feasibility of in-browser wake word detection with Honkling (Lee et al., 2019). Our application is written purely in JavaScript and supports different models using TensorFlow.js. Since our task is to provide an accurate wake word detection system for Firefox Voice, we rewrite the audio processing logic to match the new Python pipeline and optimize various preprocessing routines to substantially reduce the computational burden.

To measure the performance of our application, we refer to the built-in energy impact metric of Firefox, which reports the CPU consumption of each open tab. To establish a reference, playing a YouTube video reports an average energy impact of 10, while a static Google search reports 0.1. Our wake word detection model yields an energy impact of only 3, which efficiently enables hands-free interaction for initiating the speech recognition engine. Our wake word detection demo and browser-side integration details can be found at `https://github.com/castorini/howl-deploy`.

6 Conclusions and Future Work

This paper introduces Howl, the first in-browser wake word detection system which powers a widely deployed application, Firefox Voice. Leveraging a continuously growing speech dataset, Howl enables a community-based endeavour for building a privacy-respecting and non-eavesdropping wake word detection system. To expand the scope of Howl, our future work includes embedded systems as deployment targets, where the computational resources are even more constrained, with some systems lacking even modern memory managers.

7 Acknowledgments

This work was supported by the Canada First Research Excellence Fund and the Natural Sciences and Engineering Research Council of Canada.

References

Douglas Coimbra de Andrade, Sabato Leo, Martin Loesener Da Silva Viana, and Christoph Bernkopf. 2018. A neural attention model for speech command recognition. *arXiv:1808.08929*.

Rosana Ardila, Megan Branson, Kelly Davis, Michael Henretty, Michael Kohler, Josh Meyer, Reuben Morais, Lindsay Saunders, Francis M. Tyers, and Gregor Weber. 2019. Common Voice: A massively-multilingual speech corpus. *arXiv:1912.06670*.

William Chan, Navdeep Jaitly, Quoc V. Le, and Oriol Vinyals. 2015. Listen, attend and spell. *arXiv:1508.01211*.

Alice Coucke, Mohammed Chlieh, Thibault Gisselbrecht, David Leroy, Mathieu Poumeyrol, and Thibaut Lavril. 2019. Efficient keyword spotting using dilated convolutions and gating. In *Proceedings of the IEEE International Conference on Acoustics, Speech and Signal Processing*.

Navdeep Jaitly and Geoffrey E. Hinton. 2013. Vocal Tract Length Perturbation (VTLP) improves speech recognition. In *Proceedings of the ICML Workshop on Deep Learning for Audio, Speech and Language*.

Jaejun Lee, Raphael Tang, and Jimmy Lin. 2019. Honkling: In-browser personalization for ubiquitous keyword spotting. In *Proceedings of the 2019 Conference on Empirical Methods in Natural Language Processing*.

Zhong Qiu Lin, Audrey G. Chung, and Alexander Wong. 2018. EdgeSpeechNets: Highly efficient deep neural networks for speech recognition on the edge. *arXiv:1810.08559*.

Michael McAuliffe, Michaela Socolof, Sarah Mihuc, Michael Wagner, and Morgan Sonderegger. 2017. Montreal Forced Aligner: Trainable text-speech alignment using Kaldi. In *Proceedings of the Eighteenth Annual Conference of the International Speech Communication Association*.

Brian McFee, Colin Raffel, Dawen Liang, Daniel P. W. Ellis, Matt McVicar, Eric Battenberg, and Oriol Nieto. 2015. librosa: Audio and music signal analysis in Python. In *Proceedings of the 14th Python in Science Conference*.

Vassil Panayotov, Guoguo Chen, Daniel Povey, and Sanjeev Khudanpur. 2015. LibriSpeech: An ASR corpus based on public domain audio books. In *Proceedings of the IEEE International Conference on Acoustics, Speech and Signal Processing*.

Daniel S. Park, William Chan, Yu Zhang, Chung-Cheng Chiu, Barret Zoph, Ekin Dogus Cubuk, and Quoc V. Le. 2019. SpecAugment: A simple augmentation method for automatic speech recognition. In *Proceedings of the Twentieth Annual Conference of the International Speech Communication Association*.

Adam Paszke, Sam Gross, Francisco Massa, Adam Lerer, James Bradbury, Gregory Chanan, Trevor Killeen, Zeming Lin, Natalia Gimelshein, Luca Antiga, et al. 2019. PyTorch: An imperative style, high-performance deep learning library. In *Advances in Neural Information Processing Systems*, pages 8024–8035.

Chandan K. A. Reddy, Ebrahim Beyrami, Jamie Pool, Ross Cutler, Sriram Srinivasan, and Johannes Gehrke. 2019. A scalable noisy speech dataset and online subjective test framework. In *Proceedings of the Twentieth Annual Conference of the International Speech Communication Association*.

Tara N. Sainath and Carolina Parada. 2015. Convolutional neural networks for small-footprint keyword spotting. In *Proceedings of the Sixteenth Annual Conference of the International Speech Communication Association*.

Mark Sandler, Andrew Howard, Menglong Zhu, Andrey Zhmoginov, and Liang-Chieh Chen. 2018. MobileNetv2: Inverted residuals and linear bottlenecks. In *Proceedings of the IEEE Conference on Computer Vision and Pattern Recognition*.

David Snyder, Guoguo Chen, and Daniel Povey. 2015. MUSAN: A music, speech, and noise corpus. *arXiv:1510.08484*.

Raphael Tang and Jimmy Lin. 2017. Honk: A PyTorch reimplementation of convolutional neural networks for keyword spotting. *arXiv:1710.06554*.

Raphael Tang and Jimmy Lin. 2018. Deep residual learning for small-footprint keyword spotting. In *Proceedings of the IEEE International Conference on Acoustics, Speech and Signal Processing*.

Pete Warden. 2018. Speech commands: A dataset for limited-vocabulary speech recognition. *arXiv:1804.03209*.

Mengjun Zeng and Nanfeng Xiao. 2019. Effective combination of DenseNet and BiLSTM for keyword spotting. *IEEE Access*.

iNLTK: Natural Language Toolkit for Indic Languages

Gaurav Arora
Jio Haptik
`gaurav@haptik.ai`

Abstract

We present iNLTK, an open-source NLP library consisting of pre-trained language models and out-of-the-box support for Data Augmentation, Textual Similarity, Sentence Embeddings, Word Embeddings, Tokenization and Text Generation in 13 Indic Languages. By using pre-trained models from iNLTK for text classification on publicly available datasets, we significantly outperform previously reported results. On these datasets, we also show that by using pre-trained models and data augmentation from iNLTK, we can achieve more than 95% of the previous best performance by using less than 10% of the training data. iNLTK is already being widely used by the community and has 40,000+ downloads, 600+ stars and 100+ forks on GitHub. The library is available at https://github.com/goru001/inltk.

1 Introduction

Deep learning offers a way to harness large amounts of computation and data with little engineering by hand (LeCun et al., 2015). With distributed representation, various deep models have become the new state-of-the-art methods for NLP problems. Pre-trained language models (Devlin et al., 2019) can model syntactic/semantic relations between words and reduce feature engineering. These pre-trained models are useful for initialization and/or transfer learning for NLP tasks. Pre-trained models are typically learned using unsupervised approaches from large, diverse monolingual corpora (Kunchukuttan et al., 2020). While we have seen exciting progress across many tasks in natural language processing over the last years, most such results have been achieved in English and a small set of other high-resource languages (Ruder, 2020).

Indic languages, widely spoken by more than a billion speakers, lack pre-trained deep language models, trained on a large corpus, which can provide a headstart for downstream tasks using transfer learning. Availability of such models is critical to build a system that can achieve good results in "low-resource" settings - where labeled data is scarce and computation is expensive, which is the biggest challenge for working on NLP in Indic Languages. Additionally, there's lack of Indic languages support in NLP libraries like spacy[1], nltk[2] - creating a barrier to entry for working with Indic languages.

iNLTK, an open-source natural language toolkit for Indic languages, is designed to address these problems and to significantly lower barriers to doing NLP in Indic Languages by

- sharing pre-trained deep language models, which can then be fine-tuned and used for downstream tasks like text classification,

- providing out-of-the-box support for Data Augmentation, Textual Similarity, Sentence Embeddings, Word Embeddings, Tokenization and Text Generation built on top of pre-trained language models, lowering the barrier for doing applied research and building products in Indic languages

iNLTK library supports 13 Indic languages, including English, as shown in Table 2. GitHub repository[3] for the library contains source code, links to download pre-trained models, datasets and API documentation[4]. It includes reference implementations for reproducing text-classification results shown in Section 2.4, which can also be easily adapted to new data. The library has a permissive MIT License and is easy to download and install via pip or by cloning the GitHub repository.

---

[1] https://spacy.io/
[2] https://www.nltk.org/
[3] https://github.com/goru001/inltk
[4] https://inltk.readthedocs.io/

Proceedings of Second Workshop for NLP Open Source Software (NLP-OSS), pages 66–71
Virtual Conference, November 19, 2020. ©2020 Association for Computational Linguistics

Language	# Wikipedia Articles		# Tokens	
	Train	**Valid**	**Train**	**Valid**
Hindi	137,823	34,456	43,434,685	10,930,403
Bengali	50,661	21,713	15,389,227	6,493,291
Gujarati	22,339	9,574	4,801,796	2,005,729
Malayalam	8,671	3,717	1,954,174	926,215
Marathi	59,875	25,662	7,777,419	3,302,837
Tamil	102,126	25,255	14,923,513	3,715,380
Punjabi	35,637	8,910	9,214,502	2,276,354
Kannada	26,397	6,600	11,450,264	3,110,983
Oriya	12,446	5,335	2,391,168	1,082,410
Sanskrit	18,812	6,682	11,683,360	4,274,479
Nepali	27,129	11,628	3,569,063	1,560,677
Urdu	107,669	46,145	15,421,652	6,773,909

Table 1: Statistics of Wikipedia Articles Dataset used for training Language Models

Language	Code	Language	Code
Hindi	hi	Marathi	mr
Punjabi	pa	Bengali	bn
Gujarati	gu	Tamil	ta
Kannada	kn	Urdu	ur
Malayalam	ml	Nepali	ne
Oriya	or	Sanskrit	sa
English	en		

Table 2: Languages supported in iNLTK

Language	Vocab size	Language	Vocab size
Hindi	30,000	Marathi	30,000
Punjabi	30,000	Bengali	30,000
Gujarati	20,000	Tamil	8,000
Kannada	25,000	Urdu	30,000
Malayalam	10,000	Nepali	15,000
Oriya	15,000	Sanskrit	20,000

Table 3: Vocab size for languages supported in iNLTK

2 iNLTK Pretrained Language Models

iNLTK has pre-trained ULMFiT (Howard and Ruder, 2018) and TransformerXL (Dai et al., 2019) language models for 13 Indic languages. All the language models (LMs) were trained from scratch using PyTorch (Paszke et al., 2017) and Fastai[5], except for English. Pre-trained LMs were then evaluated on downstream task of text classification on public datasets. Pre-trained LMs for English were borrowed from Fastai directly. This section describes training of language models and their evaluation.

2.1 Dataset preparation

We obtained a monolingual corpora for each one of the languages from Wikipedia for training LMs from scratch. We used the wiki extractor[6] tool and BeautifulSoup[7] for text extraction from Wikipedia. Wikipedia articles were then cleaned and split into train-validation sets. Table 1 shows statistics of

the monolingual Wikipedia articles dataset for each language. Hindi Wikipedia articles dataset is the largest one, while Malayalam and Oriya Wikipedia articles datasets have the least number of articles.

2.2 Tokenization

We create subword vocabulary for each one of the languages by training a SentencePiece[8] tokenization model on Wikipedia articles dataset, using unigram segmentation algorithm (Kudo and Richardson, 2018). An important property of SentencePiece tokenization, necessary for us to obtain a valid subword-based language model, is its reversibility. We do not use subword regularization as the available training dataset is large enough to avoid overfitting. Table 3 shows subword vocabulary size of the tokenization model for each one of the languages.

2.3 Language Model Training

Our model is based on the Fastai implementation of ULMFiT and TransformerXL. Hyperparameters

[5]https://github.com/fastai/fastai
[6]https://github.com/attardi/wikiextractor
[7]https://www.crummy.com/software/BeautifulSoup

[8]https://github.com/google/sentencepiece

Language	Dataset	FT-W	FT-WC	INLP	iNLTK
	BBC Articles	72.29	67.44	74.25	**78.75**
Hindi	IITP+Movie	41.61	44.52	45.81	**57.74**
	IITP Product	58.32	57.17	63.48	**75.71**
Bengali	Soham Articles	62.79	64.78	72.50	**90.71**
Gujarati		81.94	84.07	90.90	**91.05**
Malayalam	iNLTK	86.35	83.65	93.49	**95.56**
Marathi	Headlines	83.06	81.65	89.92	**92.40**
Tamil		90.88	89.09	93.57	**95.22**
Punjabi		94.23	94.87	96.79	**97.12**
Kannada	IndicNLP News Category	96.13	96.50	97.20	**98.87**
Oriya		94.00	95.93	98.07	**98.83**

Table 4: Text classification accuracy on public datasets

Language	Perplexity	
	ULMFiT	**TransformerXL**
Hindi	34.0	26.0
Bengali	41.2	39.3
Gujarati	34.1	28.1
Malayalam	26.3	25.7
Marathi	17.9	17.4
Tamil	19.8	17.2
Punjabi	24.4	14.0
Kannada	70.1	61.9
Oriya	26.5	26.8
Sanskrit	5.5	2.7
Nepali	31.5	29.3
Urdu	13.1	12.5

Table 5: Perplexity on validation set of Language Models in iNLTK

Language	Dataset	N	# Examples	
			Train	**Test**
Hindi	BBC Articles	6	3467	866
	IITP+Movie	3	2480	310
	IITP Product	3	4182	523
Bengali	Soham Articles	6	11284	1411
Gujarati		3	5269	659
Malayalam	iNLTK	3	5036	630
Marathi	Headlines	3	9672	1210
Tamil		3	5346	669
Punjabi	IndicNLP	4	2496	312
Kannada	News	3	24000	3000
Oriya	Category	4	24000	3000

Table 6: Statistics of publicly available classification datasets (N is the number of classes)

of the final model are accessible from the GitHub repository of the library. Table 5 shows perplexity of language models on validation set. TransformerXL consistently performs better for all languages.

2.4 Text Classification Evaluation

We evaluated pre-trained ULMFiT language models on downstream task of text-classification using following publicly available datasets: (a) IIT-Patna Sentiment Analysis dataset (Akhtar et al., 2016), (b) BBC News Articles classification dataset[9], (c) iNLTK Headlines dataset[10], (d) Soham Bengali News classification dataset[11], (e) IndicNLP

News Category classification dataset (Kunchukuttan et al., 2020). Train and test splits, derived by the authors (Kunchukuttan et al., 2020) from the above mentioned corpora and used for benchmarking, are available on the IndicNLP corpus website[12]. Table 6 shows statistics of these datasets.

iNLTK results were compared against results reported in (Kunchukuttan et al., 2020) for pre-trained embeddings released by the Fast-Text project trained on Wikipedia (FT-W) (Bojanowski et al., 2016), Wiki+CommonCrawl (FT-WC) (Grave et al., 2018) and INLP embeddings (Kunchukuttan et al., 2020). Table 4 shows that iNLTK significantly outperforms other models across all languages and datasets[13].

---

[9]https://github.com/NirantK/hindi2vec/releases/tag/bbc-hindi-v0.1
[10]https://github.com/goru001/inltk
[11]https://www.kaggle.com/csoham/classification-bengali-news-articles-indicnlp

[12]https://github.com/AI4Bharat/indicnlp_corpus
[13]Refer GitHub repository of the library for instructions to reproduce results

68

Language	Dataset	# Training Examples		%age reduction	INLP Accuracy	iNLTK Accuracy		
		Full	Reduced		Full	Full	Reduced	
							Without Data Aug	With Data Aug
Hindi	IITP+Movie	2,480	496	80%	45.81	57.74	47.74	56.13
Bengali	Soham Articles	11,284	112	99%	72.50	90.71	69.88	74.06
Gujarati	iNLTK Headlines	5,269	526	90%	90.90	91.05	80.88	81.03
Malayalam		5,036	503	90%	93.49	95.56	82.38	84.29
Marathi		9,672	483	95%	89.92	92.40	84.13	84.55
Tamil		5,346	267	95%	93.57	95.22	86.25	89.84
	Average	6514.5	397.8	91.5%	81.03	87.11	75.21	78.31

Table 7: Comparison of Accuracy on INLP trained on Full Training set vs Accuracy on iNLTK, using data augmentation, trained on reduced training set

3 iNLTK API

iNLTK is designed to be simple for practitioners in order to lower the barrier for doing applied research and building products in Indic languages. This section discusses various NLP tasks for which iNLTK provides out-of-the-box support, under a unified API.

Data Augmentation helps in improving the performance of NLP models (Duboue and Chu-Carroll, 2006; Marton et al., 2009). It is even more important in "low-resource" settings, where labeled data is scarce. iNLTK provides augmentations[14] for a sentence while preserving its semantics following a two step process. Firstly, it generates candidate paraphrases by replacing original sentence tokens with tokens which have closest embeddings from the embedding layer of pre-trained language model. And then, it chooses top paraphrases which are similar to original sentence, where similarity between sentences is calculated as the cosine similarity of sentence embeddings, obtained from pre-trained language model's encoder.

To evaluate the effectiveness of using data augmentation from iNLTK in low resource settings, we prepare[15] **reduced train sets** of publicly available text-classification datasets by picking first N examples from the full train set[16], where N is equal to size of reduced train set and compare accuracy of the classifier trained *with* vs *without* data augmentation. Table 7 shows reduced dataset statistics and comparison of results obtained on full and reduced datasets using iNLTK. Using data augmentation from iNLTK gives significant increase in accuracy on Hindi, Bengali, Malayalam and Tamil dataset, and minor improvements in Gujarati and Marathi datasets. Additionally, Table 7 compares previously obtained best results on these datasets using INLP embeddings (Kunchukuttan et al., 2020) with results obtained using iNLTK pretrained models and iNLTK's data augmentation utility. On an average, with iNLTK we are able to achieve more than 95% of the previous accuracy using less than 10% of the training data[17].

Semantic Textual Similarity (STS) assesses the degree to which the underlying semantics of two segments of text are equivalent to each other (Agirre et al., 2016). iNLTK compares[18] sentence embeddings of the two segments of text, obtained from pre-trained language model's encoder, using a comparison function, to evaluate semantic textual similarity. Cosine similarity between sentence embeddings is used as the default comparison function.

Distributed representations are the cornerstone of modern NLP, which have led to significant advances in many NLP tasks. iNLTK provides utilities to obtain distributed representations for **words**[19], **sentences and documents**[20] obtained

---

[14]https://inltk.readthedocs.io/en/latest/api_docs.html#get-similar-sentences

[15]Notebooks to prepare reduced datasets are accessible from the GitHub repository of the library

[16]Labels in publicly available full train sets were not grouped together, instead were randomly shuffled

[17]Refer GitHub repository of the library for instructions to reproduce results on full and reduced dataset

[18]https://inltk.readthedocs.io/en/latest/api_docs.html#get-sentence-similarity

[19]https://inltk.readthedocs.io/en/latest/api_docs.html#get-embedding-vectors

[20]https://inltk.readthedocs.io/en/latest/api_docs.html#get-

from embedding layer and encoder output of pre-trained language models, respectively.

Additionally, iNLTK provides utilities to **generate text**[21] given a prompt, using pre-trained language models, **tokenize**[22] text using sentencepiece tokenization models described in Section 2.2, identify[23] which one of the supported Indic languages is given `text` in and remove tokens of a foreign language[24] from given `text`.

4 Related Work

NLP and ML communities have a strong culture of building open-source tools. There are lots of easy-to-use, user-facing libraries for general-purpose NLP like NLTK (Loper and Bird, 2002), Stanford CoreNLP (Manning et al., 2014), Spacy (Honnibal and Montani, 2017), AllenNLP (Gardner et al., 2018), Flair (Akbik et al., 2019), Stanza (Qi et al., 2020) and Huggingface Transformers (Wolf et al., 2019). But most of these libraries have limited or no support for Indic languages, creating a barrier to entry for working with Indic languages. Additionally, for many Indic languages word embeddings have been trained, but they still lack richer pre-trained representations from deep language models (Kunchukuttan et al., 2020). iNLTK tries to solve these problems by providing pre-trained language models and out-of-the-box support for a variety of NLP tasks in 13 Indic languages.

5 Conclusion and Future Work

iNLTK provides pre-trained language models and supports Data Augmentation, Textual Similarity, Sentence Embeddings, Word Embeddings, Tokenization and Text Generation in 13 Indic Languages. Our results significantly outperform other methods on text-classification benchmarks, using pre-trained models from iNLTK. These pre-trained models from iNLTK can be used as-is for a variety of NLP tasks, or can be fine-tuned on domain specific datasets. iNLTK is being widely[25] used[26] and

appreciated[27] by the community[28].

We are working on expanding the supported languages in iNLTK to include other Indic languages like Telugu, Maithili; code mixed languages like Hinglish (Hindi and English), Manglish (Malayalam and English) and Tanglish (Tamil and English); expanding supported model architectures to include BERT. Additionally, we want to mitigate any possible unwarranted biases which might exist in pre-trained language models (Lu et al., 2019), because of training data, which might propagate into downstream systems using these models. While these tasks are work in progress, we hope this library will accelerate NLP research and development in Indic languages.

Acknowledgments

We are thankful to Anurag Singh[29] and Ravi Annaswamy[30] for their contributions to support Urdu and Tamil in the iNLTK library, respectively.

References

Eneko Agirre, Carmen Banea, Daniel Cer, Mona Diab, Aitor Gonzalez-Agirre, Rada Mihalcea, German Rigau, and Janyce Wiebe. 2016. SemEval-2016 task 1: Semantic textual similarity, monolingual and cross-lingual evaluation. In *Proceedings of the 10th International Workshop on Semantic Evaluation (SemEval-2016)*, pages 497–511, San Diego, California. Association for Computational Linguistics.

Alan Akbik, Tanja Bergmann, Duncan Blythe, Kashif Rasul, Stefan Schweter, and Roland Vollgraf. 2019. FLAIR: An easy-to-use framework for state-of-the-art NLP. In *Proceedings of the 2019 Conference of the North American Chapter of the Association for Computational Linguistics (Demonstrations)*, pages 54–59, Minneapolis, Minnesota. Association for Computational Linguistics.

Md Shad Akhtar, Ayush Kumar, Asif Ekbal, and Pushpak Bhattacharyya. 2016. A hybrid deep learning architecture for sentiment analysis. In *Proceedings of COLING 2016, the 26th International Conference on Computational Linguistics: Technical Papers*, pages 482–493, Osaka, Japan. The COLING 2016 Organizing Committee.

Piotr Bojanowski, Edouard Grave, Armand Joulin, and Tomas Mikolov. 2016. Enriching word vectors with subword information. *CoRR*, abs/1607.04606.

---

sentence-encoding

[21] https://inltk.readthedocs.io/en/latest/api_docs.html#predict-next-n-words

[22] https://inltk.readthedocs.io/en/latest/api_docs.html#tokenize

[23] https://inltk.readthedocs.io/en/latest/api_docs.html#identify-language

[24] https://inltk.readthedocs.io/en/latest/api_docs.html#remove-foreign-languages

[25] https://github.com/goru001/inltk/network/members

[26] https://pepy.tech/project/inltk

[27] https://github.com/goru001/inltk/stargazers

[28] https://github.com/goru001/inltk#inltks-appreciation

[29] https://github.com/anuragshas

[30] https://github.com/ravi-annaswamy

Zihang Dai, Zhilin Yang, Yiming Yang, Jaime G. Carbonell, Quoc V. Le, and Ruslan Salakhutdinov. 2019. Transformer-xl: Attentive language models beyond a fixed-length context. *CoRR*, abs/1901.02860.

Jacob Devlin, Ming-Wei Chang, Kenton Lee, and Kristina Toutanova. 2019. BERT: Pre-training of deep bidirectional transformers for language understanding. In *Proceedings of the 2019 Conference of the North American Chapter of the Association for Computational Linguistics: Human Language Technologies, Volume 1 (Long and Short Papers)*, pages 4171–4186, Minneapolis, Minnesota. Association for Computational Linguistics.

Pablo Duboue and Jennifer Chu-Carroll. 2006. Answering the question you wish they had asked: The impact of paraphrasing for question answering. In *Proceedings of the Human Language Technology Conference of the NAACL, Companion Volume: Short Papers*, pages 33–36.

Matt Gardner, Joel Grus, Mark Neumann, Oyvind Tafjord, Pradeep Dasigi, Nelson F. Liu, Matthew E. Peters, Michael Schmitz, and Luke Zettlemoyer. 2018. Allennlp: A deep semantic natural language processing platform. *CoRR*, abs/1803.07640.

Edouard Grave, Piotr Bojanowski, Prakhar Gupta, Armand Joulin, and Tomas Mikolov. 2018. Learning word vectors for 157 languages. *CoRR*, abs/1802.06893.

Matthew Honnibal and Ines Montani. 2017. spaCy 2: Natural language understanding with Bloom embeddings, convolutional neural networks and incremental parsing. To appear.

Jeremy Howard and Sebastian Ruder. 2018. Fine-tuned language models for text classification. *CoRR*, abs/1801.06146.

Taku Kudo and John Richardson. 2018. Sentencepiece: A simple and language independent subword tokenizer and detokenizer for neural text processing. *CoRR*, abs/1808.06226.

Anoop Kunchukuttan, Divyanshu Kakwani, Satish Golla, Gokul N.C., Avik Bhattacharyya, Mitesh M. Khapra, and Pratyush Kumar. 2020. Ai4bharat-indicnlp corpus: Monolingual corpora and word embeddings for indic languages. *arXiv preprint arXiv:2005.00085*.

Yann LeCun, Y. Bengio, and Geoffrey Hinton. 2015. Deep learning. *Nature*, 521:436–44.

Edward Loper and Steven Bird. 2002. Nltk: the natural language toolkit. *CoRR*, cs.CL/0205028.

Kaiji Lu, Piotr Mardziel, Fangjing Wu, Preetam Amancharla, and Anupam Datta. 2019. Gender bias in neural natural language processing.

Christopher Manning, Mihai Surdeanu, John Bauer, Jenny Finkel, Steven Bethard, and David McClosky. 2014. The Stanford CoreNLP natural language processing toolkit. In *Proceedings of 52nd Annual Meeting of the Association for Computational Linguistics: System Demonstrations*, pages 55–60, Baltimore, Maryland. Association for Computational Linguistics.

Yuval Marton, Chris Callison-Burch, and Philip Resnik. 2009. Improved statistical machine translation using monolingually-derived paraphrases. In *Proceedings of the 2009 Conference on Empirical Methods in Natural Language Processing*, pages 381–390.

Adam Paszke, S. Gross, Soumith Chintala, G. Chanan, E. Yang, Zachary Devito, Zeming Lin, Alban Desmaison, L. Antiga, and A. Lerer. 2017. Automatic differentiation in pytorch.

Peng Qi, Yuhao Zhang, Yuhui Zhang, Jason Bolton, and Christopher D Manning. 2020. Stanza: A python natural language processing toolkit for many human languages. *arXiv preprint arXiv:2003.07082*.

Sebastian Ruder. 2020. Why You Should Do NLP Beyond English. http://ruder.io/nlp-beyond-english.

Thomas Wolf, Lysandre Debut, Victor Sanh, Julien Chaumond, Clement Delangue, Anthony Moi, Pierric Cistac, Tim Rault, R'emi Louf, Morgan Funtowicz, and Jamie Brew. 2019. Huggingface's transformers: State-of-the-art natural language processing. *ArXiv*, abs/1910.03771.

KLPT – Kurdish Language Processing Toolkit

Sina Ahmadi
Insight Centre for Data Analytics
National University of Ireland Galway
`ahmadi.sina@outlook.com`

Abstract

Despite the recent advances in applying language-independent approaches to various natural language processing tasks thanks to artificial intelligence, some language-specific tools are still essential to process a language in a viable manner. Kurdish language is a less-resourced language with a notable diversity in dialects and scripts and lacks basic language processing tools. To address this issue, we introduce a language processing toolkit to handle such a diversity in an efficient way. Our toolkit is composed of fundamental components such as text preprocessing, stemming, tokenization, lemmatization and transliteration and is able to get further extended by future developers. This project is publicly available[1].

1 Introduction

Language technology is an increasingly important field in our information era which is dependent on our knowledge of the human language and computational methods to process it. Unlike the latter which undergoes constant progress with new methods and more efficient techniques being invented, the processability of human languages does not evolve with the same pace. This is particularly the case of languages with scarce resources and limited grammars, also known as less-resourced languages.

Various natural language processing (NLP) tasks are of pipeline architecture; that is, to address a specific task, a few other language processing tasks may be initially required (Manning et al., 2014). With the current advances in the open-source movements, more researchers and industrial developers are encouraged to share their knowledge in an open-source manner, accessible under certain conditions (Ljungberg, 2000).

Therefore, the development of underlying tasks in NLP for a specific language will potentially pave the way for further contributions to the field, by either improving the current tools or further progress in new tasks. For instance, tokenization as a fundamental task is widely required in many other applications such as part-of-speech tagging, machine translation and syntactic analysis. Once addressed, future researchers can build upon it for more advanced tasks or eventually improve it.

Despite a plethora of performant tools and specific frameworks for NLP, such as NLTK (Loper and Bird, 2002), Stanza (Qi et al., 2020), Teanga (Ziad et al., 2018) and spaCy[2], the progress with respect to less-resourced languages is often hindered by not only the lack of basic tools and resources but also the accessibility of the previous studies under an open-source licence. This is particularly the case of Kurdish, a less-resourced Indo-European language that is the focus of the current paper. As an example, although the task of spell-checking and stemming for Kurdish have been addressed by many previous studies, (Jaf and Ramsay, 2014; Salavati and Ahmadi, 2018; Mustafa and Rashid, 2018; Saeed et al., 2018a; Hawezi et al., 2019) to mention but a few, none of them provides an implementation of their tool under any licence.

On the other hand, some previous studies use specific frameworks that are hardly integrable and inter-operable. For instance, (Walther and Sagot, 2010) and (Walther et al., 2010) describe their efforts in developing a large-scale morphological lexicon and a part-of-speech tagger for Kurdish within the *Alexina* framework under the LGPL-LR licence. Despite the valuable impact of this study in the field, for example in (Cotterell et al., 2017) and (Gökırmak and Tyers, 2017), the tool does not

---

[1] `https://github.com/sinaahmadi/klpt`

[2] `https://github.com/explosion/spaCy`

Proceedings of Second Workshop for NLP Open Source Software (NLP-OSS), pages 72–84
Virtual Conference, November 19, 2020. ©2020 Association for Computational Linguistics

IPA	b	t͡ʃ	d͡ʒ	d	f	g	h	ʒ	k	l	ɫ	m	n	p	q	ɾ	r	s	ʃ	t	v	w	x	j	z	ʕ	ħ	ɣ	ʔ
Latin	b	ç	c	d	f	g	h	j	k	l	ł/ll	m	n	p	q	r	ř/rr	s	ş	t	v	w	x	y	z	'/'e/ë	ḧ/'h	x/x	'
Arabic	ب	چ	ج	د	ف	گ	ه	ژ	ک	ل	ڵ	م	ن	پ	ق	ر	ڕ	س	ش	ت	ف	و	خ	ى	ز	ع	ح	غ	ئ

(a) Consonants

IPA	aː	æ	eː	ɪ	iː	oː	uː	ʊ	ʉː
Latin	a	e	ê	i	î	o	û	u	ü
Arabic	ا	ە	ێ		ی	ۆ	وو	و	ۊ

(b) Vowels

Table 1: A comparison of the Kurdish alphabets. Variations are specified with "/"

seem to be widely used in the subsequent projects. As such, projects such as (Jaf and Ramsay, 2014) and (Ahmadi and Hassani, 2020a) tackle the very same topic from scratch.

Language-specific toolkits have been previously designed for various languages, such as IceNLP for Icelandic (Loftsson and Rögnvaldsson, 2007), VnCoreNLP for Vietnamese (Vu et al., 2018), FudanNLP for Chinese (Qiu et al., 2013), PSI-Toolkit for Polish (Graliński et al., 2013) and ParsiPardaz for Persian (Sarabi et al., 2013). In the same vein, in order to facilitate the basic language processing tasks for Kurdish in an organized and methodical way and aware of the increasing importance of open-source and inter-operable tools for building more efficient systems and get further advanced in the field, we present KLPT–the Kurdish language processing toolkit. This toolkit is developed in Python and is composed of core modules and is extendable by future developers.

2 Kurdish Language

Kurdish belongs to the Northwestern branch of the Iranian languages within the Indo-European language family which is spoken by 20-30 million speakers in the Kurdish regions of Turkey, Iraq, Iran and Syria and also, among the Kurdish diaspora around the world (Ahmadi et al., 2019). The division of Kurdish into Northern Kurdish (or Kurmanji), Central Kurdish (or Sorani), Southern Kurdish and Laki, respectively with kmr, ckb, sdh and lki ISO 639-3 language codes, has been widely studied previously (Edmonds, 2013). Based on the structural differences between these, some scholars believe that they are distinct languages and therefore, refer to them as Kurdish languages (Kreyenbroek, 2005). On the other hand, it is also commonly believed by both scholars and

Kurdish people that those are in fact different dialects of the Kurdish language (Haig and Matras, 2002; Matras, 2017). In this study, we remain with this theory and refer to them as Kurdish dialects. It is worth mentioning that despite the linguistic similarities of Zazaki, also known as Dimlî, and Gorani languages and the popular belief that they are dialects of Kurdish, studies show that they belong to the Zaza-Gorani language family which is independent from the Kurdish language (Paul, 1998; Jugel, 2014; Ahmadi, 2020c).

Kurdish has been historically written in various scripts, namely Cyrillic, Armenian, Latin and Arabic among which the latter two are still widely in use. Efforts in standardization of the Kurdish alphabets and orthographies have not succeeded to be globally followed by all Kurdish speakers in all regions (Tavadze, 2019; Haig and Matras, 2002; Aydoğan, 2012). As such, the Kurmanji dialect is mostly written in the Latin-based script while the Sorani, Southern Kurdish and Laki are mostly written in the Arabic-based script. That, not only scatters readers and speakers to communicate together, but also creates further challenges in processing the language (Esmaili, 2012; Ahmadi, 2019). Table 1 provides the Latin-based and Arabic-based Kurdish alphabets used for all the dialects.

Kurdish language is a highly inflectional language, particularly due to a high number of affixes and clitics (Ahmadi and Hassani, 2020b). Regarding nouns, although Sorani does not have gender or grammatical cases, it has a full article marking system for definite, indefinite and demonstrative in singular and plural forms (Jugel, 2014). On the other hand, Kurmanji has a fewer number of article markers for feminine and masculine genders (Thackston, 2006). With respect to the

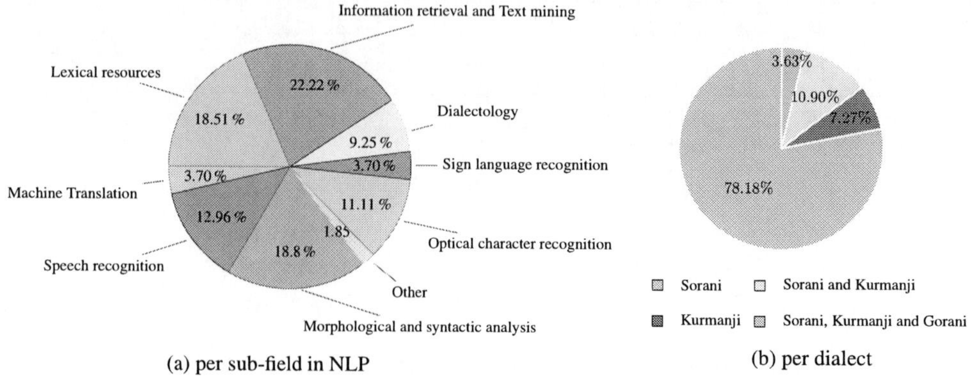

(a) per sub-field in NLP   (b) per dialect

Figure 1: Proportion of publications related to Kurdish language processing

verbs, Kurdish has a few number of around 300 single-word verbs (Walther and Sagot, 2010), e.g. *kirdin/kirin* "to do", which are inflected based on person (1,2,3, SG, PL), tense (past, present, future), aspect (indefinite, perfect, progressive, imperfective) and mood (indicative, subjunctive, conditional). Unlike Kurmanji, Sorani Kurdish does not have future tense and uses adverbs for this purpose. However, Kurdish extensively takes use of compound constructions for creating new verb forms, particularly with (Noun + Verb), (Adjective + Verb) and (Preposition + Verb) forms (Traida, 2007). For instance, *siław* 'hi (n)', *pîroz* 'holy' (adj) and *heł* (verbal particle denoting 'up') with the single-word verb *kirdin* can respectively form compound verbs *siław kirdin* "to greet", *pîroz kirdin* "to congratulate" and *heł kirdin* "to turn on". The stringing characteristic of the Arabic-based script of Kurdish further adds to this morphological complexity in such a way that several word forms may be concatenated together (Ahmadi, 2020b).

Regarding syntax, Kurdish has a subject–object–verb word order and is a null-subject (or pro-drop) language. The presence of grammatical markers for nominative and oblique cases varies within dialects and subdialects. For instance, in the Sorani subdialects of Sulaymaniyah and Erbil, respectively categorized as Southern Sorani and Northern Sorani by (Matras, 2017), the oblique case is marked differently. Another particularity of the Kurdish language is its morphosyntactic alignment in the past tense of transitive verbs. In such tenses, an ergative–absolutive alignment occurs where the subject of intransitive verbs behaves like the patient of the transitive verb in the past (Haig,

1998; Karimi, 2014). Unlike Kurmanji which uses oblique cases for this purpose, Sorani only uses different pronominal markers to specify ergativity, therefore it is called split-ergative (Esmaili and Salavati, 2013). Except the past tenses, a nominative-accusative alignment is observed in other tenses.

Not being equally documented and used, Kurdish dialects have different levels of linguistic resourcefulness. In comparison to Sorani and Kurmanji which are widely used by the media and press, Southern Kurdish and Laki are under-documented and lack basic language resources such as electronic dictionaries and corpora (Fattah, 2000; Ahmadi et al., 2019; Ahmadi, 2020c).

3 Current State of Kurdish Language Processing

The earliest works in the field of Kurdish language processing date back to 2009. Our literature review indicates that some of these contributions fail to provide open-source solutions. Despite financial and scientific constraints in Kurdish language processing, the Kurdish Language Processing Project (KLPP) (Esmaili et al., 2013) in 2012[3] and Kurdish Basic Language Resource Kit (Kurdish BLARK) (Hassani, 2018) in 2014[4] have succeeded to promote an open-source vision based on research volunteering within the Kurdish scientific communities. However, the outcomes of these projects are mostly released in an unorganized manner for individual tasks.

In order to understand the current state of the Kurdish language in the realm of NLP and com-

---

[3]http://klpp.github.io
[4]https://kurdishblark.github.io

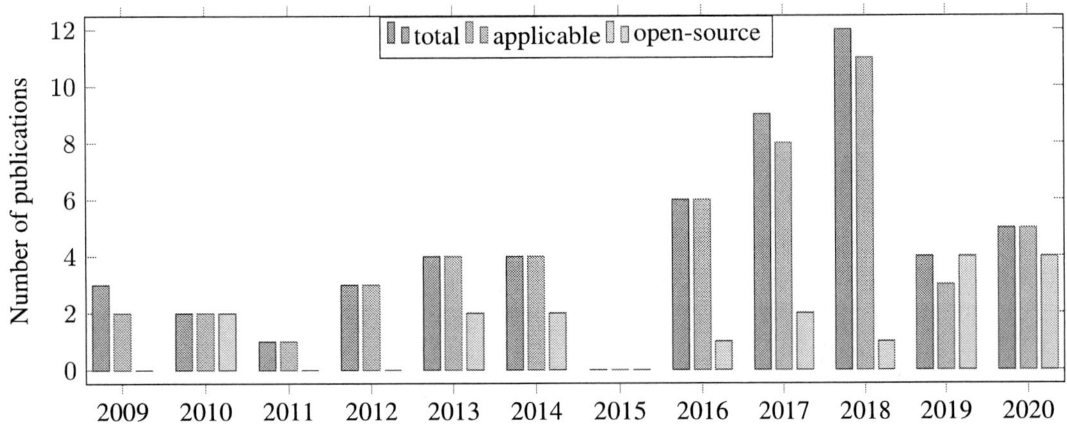

Figure 2: Number of scientific publications directly related to Kurdish language processing per year

putational linguistics, we reviewed the scientific publications that directly address an issue in those fields. A total number of 53 publications are collected from the widely-used academic databases and search engines such as Google Scholar[5], and then classified based on their discussed sub-fields which are illustrated in Figure 1. The Kurdish dialects are not evenly discussed in the previous studies, with Sorani making up a predominant proportion of almost 90%. Although a smaller proportion represents the Kurmanji dialect, no publication is found with respect to processing of the Southern Kurdish or Laki dialects. Regarding the research focus of the previous works, a range of NLP sub-fields has been addressed, particularly in text mining, morphological and syntactic analysis and, creation of lexical resources. We exceptionally included optical character recognition as it is of importance for converting printed material to electronic forms (Ahmadi et al., 2019). The full list of the surveyed papers can be found in Appendix A.2.

More importantly, we analyze previous publications from the following two perspectives:

- Open-source: Does the paper provide the discussed resource or tool under an open-source license? To this end, we verified the content of the papers and also, checked the Web, particularly major distributed version control systems such as GitHub[6], GitLab[7] and Bit-Bucket[8].

- Applicability: Does the paper, implicitly or explicitly, propose an approach or methodology that can be applied to solve the same problem in the other dialects of Kurdish? For the choice of the word, we were inspired by (Årdal et al., 2011) where the possibility of applying common practices of software development for drug discovery are investigated. For instance, (Ahmadi et al., 2019) is deemed an applicable contribution where lexicographical resources can be created for other dialects. On the other hand, (Ahmadi, 2019) is not applicable to other dialects due to its ad-hoc solution for transliterating Sorani texts according to its phonological and phonetic rules.

Figure 2 provides the number of previous publications in the Kurdish language processing field per year, and specifies their open-source status and their applicability. Although most of these publications are applicable to other dialects, only 18 out of 53 of them provide their resources or tools under an open-source license. Among the open-source ones, 11 are outcomes of volunteering projects, KLPP and Kurdish-BLARK. Given the small number of non-scientific contributions, we did not include them in this survey. A few notable examples of such contributions are Kurdînûs[9], Vejin Dictionaries[10] and VejinBooks[11] which mostly focus on Sorani Kurdish and script conversion tasks.

[5]https://scholar.google.com
[6]https://github.com
[7]https://gitlab.com
[8]https://bitbucket.org

[9]https://github.com/aso-mehmudi/kurdinus
[10]https://lex.vejinbooks.com
[11]https://books.vejin.net

4   KLPT Architecture

KLPT is implemented in Python and is composed of four core modules with specific tasks. Although we were inspired by the functionality of relevant NLP toolkits, particularly NLTK and spaCy, no external library is used in this toolkit. Regarding the toolkit design, we followed the rules of scientific software development suggested by (Prlić and Procter, 2012) along with common practices in Python programming language. Figure 3 provides the structure of the toolkit. In order to facilitate the integration of variations specific to dialects and scripts and more importantly, to avoid hard-coding, required files are provided in the `data` folder. For instance, the data required for the `preprocess` module is imported from `preprocess.json`. In addition, third-party programs can be provided in `bin`. `test` and `docs` respectively contain test cases and project documentation. Regarding the latter, we use Sphinx documentation generator[12].

It is worth noting that each module within the `klpt` package has been previously studied and evaluated separately. Our goal is to introduce the functionality of the modules within the toolkit in this section.

4.1   Preprocess

Many keyboard layouts are specifically designed for Kurdish where different character encoding are assigned to visually-similar graphemes. In addition to the usage of non-Kurdish keyboards, such as Arabic, Turkish and Persian keyboards, such diversity creates abnormality across texts in Kurdish writing. For instance, the grapheme ی (*î/y*), can be represented as ي (U+064A), ى (U+0649), ﻲ (U+FEF2), ي (U+FEF1) and ی (U+06CC), among which only the latter should be used in the Arabic-based script of Kurdish. Moreover, various writing conventions are used for each dialect and script. For instance, in Kurmanji, when dates are affixed with a morpheme, the suffix may be separated by ', - or without any marker as in *2020'an*, *2020-an* and *2020an*.

To remedy such issues in an automatic and structured manner, the `preprocess` module provides two main functions: `normalize()` for normalizing encoding abnormalities by unifying characters in such a way that only one specific encoding is used for each grapheme and,

standardize() which applies orthographic conventions to the text. For example, when *hêvî* 'hope' is suffixed with the vowel *a* (*Izafa*, meaning 'of'), a semi-vowel *y* appears between the two vowels and is usually written as *hêviya* or *hêvîya* 'hope of'. As the latter form is considered less ambiguous, this function converts the first form accordingly. Although defining a universal orthography for Kurdish is out of scope of our project, we believe that writing conventions and orthographies should be addressed to some extent. Therefore, in this initial version, we follow the writing conventions proposed by (Aydoğan, 2012) for Kurmanji and (Hashemi, 2016) for Sorani.

In addition to these two functions, `unify_numeral()` is provided to convert numerals, namely in Farsi (۰۱۲۳۴۵۶۷۸۹), Eastern Arabic (٠١٢٣٤٥٦٧٨٩) and Western Arabic (0123456789). Although we set the latter as default for all scripts, users will have the

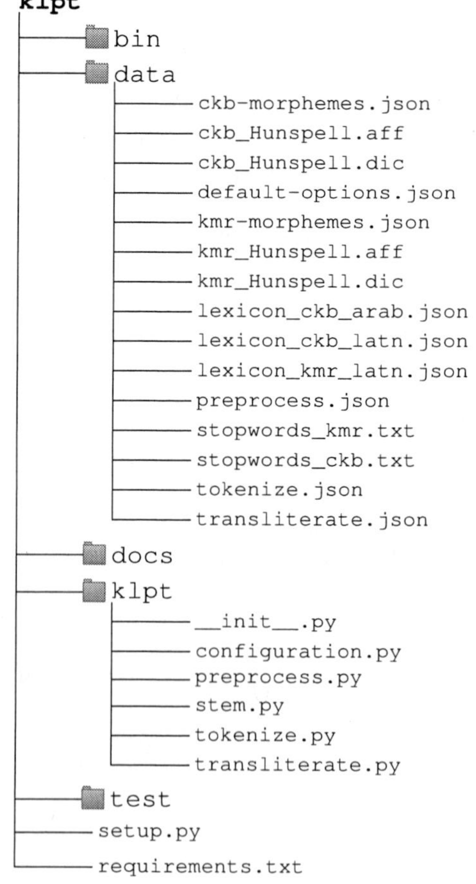

Figure 3: Structure of KLPT

---

[12]https://www.sphinx-doc.org

choice to modify the numerals according to the administrations in the Kurdish regions. All these three functions are then evoked within `preprocess()` function which normalizes, standardizes and unifies the text according to the given arguments.

The general procedure followed in this module can be summarized as string replacement. For this purpose, we define regular expressions for each dialect and script. The regular expressions along with the character mappings are provided in `preprocess.json` in such an order that the intended normalization and standardization are carried out correctly. Although this module is not explicitly evoked within other modules, except in the `transliterate` module, it is recommended that the output of the preprocessing module be used as the input of other modules by the user.

4.2 Transliterate

Given the diversity of the alphabets used in Kurdish, transliteration is a necessity to facilitate the communication between speakers and is also beneficial to various NLP tasks, such as named-entity recognition and machine translation. Although Kurdish orthographies are phonemic, i.e. each grapheme is supposed to represent a single phoneme, transliterating characters within the alphabets is more challenging than it appears. This is particularly due to و (U+0648) and ی (U+06CC) in the Arabic-based alphabet which can be respectively mapped to 'u/w' and 'î/y'. For instance, و in بیور and کورت is transliterated as *bîwir* 'axe' and *kurt* 'short', respectively. Moreover, there is no grapheme for the vowel *i*, also known as *Bizroke* "the little furtive", in the Arabic-based script which creates further challenges in the morphological analysis of the language (Ahmadi, 2019).

In this module, we focus on transliterating Arabic-based and Latin-based scripts of Kurdish using WERGOR transliterator[13] (Ahmadi, 2019). This tool uses a rule-based approach based on the phonological and syllabic characteristics of Kurdish for distinguishing double-usage characters, i.e. و and ی, and predicting the placement of *i*. Although the algorithm efficiently transliterates double-usage characters, it has been evaluated to detect *i* with a low accuracy of 39%.

4.3 Stem

Although the task of stemming has been previously addressed in the literature, no open-source viable solution was available for Kurdish. Therefore, we developed morphological rules containing combinations of Kurdish morphemes in Sorani and Kurmanji, and also an annotated lexicon containing lemmas with specific flags such as part-of-speech tags and stems. The morphological rules and the lexicons are then used to develop a morphological analyzer and spell-checker in HUNSPELL (Ooms, 2017) for Kurdish, where they are respectively known as affixes (`.aff`) and dictionary (`.dic`). Thanks to the wide usage of HUNSPELL in open-source text editors such as Apache OpenOffice, our development will be also beneficial for general purposes such as spell-checking in text editors. More importantly, we integrate HUNSPELL in KLPT for this module using a wrapper program[14].

The Stem module comes with two classes: `Stem` and `Spellcheck`. Although these two classes focus on two different tasks, they are provided in the same module as they are both based on the same implementation in Hunspell. Given a word, the `Stem` class provides four main functions, namely `stem()` for retrieving word-form stem, e.g. *kirdin/kirin* (do.INF) → *kir*, `lemmatize()` for lemmatization, e.g. *kirdbûm* (do.1SG.PST.PFV) → *kirdin*, `analyze()` for morphological analysis which returns a dictionary containing the flags according to HUNSPELL such as part-of-speech, terminal suffixes and inflectional suffixes and finally, `suffix_suggest()` which returns all the possible suffixes that can appear with a given lexeme. In addition to these, `generate()` will also be added to the module which generates a word-form given morphemes.

On the other hand, the `Spellcheck` class provides `check_spelling()` and `correct_spelling()` which are respectively used for spell checking (Boolean output) and spell correction. For instance, given خواردووماته (*xwardûmate*), `check_spelling()` detects that it is incorrectly written and a few suggestions are provided by `correct_spelling()`, among which خواردوومانه (*xwardûmane*) "(we) have eaten". The performance of the tool is further described in (Ahmadi, 2020d,a).

---

[13]`https://github.com/sinaahmadi/wergor`

[14]`https://github.com/MSeal/cython_hunspell`

4.4 Tokenize

Although both Arabic-based and Latin-based alphabets use spaces to delimit word boundaries, not all words correspond to a token in Kurdish. This is particularly due to the complex morphology, e.g. article marking suffixes, and the writing traditions. In the Arabic-based alphabet, there is a tendency to concatenate clitics, affixes and words together which results many tokens being written as one single word-form without any space as in هیواشیانه (*hîwaşyane*) "(it) is also their hope" which is composed of four tokens, noun *hîwa*, endoclitic =ş, pronominal enclitic -*yan* and present copula *e*. The Latin-based script, particularly when used for writing Kurmanji, respects word boundaries in a better way. For instance, the same phrase is written as "*hêvîya wan jî ew e*".

In this module, we use the tokenization approach proposed by (Ahmadi, 2020b). This approach uses an annotated lexicon with a morphological analyzer to tokenize words in Sorani and Kurmanji. Given the wide usage of compound forms in word formation in Kurdish, a lexicon is also provided for multi-word expressions (MWEs) and their possible forms, with and without space. That way, the inconsistencies in writing compound words is tackled efficiently. In addition to `mwe_tokenize()` and `word_tokenize()` which are respectively provided for the tokenization of words and MWEs, `sent_tokenize()` is a third function which tokenizes a given text into sentences based on punctuation marks. It is worth mentioning that words and MWEs are respectively separated by __ and _____ by default which can be customized by the user.

4.5 Configuration

Given the combination of scripts and dialects of the input data, verification of the several configurations of each class can be complex. Therefore, we provide the `configuration` module which is used internally within the modules when an object of a class is initialized. This way, the class constructors validate the arguments by evoking this module and the error-handling is carried out only in the `Configuration` class.

For further clarification on the interaction of the individual modules within the KLPT package, Figure A.5 shows its package and class diagrams in the Unified Modeling Language (UML).

5 Usages

In this section, we provide basic usages of the application programming interface (API) of the KLPT package. The package is available on the Python Package Index (PyPI)[15] in Python 3.5 and later and, can be installed as follows:

```
pip install klpt
```

The installation of the package comes with the data files, i.e. `data` folder, and requirements which are also installed. Once the package installed, each module can be imported and used as described above. Figure 4 provides an example on how to work with various modules of the package.

```
>>> from klpt.preprocess import Preprocess
>>> from klpt.transliterator import Transliterate
>>> from klpt.tokenize import Tokenize
>>> from klpt.stem import Stem

# Preprocess module
>>> preprocessor = Preprocess("Sorani", "Arabic",
numeral="Latin")
>>> preprocessor.normalize("له ســــاڵەکانی ١٩٥٠دا")
له ساڵەکانی 1950دا
>>> preprocessor.standardize("راسۆه له و ووڵاتەدا")
راسۆه له و وڵاتەدا

# Transliterate module
>>> transliterator = Transliterate("Kurmanji", "Latin",
target_script="Arabic")
>>> transliterator.transliterate("rojhilata navîn")
'رۆژهلاتا ناڤین'

# Stem module
>>> stemmer = Stem("Sorani", "Arabic")
>>> stemmer.check_spelling("سووناندبووت")
False
>>> stemmer.correct_spelling("سووناندبووت")
('سووناندبووت', 'سووناندت', 'سوواندن', 'سووانداد')
>>> stemmer.stem("سووناندبووت")
('سووت',)
>>> stemmer.analyze("دەینبامن")
{'pos': 'verb', 'is': 'past_intransitive', 'stem':
'دی', 'verb_stem': 'دین', 'terminal_suffix': 'بامن'}

# Tokenize module
>>> tokenizer = Tokenize("Kurmanji", "Latin")
>>> tokenizer.word_tokenize("endamên encûmena wezîrên")
['_endam_ên', '_encûmen_a', '_wezîr_ên']
```

Figure 4: Basic usage of the KLPT package for the Sorani and Kurmanji dialects

6 Conclusion and Future Work

In this paper, we present KLPT, an open-source toolkit developed in Python and composed of core modules, namely `Preprocess`, `Stem`,

---

[15] https://pypi.org

`Tokenize` and `Transliterate` for processing the Sorani and Kurmanji dialects of Kurdish. In addition to the provided modules, the toolkit enables future researchers to contribute their work by extending the modules for more advanced tasks and other dialects. We believe that recognizing every single contribution to the toolkit is encouraging for researchers and also, beneficial to help Kurdish to pass over its less-resourced status.

As a future work, we would like to extend the current version to include syntactic and semantic parsing for Sorani and Kurmanji. Given the scarcity of resources regarding computational linguistics and natural language processing, we believe that the KLPT package will create a new field of interest for Kurdish linguists as well. Therefore, we are aiming at creating educational content to introduce the field to non-expert public too.

Acknowledgments

The author would like to thank his two colleagues, Dr. Kyumars Sheykh Esmaili and Dr. Hossein Hassani who respectively initiated the Kurdish Language Processing Project and Kurdish-BLARK. Despite the lack of financial support of Kurdish-related projects, these initiatives have made huge contributions thanks to volunteer researchers. Similarly, the constructive comments of the three anonymous reviewers were very useful and are much appreciated.

References

Roshna Abdulrahman, Hossein Hassani, and Sina Ahmadi. 2019. Developing a Fine-grained Corpus for a Less-resourced Language: the case of Kurdish. In *Proceedings of the 2019 Workshop on Widening NLP*, pages 106–109.

Roshna Omer Abdulrahman and Hossein Hassani. 2020. Using Punkt for Sentence Segmentation in non-Latin Scripts: Experiments on Kurdish (Sorani) Texts. *arXiv preprint arXiv:2004.14134*.

Sina Ahmadi. 2019. A Rule-based Kurdish Text Transliteration System. *Asian and Low-Resource Language Information Processing (TALLIP)*, 18(2):18:1–18:8.

Sina Ahmadi. 2020a. A Lemmatization System for Sorani Kurdish. under review.

Sina Ahmadi. 2020b. A Tokenization System for the Kurdish Language. In *the Proceedings of the Seventh Workshop on NLP for Similar Languages, Varieties and Dialects (VarDial 2020)*.

Sina Ahmadi. 2020c. Building a Corpus for the Zaza–Gorani Language Family. In *the Proceedings of the Seventh Workshop on NLP for Similar Languages, Varieties and Dialects (VarDial 2020)*.

Sina Ahmadi. 2020d. Hunspell for Sorani Kurdish Spell-checking and Morphological Analysis. under review.

Sina Ahmadi and Hossein Hassani. 2020a. Towards Finite-State Morphology of Kurdish. *arXiv preprint arXiv:2005.10652*.

Sina Ahmadi and Hossein Hassani. 2020b. Towards Finite-State Morphology of Kurdish. *(under review) ACM Transactions on Asian and Low-Resource Language Information Processing (TALLIP)*.

Sina Ahmadi, Hossein Hassani, and Kamaladdin Abedi. 2020. A corpus of the Sorani Kurdish folkloric lyrics. In *Proceedings of the 1st Joint Spoken Language Technologies for Under-resourced languages (SLTU) and Collaboration and Computing for Under-Resourced Languages (CCURL) Workshop at the 12th International Conference on Language Resources and Evaluation (LREC)*.

Sina Ahmadi, Hossein Hassani, and John P McCrae. 2019. Towards electronic lexicography for the Kurdish language. In *Proceedings of the sixth biennial conference on electronic lexicography (eLex)*. eLex 2019.

Abdulbasit Al-Talabani, Zrar Abdul, and Azad Ameen. 2017. Kurdish dialects and neighbor languages automatic recognition. *ARO-The Scientific Journal of Koya University*, 5(1):20–23.

Purya Aliabadi. 2014. Semi-automatic development of KurdNet, the Kurdish Wordnet. In *Proceedings of the ACL 2014 Student Research Workshop*, pages 94–99.

Purya Aliabadi, Mohammad Sina Ahmadi, Shahin Salavati, and Kyumars Sheykh Esmaili. 2014. Towards building kurdnet, the Kurdish Wordnet. In *Proceedings of the Seventh Global Wordnet Conference*, pages 1–6.

Christine Årdal, Annette Alstadsæter, and John-Arne Røttingen. 2011. Common characteristics of open source software development and applicability for drug discovery: a systematic review. *Health Research Policy and Systems*, 9(1):36.

Duygu Ataman. 2018. Bianet: A parallel news corpus in turkish, kurdish and english. *arXiv preprint arXiv:1805.05095*.

Mustafa Aydoğan. 2012. *Rêbera rastnivîsînê*. Weşanxaneya Rûpelê. Ziman. Rûpel.

Anvar Bahrampour, Wafa Barkhoda, and Bahram Zahir Azami. 2009. Implementation of three text to speech systems for Kurdish language. In *Iberoamerican Congress on Pattern Recognition*, pages 321–328. Springer.

Wafa Barkhoda, Bahram ZahirAzami, Anvar Bahrampour, and Om-Kolsoom Shahryari. 2009. A comparison between allophone, syllable, and diphone based TTS systems for Kurdish language. In *Signal Processing and Information Technology (ISSPIT), 2009 IEEE International Symposium on*, pages 557–562. IEEE.

Ryan Cotterell, Christo Kirov, John Sylak-Glassman, Géraldine Walther, Ekaterina Vylomova, Patrick Xia, Manaal Faruqui, Sandra Kübler, David Yarowsky, Jason Eisner, et al. 2017. CoNLL-SIGMORPHON 2017 Shared Task: Universal Morphological Reinflection in 52 Languages. In *Proceedings of the CoNLL SIGMORPHON 2017 Shared Task: Universal Morphological Reinflection*, pages 1–30.

Fatemeh Daneshfar, Wafa Barkhoda, and Bahram Zahir Azami. 2009. Implementation of a Text-to-Speech System for Kurdish Language. In *Digital Telecommunications, 2009. ICDT'09. Fourth International Conference on*, pages 117–120. IEEE.

Özlem Batur Dinler and Nizamettin Aydin. 2018a. Extraction of the acoustic features of semi-vowels in the Kurdish language. *The Online Journal of Science and Technology-April*, 8(2).

Özlem Batur Dinler and Nizamettin Aydin. 2018b. Kurdish recognition system digit. *The Online Journal of Science and Technology*, 8(1):101.

Özlem Batur Dinler and Fatih Karabıber. 2017. Formant analysis of vowels in Kurdish language. In *Signal Processing and Communications Applications Conference (SIU), 2017 25th*, pages 1–4. IEEE.

Alexander Johannes Edmonds. 2013. The Dialects of Kurdish. *Ruprecht-Karls-Universität Heidelberg*.

Kyumars Sheykh Esmaili. 2012. Challenges in Kurdish text processing. *arXiv preprint arXiv:1212.0074*.

Kyumars Sheykh Esmaili, Donya Eliassi, Shahin Salavati, Purya Aliabadi, Asrin Mohammadi, Somayeh Yosefi, and Shownem Hakimi. 2013. Building a test collection for Sorani Kurdish. In *Computer Systems and Applications (AICCSA), 2013 ACS International Conference on*, pages 1–7. IEEE.

Kyumars Sheykh Esmaili and Shahin Salavati. 2013. Sorani kurdish versus kurmanji kurdish: An empirical comparison. In *Proceedings of the 51st Annual Meeting of the Association for Computational Linguistics (Volume 2: Short Papers)*, volume 2, pages 300–305.

Kyumars Sheykh Esmaili, Shahin Salavati, and Anwitaman Datta. 2014. Towards Kurdish information retrieval. *ACM Transactions on Asian Language Information Processing (TALIP)*, 13(2):7.

Ismaïl Kamandâr Fattah. 2000. *Les dialectes kurdes méridionaux: étude linguistique et dialectologique*. Acta Iranica : Encyclopédie permanente des études iraniennes. Peeters.

Memduh Gökırmak and Francis M Tyers. 2017. A dependency treebank for Kurmanji Kurdish. In *Proceedings of the Fourth International Conference on Dependency Linguistics (Depling 2017)*, pages 64–72.

Filip Graliński, Krzysztof Jassem, and Marcin Junczys-Dowmunt. 2013. PSI-toolkit: A natural language processing pipeline. In *Computational Linguistics*, pages 27–39. Springer.

Geoffrey Haig. 1998. On the interaction of morphological and syntactic ergativity: Lessons from Kurdish. *Lingua*, 105(3-4):149–173.

Geoffrey Haig and Yaron Matras. 2002. Kurdish linguistics: a brief overview. *STUF-Language Typology and Universals*, 55(1):3–14.

Dyako Hashemi. 2016. Kurdish orthography [In Kurdish]. `http://yageyziman.com/Renusi_Kurdi.htm`. Accessed: 2020-07-25.

Abdulla D Hashim and Fattah Alizadeh. 2018. Kurdish sign language recognition system. *UKH Journal of Science and Engineering*, 2(1):1–6.

Hossein Hassani. 2017a. Kurdish interdialect machine translation. In *Proceedings of the fourth workshop on NLP for similar languages, varieties and dialects (VarDial)*, pages 63–72.

Hossein Hassani. 2017b. A method for proper noun extraction in Kurdish. In *OASIcs-OpenAccess Series in Informatics*, volume 56. Schloss Dagstuhl-Leibniz-Zentrum fuer Informatik.

Hossein Hassani. 2018. BLARK for multi-dialect languages: towards the Kurdish BLARK. *Language Resources and Evaluation*, 52(2):625–644.

Hossein Hassani and Rahel Kareem. 2011. Kurdish text to speech (ktts). *Designing for Global Markets*, 10:79–89.

Hossein Hassani and Dzejla Medjedovic. 2016. Automatic Kurdish dialects identification. *Computer Science & Information Technology*, 6(2):61–78.

Roojwan Sc Hawezi, Muhammed Y Azeez, and Ahmed A Qadir. 2019. Spell checking algorithm for agglutinative languages "Central Kurdish as an example". In *2019 International Engineering Conference (IEC)*, pages 142–146. IEEE.

Sardar Jaf. 2016. A simple approach to unify ambiguously encoded Kurdish characters. In *Proceedings of the International Conference Computational Linguistics in Bulgaria (CLIB 2016).*, pages 86–94. Institute for Bulgarian Language, Bulgarian Academy of Sciences.

Sardar Jaf and Allan Ramsay. 2014. A Stemmer and a POS tagger for Sorani Kurdish. In *6th International Conference on Corpus Linguistics (CILC-14)*. Gran Canaria, Spain, Cambridge Scholars.

Sardar Jaf and Allan Ramsay. 2016. A Rule-based Part-of-speech Tagger For Sorani Kurdish. *Input a Word, Analyze the World: Selected Approaches to Corpus Linguistics*, page 39.

Thomas Jugel. 2014. On the linguistic history of Kurdish. *Kurdish Studies*, 2(2):123–142.

Kanaan M Kaka-Khan. 2017. Building Kurdish chatbot using free open source platforms. *UHD Journal of Science and Technology*, 1(2):46–50.

Kanaan M Kaka-Khan. 2018. English to Kurdish Rulebased Machine Translation System. *UHD Journal of Science and Technology*.

Zina Kamal and Hossein Hassani. 2020. Towards Kurdish text to sign translation. In *Proceedings of the LREC2020 9th Workshop on the Representation and Processing of Sign Languages: Sign Language Resources in the Service of the Language Community, Technological Challenges and Application Perspectives*, pages 117–122, Marseille, France. European Language Resources Association (ELRA).

Yadgar Karimi. 2014. On the syntax of ergativity in Kurdish. *Poznan Studies in Contemporary Linguistics*, 50(3):231–271.

Philip G Kreyenbroek. 2005. On the Kurdish language. In *The Kurds*, pages 62–73. Routledge.

Patrick Littell, Kartik Goyal, David R Mortensen, Alexa Little, Chris Dyer, and Lori Levin. 2016. Named entity recognition for linguistic rapid response in low-resource languages: Sorani Kurdish and Tajik. In *Proceedings of COLING 2016, the 26th International Conference on Computational Linguistics: Technical Papers*, pages 998–1006.

Jan Ljungberg. 2000. Open source movements as a model for organising. *European Journal of Information Systems*, 9(4):208–216.

Hrafn Loftsson and Eiríkur Rögnvaldsson. 2007. IceNLP: A natural language processing toolkit for Icelandic. In *Eighth Annual Conference of the International Speech Communication Association*.

Edward Loper and Steven Bird. 2002. NLTK: The Natural Language Toolkit. In *Proceedings of the ACL-02 Workshop on Effective Tools and Methodologies for Teaching Natural Language Processing and Computational Linguistics*, pages 63–70.

Shervin Malmasi. 2016. Subdialectal differences in Sorani Kurdish. In *Proceedings of the third workshop on nlp for similar languages, varieties and dialects (vardial3)*, pages 89–96.

Christopher D Manning, Mihai Surdeanu, John Bauer, Jenny Rose Finkel, Steven Bethard, and David McClosky. 2014. The Stanford CoreNLP natural language processing toolkit. In *Proceedings of 52nd annual meeting of the association for computational linguistics: system demonstrations*, pages 55–60.

Yaron Matras. 2017. Revisiting Kurdish dialect geography: Preliminary findings from the Manchester Database. `http://kurdish.humanities.manchester.ac.uk/wp-content/uploads/2017/07/PDF-Revisiting-Kurdish-dialect-geography.pdf`. [Online; accessed 04-Mar-2019].

Bayan Omar Mohammed. 2012. Uniqueness in Kurdish handwriting. *International Journal of Engineering & Computer Science IJECS-IJENS*, 12(06):42–50.

Bayan Omar Mohammed. 2013. Handwritten Kurdish character recognition using geometric discertization feature. *Volume*, 4:51–55.

FS Mohammed, L Zakaria, Nazlia Omar, and MY Albared. 2012. Automatic Kurdish Sorani text categorization using n-gram based model. In *Computer & Information Science (ICCIS), 2012 International Conference on*, volume 1, pages 392–395. IEEE.

Arazo M Mustafa and Tarik A Rashid. 2018. Kurdish stemmer pre-processing steps for improving information retrieval. *Journal of Information Science*, 44(1):15–27.

Jeroen Ooms. 2017. hunspell: High-Performance Stemmer, Tokenizer, and Spell Checker. *https://hunspell.github.io/*.

Ludwig Paul. 1998. The position of Zazaki among West Iranian languages. *Old and Middle Iranian Studies*, pages 163–176.

Andreas Prlić and James B Procter. 2012. Ten simple rules for the open development of scientific software. *PLoS Comput Biol*, 8(12):e1002802.

Akam Qader and Hossein Hassani. 2019. Kurdish (sorani) speech to text: Presenting an experimental dataset. *arXiv preprint arXiv:1911.13087*.

Peng Qi, Yuhao Zhang, Yuhui Zhang, Jason Bolton, and Christopher D Manning. 2020. Stanza: A python natural language processing toolkit for many human languages. *arXiv preprint arXiv:2003.07082*.

Xipeng Qiu, Qi Zhang, and Xuan-Jing Huang. 2013. Fudannlp: A toolkit for chinese natural language processing. In *Proceedings of the 51st Annual Meeting of the Association for Computational Linguistics: System Demonstrations*, pages 49–54.

Tarik A Rashid, Arazo M Mustafa, and A Saeed. 2017a. A robust categorization system for Kurdish Sorani text documents. *Inf. Technol. J*, 16(1):27–34.

Tarik A Rashid, Arazo M Mustafa, and Ari M Saeed. 2017b. Automatic Kurdish text classification using kdc 4007 dataset. In *International Conference on Emerging Internetworking, Data & Web Technologies*, pages 187–198. Springer.

Ari M Saeed, Tarik A Rashid, Arazo M Mustafa, Rawan A Al-Rashid Agha, Ahmed S Shamsaldin, and Nawzad K Al-Salihi. 2018a. An evaluation of Reber stemmer with longest match stemmer technique in Kurdish Sorani text classification. *Iran Journal of Computer Science*, 1(2):99–107.

Ari M Saeed, Tarik A Rashid, Arazo M Mustafa, Polla Fattah, and Birzo Ismael. 2018b. Improving Kurdish Web Mining through Tree Data Structure and Porter's Stemmer Algorithms. *UKH Journal of Science and Engineering*, 2(1):48–54.

Shahin Salavati and Sina Ahmadi. 2018. Building a Lemmatizer and a Spell-checker for Sorani Kurdish. In *Proceedings of the 8th Language & Technology Conference: Human Language Technologies as a Challenge for Computer Science and Linguistics*, Poznan, Poland.

Shahin Salavati, Kyumars Sheykh Esmaili, and Fardin Akhlaghian. 2013. Stemming for Kurdish information retrieval. In *Asia Information Retrieval Symposium*, pages 272–283. Springer.

Zahra Sarabi, Hooman Mahyar, and Mojgan Farhoodi. 2013. ParsiPardaz: Persian language processing toolkit. In *ICCKE 2013*, pages 73–79. IEEE.

Abdusalam Abdulla Shaltooki and Mzhda Hiwa Hama. 2016. Sentiment analyses for Kurdish social network texts using Naive Bayes classifier. *Journal of Human Development*, 1(4):393–397.

Givi Tavadze. 2019. Spreading of the Kurdish Language Dialects and Writing Systems Used in the Middle East. *Bull. Georg. Natl. Acad. Sci*, 13(1).

Wheeler M Thackston. 2006. *Kurmanji Kurdish:A Reference Grammar with Selected Readings*. Harvard University.

Sandrine Traida. 2007. *Morphosyntactic Study of the compound verbs in Sorani Kurdish Étude morphosyntaxique des verbes composés (nom-verbe) en kurde (dialecte sorani) [in French]*. PhD thesis at the Université Paris 3 - Sorbonne Nouvelle.

Hadi Veisi, Mohammad MohammadAmini, and Hawre Hosseini. 2020. Toward kurdish language processing: Experiments in collecting and processing the asosoft text corpus. *Digital Scholarship in the Humanities*, 35(1):176–193.

Thanh Vu, Dat Quoc Nguyen, Mark Dras, Mark Johnson, et al. 2018. VnCoreNLP: A Vietnamese Natural Language Processing Toolkit. In *Proceedings of the 2018 Conference of the North American Chapter of the Association for Computational Linguistics: Demonstrations*, pages 56–60.

Géraldine Walther and Benoît Sagot. 2010. Developing a large-scale lexicon for a less-resourced language: General methodology and preliminary experiments on Sorani Kurdish. In *Proceedings of the 7th SaLTMiL Workshop on Creation and use of basic lexical resources for less-resourced languages (LREC 2010 Workshop)*.

Géraldine Walther, Benoît Sagot, and Karën Fort. 2010. Fast development of basic nlp tools: Towards a lexicon and a pos tagger for Kurmanji Kurdish. In *International conference on lexis and grammar*, page 0.

Rasty Yaseen and Hossein Hassani. 2018. Kurdish optical character recognition. *UKH Journal of Science and Engineering*, 2(1):18–27.

Rina D Zarro and Mardin A Anwer. 2017. Recognition-based online Kurdish character recognition using hidden Markov model and harmony search. *Engineering Science and Technology, an International Journal*, 20(2):783–794.

Housam Ziad, John Philip McCrae, and Paul Buitelaar. 2018. Teanga: a linked data based platform for natural language processing. In *Proceedings of the Eleventh International Conference on Language Resources and Evaluation (LREC 2018)*.

A   Appendix

Reference	Year	Field	open-source	applicable	dialects
(Mohammed et al., 2012)	2012	Dialectology	no	no	Sorani
(Esmaili and Salavati, 2013)	2013	Dialectology	no	yes	Sorani, Kurmanji
(Hassani and Medjedovic, 2016)	2016	Dialectology	no	yes	Sorani, Kurmanji
(Malmasi, 2016)	2016	Dialectology	yes	yes	Sorani
(Al-Talabani et al., 2017)	2017	Dialectology	no	yes	Sorani, Kurmanji, Gorani
(Littell et al., 2016)	2016	Information retrieval and Text mining	no	yes	Sorani
(Hassani, 2017b)	2017	Information retrieval and Text mining	yes	yes	Sorani, Kurmanji
(Esmaili, 2012)	2012	Information retrieval and Text mining	no	no	Sorani
(Esmaili et al., 2014)	2014	Information retrieval and Text mining	yes	yes	Sorani, Kurmanji
(Jaf, 2016)	2016	Information retrieval and Text mining	no	yes	Sorani
(Rashid et al., 2017a)	2017	Information retrieval and Text mining	no	yes	Sorani
(Rashid et al., 2017b)	2017	Information retrieval and Text mining	no	yes	Sorani
(Ahmadi, 2019)	2019	Information retrieval and Text mining	yes	no	Sorani
(Saeed et al., 2018b)	2018	Information retrieval and Text mining	no	yes	Sorani
(Saeed et al., 2018b)	2018	Information retrieval and Text mining	no	yes	Sorani
(Mustafa and Rashid, 2018)	2018	Information retrieval and Text mining	no	yes	Sorani
(Saeed et al., 2018a)	2018	Information retrieval and Text mining	no	no	Sorani
(Ahmadi et al., 2020)	2020	Lexical resources	yes	yes	Sorani
(Esmaili et al., 2013)	2013	Lexical resources	yes	yes	Sorani
(Aliabadi et al., 2014)	2014	Lexical resources	yes	yes	Sorani
(Aliabadi, 2014)	2014	Lexical resources	no	yes	Sorani
(Veisi et al., 2020)	2020	Lexical resources	yes	yes	Sorani
(Ahmadi et al., 2019)	2019	Lexical resources	yes	yes	Sorani, Kurmanji, Gorani
(Abdulrahman et al., 2019)	2019	Lexical resources	yes	yes	Sorani
(Abdulrahman and Hassani, 2020)	2020	Lexical resources	yes	yes	Sorani
(Ataman, 2018)	2018	Lexical resources	yes	yes	Kurmanji
(Hassani, 2017a)	2017	Machine Translation	no	yes	Sorani, Kurmanji
(Kaka-Khan, 2018)	2018	Machine Translation	no	yes	Sorani
(Walther and Sagot, 2010)	2010	Morphological and syntactic analysis	yes	yes	Sorani
(Walther et al., 2010)	2010	Morphological and syntactic analysis	yes	yes	Kurmanji
(Salavati et al., 2013)	2013	Morphological and syntactic analysis	yes	yes	Sorani
(Jaf and Ramsay, 2014)	2014	Morphological and syntactic analysis	no	yes	Sorani
(Jaf and Ramsay, 2016)	2016	Morphological and syntactic analysis	no	yes	Sorani
(Gökırmak and Tyers, 2017)	2017	Morphological and syntactic analysis	yes	yes	Kurmanji
(Salavati and Ahmadi, 2018)	2018	Morphological and syntactic analysis	no	yes	Sorani
(Mustafa and Rashid, 2018)	2018	Morphological and syntactic analysis	no	yes	Sorani
(Ahmadi and Hassani, 2020a)	2020	Morphological and syntactic analysis	no	yes	Sorani
(Mohammed, 2012)	2012	Optical character recognition	no	no	Sorani
(Mohammed, 2013)	2013	Optical character recognition	no	yes	Sorani
(Shaltooki and Hama, 2016)	2016	Optical character recognition	no	yes	Sorani
(Zarro and Anwer, 2017)	2017	Optical character recognition	no	yes	Sorani
(Yaseen and Hassani, 2018)	2018	Optical character recognition	no	yes	Sorani
(Dinler and Aydin, 2018b)	2018	Optical character recognition	no	yes	Sorani
(Kaka-Khan, 2017)	2017	Other	no	yes	Sorani
(Hashim and Alizadeh, 2018)	2018	Sign language recognition	no	yes	Sorani
(Kamal and Hassani, 2020)	2020	Sign language recognition	yes	yes	Sorani
(Daneshfar et al., 2009)	2009	Speech recognition	no	yes	Sorani
(Barkhoda et al., 2009)	2009	Speech recognition	no	no	Sorani
(Bahrampour et al., 2009)	2009	Speech recognition	no	yes	Sorani
(Hassani and Kareem, 2011)	2011	Speech recognition	no	yes	Sorani
(Dinler and Karabıber, 2017)	2017	Speech recognition	no	no	Kurmanji
(Dinler and Aydin, 2018a)	2018	Speech recognition	no	yes	Sorani, Kurmanji
(Qader and Hassani, 2019)	2019	Speech recognition	yes	yes	Sorani

Table A.2: Classification of the publications in the field of Kurdish language processing

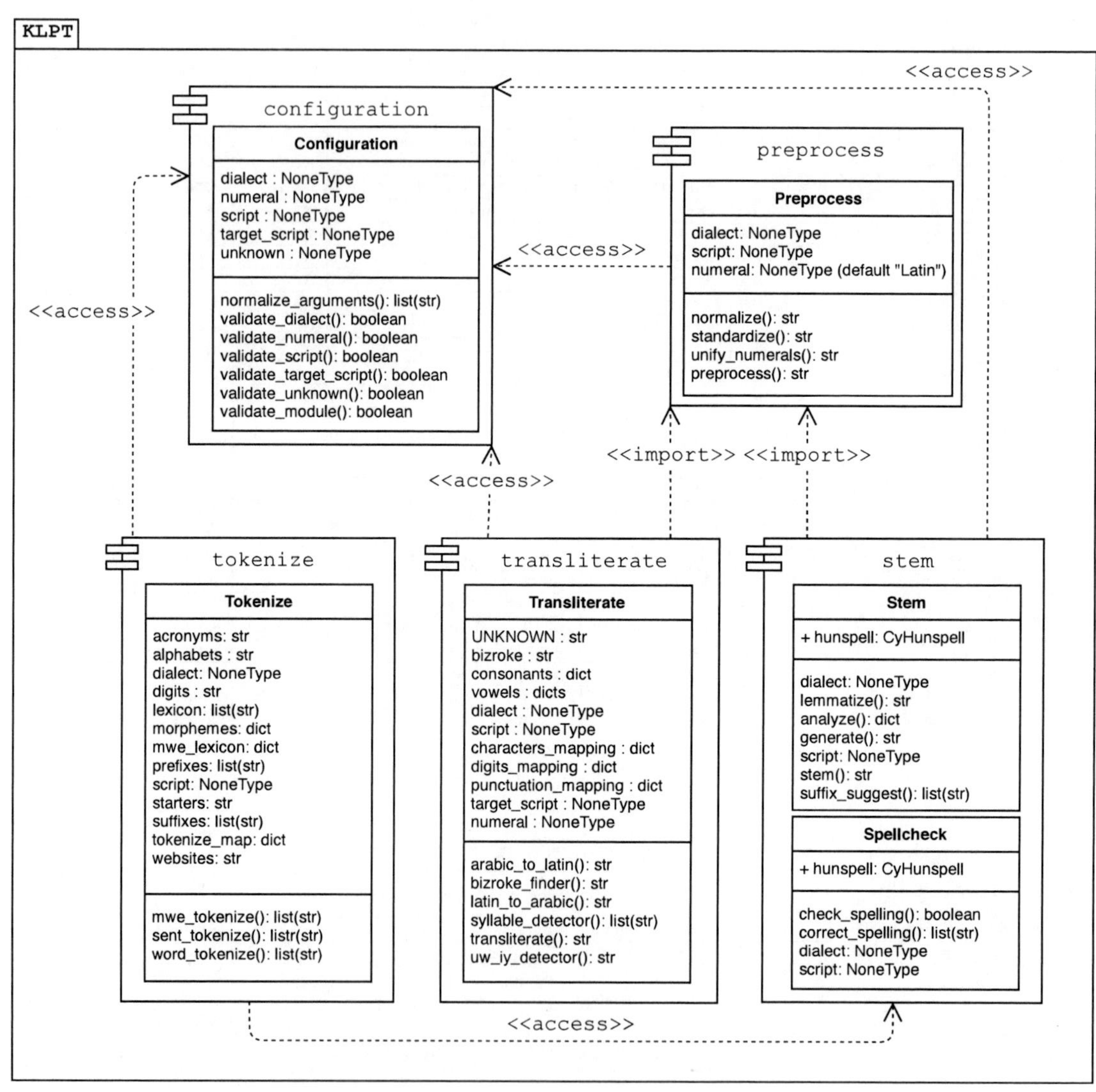

Figure A.5: The Package and class models of KLPT in the Unified Modeling Language (UML)

Open Korean Corpora: A Practical Report

Won Ik Cho
Seoul National University
Seoul, Korea

wicho@hi.snu.ac.kr

Sangwhan Moon
Tokyo Institute of Technology
Odd Concepts Inc.
Tokyo, Japan

sangwhan@iki.fi

Youngsook Song
Kyung Hee University
Seoul, Korea

youngsoksong@khu.ac.kr

Abstract

Korean is often referred to as a low-resource language in the research community. While this claim is partially true, it is also because the availability of resources is inadequately advertised and curated. This work curates and reviews a list of Korean corpora, first describing institution-level resource development, then further iterate through a list of current open datasets for different types of tasks. We then propose a direction on how open-source dataset construction and releases should be done for less-resourced languages to promote research.

1 Introduction

The Korean language is less explored in terms of corpus and computational linguistics, but its prevalence is often underrated. It regards about 80 million language users and is recently adopted in multilingual research as it is bound to CJK (Chinese, Japanese, and Korean), also handling a distinguished writing system.

However, compared to the industrial need, the interest in Korean natural language processing (NLP) has not been developed much in international viewpoints, which recurrently hinders the related publication and further academic extension. Besides, in the recent NLP, where the benchmark practice is a trend, such systems lack at this point, deterring abroad and even native researchers who start Korean NLP from finding directions. Park et al. (2016) has shown a decent survey, but it seems that the techniques are mainly on the NLP pipeline. Also, albeit some curations on Korean NLP[1] and datasets[2], we considered that little more organization is required, and better if internationally available. Our attempts are expected to mitigate the challenges that the researchers who handle Korean from a multi- or cross-lingual viewpoint may face.

In this paper, we scrutinize the struggles of government, institutes, industry, and individuals to construct public Korean NLP resources. First, we state how the institutional organizations have tackled the issue by making up the accessible resources, and point out the limitation thereof regarding international availability and license, to finally introduce and curate the fully public datasets along with the proposed criteria. Through this, we want to find out the current state of Korean corpora across the NLP tasks and whether they are freely or conditionally available. Our survey is to be curated and updated in the public repository[3].

2 Accessible Resources

With the increase in popularity of machine learning-driven methods in NLP, constructing a novel dataset and releasing it to the public can be considered the cornerstone of advancing research of a given language. While we believe many useful datasets exist behind industry walls, this is not particularly useful for advancing open research. Fortunately, there are organizations that construct and distribute cleaned, pre-processed datasets which are occasionally accompanied by a task and the annotation. In the context of Korean, there are numerous efforts in this field driven by government-affiliated organizations.

2.1 Datasets from public institutions

National Institute of Korean Language (NIKL) is an institution that establishes the norm for Korean linguistics[4]. However, at the same time, it usually undergoes the massive dataset construction from the view of computational

---

[1] https://github.com/datanada/
Awesome-Korean-NLP
[2] https://littlefoxdiary.tistory.com/42

[3] https://github.com/ko-nlp/
Open-korean-corpora
[4] https://www.korean.go.kr/

Proceedings of Second Workshop for NLP Open Source Software (NLP-OSS), pages 85–93
Virtual Conference, November 19, 2020. ©2020 Association for Computational Linguistics

linguistics, to apt to the new wave of language artificial intelligence (AI). Widely known ones include Korean word dictionaries[5] and Sejong Corpus (Kim, 2006). The dictionary contains fundamental and new lexicons that make up Korean (along with the content), and the Sejong Corpus is a large-scale labeled NLP pipeline corpus for the tasks such as constituency and dependency parsing, mainly provided in *.json* format. Besides, recently, labeled corpora of about 300 million word size is released[6], covering inter-sentence tasks such as similarity and entailment.

Electronics and Telecommunications Research Institute (ETRI) has been collecting, refining, and tagging language processing and speech learning data over a long period of time[7]. Aside from NIKL, which mainly focuses on classical NLP pipelines, ETRI has also built a database for semantic analysis and question answering (QA), which are the outcome of a project Exo-brain[8]. The project includes syntax-semantic ones such as part of speech (POS) tagging and semantic role labeling (SRL), simultaneously providing construction guidelines for the corpora.

AI HUB is a platform organized by National Information Society Agency (NIA) in which a large-scale dataset are integrated[9]. The datasets are built for various tasks at the government level, to promote the development of the AI industry. Provided resources are labeled or parallel corpora in real-life domains. Here, the domains are law, patent, common sense, open dialog, machine reading comprehension, and machine translation. Also, about 1,200 hours of speech corpus is provided to be used in spoken language modeling[10]. Recently, some new datasets have been distributed on wellness and emotional dialog, so that many people can have trials for social good and public AI. Also, open dictionary NIAdic[11] is freely available, provided by K-ICT Big Data Center.

2.2 Accessibility

The above datasets guarantee high quality, along with well-defined guidelines and the well-educated workers. However, their usage is often unfortunately confined to domestic researchers for procedural issues. Researchers abroad can indeed access the data, but they may face difficulty filling out and submitting the particular application form, instead of the barrier-free downloading system. Also, in most cases, modification and redistribution are restricted, making them uncompetitive in view of quality enhancement (Han et al., 2017).

Here, we want to introduce datasets that can be utilized as an alternative to the limitedly accessible Korean NLP resources. Instead of scrutinizing all available corpora, we are going to curate them under specific criteria.

3 Open Datasets

All the datasets to be introduced from now on are fully open access. This means that the dataset is downloadable with a single click or cloning, or at least one can acquire the dataset with simple signing. We set three checklists for the status of the corpus, namely *documentation*, *usage*, and *redistribution*. The first one is on how fine-grained the corpus description is.

- Does the corpus have any documentation on the usage? (**doc**)
- Does the corpus have a related article?[12] (**art**)
- Does the corpus have a internationally available publication? (**inter**)

Next, we check whether the dataset is commercially available, academic use only, or unknown (**com, acad, unk**). For the last one, We also investigate if redistribution is available with or without modification, if neither, or unknown (**rd, rd/mod-x, no, unk**). These attributes are noted along with each corpus title.

3.1 Parsing and tagging

KAIST Morpho-Syntactically Annotated Corpus [art, acad, no] applies morphological analysis to freely available KAIST raw corpus[13]. The scale is about 70M words and the domain includes novel, non-literature, article, etc.

---

[5]The search portal is provided in `https://stdict.korean.go.kr/main/main.do` while the full word and content list are available at `https://github.com/korean-word-game/db`

[6]`https://corpus.korean.go.kr/`

[7]`https://www.etri.re.kr/intro.html`

[8]`http://exobrain.kr/pages/ko/result/outputs.jsp`

[9]`http://www.aihub.or.kr/`

[10]`https://www.aihub.or.kr/aidata/105`

[11]`https://kbig.kr/portal/kbig/knowledge/files/bigdata_report.page?bltnNo=10000000016451`

[12]Article is here more a complete form of document than *doc* above, and some domestic publications are included here since they are not internationally available.

[13]`http://semanticweb.kaist.ac.kr/home/index.php/KAIST_Corpus`

KAIST Korean Tree-Tagging Corpus [inter, acad, no] Choi et al. (1994)[14] bases on independently collected 30K sentences that are annotated according to the tree tagging scheme for Korean.

UD Korean KAIST [inter, acad, no] Chun et al. (2018)[15] applies universal dependency (UD) parsing (McDonald et al., 2013) to the Korean Tree-Tagging Corpus (Choi et al., 1994).

PKT-UD [inter, acad, no] Chun et al. (2018); Oh et al. (2020)[16] applies UD parsing to the Penn Korean Treebank (Han et al., 2001)[17].

KMOU NER [art, acad, rd] is a named entity recognition (NER) dataset built by Korean Marine and Ocean University[18]. The named entities are tagged for about 24K utterances according to name, time, and number. The data source are Exo-brain (by ETRI) and their own data combined, while the redistribution is available only for the latter.

AIR×NAVER NER/SRL [doc, acad, no] adopted the NER[19] and SRL[20] data constructed by Changwon National University for the purpose of a public competition[21], and is annotated according to CoNLL format (Tjong Kim Sang and De Meulder, 2003). Corpus size is about 90K and 35K each.

3.2 Entailment and sentence similarity

Question Pair [doc, com, rd] consists of about 10,000 open domain sentence pairs[22], with the binary labels that are hand-annotated on whether the sentences are paraphrase or irrelevant.

KorNLI/KorSTS [inter, com, rd] Ham et al. (2020) is a natural language inference (NLI) and sentence textual similarity (STS) dataset for Korean[23]. For KorNLI, the train set was constructed by machine translating SNLI (Bowman et al., 2015) and MNLI (Williams et al., 2018), and the valid

and test set were constructed by human translation of XNLI (Conneau et al., 2018). Just as in the original dataset, the pairs are labelled with entailment, contradiction, or neutral. About 940K examples are provided for training, and 2,490 and 5,010 respectively for dev and test. For KorSTS, the scoring was done from 0 to 5 to elaborate rather than the binary label that determines paraphrase. Following the scheme of NLI, 5,749 training data were machine translated using the STS-B dataset (Cer et al., 2017) as a source, while 1,500 dev set and 1,379 test set pairs are human translated.

ParaKQC [inter, com, rd] Cho et al. (2020)[24] originally consists of 10,000 questions and commands, and each instance is labeled with 4 topics (mail, smart agent, scheduling, and weather) and 4 speech acts (*wh*-question, alternative question, prohibition, and requirement). The sentence set can be extended to about 540K sentence pairs that determine sentence similarity and paraphrase.

3.3 Sentence classification and QA

NSMC [doc, com, rd] is a review sentiment corpus[25] of size 200K, which consists of Naver movie comments automatically labeled according to the methodology of Maas et al. (2011). It adopts pos/neg binary labels, and it has been widely used as a benchmark for pretrained language models.

BEEP! [inter, com, rd] Moon et al. (2020) is a hand-labeled, crowd-sourced dataset of about 9.4K Naver entertainment news comments with hate speech and social bias[26]. Bias and hate attribute consists of 3 labels, namely gender/others/none and hate/offensive/none, respectively.

3i4K [inter, com, rd] Cho et al. (2018) aims an utterance-level speech act classification of the Korean language[27]. The volume reaches 61K, hand-labeled with 7 classes, namely fragment, statement, question, command, rhetorical question/command, and intonation-dependent utterances.

KorQuAD 1.0, 2.0 [inter, com, rd/mod-x] provides human-generated QA corpus and leaderboard for Korean[28]. KorQuAD 1.0 (Lim et al., 2019) benchmarks SQuAD 1.0 (Rajpurkar et al., 2016)

---

[14]http://semanticweb.kaist.ac.kr/home/index.php/Corpus4

[15]https://github.com/emorynlp/ud-korean

[16]Also available at UD-Korean repository, but currently previous version. PKT v2020 data will be uploaded.

[17]https://catalog.ldc.upenn.edu/LDC2006T09 LDC materials are not curated here.

[18]https://github.com/kmounlp/NER

[19]http://air.changwon.ac.kr/?page_id=10

[20]http://air.changwon.ac.kr/?page_id=14

[21]https://github.com/naver/nlp-challenge

[22]https://github.com/songys/Question_pair

[23]https://github.com/kakaobrain/KorNLUDatasets

[24]https://github.com/warnikchow/paraKQC

[25]https://github.com/e9t/nsmc

[26]https://github.com/kocohub/korean-hate-speech

[27]https://github.com/warnikchow/3i4k

[28]https://korquad.github.io/

and consists of total 70K questions. KorQuAD 2.0 of size 100K aims at machine reading comprehension for structured HTML natural questions, which was created referring to the scheme of Google Natural Questions (Kwiatkowski et al., 2019).

3.4 Parallel corpora

Sci-news-sum-kr [doc, acad, rd] contains about 50 Korean news summarizations generated by two Korean natives[29]. Since the size is not large, it is recommended to be used as a dev set.

sae4K [inter, com, rd] Cho et al. (2019b) contains the directive sentence summarization of the sentence level. It includes about 50K pairs of utterance and natural language query pair for questions and commands, where the data is partly based on 3i4K (Cho et al., 2018) and some are human-generate in concurrence with Cho et al. (2020).

Korean Parallel Corpora [inter, acad, rd/mod-x] Park et al. (2016) contains about 100K en-ko sentence pairs for machine translation (MT). The data mainly bases on news articles, and now also provides the data on North Korean[30].

KAIST Translation Evaluation Set [doc, acad, no] is an evaluation set of size about 3,000 for en-ko MT[31], augmented with index, original sentence, translation, related articles, and text source.

KAIST Chinese-Korean Multilingual Corpus [doc, acad, no] contains 60K short sentence pairs for zh-ko MT[32].

Transliteration Dataset [doc, com, rd] is not an official data repository[33], but en-ko transliteration is collected from public dictionaries such as NIKL or Wiktionary[34]. A total of about 35K en (word) - ko (pronunciation) pairs are included.

KAIST Transliteration Evaluation Set [doc, acad, no] is a word-pronunciation pair for phono-

tactics in en-ko[35], and consists of 7,186 words excerpted from the loanword dictionary[36].

3.5 Korean in multilingual corpora

Multilingual G2P Conversion [inter, com, rd] Gorman et al. (2020) is a shared task of SIGMORPHON 2020[37], which aims to transform grapheme sequence into a phoneme sequence. The dataset was created with WikiPron[38] (Lee et al., 2020), and has been built for 10 languages including Korean (3,600 pairs for train, and 450 for dev/test each).

PAWS-X [inter, com, rd] Yang et al. (2019) is a dataset that consists of 23,659 human translated PAWS evaluation pairs (Zhang et al., 2019) and about 300K machine-translated ones, for 6 languages including Korean[39]. Among them, Korean occupies about 5K train pairs, and 1,965 and 1,972 for dev/test each.

TyDi-QA [inter, com, rd] Clark et al. (2020) pursues typological diversity in QA, and provides a total of 200,000 question-answer pairs for 11 linguistically diverse languages, including Korean[40]. Among them, Korean occupies about 11K train pairs, and 1,698/1,722 for dev/test each.

XPersona [inter, com, rd] Lin et al. (2020) is a dataset for evaluating personalized chatbots[41]. It provides the dataset of Zhang et al. (2018) translated to 7 languages, including Korean, where Korean displays 299 dialogues with 4,684 utterances.

3.6 Speech corpora

Speech datasets are usually massive, that a downloading via a single click is not necessarily guaranteed. Thus, we listed some of them as open even if they require some application form.

KSS [doc, acad, rd] Park (2018) is a book corpus read by a female voice actress. 12K speech

---

[29] https://github.com/theeluwin/
sci-news-sum-kr-50

[30] https://github.com/jungyeul/
korean-parallel-corpora

[31] http://semanticweb.kaist.ac.kr/home/
index.php/Evaluateset2

[32] http://semanticweb.kaist.ac.kr/home/
index.php/Corpus9

[33] https://github.com/muik/
transliteration

[34] https://en.wiktionary.org/wiki/
Wiktionary:Main_Page

[35] http://semanticweb.kaist.ac.kr/home/
index.php/Evaluateset3

[36] http://www-lib.tufs.ac.jp/opac/xc/
openurl/search?rft.issn=0000200626

[37] https://sigmorphon.github.io/
sharedtasks/2020/task1/

[38] https://github.com/kylebgorman/
wikipron

[39] https://github.com/
google-research-datasets/paws/tree/
master/pawsx

[40] https://github.com/
google-research-datasets/tydiqa

[41] https://github.com/HLTCHKUST/Xpersona

utterances and transcriptions are provided[42].

Zeroth [doc, com, rd] is an automatic speech recognition (ASR) dataset that contains approximately 50 hours of well-refined training data[43]. The speech corpus is provided free upon request and can be utilized for both research and commercial purposes.

ClovaCall [inter, acad, no] Ha et al. (2020) is an ASR dataset that consists of approximately 80 hours of telephone speech. The corpus is provided upon request, for only research purposes[44].

Pansori-TED×KR [inter, acad, rd/mod-x] Choi and Lee (2018) is an ASR dataset obtained by extracting the voices of Korean speakers from Pansori (Korean traditional song in colloquial style) and TED videos, with the transcription augmented[45]. The total reaches 3 hours, but it incorporates unique phonations that are not viable in other datasets.

ProSem [inter, com, rd] Cho et al. (2019a) is a spoken language understanding corpus for syntactic ambiguity resolution in Korean, classifying spoken utterances into 7 speech acts[46]. For about 7,100 utterances recorded by two speakers, namely a male and a female, the ground truth text and label are annotated along with the English translation.

4 Summary

In total, we surveyed 32 corpora, namely 18 Korean text corpora, 9 multilingual corpora, and 5 speech corpora. They are composed of 7 datasets on parsing and tagging, 7 datasets on entailment, paraphrasing, and summarization, 8 datasets on (spoken language) classification, QA, and dialog, 5 datasets on machine translation/transliteraion, and 5 datasets on speech (pre-)processing[47]. We provide the full specification in Table 1 in the Appendix A.

Documentation Ensuring that a curated list of resources is up-to-date is a challenge. In this regard, we aim to make our work open and canonical, as an online repository of curated resources for Korean. For the research community to have unconstrained access to all current open resources, while endorsing community contributions, the following criteria are crucial:

- The canonical, current version of this paper will be regularly published as a revision, e.g., on `arxiv.org`, based on a community-open version of this paper.
- The resources will also have a corresponding registry, following the same metadata protocol for usability in different types of research, as we used in this protocol.
- Each new contribution to the resource list will have a corresponding entry in the acknowledgments section.

We will make the registry machine parseable, so that other curated sites such as `nlpprogress.org`, can utilize the registry to automate updates. The project will be maintained as an open-source project, under a permissive license. A living document is a new territory for the field of academia, but we strongly believe that given the rapid progress of NLP research, this is an experiment worth attempting; and hope that a successful effort can inspire other languages to follow the same approach. Our approach is to be described in the public repository, guaranteeing the accessibility for domestic and abroad researchers. Also, a large portion of the data are expected to be more easily accessible via Koco[48] and Korpora[49], the recently constructed dataset wrappers for Korean NLP.

5 Conclusion

In this paper, we investigated the Korean NLP datasets constructed and released as public resources. Our curation suggests a variety of open corpora that are freely available. This information will not only be helpful for the Korean researchers who want to start NLP, but also for the abroad ones who are interested in Korean NLP. Nonetheless, we think that Korean open corpora are still less disclosed or not yet sufficient. It is notable that the Korean government is currently supplying substantial funds to build a database. To guide this well, appropriate management and documentation should be guaranteed, so that the construction is meaningful and the outcome is internationally available.

---

[42]`https://www.kaggle.com/bryanpark/korean-single-speaker-speech-dataset`
[43]`https://github.com/goodatlas/zeroth`
[44]`https://github.com/clovaai/ClovaCall`
[45]`https://github.com/yc9701/pansori-tedxkr-corpus`
[46]`https://github.com/warnikchow/prosem`
[47]Note that these statistics do not incorporate the datasets provided by NIKL, ETRI, and AI HUB.

[48]`https://github.com/inmoonlight/koco`
[49]`https://github.com/ko-nlp/Korpora`

Acknowledgments

The authors are grateful for all the contributors of the open Korean corpora. Special thanks goes to Seungyoung Lim, Jiyeon Ham, Jiyoon Han, Hyunjoong Kim and Jihyung Moon for checking and proofreading. We also appreciate team Ko-NLP for accommodating the public repository of our project.

References

Samuel R. Bowman, Gabor Angeli, Christopher Potts, and Christopher D. Manning. 2015. A large annotated corpus for learning natural language inference. pages 632–642.

Daniel Cer, Mona Diab, Eneko Agirre, Iñigo Lopez-Gazpio, and Lucia Specia. 2017. SemEval-2017 task 1: Semantic textual similarity multilingual and crosslingual focused evaluation. pages 1–14.

Won Ik Cho, Jeonghwa Cho, Jeemin Kang, and Nam Soo Kim. 2019a. Prosody-semantics interface in Seoul Korean: Corpus for a disambiguation of wh-intervention. In *Proceedings of the 19th International Congress of the Phonetic Sciences (ICPhS 2019)*, pages 3902–3906.

Won Ik Cho, Jong In Kim, Young Ki Moon, and Nam Soo Kim. 2020. Discourse component to sentence (DC2S): An efficient human-aided construction of paraphrase and sentence similarity dataset. In *Proceedings of The 12th Language Resources and Evaluation Conference*, pages 6819–6826.

Won Ik Cho, Hyeon Seung Lee, Ji Won Yoon, Seok Min Kim, and Nam Soo Kim. 2018. Speech intention understanding in a head-final language: A disambiguation utilizing intonation-dependency. *arXiv preprint arXiv:1811.04231*.

Won Ik Cho, Young Ki Moon, Sangwhan Moon, Seok Min Kim, and Nam Soo Kim. 2019b. Machines getting with the program: Understanding intent arguments of non-canonical directives. *arXiv preprint arXiv:1912.00342*.

Key-Sun Choi, Young S Han, Young G Han, and Oh W Kwon. 1994. KAIST tree bank project for Korean: Present and future development. In *Proceedings of the International Workshop on Sharable Natural Language Resources*, pages 7–14. Citeseer.

Yoona Choi and Bowon Lee. 2018. Pansori: ASR corpus generation from open online video contents. *arXiv preprint arXiv:1812.09798*.

Jayeol Chun, Na-Rae Han, Jena D Hwang, and Jinho D Choi. 2018. Building universal dependency treebanks in Korean. In *Proceedings of the Eleventh International Conference on Language Resources and Evaluation (LREC 2018)*.

Jonathan H. Clark, Eunsol Choi, Michael Collins, Dan Garrette, Tom Kwiatkowski, Vitaly Nikolaev, and Jennimaria Palomaki. 2020. TyDi QA: A benchmark for information-seeking question answering in typologically diverse languages. *Transactions of the Association for Computational Linguistics*, 8:454–470.

Alexis Conneau, Ruty Rinott, Guillaume Lample, Adina Williams, Samuel Bowman, Holger Schwenk, and Veselin Stoyanov. 2018. XNLI: Evaluating cross-lingual sentence representations. pages 2475–2485.

Kyle Gorman, Lucas FE Ashby, Aaron Goyzueta, Arya D McCarthy, Shijie Wu, and Daniel You. 2020. The SIGMORPHON 2020 shared task on multilingual grapheme-to-phoneme conversion. In *Proceedings of the 17th SIGMORPHON Workshop on Computational Research in Phonetics, Phonology, and Morphology*, pages 40–50.

Jung-Woo Ha, Kihyun Nam, Jin Gu Kang, Sang-Woo Lee, Sohee Yang, Hyunhoon Jung, Eunmi Kim, Hyeji Kim, Soojin Kim, Hyun Ah Kim, et al. 2020. ClovaCall: Korean goal-oriented dialog speech corpus for automatic speech recognition of contact centers. *arXiv preprint arXiv:2004.09367*.

Jiyeon Ham, Yo Joong Choe, Kyubyong Park, Ilji Choi, and Hyungjoon Soh. 2020. KorNLI and KorSTS: New benchmark datasets for Korean natural language understanding. *arXiv preprint arXiv:2004.03289*.

Chung-hye Han, Na-Rae Han, Eon-Suk Ko, Martha Palmer, and Heejong Yi. 2001. Penn Korean Treebank: Development and evaluation. In *Proceedings of the 16th Pacific Asia Conference on Language, Information and Computation*, pages 69–78.

Gyeong-Eun Han, Seul-Ye Baek, and Jae-Soo Lim. 2017. Open sourced and collaborative method to fix errors of Sejong morphologically annotated corpora. In *Annual Conference on Human and Language Technology*, pages 228–232. Human and Language Technology.

Hansaem Kim. 2006. Korean national corpus in the 21st century Sejong project. In *Proceedings of the 13th NIJL International Symposium*, pages 49–54. National Institute for Japanese Language Tokyo.

Tom Kwiatkowski, Jennimaria Palomaki, Olivia Redfield, Michael Collins, Ankur Parikh, Chris Alberti, Danielle Epstein, Illia Polosukhin, Jacob Devlin, Kenton Lee, et al. 2019. Natural questions: a benchmark for question answering research. *Transactions of the Association for Computational Linguistics*, 7:453–466.

Jackson L. Lee, Lucas F.E. Ashby, M. Elizabeth Garza, Yeonju Lee-Sikka, Sean Miller, Alan Wong, Arya D. McCarthy, and Kyle Gorman. 2020. Massively multilingual pronunciation modeling with WikiPron.

In *Proceedings of the 12th Language Resources and Evaluation Conference*, pages 4223–4228, Marseille, France. European Language Resources Association.

Seungyoung Lim, Myungji Kim, and Jooyoul Lee. 2019. KorQuAD 1.0: Korean QA dataset for machine reading comprehension. *arXiv preprint arXiv:1909.07005*.

Zhaojiang Lin, Zihan Liu, Genta Indra Winata, Samuel Cahyawijaya, Andrea Madotto, Yejin Bang, Etsuko Ishii, and Pascale Fung. 2020. XPersona: Evaluating multilingual personalized chatbot. *arXiv preprint arXiv:2003.07568*.

Andrew L. Maas, Raymond E. Daly, Peter T. Pham, Dan Huang, Andrew Y. Ng, and Christopher Potts. 2011. Learning word vectors for sentiment analysis. In *Proceedings of the 49th Annual Meeting of the Association for Computational Linguistics: Human Language Technologies*, pages 142–150, Portland, Oregon, USA. Association for Computational Linguistics.

Ryan McDonald, Joakim Nivre, Yvonne Quirmbach-Brundage, Yoav Goldberg, Dipanjan Das, Kuzman Ganchev, Keith Hall, Slav Petrov, Hao Zhang, Oscar Täckström, et al. 2013. Universal dependency annotation for multilingual parsing. In *Proceedings of the 51st Annual Meeting of the Association for Computational Linguistics (Volume 2: Short Papers)*, pages 92–97.

Jihyung Moon, Won Ik Cho, and Junbum Lee. 2020. BEEP! Korean corpus of online news comments for toxic speech detection. pages 25–31.

Tae Hwan Oh, Ji Yoon Han, Hyonsu Choe, Seokwon Park, Han He, Jinho D. Choi, Na-Rae Han, Jena D. Hwang, and Hansaem Kim. 2020. Analysis of the Penn Korean Universal Dependency treebank (PKT-UD): Manual revision to build robust parsing model in Korean. pages 122–131.

Jungyeul Park, Jeen-Pyo Hong, and Jeong-Won Cha. 2016. Korean language resources for everyone. In *Proceedings of the 30th Pacific Asia conference on language, information and computation: Oral Papers*, pages 49–58.

Kyubyong Park. 2018. KSS dataset: Korean single speaker speech dataset.

Pranav Rajpurkar, Jian Zhang, Konstantin Lopyrev, and Percy Liang. 2016. SQuAD: 100,000+ questions for machine comprehension of text. In *Proceedings of the 2016 Conference on Empirical Methods in Natural Language Processing*, pages 2383–2392.

Erik F Tjong Kim Sang and Fien De Meulder. 2003. Introduction to the CoNLL-2003 shared task: language-independent named entity recognition. In *Proceedings of the seventh conference on Natural language learning at HLT-NAACL 2003-Volume 4*, pages 142–147.

Adina Williams, Nikita Nangia, and Samuel Bowman. 2018. A broad-coverage challenge corpus for sentence understanding through inference. pages 1112–1122.

Yinfei Yang, Yuan Zhang, Chris Tar, and Jason Baldridge. 2019. PAWS-X: A cross-lingual adversarial dataset for paraphrase identification. pages 3687–3692.

Saizheng Zhang, Emily Dinan, Jack Urbanek, Arthur Szlam, Douwe Kiela, and Jason Weston. 2018. Personalizing dialogue agents: I have a dog, do you have pets too? *arXiv preprint arXiv:1801.07243*.

Yuan Zhang, Jason Baldridge, and Luheng He. 2019. PAWS: Paraphrase adversaries from word scrambling. pages 1298–1308.

A Specification

The labels in Docu. denote the level of description.

- *doc*: If exists any document for the usage
- *art*: If exists any complete form of article
- *inter*: If exists a globally readable publication

Other attributes regarding license has the following order of usage and redistribution availability:

- *com > acad > unk*
- *rd > rd/mod-x > no > unk*

while no *unk* at this moment.

Dataset	Typical Usage	Provider	Docu.	License	Volume	Goal	Lang.
KAIST Morpho-Syntactically Annotated Corpus	Morphological analysis	Academia	art	acad/no	70M (w)	-	ko
KAIST Korean Tree-Tagging Corpus	Tree parsing	Academia	inter	acad/no	30K (s)	-	ko
UD Korean KAIST	Dependency parsing	Academia	inter	acad/rd	27K (s)	-	ko
PKT-UD	Dependency parsing	Academia	inter	acad/no	5K (s)	-	ko
KMOU NER	NER	Academia	art	acad/rd	24K (s)	-	ko
AIR×NAVER NER	NER	Competition	doc	acad/no	90K (s)	-	ko
AIR×NAVER SRL	SRL	Competition	doc	acad/no	35K (s)	-	ko
Question Pair	Paraphrase detection	Academia	doc	com/rd	10K (p)	-	ko
KorNLI	NLI	Industry	inter	com/rd	1,000K (p)	-	ko
KorSTS	STS	Industry	inter	com/rd	8,500 (p)	-	ko
ParaKQC	STS	Academia	inter	com/rd	540K (p)	-	ko
NSMC	Sentiment analysis	Academia	doc	com/rd	150K / 50K (s)	-	ko
BEEP!	Hate speech detection	Academia	inter	com/rd	8K / 500 / 1,000 (s)	-	ko
3i4K	Speech act classification	Academia	inter	com/rd	55K / 6K (s)	-	ko
KorQuAD 1.0	QA	Industry	inter	com/rd (mod-x)	60K / 5K / 4K (p)	-	ko
KorQuAD 2.0	QA	Industry	art	com/rd (mod-x)	80K / 10K / 10K (p)	-	ko
Sci-news-sum-kr	Summarization	Academia	doc	acad/rd	50 (p)	Eval	ko
sae4K	Summarization	Academia	inter	com/rd	50K (p)	-	ko
Korean Parallel Corpora	MT	Academia	inter	acad/rd (mod-x)	97K (p)	-	ko, en
KAIST Translation Evaluation Set	MT	Academia	doc	acad/no	3K (p)	Eval	ko, en

Dataset	Typical Usage	Provider	Docu.	License	Volume	Goal	Lang.
KAIST Chinese-Korean Multilingual Corpus	MT	Academia	doc	acad/no	60K (p)		ko, zh
Transliteration Dataset	Transliteration	Academia	doc	com/rd	35K (p)	-	ko, en
KAIST Transliteration Evaluation Set	Transliteration	Academia	doc	acad/no	7K (p)	Eval	ko, en
SIGMORPHON G2P	G2P conversion	Competition	inter	com/rd	3,600 / 450 / 450 (p)	-	ko, en, hy, bg, fr, ka, hi, hu, is, lt, el
PAWS-X	Paraphrase detection	Industry	inter	com/rd	5K / 2K / 2K (p)	-	ko, fr, es, de, zh, ja
TyDi-QA	QA	Industry	inter	com/rd	11K / 1,698 / 1,722 (p)	-	ko, en, ar, bn, fi, ja, id, sw, ru, te, th
XPersona	Dialog	Academia	inter	com/rd	299 (d) / 4,684 (s)	-	ko, en, it, fr, id, zh, ja
KSS	ASR	Academia	doc	acad/rd	12+ (h) / 13K (u) / 1 speaker	-	ko
Zeroth	ASR	Industry	doc	com/rd	51+ (h) / 27K (s) / 46K (u) / 181 speakers	-	ko
ClovaCall	ASR	Industry	inter	acad/no	80+ (h) / 60K (u) / 11K speakers	-	ko
Pansori-TED×KR	ASR	Academia	inter	acad/rd (mod-x)	3+ (h) / 3K (u) / 41 speakers	-	ko
ProSem	SLU	Academia	inter	com/rd	6+ (h) / 3,500 (s) / 7K (u) / 2 speakers	-	ko

Table 1: The specification on open Korean corpora. In *Provider*, *Academia* denotes universities and institutes, as well as the independent researchers who contribute to the community, while *Industry* means the companies or the research group thereof. *Competition* indicates the data used for the public competition, usually concerning both academia and industry. In *Volume*, (w) denotes words, (s) denotes sentences, (p) denotes pairs (either document or sentence pairs), (d) denotes dialogues, (h) denotes hours, and (u) denotes speech utterances. We note *Eval* only if the dataset is not for the training purpose.

Open-Source Morphology for Endangered Mordvinic Languages

Jack Rueter
Dept. of Digital Humanities
University of Helsinki
jack.rueter@helsinki.fi

Mika Hämäläinen
Dept. of Digital Humanities
University of Helsinki
and Rootroo Ltd
mika@rootroo.com

Niko Partanen
Dept. of Finnish,
Finno-Ugrian
and Scandinavian Studies
University of Helsinki
niko.partanen@helsinki.fi

Abstract

This document describes shared development of finite-state description of two closely related but endangered minority languages, Erzya and Moksha. It touches upon morpholexical unity and diversity of the two languages and how this provides a motivation for shared open-source FST development. We describe how we have designed the transducers so that they can benefit from existing open-source infrastructures and are as reusable as possible.

1 Introduction

There are over 5000 languages spoken world wide, and a vast majority of them are endangered (see Moseley 2010). The Mordvinic languages Erzya and Moksha are no exception. One of the first NLP solutions that are typically developed along with lexical resources for any low-resourced language is a morphological analyzer (cf Zueva et al. 2020; Tyers et al. 2019; Lovick et al. 2018).

In this paper, we describe the development of an open-source FST (finite-state transducer) based morphological analyzer, lemmatizer and generator for Erzya and Moksha. We highlight the importance of certain design decisions to ensure the compatibility of our transducers with existing systems. In addition, we will describe how the transducers can be edited in a system that creates an abstraction layer behind a graphical user interface for FST development.

The unity and diversity of the Mordvin literary languages of today, Erzya and Moksha, has been a subject of research for over two hundred years. The first grammars were published in 1830s – Moksha in 1838 (Ornatov, 1838) and Erzya in 1838–1839 (Gabelentz, 1839). The subsequent 180 years brought scholars for fieldwork, grammars, dictionaries, and the popularization of the languages. 2002 saw the publication of the first monolingual dictionary of Erzya (Abramov, 2002), and the manuscript was proclaimed open by the author for future development. The Mordvin languages have continued to receive a fair share of linguistic research interest in the recent years (Luutonen, 2014; Hamari and Aasmäe, 2015; Kashkin and Nikiforova, 2015; Grünthal, 2016).

After the release first finite-state transducer for the closely related Komi-Zyrian (Rueter, 2000), it was only obvious that similar work should be done for Erzya Mordvin. Fortunately, over the past decade there has been an increasing number of publications on Erzya, relating to its morphology (Rueter, 2010), its OCR tools (Silfverberg and Rueter, 2015) and universal dependencies (Rueter and Tyers, 2018).

This document discusses open-source morphology development, which has greatly benefited from open-source projects, most notably achievements attributed to the GiellaLT infrastructure (Moshagen et al., 2014), i.e. Giellatekno & Divvun at the Norwegian Arctic University in Tromsø, Norway.

It is also very important that people new to language documentation be given opportunities to develop their understanding of languages through participation in projects. Here we must mention an important span of time 1988–1997, during which the first author did word processing for the 2073-page 'Dictionary of Mordvin Dialects' by Heikki Paasonen.

The transducers are available on GitHub for Erzya [1] and Moksha [2]. The nightly builds are available through a Python library called UralicNLP[3] (Hämäläinen, 2019).

---

[1] https://github.com/giellalt/lang-myv
[2] https://github.com/giellalt/lang-mdf
[3] https://github.com/mikahama/uralicNLP

Proceedings of Second Workshop for NLP Open Source Software (NLP-OSS), pages 94–100
Virtual Conference, November 19, 2020. ©2020 Association for Computational Linguistics

2 Designing for a Reusable API

It is not uncommon that similar tools and methods are developed by different research groups in different parts of the world for language documentation purposes. To name a few, there are projects developing similar language documentation systems for African languages (Jones and Muftic, 2020), Indonesian languages (Nasution et al., 2018) and Yupik (Hunt et al., 2019), while at the same time, it has been shown that digital humanities projects that are seemingly different, still face the very same technical problems (Mäkelä et al., 2020). In arguably, any work conducted with endangered languages to document them and better serve the small community of speakers has a lot of value. However, the fact that the wheel gets reinvented over and over again leads to fragmentation in the resources available for smaller languages and makes their use more difficult as each individual tool exposes an API of their own.

Rule-based morphology can be implemented in many different systems. Popular tools include XFST (Karttunen et al., 1997), Foma (Hulden, 2009) and OpenFST (Allauzen et al., 2007). However, we use HFST (Helsinki-Finite State Technology) (Lindén et al., 2009) because it is the system used in GiellaLT (Moshagen et al., 2014).

GiellaLT provides our transducers with a list of quality attributes. Their infrastructure consists of work done for multiple endangered languages in such a way that the morphological resources can be used in a multitude of different contexts such as disambiguation (Trosterud, 2004; Ens et al., 2019), dependency parsing (Antonsen et al., 2010), online dictionaries (Rueter and Hämäläinen, 2019), spell checkers (Wiechetek et al., 2019), online creative writing tools (Hämäläinen, 2018), automated news generation (Alnajjar et al., 2019) and language learning tools (Antonsen and Argese, 2018).

In order to gain the added benefit from the GiellaLT infrastructure, we have to design our transducers so that they are compatible with HFST and that they follow a certain morphological tagset and that they take the input and output in a certain format. These requirements define the API our transducers need to implement. An example of this can be seen in Table 1.

Apertium (Forcada et al., 2011) is another open-source system that uses FST transducers for rule-based machine translation. They use their own transducer format, but fortunately also support

	input	output
analyzer	вирев	вирев+A+Sg+Nom+Indef вирь+N+SP+Lat+Indef
generator	вирев+A+Sg+Nom+Indef	вирев

Table 1: Examples of GiellaLT style input and output

HFST based transducers, and in fact Apertium type transducers can be compiled to HFST form as well (Pirinen and Tyers, 2012). However, their tagset is different from that of GiellaLT. This is solved by applying filters at the time the FST is compiled to produce a separate, Apertium-compatible, transducer automatically.

3 Erzya and Moksha language pair

At the moment Erzya and Moksha infrastructure in GiellaLT can be considered to be in nearly equal standing, despite the fact that work on Erzya was started considerably earlier. This does not mean, however, that the resources for both languages are identical in all measures, although in basic numeric levels their sizes are comparable. There are many situations where additional consistency between the infrastructures for these two languages would be quite desirable and beneficial. We discuss next what these instances could be, and outline some of the major questions while working with this language pair.

The open-source machine translation infrastructure Apertium uses a shallow-transfer strategy. By definition, shallow transfer makes a morphosyntactic analysis of the source language, translates the lemmas from source to target language, generates morphology acquired from the source language in the target language and makes adjustments to the syntax of the target language. This concept of parallel lexica, morphology and syntax, would therefore, seem most effective in translation between closely related languages. In the case of the Mordvin pair, this means the use of mutual tags for describing mutual phenomena.

Mutual phenomena in Erzya and Moksha, however, can be distinguished as exact matches and fuzzy matches, as it were. While there is no doubt that the two languages share nearly the same categories of case, person, number and definiteness, it must also be noted that the paradigms do not share the same cellular structure (Keresztes 1999; Trosterud 2006; Rueter 2016). When the paradigm structure is diverse, it is suggested that a union of morphological tags be taken as a starting point. When one language distinguishes a category of

	+Nom	+Gen	+Dat
Sg+PxSg1 (my son)	цёразе	цёразень	цёразти
Sg+PxSg1 (my sons)	цёране	цёранень	цёраненди
Sg+PxSg2 (your son)	цёраце	цёрацень	цёрацти
Pl+PxSg2 (your sons)	цёратне	цёратнень	цёратненди
Sg+PxSg3 (his/her son)	цёрац	цёранц	цёранцты
Pl+PxSg3 (his/her son)	цёранза	цёранзон	цёранзонды
SP+PxPl1 (our son/sons)	цёраньке	цёраньконь	цёраньконди
SP+PxPl2 (your son/sons)	цёранте	цёрантень	цёрантенди
SP+PxPl3 (their son/sons)	цёрасна	цёраснон	цёраснонды

Table 2: Symmetric possessive declension of Moksha core cases

	+Nom	+Gen	+Dat
Sg+PxSg1 (my son)	цёрам	цёрам ~ цёрань	цёрам туртов ~ цёрань туртов ~ цёранень
Pl+PxSg1 (my sons)	цёран ~ цёрам	цёран ~ цёрам	цёран туртов цёрам туртов
Sg+PxSg2 (your son)	цёрат	цёрать ~ цёрат	цёрать туртов ~ цёратень
PxSg2 Pl (your son)	цёрат	цёрат	цёрат туртов
PxSg3 Sg (his/her son)	цёразо	цёранзо	цёранстэнь ~ цёранзо туртов
PxSg3 Pl (his/her sons)	цёранзо	цёранзо	цёранстэнь ~ цёранзо туртов
SP+PxPl1 (our son/sons)	цёранок	цёранок	цёранк туртов
SP+PxPl2 (your son/sons)	цёранк	цёранк	цёранк туртов
SP+PxPl3 (their son/sons)	цёраст	цёраст	цёранстэнь ~ цёраст туртов

Table 3: Asymmetric possessive declension of Erzya core cases

number, for instance, and the other does not, there comes a point where number must be determined. And, in order to facilitate a transition from the absence of the category of number to its presence and vice versa, the rudiments of tagging this category must be put in place, e.g. for the category of number we use SG 'singular', PL 'plural' and SP 'singular or plural'.

Diversity in the Erzya-Moksha language pair can be found in the core ranges of the categories definiteness, person and number. Both languages have an indefinite or basic declension, a definite or determiner declension and a possessive declension. For both languages, it can be stated that the indefinite declension distinguishes the category of number in the nominative alone, whereas number is always specified in the definite declension paradigms. The possessive declension, however, exhibits a salient rift in unity. Moksha has a symmetric paradigm in the core cases, nominative, genitive and dative (see Table 2), with distinct word forms for each case-possessor combination slot and an additional distinction for number of possessa when the possessor is singular, whereas Erzya makes virtually no consistent distinction for case or number in the nominative and genitive – with one exception the specific nominative singular reading of the third person singular +N+SG+NOM+PXSG3 and optionally in the first and second person singular of modern written literature (see Table 3).

Additional diversity is found in the subject-object paradigm, where portmanteau morphology enables the specification of first, second and third person subject and object provided both arguments are singular. When one or both of the arguments is not specifically singular, however, one form may serve to indicate more than one set of arguments, e.g. Erzya has a default non-past form *-samiź* which simply indicates a first person object with a second or third person subject when it is not true that both subject and object are specified, singular entities

	Obj+Sg1	Obj+Pl1
Subj+Sg2	NA	*-samiź*
Subj+Pl2	*-samiź*	*-samiź*
Subj+Sg3	NA	*-samiź*
Subj+Pl3	*-samiź*	*-samiź*

Table 4: Erzya default first person object

(see Table 4).

Moksha, however, makes a further semantic split with regard to the category of person in the subject, namely, the form *-samaśt'* is used to indicate a second person subject, and *-samaź* is used to indcate a third or indefinite person subject (see Table 5).

The differences outlined here are not the same, but comparable, to those found in a recent study that evaluated the morphological differences between Komi-Zyrian and Komi-Permyak within the context of FST and treebank development (Rueter et al., 2020). With closely related languages any kind of resource reuse or transfer is rarely trivial, but through careful evaluation of linguistic features and differences we show that these goals are certainly possible and realistic.

4 Current State and Ensuring Maintainability

At the time of writing the transducers lemmas, stems and glosses were acquired through several channels. Statistics on the coverage of the Erzya FST can be seen on Table 6. The same statistics for

	Obj+Sg1	Obj+Pl1
Subj+Sg2	NA	*-samaśt'*
Subj+Pl2	*-samaśt'*	*-samaśt'*
Subj+Sg3	NA	*-samaź*
Subj+Pl3	*-samaź*	*-samaź*

Table 5: Moksha default first person object

word class	total	glossed	inflections	derivations
common nouns	24723	10754	450	8
proper nouns	50566	146	(450)	8
adjectives	12938	446	(450)	1
verbs	16133	4123	356	20
lemma:stem pairs	106293	15908		36

Table 6: Statistics for Erzya transducers

word class	total	glossed	inflections	derivations
common nouns	12851	9056	426	6
proper nouns	50070	267	(426)	6
adjectives	12043	4083	(426)	1
verbs	13449	11577	337	10
lemma:stem pairs	92716	26572		23

Table 7: Statistics for Moksha transducers

Moksha are shown in Table 7.

Although the largest bilingual dictionaries for Erzya and Moksha provide declension information, classification of declension for other nominals has not been dealt with. In the noun phrase, adjectives are declined only when they are promoted to NP head in ellipsis or in the predicative. Hence, adjectives, by nature, might be declined to virtually the same extent as common nouns, but they are subject to fewer derivations. Proper nouns, although most commonly encountered in the singular, may, in fact, be declined in the plural – place names when declined in the plural are down cased and their new semantics refer to inhabitants. Person names gain a sense of associative plural.

Derivations include morphologically new forms and orthographic compounds. Most salient are the ever present diminutive, which has a sense of endearment, diminutive and even partitive measure. Orthographic derivation can be observed in compound nouns, with collective sense, and verbs, expressing simultaneous activities. The challenge of orthographic compounds lies in the hyphened pair where both elements are inflected for the same grammatical categories, such that copula forms of compound nouns are included in the morphology of both stems, but the additive clitic attaches only to the second.

The transducer development is conducted in an agile fashion with nightly builds available for the end user via an open-source Python library called UralicNLP (Hämäläinen, 2019). The quality of the transducers is ensured by unit testing. We use test scripts written in YAML that contain a list of inputs and accepted outputs. Any changes in the transducers that break the tests will be immediately noticed and acted upon.

The source code of an FST is not the easiest to write for an average linguist or an NLP researcher. In the context of endangered languages, however, one would hope that people working on language documentation with a limited technical background or even community members could make an active contribution to the morphological tools. In order to address this need, we have embraced two levels of abstraction for FST development.

The first level of abstraction is the use of an XML-based dictionary. Lexical data is stored in XML form in the GiellaLT infrastructure, and to a great extent, they contain similar information to the lexicon of an FST: words (lemmas and stems) and their continuation lexicons that indicate how they are inflected. For this reason, we actually compile the FST lexicon from the XML-based dictionary. The XML dictionaries are, in fact, also used as source files for online dictionaries, and therefore they are an attempt to address the matter of reuse, i.e. transducer construction, online morphological dictionaries, source material for ICALL projects as well as rule-based machine translation.

With a recent effort of a TEI (Text-Encoding Initiative) compatibility layer in the GiellaLT XML dictionaries (Rueter and Hämäläinen, 2019), it was decided that editing the FSTs in the XML dictionaries should be open for a majority of people using modern lexicographic tools. This compatibility layer is important as TEI is an ISO-standard, which means that it will most likely outlive any individual project and remain usable in the future as well.

The second layer of abstraction is the open-source online user interfaces Ve'rdd (Alnajjar et al., 2020) and Akusanat (Hämäläinen and Rueter, 2018) that make it possible to edit XML based dictionaries for anyone without any technical background. This is important since direct edits to an XML might be daunting for a language community member who has no programming background. These two different levels of abstraction ultimately produce XMLs in the GiellaLT format that can be directly used to enhance the transducers.

To provide further comparison, a very similar mechanism to store lexicon externally from the FST has also been used successfully by Wilbur (2018) with Pite Saami. Also in this case same lexicon is used in FST, in a published dictionary (Wilbur, 2016), and in an online dictionary[4]. This shows that approach described here is practical,

---

and already used, in different endangered language contexts.

5 Conclusions

In this paper we have presented our work on opensource FSTs for Erzya and Moksha. Leveraging existing open source platforms has been the core design principle throughout the development. Without GiellaLT support, our transducer would be left out of a plethora of higher level services provided by the infrastructure such as spell-checking, constraint grammar based syntax, language learning tools etc. This would mean that we would need to build these resources from the ground up.

Another important design principle has been accessibility of the FSTs. Continuous integration makes it possible to commit to the nightly builds of the UralicNLP library, which makes our FSTs usable through a generic multilingual Python API. Accessibility has also been thought of from the point of view of the development. Using an XML based dictionary to generate the FST lexicon with a compatibility with the ISO-standardized TEI XML makes it easier for non-FST savvy people to contribute to the work. Furthermore, integration with a GUI such as Ve'rdd, makes it possible to crowdsource the development in the future by evoking community involvement of the native speakers.

We have had positive experiences from building on top of these other open-source solutions and would strongly recommend that other researchers working on the morphology of endangered languages investigate the existing open-source platforms before starting to build everything from scratch. The GiellaLT infrastructure could save you from two to three years of development. At the same time attention has to be paid to general APIs and interfaces that allow access to these tools at various levels of abstraction.

References

Kuzma Abramov. 2002. Валонь ёвтнема валкс. Mordovskoj knizhnoj izdateljstvasj. The manuscript of this dictionary was compiled by the Erzya national writer Kuz'ma Grigorievich Abramov, 1914-2008, whose activities as an Erzya writer spanned nearly 70 years.

Cyril Allauzen, Michael Riley, Johan Schalkwyk, Wojciech Skut, and Mehryar Mohri. 2007. Openfst: A general and efficient weighted finite-state transducer library. In *Proceedings of the Ninth International Conference on Implementation and Application of Automata, (CIAA 2007)*, volume 4783 of *Lecture Notes in Computer Science*, pages 11–23. Springer.

Khalid Alnajjar, Mika Hämäläinen, and Jack Rueter. 2020. On editing dictionaries for uralic languages in an online environment. In *Proceedings of the Sixth International Workshop on Computational Linguistics of Uralic Languages*, pages 26–30.

Khalid Alnajjar, Leo Leppänen, and Hannu Toivonen. 2019. No time like the present: methods for generating colourful and factual multilingual news headlines. In *Proceedings of the 10th International Conference on Computational Creativity*. Association for Computational Creativity.

Lene Antonsen and Chiara Argese. 2018. Using authentic texts for grammar exercises for a minority language. In *Proceedings of the 7th workshop on NLP for Computer Assisted Language Learning*, pages 1–9.

Lene Antonsen, Trond Trosterud, and Linda Wiechetek. 2010. Reusing grammatical resources for new languages. In *Proceedings of the Seventh conference on International Language Resources and Evaluation (LREC'10)*.

Jeff Ens, Mika Hämäläinen, Jack Rueter, and Philippe Pasquier. 2019. Morphosyntactic disambiguation in an endangered language setting. In *Proceedings of the 22nd Nordic Conference on Computational Linguistics*, pages 345–349.

Mikel L Forcada, Mireia Ginestí-Rosell, Jacob Nordfalk, Jim O'Regan, Sergio Ortiz-Rojas, Juan Antonio Pérez-Ortiz, Felipe Sánchez-Martínez, Gema Ramírez-Sánchez, and Francis M Tyers. 2011. Apertium: a free/open-source platform for rule-based machine translation. *Machine translation*, 25(2):127–144.

Herr Conon von der Gabelentz. 1839. Versuch einer mordwinischen grammatik. In *Zeitschrift für die Kunde des Morgenlandes.*, II. 2–3., pages 235–284, 383–419. Druck und Verlag der Dieterlichschen Buchhandlung.

Riho Grünthal. 2016. *Transitivity in Erzya: Second language speakers in a grammatical focus*, Uralica Helsingiensia, page 291–318. Finno-Ugrian Society, Finland.

Mika Hämäläinen. 2018. Poem machine-a co-creative nlg web application for poem writing. In *The 11th International Conference on Natural Language Generation Proceedings of the Conference*. The Association for Computational Linguistics.

Mika Hämäläinen and Jack Rueter. 2018. Advances in synchronized xml-media wiki dictionary development in the context of endangered uralic languages. In *Proceedings of the XVIII EURALEX International Congress: Lexicography in Global Contexts 17-21 July 2018, Ljubljana*. Ljubljana University Press.

Arja Hamari and Niina Aasmäe. 2015. Negation in erzya. *Negation in Uralic languages*, 108:293.

Mans Hulden. 2009. Foma: a finite-state compiler and library. In *Proceedings of the 12th Conference of the European Chapter of the Association for Computational Linguistics*, pages 29–32. Association for Computational Linguistics.

Benjamin Hunt, Emily Chen, Sylvia L.R. Schreiner, and Lane Schwartz. 2019. Community lexical access for an endangered polysynthetic language: An electronic dictionary for st. lawrence island yupik. In *Proceedings of the 2019 Conference of the North American Chapter of the Association for Computational Linguistics (Demonstrations)*, pages 122–126, Minneapolis, Minnesota. Association for Computational Linguistics.

Mika Hämäläinen. 2019. UralicNLP: An NLP library for Uralic languages. *Journal of Open Source Software*, 4(37):1345.

Kerry Jones and Sanjin Muftic. 2020. Endangered African languages featured in a digital collection: The case of the Ç,Khomani San, Hugh Brody Collection. In *Proceedings of the first workshop on Resources for African Indigenous Languages*, pages 1–8, Marseille, France. European Language Resources Association (ELRA).

Lauri Karttunen, Tamás Gaál, and André Kempe. 1997. Xerox finite-state tool. *Rapport technique, Centre de recherche Xerox de Grenoble*.

Egor Kashkin and Sofya Nikiforova. 2015. Verbs of sound in the moksha language: a typological account. *Nyelvtudományi Közlemények*, 111:341–362.

László Keresztes. 1999. *Development of Mordvin definite conjugation.* Suomalais-Ugrilaisen Seuran toimituksia, 233. Suomalais-Ugrilainen Seura, Helsinki.

Krister Lindén, Miikka Silfverberg, and Tommi Pirinen. 2009. Hfst tools for morphology–an efficient open-source package for construction of morphological analyzers. In *International Workshop on Systems and Frameworks for Computational Morphology*, pages 28–47. Springer.

Olga Lovick, Christopher Cox, Miikka Silfverberg, Antti Arppe, and Mans Hulden. 2018. A computational architecture for the morphology of upper tanana. In *Proceedings of the Eleventh International Conference on Language Resources and Evaluation (LREC 2018)*, Miyazaki, Japan. European Language Resources Association (ELRA).

Jorma Luutonen. 2014. Kahden sukupolven ersää – kielenhuoltoa ja muutoksen merkkejä. *Memoires de la Societe Finno-Ougrienne*, 270:187—201.

Eetu Mäkelä, Krista Lagus, Leo Lahti, Tanja Säily, Mikko Tolonen, Mika Hämäläinen, Samuli Kaislaniemi, and Terttu Nevalainen. 2020. Wrangling with non-standard data. In *Proceedings of the Digital Humanities in the Nordic Countries 5th Conference.*

Christopher Moseley, editor. 2010. *Atlas of the World′s Languages in Danger*, 3rd edition. UNESCO Publishing. Online version: http://www.unesco.org/languages-atlas/.

Sjur Moshagen, Jack Rueter, Tommi Pirinen, Trond Trosterud, and Francis M. Tyers. 2014. Open-source infrastructures for collaborative work on under-resourced languages. The LREC 2014 Workshop "CCURL 2014 - Collaboration and Computing for Under-Resourced Languages in the Linked Open Data Era".

Arbi Haza Nasution, Yohei Murakami, and Toru Ishida. 2018. Designing a collaborative process to create bilingual dictionaries of Indonesian ethnic languages. In *Proceedings of the Eleventh International Conference on Language Resources and Evaluation (LREC 2018)*, Miyazaki, Japan. European Language Resources Association (ELRA).

Pavel Ornatov. 1838. *Mordovskaja grammatika / sostavlennaja na narechij mordvy mokshi Pavlom Ornatovym.* V Sinodalnoj tip., Moskva.

Tommi A Pirinen and Francis M Tyers. 2012. Compiling apertium morphological dictionaries with hfst and using them in hfst applications. *Language Technology for Normalisation of Less-Resourced Languages*, page 25.

Jack Rueter. 2010. *Adnominal person in the morphological system of Erzya.* Suomalais-ugrilaisen seuran toimituksia. Suomalais-Ugrilainen Seura, Finland.

Jack Rueter and Mika Hämäläinen. 2019. On xml-mediawiki resources, endangered languages and tei compatibility, multilingual dictionaries for endangered languages. *Rachel Edita O. ROXAS President National University (The Philippines)*, page 350.

Jack Rueter, Niko Partanen, and Larisa Ponomareva. 2020. On the questions in developing computational infrastructure for komi-permyak. In *Proceedings of the Sixth International Workshop on Computational Linguistics of Uralic Languages*, pages 15–25.

Jack M. Rueter. 2000. Xeljsinkisa universitetsa kyv tujalysj izhkaryn perymsa kyvjas simpozium vylyn lyddjomtor. In *V sbornike Permistika 6: Problemy sinxronii i diaxronii permskix jazykov i ix dialektov [Permistika 6: Problems in the synchrony and diachrony of the Permic languages and their dialects]*, volume 6 of *Permistika*, pages 154–158.

Jack Michael Rueter. 2016. *Towards a systematic characterization of dialect variation in the Erzya-speaking world: Isoglosses and their reflexes attested in and around the Dubyonki Raion*, number 10 in Uralica Helsingiensia, pages 109–148. University of Helsinki, Finland.

Jack Michael Rueter and Francis M Tyers. 2018. Towards an open-source universal-dependency treebank for erzya. In *International Workshop for Computational Linguistics of Uralic Languages*.

Miikka Silfverberg and Jack Rueter. 2015. Can morphological analyzers improve the quality of optical character recognition? In *First International Workshop on Computational Linguistics for Uralic Languages*, volume 2 of *Septentrio Conference Series*, pages 45–56, Norway. Septentrio Academic Publishing. Volume: Proceeding volume: 2.

Trond Trosterud. 2004. Porting morphological analysis and disambiguation to new languages. In *SALTMIL Workshop at LREC 2004: First Steps in Language Documentation for Minority Languages*, pages 90–92. Citeseer.

Trond Trosterud. 2006. *Homonymy in the Uralic Two-Argument Agreement Paradigms*. Suomalais-Ugrilaisen Seuran Toimituksia 251. Suomalais-Ugrilainen Seura, Helsinki.

Francis M. Tyers, Jonathan Washington, Darya Kavitskaya, Memduh Gökırmak, Nick Howell, and Remziye Berberova. 2019. A biscriptual morphological transducer for crimean Tatar. In *Proceedings of the 3rd Workshop on the Use of Computational Methods in the Study of Endangered Languages Volume 1 (Papers)*, pages 74–80, Honolulu. Association for Computational Linguistics.

Linda Wiechetek, Sjur Moshagen, Børre Gaup, and Thomas Omma. 2019. Many shades of grammar checking – launching a constraint grammar tool for north sámi. In *Proceedings of the NoDaLiDa 2019 Workshop on Constraint Grammar - Methods, Tools and Applications*.

Joshua Wilbur. 2016. *Pitesamisk ordbok: samt stavingsregler*. Department of Scandinavian Studies, University of Freiburg.

Joshua Wilbur. 2018. Extracting inflectional class assignment in pite saami: Nouns, verbs and those pesky adjectives. In *Proceedings of the Fourth International Workshop on Computational Linguistics of Uralic Languages*, pages 154–168.

Anna Zueva, Anastasia Kuznetsova, and Francis Tyers. 2020. A finite-state morphological analyser for evenki. In *Proceedings of The 12th Language Resources and Evaluation Conference*, pages 2581–2589, Marseille, France. European Language Resources Association.

Pimlico: A toolkit for corpus-processing pipelines and reproducible experiments

Mark Granroth-Wilding
University of Helsinki
mark.granroth-wilding@helsinki.fi

Abstract

We present Pimlico, an open source toolkit for building pipelines for processing large corpora. It is especially focused on processing linguistic corpora and provides wrappers around existing, widely used NLP tools. A particular goal is to ease distribution of reproducible and extensible experiments by making it easy to document and re-run all steps involved, including data loading, pre-processing, model training and evaluation. Once a pipeline is released, it is easy to adapt, for example, to run on a new dataset, or to re-run an experiment with different parameters. The toolkit takes care of many common challenges in writing and distributing corpus-processing code, such as managing data between the steps of a pipeline, installing required software and combining existing toolkits with new, task-specific code.

1   Introduction

It is becoming more and more common for conferences and journals in NLP and other computational areas to encourage, or even require, authors to make publicly available the code and data required to reproduce their reported results. It is now widely acknowledged that such practices lie at the center of open science and are essential to ensuring that research contributions are verifiable, extensible and useable in applications. However, this requires extensive additional work. And, even when researchers do this, it is all too common for others to have to spend large amounts of time and effort preparing data, downloading and installing tools, configuring execution environments and picking through instructions and scripts before they can reproduce the original results, never mind apply the code to new datasets or build upon it in novel research. Whilst sometimes it may be sufficient to release a script that performs all of the data processing, model training and experimental evaluation steps, often this is not a practical approach to multi-stage processing of large corpora.

We present a toolkit, *Pimlico* (**Pi**pelined **M**odular **L**inguistic **C**orpus processing), that addresses these problems. It allows users to write and run potentially complex processing pipelines, with the key goals of making it easy to:

- clearly document what was done;

- incorporate standard NLP and data-processing tasks with minimal effort;

- integrate non-standard code, specific to the task at hand, into the same pipeline; and

- distribute code for later reproduction or application to other datasets or experiments.

The toolkit is written in Python and released under the open source LGPLv3 license[1]. It comes with pre-defined modules to wrap a number of existing NLP toolkits (including non-Python code) and carry out many other common pre-processing or data manipulation tasks. Comprehensive documentation is maintained online[2].

In this paper, we describe the core concepts that Pimlico is built around and some of its key features. We also describe a number of the core modules that come built into the toolkit and we present an example pipeline. Finally, we explain how the toolkit addresses the stated goals and outline plans for future development.

2   Building pipelines

Pimlico addresses the task of building of pipelines to process large datasets. It allows you to run one or several steps of processing at a time, with high-level control over how each step is run, manages

---

[1] https://github.com/markgw/pimlico/
[2] https://pimlico.readthedocs.io/

Proceedings of Second Workshop for NLP Open Source Software (NLP-OSS), pages 101–109
Virtual Conference, November 19, 2020. ©2020 Association for Computational Linguistics

```
[split]
type=pimlico.modules.corpora.split
input=tokenized_corpus
set1_size=0.8
```

Figure 1: Example configuration section specifying a single module in a pipeline. The module has a single input, taken from an earlier module's output, and a single parameter.

the data produced by each step, and lets you observe these intermediate outputs. Pimlico provides simple, powerful tools to give this kind of control, without needing to write any code.

Developing a pipeline with Pimlico involves defining the structure of the pipeline itself in terms of *modules* to be executed and connections between their inputs and outputs describing the flow of data. Modules correspond to some data-processing code, with some parameters. They may be of a standard type, so-called *core* modules, for which code is provided as part of Pimlico. A pipeline may also incorporate custom module types, for which metadata and data-processing code must be provided by the author.

2.1 Pipeline configuration

At the heart of Pimlico is the concept of a pipeline configuration, defined by a configuration (or *conf*) file, which can be loaded and executed. This specifies some general parameters and metadata regarding the pipeline and then a sequence of modules to be executed.

Each pipeline module is defined by a named section in the file, which specifies the module type, inputs to be read from the outputs of other, previous modules, and parameters. For example, the configuration section in Fig. 1 defines a module called `split`. Its type is the core Pimlico module type *corpus split*[3], which splits a corpus by documents into two randomly sampled subsets (as is typically done to produce training and test sets). The option `input` specifies where the module's only input comes from and refers by name to a module defined earlier in the pipeline whose output provides the data. The option `set1_size` tells the module to put 80% of documents into the first set and 20% in the second. Two outputs are produced, which can be referred to later in the pipeline as `split.set1` and `split.set2`.

---

[3]`https://pimlico.readthedocs.io/en/latest/modules/pimlico.modules.corpora.split.html`

The first module(s) of a pipeline have no inputs, but load datasets, with parameters to specify where the input data can be found on the filesystem. A number of standard **input readers** are among Pimlico's core module types to support reading of simple datasets, such as text files in a directory, and some standard input formats for data such as word embeddings. The toolkit also provides a factory to make it easy to define custom routines for reading other types of input data.

The **type** of a module is given as a fully qualified Python path to a Python package. The package provides separately the module type's metadata, referred to as its 'module info' – input datatypes, options, etc. – and the code that is executed when it is run, the 'module executor'. The example in Fig. 1 uses one of Pimlico's core module types. A pipeline will usually also include non-standard module types, distributed together with the conf file. These are defined and used in exactly the same way as the core module types. Where custom module types are used, the pipeline conf file specifies a directory where the source code can be found.

An example of a complete pipeline conf, using both core and custom module types, is shown in Fig. 2 and is described in more detail in Section 6.

2.2 Datatypes

When a module is run, its output is stored ready for use by subsequent modules. Pimlico takes care of storing each module's output in separate locations and providing the correct data as input.

The module info for a module type defines a **datatype** for each input and each output. Pimlico includes a system of datatypes for the datasets that are passed between modules. When a pipeline is loaded, type-checking is performed on the connections between modules' outputs and subsequent modules' inputs to ensure that appropriate datatypes are provided.

For example, a module may require a vocabulary as an input, for which Pimlico provides a standard datatype. The pipeline will only pass checks if this input is connected to an output that supplies a compatible type. The supplying module does not need to define how to store a vocabulary, since the datatype defines the necessary routines for writing a vocabulary to disk. The subsequent module does not need to define how to read the data, since the datatype takes care of that too, providing the module executor with suitable Python data structures.

```
# Options for the whole pipeline
[pipeline]
name=custom_module_example
# Pimlico version this is designed to work with
release=0.9.23
# Python source dir, relative to config file:
# needed for the custom module type
python_path=src/

# Specify input paths, etc at the top
[vars]
text_path=%(pimlico_root)s/examples/data/input/bbc/data

# Read in the raw text files
[input_text]
type=pimlico.modules.input.text.raw_text_files
files=%(text_path)s/*

# Tokenize the text using the spaCy tokenizer
[tokenize]
type=pimlico.modules.spacy.tokenize
input=input_text

# Rough filter to remove proper nouns: custom module
[filter_prop_nns]
type=pim_example.modules.filter_prop_nns
input=tokenize

# Build vocabulary from words used:
# can be used to map words to IDs
[vocab]
type=pimlico.modules.corpora.vocab_builder
input=filter_prop_nns
# Only include words that occur >=5 times
threshold=5
```

```
input_text
```
Input reader

↓

```
tokenize
```
spaCy tokenizer

↓

```
filter_prop_nns
```
Custom document-
map module

↓

```
vocab
```
Vocab builder

Figure 2: Full example pipeline which loads a dataset from raw text files, tokenizes it and applies some custom processing. The file, together with the source code for the custom module type, are available at `https://github.com/markgw/pimlico/tree/master/examples`. Alongside is a graphical representation of the pipeline structure.

Often modules read and write *corpora*, consisting of a large number of documents. Pimlico provides a datatype for representing such corpora and a further type system for the **types of the documents** stored within a corpus (rather like Java's *generic* types). For example, a module may specify that it requires as input a corpus whose documents contain tokenized text. All tokenizer modules (of which there are several) provide output corpora with this document type. The corpus datatype takes care of reading and writing large corpora, preserving the order of documents, storing corpus metadata, and much more.

The datatype system is also extensible in custom code. As well as defining custom module types, a pipeline author may wish to define new datatypes to represent the data required as input to the modules or provided as output.

2.3 Running the pipeline

Pimlico provides a command-line interface for parsing and executing pipelines. The interface provides sub-commands to perform different operations relating to a given pipeline. The conf file defining the pipeline is always given as an argument and the first operation is therefore to parse the pipeline and check it for validity. We describe here a few of the most important sub-commands.

status. Outputs a list of all of the modules in the pipeline, reporting the execution status of each. This indicates whether the module has been run; if so, whether it completed successfully or failed; if not, whether it is ready to be run (i.e. all of its input data is available).

Each of the modules is numbered in the list, and this number can be used instead of the module's full name in arguments to all sub-commands.

Given the name of a module, the command out-

103

puts a detailed report on the status of that module and its input and output datasets.

run. Executes a module. An option `--dry` runs all pre-execution checks for the module, without running it. These include checking that required software is installed (see Section 3.2) and performing automatic installation if not.

If all requirements are satisfied, the module will be executed, outputting its progress to the terminal and to module-specific log files. Output datasets are written to module-specific directories, ready to be used by subsequent modules later.

Multiple modules can be run in sequence, or even the entire pipeline. A switch `--all-deps` causes any unexecuted modules upon whose output the specified module(s) depend to be run.

browse. Inspects the data output by a module, stored in its pipeline-internal storage. Inspecting output data by loading the files output by the module would require knowledge of both the Pimlico data storage system and the specific storage formats used by the output datatypes. Instead, this command lets the user inspect the data from a given module (and a given output, if there are multiple).

Datatypes, as part of their definition, along with specification of storage format reading and writing, define how the data can be formatted for display. Multiple formatters may be defined, giving alternative ways to inspect the same data.

For some datatypes, browsing is as simple as outputting some statistics about the data, or a string representing its contents. For corpora, a document-by-document browser is provided, using the Urwid[4] library. Furthermore, the definition of corpus document types determines how an individual document should be displayed in the corpus browser. For example, the tokenized text type shows each sentence on a separate line, with spaces between tokens.

2.4 Document map modules

A common type of module is one that takes input from one or more corpora, applies some independent processing to each document in turn and outputs a new corpus containing the processed data for the same set of documents. For example, we might lower-case the text of each document; map words to IDs from a vocabulary; or perform document-level topic inference using a pre-trained topic model.

---

[4]`http://urwid.org/`

Pimlico makes it easy to define such modules, referred to as *document map modules*. The module executor can be defined using a factory, simply specifying a function to be applied independently to each document. It may also define pre- and post-processing functions to be run before and after the document mapping process.

Such modules lend themselves naturally to parallelization, since separate documents can be processed independently by worker processes in a pool. When a document map module is defined using the factory, this simple type of parallelization is provided by default, using Python's `multiprocessing` module. The user simply needs to specify when running a module how many processes Pimlico should use and this number of workers will be launched to process documents.

Furthermore, any document map module can be set to run in *filter* mode, using the `filter=T` option. This causes its processing to be performed on the fly as required by subsequent modules, instead of being stored to disk. The module then no longer appears in the list of executable modules, since it will be executed as necessary to provide inputs to subsequent modules when they are run. If an output corpora is used a number of times, this approach is inefficient, but if not, and especially if the per-document processing is fast, this can lead to a more streamlined workflow.

3 Some key features

3.1 Data management

Data output by a module is stored ready for other modules to use. Pimlico manages storage locations specific to the pipeline, module and output, and provides the correct version of the data to modules that use the data as input.

Pimlico can be configured to use any location on the filesystem for pipeline-internal storage. Beyond this, the user does not need to concern themselves with the storage structure, nor data storage formats, which are managed by the datatype system.

The command-line interface provides a `reset` command to remove the output data of a given module and any subsequent modules that depend on it. This is useful, for example, if changing a module parameter and rerunning it.

3.2 Software dependencies

Executing a module will often depend on having some software installed. This may be Python pack-

```
[model_train]
type=mycode.modules.train_model
input=tokenized_text
regularization=0.1
layers=5|10

[model_eval]
type=mycode.modules.eval_model
input=model_train
```

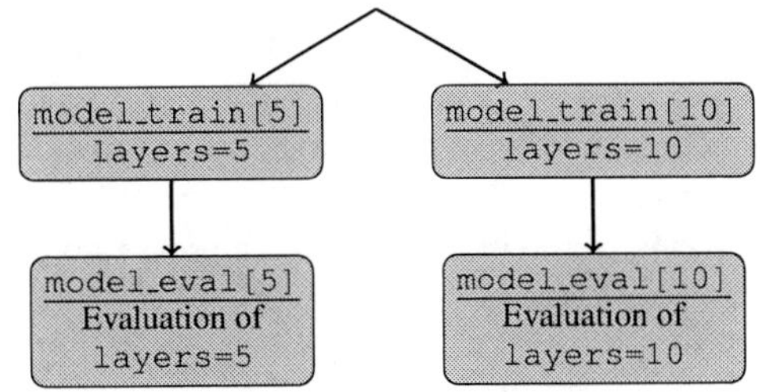

Figure 3: Example pipeline fragment defining a module with alternative values for an option. The diagram shows how the two modules are expanded into branches for the alternatives.

ages, for pure Python modules, or other types of software. For example, Pimlico's core modules include wrappers around the OpenNLP Java toolkit, so running modules of one of these types requires the Java Runtime Environment (JRE) as well as the OpenNLP jar packages.

Pimlico includes a software dependency management system. Software dependencies of many different types can be defined, such as Python packages, Java libraries, compiled C++ binaries and so on. A software dependency definition includes a routine to test whether the software is available and, wherever possible, a routine to automatically install the software in a location that is local to the pipeline's execution environment. For example, Python dependencies can be simply defined by reference to a Pip[5] package, which can be automatically downloaded and installed within a Python virtual environment using the Pip library.

Each module type lists software that it depends on to run as part of its module info. When the user attempts to run a module or checks whether it is ready to run (using the `run` subcommand, Section 2.3), Pimlico checks all the dependencies and installs the necessary software by running the installation routine. A module's executor is strictly separated from its module info and is not loaded until all dependency checks are passed. This allows a module type programmer to freely write code within the executor that loads dependent libraries.

For example, the core module for training topic models using the Gensim toolkit (Řehůřek and Sojka, 2010) can only be run when the Gensim Python library is installed. Its module info declares this dependency. When a user attempts to run a module of this type in a pipeline, Pimlico uses Pip to automatically install the library before executing. In this way, another user subsequently receiving the pipeline does not need to make sure that they have installed this package on their system before running the pipeline.

Requirements of specific versions of dependencies are currently supported for some types of dependencies. In future, this will be extended, including more sophisticated handling of conflicting versions within a pipeline.

3.3 Module alternatives

Examples so far have been of linear pipelines, where each module's output feeds into the input for the next. Pipeline structures are not restricted to this: they may branch arbitrarily by defining multiple modules that take input from the same source, or combine branches with a single module that takes multiple inputs. Several tools are provided to assist concise definition of complex pipeline structures. One we describe here is *module alternatives*.

Consider a hypothetical module type, used in Fig. 3, that takes one input corpus and trains a machine learning model on the data. It has a parameter `layers` which takes a numeric value. We wish to train models with several different values for this parameter and apply the same evaluation to each.

We could do this by defining multiple modules of this type, each training a different model. We would then need to duplicate the subsequent evaluation module to create a version for each model. Pimlico provides a more concise way to do this. We define one module, `model_train`, and specify a list of alternative values for the `layers` parameter: `layers=5|10`. The module is automatically expanded into multiple modules, one for each parameter value. Each is given a distinct name, which may be specified explicitly or automatically generated – `model_train[5]` and `model_train[10]`.

Subsequent modules can also be expanded automatically, propagating the set of alternatives through the pipeline to create separate branches. In our example, we define a single evaluation module

---

`model_eval`, which declares its input to come from `model_train` (the name of the training module prior to expansion). This is expanded into `model_eval[5]` and `model_eval[10]`, each alternative taking input from the respective model training module.

Further details of expansion, combination and naming of module alternatives are given in the documentation.

3.4 Pipeline variants

In a pipeline that processes a large corpus, it can take hours or even days to run a single module. While developing and testing the pipeline, it is not convenient to blindly write the entire configuration and module code without testing, or to have to execute long-running modules simply to get some input data to test custom code later in the pipeline. Pimlico provides a solution: pipeline *variants*.

Variants are independent pipelines, sharing no internal datasets or state, defined by a single config file. A special syntax can be used in the file to prefix lines that are to appear only in a specific variant. Other lines are included in all variants. This can be used to set different values of module parameters in different variants, or even include whole modules in only one variant. When Pimlico is run, it will by default load the standard variant, always called 'main'. A command-line option can specify another variant to load.

The most common use of this is to define a *small* variant, which only processes a small subset of the input data. It may do this, for example, by setting parameters of the input reader, or including a *subset* module to truncate the corpus. The entire pipeline can then be run to test configuration and custom code and sanity-check the resulting datasets, before setting the pipeline running on the full dataset.

Other uses of this feature include running an identical pipeline on different input corpora.

4 Code distribution

One of the key problems that Pimlico sets out to solve is the difficulty of distributing code in a way that makes it easy for others to reproduce and extend the processing. It achieves this by making the full processing pipeline explicit in the pipeline conf file. It is therefore crucial that (a) it is easy to distribute all the necessary files to re-run a pipeline; and (b) it is easy for someone else, given these files to get the pipeline running.

4.1 Releasing pipelines

Three elements of a pipeline need to be distributed: (1) a full description of the processing pipeline; (2) any code needed to run the pipeline that is not part of a standard library; and (3) input data. (1) is trivial with Pimlico, since a pipeline's conf file is all that is needed. (2) requires simply that all code in the path from which custom code is loaded is distributed. This can simply be packaged into an archive together with the conf file. Pimlico's source code does not need to be distributed, since it can be downloaded as necessary. Other libraries will generally be downloaded and installed automatically by Pimlico when the pipeline is to be run, as described in Section 3.2.

Pimlico does not attempt to address the distribution of datasets used as input data. It is usually appropriate to distribute these separately in a way that respects licenses and handles distribution of large files. Much of the time, input data is not specific to a pipeline, but comes from existing corpora.

4.2 Using and extending pipelines

Upon receiving the files providing (1) and (2) above, you can use Pimlico's *bootstrap* tool to set up a working environment for running the pipeline. A Python script, `bootstrap.py`, is available from the online documentation. This reads the config file to check what version of Pimlico was used when it was originally run and downloads the same release. It then prompts Pimlico to set up a Python virtual environment and install core software dependencies. After this, the pipeline is ready to be loaded and run.

Having loaded a pipeline and set up the environment, it is easy to extend or adjust the pipeline to run further experiments or build on the previous work. New modules can be added and parameters to the existing modules changed. Pimlico's system of standardized internal datatypes for passing data between modules also makes it straightforward to apply the same pipeline to a different dataset. All that is required is a suitable *input reader* for the new data (see Section 2.1). This supplies the dataset in a standard, pipeline-internal format, so the rest of the pipeline can be run without modification.

5 Core module types

Pimlico comes with a large number of *core* module types, for which a pipeline author needs to write no code, but simply define the module configuration in their config file. This set is being constantly expanded.

The following list gives some examples of core module types provided with Pimlico. The full list is available in the documentation.

- Generic corpus manipulation, including shuffling, concatenation, truncation, subsampling, random splitting

- Vocabulary building, word-to-ID mapping

- Gensim topic model training (Řehůřek and Sojka, 2010)

- Malt dependency parsing (Nivre et al., 2006)

- OpenNLP[6] tokenization, POS tagging, constituency parsing

- Word embedding (Mikolov et al., 2013) loading, manipulation, storing

- Word embedding training using `word2vec` (Mikolov et al., 2013) and *fastText* (Mikolov et al., 2018)

- Text normalization (lower-casing, etc.)

- Scikit-learn classifier training (Pedregosa et al., 2011)

The core module types also serve as a reference for defining custom module types. For example, the current release contains several module types wrapping tools from OpenNLP, but not coreference resolution. If a user wishes to use the OpenNLP coreference resolver, it is a relatively simple matter to define a custom module in their own source directory, using one of the existing wrappers as a model.

6 A worked example

An example of a full pipeline config file is shown in Fig. 2. This simple pipeline loads a corpus from a directory containing text files, each representing a single document. It applies tokenization to each document using the core document-map module that wraps spaCy's tokenizer.

Then it applies some custom processing to the tokens of each document, using a module type defined specifically for this pipeline and found in

---

the accompanying source directory[7]. The resulting corpus is finally passed through the core vocabulary builder, which builds a vocabulary from all the words used in the corpus.

7 Software licenses

Pimlico itself is released under the GNU LGPLv3 license. However, it provides access to a large number of software packages, with a wide range of different licenses. Software dependencies are installed only when required, so use of Pimlico does not fall under the terms of all of these – only those required by the modules of the user's pipeline.

It can be important to know what licenses apply to all the code used by a pipeline. The Pimlico codebase keeps track of the licenses that apply to software that may be installed to support the use of the core module types. The command `licenses` produces a list of the licenses of all of the software used by a given pipeline, or alternatively just particular modules.

8 Related toolkits

Some proprietary tools exist for similar purposes to Pimlico[8]. However, the use of a proprietary tool to build a pipeline in itself precludes easy replication and extension by other authors, so we focus here on open source tools.

Two recently released examples of toolkits for building NLP pipelines are *Forte* and *PSI*. Forte (Liu et al., 2020) is constructed around similar concepts to Pimlico and it too provides wrappers around other NLP toolkits. PSI (Gralinski et al., 2012, Platform for Situated Intelligence) is similar in its goals and design to Forte. Pimlico's focus is on control of the execution of static pipelines to process large datasets and the management of the data as it passes through the pipeline. For these purposes, it provides a powerful set of tools not built into other toolkits. It does not provide facilities to run pipelines in a way that can be dynamically integrated into other systems. We see this as a distinct use case with different design requirements, one that is well catered for by toolkits like Forte and PSI.

Many other toolkits focus specifically on NLP tools, allowing models to be trained and applied

---

[7]The source code is not shown here, but the full example, including code, can be found in the documentation.

[8]For example, I2E, https://www.linguamatics.com/products/i2e.

for standard NLP tasks. Some provide their own structures for defining pipelines that chain multiple tasks (e.g., Qi et al., 2020; Manning et al., 2014; Honnibal and Montani, 2017). Pimlico provides a general framework for processing of large datasets, incorporating NLP tasks by providing wrappers around toolkits such as these. Unlike with these toolkits, data loading, pre- and post-processing can be handled in a single pipeline definition, requiring minimal (or no) code to be written.

Other general toolkits exist for building and running data-processing pipelines, such as Bonobo[9]. An alternative approach to developing Pimlico would have been to define a library of modules for NLP-specific tasks that could be used from such a toolkit. We chose instead to develop an infrastructure tuned to the type of corpus processing and data management that is typical in NLP experiments and tasks.

9   Conclusions

We have introduced the Pimlico toolkit for building pipelines for processing large corpora. We set out to address four key goals in improving the process of writing, running and distributing pipelines.

1. Pimlico provides **clear documentation** of pipelines in the form of a simple definition in a text file, containing pipeline structure and parameters for every step.

2. It is easy to incorporate **standard NLP tasks** using the core modules provided with the toolkit, for which only a definition of inputs and parameters is required. Among these are wrappers for commonly used NLP toolkits.

3. Integrating **custom code** into the pipeline is straightforward, by defining custom module types. An extensive array of factories, tools and templates means that typically only a small amount of code is required beyond the code to be executed.

4. The resulting pipeline definition and code can easily be **packaged and distributed**. Tools are provided to make the process of setting up the execution environment and installing software quick and simple. It is then possible to **extend or adjust** the pipeline by editing the conf file, or **apply to other datasets** by replacing input modules.

---

[9]`https://www.bonobo-project.org/`

The toolkit effectively addresses common problems encountered in using NLP tools to process large datasets, releasing code for experiments or other corpus processing for others to use, and running someone else's released code in a new environment or on new data. As such, we present it as a key contribution to free distribution of code to accompany NLP research and replicability of experiments.

9.1   Future work

Pimlico is under active development and new features are constantly being added. Several planned enhancements are worth noting in particular.

We plan to continue to expand the set of core modules to include wrappers around other NLP and machine learning toolkits. Many excellent new NLP toolkits have been released in recent years and have yet to be wrapped by core Pimlico modules, or have only partial wrappers. In many case, the addition of a wrapper is quick and requires only a small amount of code. Further commonly used pre-processing methods not currently covered by core modules, like Byte-Pair Encoding, would make pipeline development for modern NLP methods faster.

Pimlico includes a number of input readers for standard formats in which corpora are stored. However, many different formats are used for NLP corpora, often specific to one corpus. We plan to expand the set of core input reader modules, to allow more corpora to be read into a pipeline without requiring custom module code.

Modules currently assume that a corpus is a fixed unit, with a known size. Whilst this is often the case, there are exceptions. For example, if data is generated on the fly, a corpus could in effect have an infinite length. In future, it may be desirable to extend Pimlico's conception of a corpus to cover such cases.

Pipeline development and use could be helped by a visual tool to inspect pipeline structure and execution status. This could take the form of a tool to output images like those in the figures of this paper, or an interactive graphical interface as an alternative to the command-line interface.

We plan to add a system similar to the management of software dependencies for fetching pre-trained models. For example, OpenNLP provides models for a number of languages for some of its components. Currently, the user must download these models themselves in order to be able to run a module that uses them. The specification of which model to use, however, is part of the pipeline config. The new model management system would be able to download the models prior to running the module in question, just as software dependencies are downloaded and installed automatically.

We have chosen not to build into the toolkit any system for storing, fetching or managing input data. However, corpora are increasingly available online in standard repositories and formats, thanks to projects like Hugging Face[10]. Pipelines using such corpora could include a specification of where their input data can be retrieved from, such that it could be automatically downloaded as part of the execution process.

10   Acknowledgements

Pimlico has been developed to support work in a number of different projects. It has been supported by: European Commission FP7 framework grant 611560 (WHIM); the Academy of Finland grant 12933481 (Digital Language Typology). European Union Horizon 2020 research and innovation programme grants 770299 (NewsEye) and 825153 (EMBEDDIA).

References

Filip Gralinski, Krzysztof Jassem, and Marcin Junczys-Dowmunt. 2012. Psi-toolkit: A natural language processing pipeline. *Computational Linguistics*, 458:27–39.

Matthew Honnibal and Ines Montani. 2017. spaCy 2: Natural language understanding with Bloom embeddings, convolutional neural networks and incremental parsing. *To appear*.

Zhengzhong Liu, Avinash Bukkittu, Mansi Gupta, Pengzhi Gao, Swapnil Singhavi, Atif Ahmed, Wei Wei, Zecong Hu, Haoran Shi, Eric P. Xing, and Zhiting Hu. 2020. Forte: Composing Diverse NLP tools For Text Retrieval, Analysis and Generation.

Christopher D. Manning, Mihai Surdeanu, John Bauer, Jenny Finkel, Steven J. Bethard, and David McClosky. 2014. The Stanford CoreNLP natural language processing toolkit. In *Association for Computational Linguistics (ACL) System Demonstrations*, pages 55–60.

Tomas Mikolov, Edouard Grave, Piotr Bojanowski, Christian Puhrsch, and Armand Joulin. 2018. Advances in pre-training distributed word representations. In *Proceedings of the International Conference on Language Resources and Evaluation (LREC 2018)*.

Tomas Mikolov, Wen-tau Yih, and Geoffrey Zweig. 2013. Linguistic regularities in continuous space word representations. In *Proceedings of the 2013 Conference of the North American Chapter of the Association for Computational Linguistics: Human Language Technologies*, pages 746–751, Atlanta, Georgia. Association for Computational Linguistics.

Joakim Nivre, Johan Hall, and Jens Nilsson. 2006. Maltparser: A data-driven parser-generator for dependency parsing.

F. Pedregosa, G. Varoquaux, A. Gramfort, V. Michel, B. Thirion, O. Grisel, M. Blondel, P. Prettenhofer, R. Weiss, V. Dubourg, J. Vanderplas, A. Passos, D. Cournapeau, M. Brucher, M. Perrot, and E. Duchesnay. 2011. Scikit-learn: Machine learning in Python. *Journal of Machine Learning Research*, 12:2825–2830.

Peng Qi, Yuhao Zhang, Yuhui Zhang, Jason Bolton, and Christopher D. Manning. 2020. Stanza: A Python natural language processing toolkit for many human languages. In *Proceedings of the 58th Annual Meeting of the Association for Computational Linguistics: System Demonstrations*.

Radim Řehůřek and Petr Sojka. 2010. Software Framework for Topic Modelling with Large Corpora. In *Proceedings of the LREC 2010 Workshop on New Challenges for NLP Frameworks*, pages 45–50, Valletta, Malta. ELRA. `http://is.muni.cz/publication/884893/en`.

---

[10]`https://huggingface.co/datasets`

PySBD: Pragmatic Sentence Boundary Disambiguation

Nipun Sadvilkar
Episource LLC
nipun.sadvilkar@episource.com

Mark Neumann
Allen Institute for Artificial Intelligence
markn@allenai.org

Abstract

In this paper, we present a rule-based sentence boundary disambiguation Python package that works out-of-the-box for 22 languages. We aim to provide a realistic segmenter which can provide logical sentences even when the format and domain of the input text is unknown. In our work, we adapt the *Golden Rules Set* (a language specific set of sentence boundary exemplars) originally implemented as a ruby gem *pragmatic_segmenter*[1] which we ported to Python with additional improvements and functionality. PySBD passes 97.92% of the Golden Rule Set examplars for English, an improvement of 25% over the next best open source Python tool.

1 Introduction

Sentence Boundary Disambiguation (SBD), also known as sentence boundary detection, is a key underlying task for natural language processing. In many NLP pipelines, gold standard SBD often assumed, and acts as a primary input to downstream NLP tasks such as machine translation, named entity recognition and coreference resolution. However, in real world scenarios, text occurs in a variety of input modalities, such as HTML forms, PDFs and word processing doccument formats.

Although SBD is considered to be a simple problem, it becomes more complex in other domains due to unorthodox use of punctuation symbols. For example, drug names in medical documents, case citations in legal text and references in academic articles all use punctuation in ways which are uncommon in newswire documents. Simple SBD approaches for English web text (treating - "?!:;." - as end of sentence markers) covers a majority of cases, but an ideal SBD system should be able

to disambiguate these edge case scenarios and be robust to *known* textual variation.

Our contributions in this paper are describing an open-source, freely available tool for pragmatic sentence boundary disambiguation. In particular, we describe the implementation details of PySBD, evaluate it in comparison to other open source SBD tools and discuss it's natural extensibility due to it's rule based nature.

2 Related Work

Sentence segmentation methods can be broadly divided into 3 approaches: i) rules-based, requiring hand crafted rules/heuristics; ii) Supervised machine learning, requiring annotated datasets, and iii) Unsupervised machine learning, requiring distributional statistics derived from raw text.

(Palmer and Hearst, 1997) use decision trees and neural networks in a supervised, feature based SBD model, requiring part of speech information and training data. (Kiss and Strunk, 2006) design punkt, an unsupervised SBD model centered around the observation that abbreviations are the main confounders for rule based sentence boundary models. Although it is unsupervised, punkt requires the computation of various co-occurence and distributional statistics of a relevant corpora; as PySBD is rule-based, it does not require a initial corpus of text. (Evang et al., 2013) cast SBD as a character sequence labelling problem and use features from a recurrent neural network language model to train a CRF labelling model.

Many SBD papers reject rule-based approaches due to non-robustness, maintainability and performance. We reject these conclusions, and instead focus on the *positive* features of rule-based systems - namely that their errors are interpretable, rules can be adjusted incrementally and their performance is often on-par with learnt statistical models.

---

[1] https://github.com/diasks2/pragmatic_segmenter

Proceedings of Second Workshop for NLP Open Source Software (NLP-OSS), pages 110–114
Virtual Conference, November 19, 2020. ©2020 Association for Computational Linguistics

Issues with benchmarks on PTB/WSJ corpora
SBD systems have historically been benchmarked
on the Wall Street Journal/Penn Treebank corpora
(Read et al., 2012). The majority of the sentences
found in the Penn Tree Bank are sentences that
end with a regular word followed by a period, testing the same sentence boundary cases repeatedly.
In the Brown Corpus 90% of potential sentence
boundaries come after a regular word. Although
the Wall Street Journal corpus is richer with numerical values, abbreviations and only 53% according to (Gale and Church, 1993) of sentences end
with a regular word followed by a period (Mikheev,
2002).

Given that commonly used training/evaluation
corpora do not contain a particularly large amount
of sentence marker variation, we use a *Golden
Rule Set* to enumerate edge cases observed in sentence boundaries. The *Golden Rule Set* contains 48
hand-constructed rules, designed to cover sentence
boundaries across a variety of domains. The GRS
is interpretable (each rule targets a specific type of
sentence boundary) and easy to extend with new
examples of particular sentence boundary markers.

3 Implementation

PySBD is divided into four high level components:
The Segmenter, Processor, Language and Cleaner
sub-modules.

The *Segmenter* class is the public API to PySBD.
It allows a user to set up a *Segmenter* in their language of choice, as well as specify additional options such as text cleaning and char_span functionality. The *Segmenter* requires a two character ISO
639-1 code[2] to process input text. Text extracted
from a PDF or obtained from OCR systems typically contains unusually formatted text, such as
line breaks in the middle of sentences. This can
be handled with the *doc_type* option, or for more
aggressive text cleaning, the *clean* functionality
performs additional pre-filtering of the input text,
removing repeated and unnecessary punctuation.

The *Processor* contains the sentence segmentation logic, using rules to segment the input text.
The *Processor* contains several groups of sentence
segmentation rules, some of which are universal
across languages, and some of which are language
specific. These are grouped as follows:

- Common

- Standard
- ListItemReplacer
- AbbreviationReplacer
- ExclamationWords
- BetweenPunctuation

The *Processor* identifies sentence boundaries by
manipulating input text in 3 stages. Firstly, rules
are applied to alter the input text by adding intermediate unicode characters as placeholders to signify
that particular pieces of punctuation are not sentence boundaries. The segment stage identifies true
sentence boundaries by bypassing unicode characters and segments text into sentences using a much
simpler regex rule. Finally, the manipulated text is
transformed into original text form by replacing the
unicode placeholders with their original characters.

The *Language* holds all the languages supported
by PySBD. Each language is built on top of two
sub-components - *Common* and *Standard* - involving basic rules prevalent across languages. *Common* rules encompass the main sentence boundary
regexes; AM-PM regexes handle numerically expressed time periods; number regexes handle pe-
riod/newline characters before or after single/multi-
digit numbers and additional rules handle quota-
tion, parenthesis, and numerical references within
the input text. The *Standard* rule set contains regex
patterns to handle single/double punctuation, geolo-
cation references, fileformat mentions and ellipsis
in input text. The *ListItemReplacer* rule set handles
itemized, ordered/unordered lists; the *AbbreviationReplacer* contains language specific common
abbreviations. Finally, the *ExclaimationWords* and
BetweenPunctuation rules handle language specific
exclamations and more complicated punctuation
cases.

In practice, text encountered in the wild is noisy,
containing extraneous line breaks, unicode characters, uncommon spacing and hangovers from document structure. In order to handle this, PySBD
provides an optional component to handle such
texts. The *Cleaner* is passed as an option through
the top-level *Segmenter* component and provides
text cleaning rules for cases like irregular newline
characters, tables of contents, URLs, HTML tags
and text involving no space between sentences. As
the text cleaning rules perform a destructive operation, this feature is incompatible with the *char_span*
functionality, as mapping back to character indices
within the original text is no longer possible.

---

[2]https://en.wikipedia.org/wiki/List_
of_ISO_639-1_codes

4 Experimental Setup

Data Contrary to the WSJ, Brown and GENIA datasets mentioned in (Read et al., 2012), we use language specific *Golden Rules Sets* for our experiments. There are total 22 Golden Rules sets for following languages - English, Marathi, Hindi, Bulgarian, Español (Spanish), Russian, Arabic, Amharic, Armenian, Persian, Urdu, Polish, Chinese, Dutch, Danish, French, Italian, Greek, Burmese, Japanese, Deutsch (Germen), Kazakh.

The *Golden Rules Sets* are devised by considering possible sentence boundaries per language as well as considering different domains. For example the English language GRS is comprised of 48 golden rules[3] from formal and informal domains to cover a wide variety of phenomena. For example, news articles are grammatically and punctually correct; scientific literature often involves numbers, abbreviations and bibliography references, and Informal domain like Web Text - E-mail, Social media text involves irregular punctuation and ellipses. To ensure our rules-based system built with respect to the *Golden Rules Set* generalizes well in the real world, we have also performed a benchmark comparison on the GENIA corpus (Kim et al., 2003), a dataset of linguistic annotations on top of the abstracts of biomedical papers. The GENIA corpus provides both raw and segmented abstracts, which we use as natural data for our evaluation.

Setup We evaluate PySBD and other segmentation tools on two corpora - the *English Golden Rules Set* and GENIA corpus.

5 Comparison to alternatives

Table 1 summarizes accuracy of PySBD and the alternative Python SBD modules on *English Golden Rules Set* and the GENIA corpus. The supervised machine learning based sentence segmenters, stanza (Qi et al., 2020) and spacy dependency parsing (spacy dep) (Honnibal and Montani, 2017) are slower compared to other python modules and seem to segment incorrectly when text contains mixed case words or abrupt punctuation within words, which is prevalent in biomedical domain. Inability to generalise on out of domain corpora is a main drawback of using supervised learning for SBD.

Tool	GRS	GENIA
blingfire	75.00	86.95
syntok	68.75	80.90
spaCy	52.08	76.80
spacy dep	54.17	39.20
stanza	72.92	63.40
NLTK	56.25	87.95
PySBD	97.92	97.00

Table 1: Accuracy (%) of PySBD compared to other open source SBD packages with respect to the English *Golden Rule Set* and the GENIA corpus.

NLTK's (Bird, 2006) *PunktSentenceTokenizer* is based on an unsupervised algorithm (Kiss and Strunk, 2006) and fails to segment text containing brackets, itemized text and abbreviations as sentence boundaries. In contrast, practically all the modules following a rules-based approach - blingfire (Bling Team, 2020), syntok (Leitner, 2020) and PySBD - appear to be faster and more accurate on both corpora. Blingfire and syntok modules struggle when text has decimal numbers, abbreviations, brackets and mixed cased words prior to or following the true sentence boundary. Lastly, the 3% drop in PySBD's accuracy on the GENIA corpus is caused by splitting itemized text into segments, whereas the GENIA abstracts contain single sentences with multiple bulleted lists. We feel that this segmentation choice comes down to preference, and both are equally valid.

Table 2 shows the runtime performance of each module on the entire text of "The Adventures of Sherlock Holmes" [4], which contains 10K lines and 100K words. The experiment was performed on Intel Core i5 processor running at 2.9 GHz clock speed. Blingfire module is the fastest since it is extremely performance oriented (at cost of reduced maintainability/extensibility). Although PySBD is slower than several alternatives, it is considerably faster than running full pipelines and is a good choice for users who require high accuracy segmentations. Our comparisons cover a variety of different implementations (C++, Cython, Pytorch), approaches (model-based, distributional, rule-based) and are representative of practical choices for an NLP practitioner.

---

[3] https://s3.amazonaws.com/
tm-town-nlp-resources/golden_rules.txt

[4] http://www.gutenberg.org/files/1661/
1661-0.txt

Tool	Speed(ms)
blingfire	85.24
syntok	1764.11
spaCy	1523.20
spacy dep	26850.69
stanza	48383.46
NLTK	780.49
PySBD	9483.96

Table 2: Speed benchmark on the entire text of "The adventures of Sherlock Holmes" for PySBD compared to other open source SBD packages.

6 Discussion

6.1 Package Development

We use Test-driven Development (TDD) whilst developing, first write a test for one of the rule from *Golden Rules Set* that fails intentionally, before writing functional code to pass the test. The approach used by our python module is rules-based. We employ Python's standard library module called re[5] which provides regular expression (regex) matching operations for text processing.

6.2 Non-destructive Segmentation

Our module does non-destructive sentence tokenization, as when dealing with noisy text, character offsets into the original documents are often desirable. The indices are obtained after postprocess stage by mapping post-processed sentence start indices into the original input text. Upon enabling this feature, the output format is a list of *TextSpan* objects containing sentence, start and end character indices. The character spans makes it easy to navigate to any sentence within the unaltered original text.

6.3 Multilingual Implementation

NLP research predominantly focuses on developing dataset and methods for English language despite the many benefits of working on other languages (Ruder, 2020). An advantage of PySBD's rule-based approach is straightforward extension to new languages. PySBD has support for 22 languages spanning many language families, each having its own *Golden Rules Set*. Adding support for a new language involves adding language specific rules to the *Golden Rules Set* and adding language specific punctuation markers to a new language

Language	Accuracy (%)
Amharic	80.95%
Arabic	70.40%
Armenian	63.75%
Bulgarian	93.35%
Burmese	48.05%
Chinese	85.35%
Danish	91.40%
Deutsch	80.95%
Dutch	91.40%
French	91.90%
Greek	91.05%
Hindi	88.50%
Italian	90.55%
Japanese	96.45%
Kazakh	63.20%
Marathi	92.60%
Persian	84.95%
Polish	55.48%
Russian	88.55%
Spanish	92.65%
Urdu	77.55%

Table 3: Accuracy of PySBD's multilingual modules on the OPUS-100 multilingual corpus test sets, containing 2000 sentences per language. Each language module build with respect to its own GRS.

module. This modular language support allows PySBD to be maintained in a community driven way by open source NLP practitioners. For example, we extended the original Ruby pragmatic segmeter by adding support for Marathi by forming the Golden Rules and identifying Marathi language specific sentence syntax, punctuations and abbreviations resulting in a usable module within 1 hour of work. If you would like to contribute to the PySBD module by updating existing GRS or by adding support for new language then refer to our contributing guidelines[6] to get you started.

We benchmarked PySBD on the OPUS-100 parallel multilingual corpus, covering 100 languages (Tiedemann, 2012). We used the test sets of 21 of the languages excluding English which contain 2000 sentences per language (Due to unavailability of the test set for Armenian, we used its train set, containing 7000 sentences). Due to noisy nature of OPUS (on inspection, multiple sentences were present on individual lines in the test sets) and lack

---

[5]https://docs.python.org/3/library/re.html

[6]https://github.com/nipunsadvilkar/pySBD/blob/master/CONTRIBUTING.md

of language specific knowledge to form rules and abbreviation list we observed weak performance in a few languages like Burmese, Polish, Kazakh, Armenian, etc. Shortcomings of such languages can be improved in community driven way by collaborating with multilingual NLP practitioners.

7   Conclusion

In this paper, we have described PySBD, a *pragmatic* sentence boundary disambiguation model. PySBD is open source, has over 98% test coverage and integrates easily with existing natural language processing pipelines. PySBD currently supports 22 languages, and is easily extensible, with 57 projects depending on it at the time of writing. Although slower than some alternatives implemented in low level languages such as C++, PySBD successfully disambiguates 97% of sentence boundaries in a *Golden Rule Set* and is robust across domains and noisy text.

References

Steven Bird. 2006. Nltk: The natural language toolkit. *ArXiv*, cs.CL/0205028.

Beyond Language Understanding Bling Team, Microsoft. 2020. Blingfire : A lightning fast finite state machine and regular expression manipulation library. https://github.com/microsoft/BlingFire/tree/master/ldbsrc/sbd.

Kilian Evang, Valerio Basile, Grzegorz Chrupała, and Johan Bos. 2013. Elephant: Sequence labeling for word and sentence segmentation. In *Proceedings of the 2013 Conference on Empirical Methods in Natural Language Processing*, pages 1422–1426, Seattle, Washington, USA. Association for Computational Linguistics.

William A. Gale and Kenneth W. Church. 1993. A program for aligning sentences in bilingual corpora. *Computational Linguistics*, 19(1):75–102.

Matthew Honnibal and Ines Montani. 2017. spaCy 2: Natural language understanding with Bloom embeddings, convolutional neural networks and incremental parsing. https://github.com/explosion/spaCy. To appear.

Jin-Dong Kim, Tomoko Ohta, Yuka Tateisi, and Jun'ichi Tsujii. 2003. Genia corpus - a semantically annotated corpus for bio-textmining. *Bioinformatics*, 19 Suppl 1:i180–2.

Tibor Kiss and Jan Strunk. 2006. Unsupervised multilingual sentence boundary detection. *Computational Linguistics*, 32(4):485–525.

Florian Leitner. 2020. Syntok : Text tokenization and sentence segmentation (segtok v2). https://github.com/fnl/syntok.

Andrei Mikheev. 2002. Periods, capitalized words, etc. *Computational Linguistics*, 28(3):289–318.

David D. Palmer and Marti A. Hearst. 1997. Adaptive multilingual sentence boundary disambiguation. *Computational Linguistics*, 23(2):241–267.

Peng Qi, Yuhao Zhang, Yuhui Zhang, Jason Bolton, and Christopher D. Manning. 2020. Stanza: A python natural language processing toolkit for many human languages. In *ACL*.

Jonathon Read, Rebecca Dridan, Stephan Oepen, and Lars Jørgen Solberg. 2012. Sentence boundary detection: A long solved problem? *Computational Linguistics*, pages 985–994.

Sebastian Ruder. 2020. Why You Should Do NLP Beyond English. http://ruder.io/nlp-beyond-english.

Jörg Tiedemann. 2012. Parallel data, tools and interfaces in opus. In *LREC*.

iobes: A Library for Span-Level Processing

Brian Lester
Independent
blester125@gmail.com

Abstract

Many tasks in natural language processing, such as named entity recognition and slot-filling, involve identifying and labeling specific spans of text. In order to leverage common models, these tasks are often recast as sequence labeling tasks. Each token is given a label and these labels are prefixed with special tokens such as `B-` or `I-`. After a model assigns labels to each token, these prefixes are used to group the tokens into spans.

Properly parsing these annotations is critical for producing fair and comparable metrics; however, despite its importance, there is not an easy-to-use, standardized, programmatically integratable library to help work with span labeling. To remedy this, we introduce our open-source library, *iobes*. *iobes* is used for parsing, converting, and processing spans represented as token level decisions.

1 Introduction

Tasks like named entity recognition, finding mentions for real world things in text, and slot-filling, finding mentions of relevant objects, often in a dialogue, require identifying contiguous sections of the input text and classifying them into one of several pre-defined classes. While some work solves span labeling by scoring all possible spans, followed by filtering with a threshold (Lee et al., 2017), most work recasts span identification as a token labeling task (Tjong Kim Sang and De Meulder, 2003; Bender et al., 2003; Collobert et al., 2011; Ma and Hovy, 2016; Lample et al., 2016). Special prefixes like `B-` are used in conjunction with token level type labels, like "PER" for person or "ORG" for organization, to signal where different spans begin and end. Once a standard sequence labeling model is used to produce tags for each token, we use these prefixes to convert the token level annotations into spans. For example, the token `B-LOC` means that we need to start a location span here. The tokens labeled with `I-LOC` are continuations of this span. Finally, a token of a different type, or the special `O` label, representing a token that is "outside" of a span, will signal the end of our span. Once we have decoded our spans, we often use a metric like exact match F1, where both the span type and the span boundaries have to match, to compare our predicted spans to the reference spans.

Unfortunately, there are many subtle places where implementations of this approach to span labeling can diverge. The semantics of these special prefixes can change. There are multiple encoding schemes that are all equally expressive but have differences in how easy it is for a model to learn them (Ratinov and Roth, 2009). Many common datasets are old and therefore distributed in older formats. Researchers often convert these datasets to newer formats, but differences or bugs in this process can introduce discrepancies in the data used to train models. Policy decisions on handling token level annotations that do not conform to the rules of the encoding scheme also introduce differences that render different models incomparable.

The problems mentioned above all stem from the lack of a community wide standardization on how to handle these edge cases. The lack of common tooling for working with these spans, represented as token level annotations, has led to many rolling their own, slightly different implementations. We introduce the *iobes* library. A Python (Van Rossum and Drake, 2009) library that encapsulates all the rough edges of processing and evaluating spans. We aim to provide the community with a single, easy-to-use toolkit whose adoption will ensure the comparability of span labeling metrics reported by different researchers.

Proceedings of Second Workshop for NLP Open Source Software (NLP-OSS), pages 115–119
Virtual Conference, November 19, 2020. ©2020 Association for Computational Linguistics

2 Formats

There are several forms that span encoding via token labeling can take. Later we will see how these multiple formats—and the conversion between them—are the cause of many problems, but for now we will summarize them here.

- **IOB**: The original span labeling format introduced by Ramshaw and Marcus (1995). In this format, tokens that are not part of a span are labeled with `O`. Tokens that are part of a span are tagged with the span type, prefixed with a `I-`; for example, `I-PER` is part of a span representing a person. The special `B-` prefix is used to demarcate two spans of the same type that touch.

- **BIO**: A simple extension of the IOB format where all entities, regardless of what entities they touch, begin with a `B-`. An advantage of this format is that it is no longer contextual. The span "Real Madrid" will always have the tags `B-ORG I-ORG`, regardless of what the previous span is. In the IOB scheme, this would be `I-ORG I-ORG` by default and would only use the `B-` tag when preceded by another span of type "ORG".

- **IOBES**: A further extension to the BIO labeling scheme. It adds two new tags types. `E-` is used to label the token that is the last item of a span. The new `S-` prefix is used for span that only include a single token. In our example the span "Real Madrid" would be labeled as `B-ORG E-ORG`. This span encoding format has several names. BILOU is the same scheme, but uses a `L-` instead of `E-` for span ending tokens and uses `U-` rather than `S-` for single token spans. There is also the BMEWO format. This was the original name for the format introduced in Borthwick (1999). It uses `W-` in place of `S-` and it actually replaces the tokens inside of the spans, using `M-` meaning middle over `I-` for inside. This format has be demonstrated to yield better performing models (Ratinov and Roth, 2009).

3 Discrepancies

Differences in how processing of these spans is done can cause discrepancies in both the datasets and the evaluation metrics used by researchers. While this section draws examples of errors from specific pieces of work, we would like to emphasize these are not failures on the part of the authors, but rather a failing of the community for not providing tested, reusable tooling.

3.1 Conversion

Many older datasets like CONLL 2003 (Tjong Kim Sang and De Meulder, 2003) are distributed in older formats such as IOB. Researchers then convert them to newer formats like IOBES. This conversion can go wrong. For example, the data used in Yang et al. (2018) contained such errors. A Github issue[1] points out that two entities, one of length one followed by one of length two, in the original IOB1 format (represented by the tag sequence `I-MISC B-MISC I-MISC`) were incorrectly converted into three separate, length-one entities. The author states that this transformed data was received from a friend, meaning that there is probably another paper—that likely did not open source their data and code—that has this same error. The authors analysis claims that the number of these mistakes are too small to affect the results when the metric is aggregated over the whole test sets. Regardless of whether this bug affected these particular results or not, it is worrying that different researchers are using different datasets. After all, the point of shared datasets is to hold the input data constant, allowing one to demonstrate the improvements are truly from their new modeling approach.

3.2 Formatting

A second place where errors can creep in is the formatting of the token level annotations. Different encoding schemes have different rules, for example, in the BIO tagging scheme each entitiy needs to start with a `B-` tag. This means that `I-` tokens can only follow `B-` tokens of the same type. In the data set for the WNUT 2017 shared task (Derczynski et al., 2017), there was an entity of type "creative-work" that incorrectly started with an `I-` token. While this has since been fixed[2], gold data that does not strictly follow the rules of the encoding scheme puts toolkits that provide tagger output modules that enforce constraints based on the tagging scheme, such as AllenNLP (Gardner et al., 2017) and Mead-Baseline (Pressel et al., 2018), at a disadvantage. If you constrain your output to follow the encoding scheme, but the answer does not

---

[1] https://github.com/jiesutd/NCRFpp/issues/36
[2] https://github.com/leondz/emerging_entities_17/pull/4

follow it, your model literally cannot get this example correct. Errors such as these can also cause problems for encoding scheme conversion code, which often assumes that the input is well-formed. Different error handling policies will create different gold data.

3.3 Entity Resolution

Yet another problem area is the handling of malformed output sequences. As we established earlier, there are rules on the allowed transitions from one tag to another that are dictated by the span encoding scheme. With the data-driven modeling approaches that dominate these tasks, there is no guarantee that the output sequence will be well-formed. How these errors are handled can cause large differences in the output entities.

The evaluation script from the CONLL 2000 shared task (Tjong Kim Sang and Buchholz, 2000) on noun-phrase chunking, `conlleval.pl`, uses a policy that can be best described as: A difference in the types of tags triggers a shift in spans. This means that when you have a `B-PER` followed by an `I-LOC` you would create two spans, one for the person and one for the location, even though the location span did not legally start. The behavior is a clear outgrowth of the fact that this script originally was designed for IOB, but it is the de facto entity resolution policy.

In the NCRF++ toolkit, Yang et al. (2018) use a different resolution strategy. As discussed in a Github issue[3], they only process legal spans. This means that they only look for `B-` tags to start entities and the corresponding `E-` tag to end it. They ignore changes in the type of intervening `I-` tags. As demonstrated in Table 1, this can produce very different entities when compared to the `conlleval.pl` outputs.

4 Our Library

To help avoid these kind of preventable mistakes, and to create a standardized policy on the creation of entities from illegal tag sequences, we introduce our library *iobes*.

4.1 Parsing

Our library includes robust parsers for turning lists of token level annotations into spans, represented by the named tuple outlined in Listing 1.

[3]https://github.com/jiesutd/NCRFpp/issues/87

```python
class Span(NamedTuple):
    type: str
    start: int
    end: int
    tokens: List[int]
```

Listing 1: Our Span class. The value of the end attribute is one more than the index of the final token in the span. This formulation allows for recovery of the tokens in the span via Python list slicing.

Our library handles the IOB, BIO, IOBES, BILOU, and BMEWO schemes.

When encountering malformed token sequences, our library follows the `conlleval.pl` method of entity resolution where new entities are created when there is a difference in type between adjacent token labels. In addition to producing a list of spans, our library also creates a list of errors. These errors can help localize where illegal transitions are occurring. Common errors are things like switching entity types within a span, ending spans without an `E-` token, and staring spans with an `I-`.

4.2 Conversion

Our library also includes tooling for conversion between all of these different formats. When converting a malformed sequence of tokens, there is inherent uncertainty in what the true sequence of spans was. We discussed multiple entity resolution above, but we found that choosing one when converting malformed gold labels was overly prescriptive. Unlike the models predictions, we can have humans fix these malformed gold sequences. Rather than making some policy decision on the handling malformed sequences, we raise an exception and return the list of errors to help the user fix their gold labels.

4.3 Legal Transitions

The span encoding formats dictate which tokens can follow others, for example, the IOBES scheme says the all entities must end with an `E-`, therefore an `O` cannot follow an `I-`. While most statistical models, especially those that have a global loss function, like the conditional random field (CRF) (Lafferty et al., 2001), learn these relations, it is not guaranteed that these rules are followed.

Our library is able to enumerate the legality of all possible transitions. While models encode these rules as soft, learned constraints embedded in the model parameters, they can also be enforced by

Index	Surface	Gold Tag	Predicted Tag	Gold	NCRF++	`conlleval.pl`
0	to	`O`	`O`			
1	First	`B-ORG`	`B-ORG`			ORG @ 1
2	National	`I-ORG`	`I-MISC`	ORG @ 1-3	ORG @ 1-3	MISC @ 2
3	Bank	`E-ORG`	`E-ORG`			ORG @ 3

Table 1: Differences in the handling of the malformed tags can yield different entities. The gold annotation is a span of type organization starting at index 1 and continuing until index 3 (inclusive). This is encoded as `B-`, `I-`, `E-` tags of type `ORG`. Our model has predicted correct tags for the tokens "First" and "Bank", but annotates "National" as a miscellaneous span. This `I-MISC` tag is illegal. This tag should only follow `B-MISC` or `I-MISC`. The handling of these illegal tags can result in very different spans. In the original evaluation script from the CONLL 2000 shared task on noun-phrase chunking, a tag of a different type will trigger the ending of the previous entity and the start of a new one. This yields three entities, none of which match the gold entities. Yang et al. (2018), on the other hand, use a different entity resolution strategy where only the beginning and end tags are used. Illegal tags within the entity are ignored and under this scheme we get the correct entity. Mismatches in the entity decoding method, and specifically the handling of illegal transitions, can result in different entities based on the same tags. This renders results incomparable.

various techniques, like filtering sequences with illegal transitions or masking the scores these transitions get. By providing the legality of transitions, our library makes it easy to ensure a well-formed output.

4.4 Engineering

```
class SpanFormat:
    BEGIN: str
    INSIDE: str
    END: str
    SINGLE: str
```

Listing 2: Our span encoding data structure. These classes allow us to reuse the same parsing code with different classes to parse IOBES, BILOU, and BMEWO labels. By checking token prefixes against values in this data structure, instead of explicit checks against strings like `"S-"` or `"E-"`, we can use the same code for all formats. Having only a single function means there is less surface area for bugs to creep in and allows us to test it much more thoroughly.

Our main goal in this library is correctness. We achieve that by reusing code as much as possible. By defining data structures that contain the special prefixes each encoding scheme uses, like the one in Listing 2, we can use a single, well-tested function to perform some action—such as span parsing or converting a span into token labels—for multiple encoding schemes. We also use property based tests and the fuzzing of inputs to ensure our code is behaving properly. Our tests are automatically run via CI/CD on multiple operating systems to ensure a smooth experience across platforms.

Our library is lightweight and has no dependencies. Keeping it small makes it as painless as possible to integrate with unique workflows.

In order to handle multiple encoding schemes, we provide both specific functions like `parse_spans_iob`, as well as functions like `parse_spans`, that dispatch on the value of the `span_type` parameter. Similarly, the legality of various transitions is available in multiple formats, including a mask that is ready to be applied to a CRF. We provide multiple interfaces like this to support as many use cases as possible.

5 Conclusion

Many span level tasks in natural language processing are recast as token-level labeling. There are many encoding schemes used to convert these tokens into spans and these schemes dictate which tokens can follow other ones. Unfortunately, processing these tokens is a common place where errors and mistakes manifest. We have shown how mistakes in conversion code, gold annotations, and entity resolution, in the presence of malformed tag sequences, render results incomparable.

To remedy these problems, we introduce *iobes*, a small, well-tested Python library that helps standardize the processing of spans. Our library helps with parsing token labels into a list of spans, identifying locations of errors in token sequences, converting between span encoding schemes, and enumerating which transitions are allowed and which are not. Our library will help avoid these errors and will ensure that results created by different researchers are comparable.

References

Oliver Bender, Franz Josef Och, and Hermann Ney. 2003. Maximum Entropy Models for Named Entity Recognition. In *Proceedings of the Seventh Conference on Natural Language Learning at HLT-NAACL 2003*, pages 148–151.

Andrew Eliot Borthwick. 1999. *A Maximum Entropy Approach to Named Entity Recognition*. Ph.D. thesis, USA. AAI9945252.

Ronan Collobert, Jason Weston, Léon Bottou, Michael Karlen, Koray Kavukcuoglu, and Pavel Kuksa. 2011. Natural Language Processing (Almost) from Scratch. *Journal of Machine Learning Research*, 12(76):2493–2537.

Leon Derczynski, Eric Nichols, Marieke van Erp, and Nut Limsopatham. 2017. Results of the WNUT2017 Shared Task on Novel and Emerging Entity Recognition. In *Proceedings of the 3rd Workshop on Noisy User-generated Text*, pages 140–147, Copenhagen, Denmark. Association for Computational Linguistics.

Matt Gardner, Joel Grus, Mark Neumann, Oyvind Tafjord, Pradeep Dasigi, Nelson F. Liu, Matthew Peters, Michael Schmitz, and Luke S. Zettlemoyer. 2017. AllenNLP: A Deep Semantic Natural Language Processing Platform.

John D. Lafferty, Andrew McCallum, and Fernando C. N. Pereira. 2001. Conditional Random Fields: Probabilistic Models for Segmenting and Labeling Sequence Data. In *Proceedings of the Eighteenth International Conference on Machine Learning*, ICML '01, page 282–289, San Francisco, CA, USA. Morgan Kaufmann Publishers Inc.

Guillaume Lample, Miguel Ballesteros, Sandeep Subramanian, Kazuya Kawakami, and Chris Dyer. 2016. Neural Architectures for Named Entity Recognition. In *Proceedings of the 2016 Conference of the North American Chapter of the Association for Computational Linguistics: Human Language Technologies*, pages 260–270, San Diego, California. Association for Computational Linguistics.

Kenton Lee, Luheng He, Mike Lewis, and Luke Zettlemoyer. 2017. End-to-end Neural Coreference Resolution. In *Proceedings of the 2017 Conference on Empirical Methods in Natural Language Processing*, pages 188–197, Copenhagen, Denmark. Association for Computational Linguistics.

Xuezhe Ma and Eduard Hovy. 2016. End-to-end Sequence Labeling via Bi-directional LSTM-CNNs-CRF. In *Proceedings of the 54th Annual Meeting of the Association for Computational Linguistics (Volume 1: Long Papers)*, pages 1064–1074, Berlin, Germany. Association for Computational Linguistics.

Daniel Pressel, Sagnik Ray Choudhury, Brian Lester, Yanjie Zhao, and Matt Barta. 2018. Baseline: A Library for Rapid Modeling, Experimentation and Development of Deep Learning Algorithms targeting NLP. In *Proceedings of Workshop for NLP Open Source Software (NLP-OSS)*, pages 34–40 Association for Computational Linguistics.

Lance Ramshaw and Mitch Marcus. 1995. Text Chunking using Transformation-Based Learning. In *Third Workshop on Very Large Corpora*.

Lev Ratinov and Dan Roth. 2009. Design Challenges and Misconceptions in Named Entity Recognition. In *Proceedings of the Thirteenth Conference on Computational Natural Language Learning (CoNLL-2009)*, pages 147–155, Boulder, Colorado. Association for Computational Linguistics.

Erik F. Tjong Kim Sang and Sabine Buchholz. 2000. Introduction to the CoNLL-2000 Shared Task Chunking. In *Fourth Conference on Computational Natural Language Learning and the Second Learning Language in Logic Workshop*.

Erik F. Tjong Kim Sang and Fien De Meulder. 2003. Introduction to the CoNLL-2003 Shared Task: Language-Independent Named Entity Recognition. In *Proceedings of the Seventh Conference on Natural Language Learning at HLT-NAACL 2003*, pages 142–147.

Guido Van Rossum and Fred L. Drake. 2009. *Python 3 Reference Manual*. CreateSpace, Scotts Valley, CA.

Jie Yang, Shuailong Liang, and Yue Zhang. 2018. Design Challenges and Misconceptions in Neural Sequence Labeling. In *Proceedings of the 27th International Conference on Computational Linguistics*, pages 3879–3889, Santa Fe, New Mexico, USA. Association for Computational Linguistics.

SacreROUGE: An Open-Source Library for Using and Developing Summarization Evaluation Metrics

Daniel Deutsch and Dan Roth
Department of Computer and Information Science
University of Pennsylvania
{ddeutsch, danroth}@seas.upenn.edu

Abstract

We present SacreROUGE, an open-source library for using and developing summarization evaluation metrics.[1] SacreROUGE removes many obstacles that researchers face when using or developing metrics: (1) The library provides Python wrappers around the official implementations of existing evaluation metrics so they share a common, easy-to-use interface; (2) it provides functionality to evaluate how well any metric implemented in the library correlates to human-annotated judgments, so no additional code needs to be written for a new evaluation metric; and (3) it includes scripts for loading datasets that contain human judgments so they can easily be used for evaluation. This work describes the design of the library, including the core `Metric` interface, the command-line API for evaluating summarization models and metrics, and the scripts to load and reformat publicly available datasets. The development of SacreROUGE is ongoing and open to contributions from the community.

1 Introduction

Evaluating models is a critical step of the machine learning workflow. However, unlike classification-based tasks, evaluating models which generate text is difficult and is a research area on its own. The basic workflow for developing a new automatic evaluation metric is to design/implement the metric, calculate its correlation to human judgments, then use that metric to evaluate text generation systems.

While there have been significant efforts to build libraries for developing machine learning models (Klein et al., 2017; Gardner et al., 2018; Ott et al., 2019), no equivalent library exists for developing evaluation metrics. In this work, we present SacreROUGE, an open-source, Python-based library for using and developing text generation metrics, with an emphasis on summarization.

SacreROUGE removes many obstacles that researchers face when they use or develop evaluation metrics. First, the official implementations of various metrics do not share a common interface or programming language, so using many metrics to evaluate a model can be frustrating and time consuming. SacreROUGE provides Python-based wrappers around many evaluation metrics so they all implement a simple, easy-to-use interface regardless of how they are implemented internally (§2).

Second, evaluating metrics themselves can be tricky. Correlations between metric values and human judgments are calculated at several different granularities, there are multiple commonly used correlation coefficients, and fairly comparing human-written references to system output requires implementing jackknifing. Since the evaluation code in SacreROUGE is shared across all of the metrics, any metric which implements the common `Metric` interface can be evaluated without writing additional code (§3).

Third, datasets that contain judgments which are commonly used to evaluate metrics do not share the same format, so writing code to load each dataset requires writing a significant amount of effort. SacreROUGE provides scripts for popular summarization datasets that load and reformat them into a common schema so they can easily be used for evaluation (§4).

The development of SacreROUGE is ongoing. We intend to add more metrics and datasets to the library as they become available. Further, we encourage researchers to use the SacreROUGE framework to use existing metrics and develop new ones. SacreROUGE is released under the Apache 2.0 license and is open to contributions from the community.

---

[1] https://github.com/danieldeutsch/sacrerouge

Proceedings of Second Workshop for NLP Open Source Software (NLP-OSS), pages 120–125
Virtual Conference, November 19, 2020. ©2020 Association for Computational Linguistics

2 The Metric Interface

The development of evaluation metrics for summarization has been an active area of research for two decades. However, the community has not converged on a consistent format for the input data, so each metric uses its own custom schema. Further, the published code for evaluation metrics is written in various programming languages based on which language was popular when the metric was proposed. These challenges make it very cumbersome to use multiple metrics to evaluate a summarization system. SacreROUGE addresses these two problems by unifying all of the metrics' implementations into a common interface called `Metric`. The interface provides a Pythonic API that allows for evaluating an individual summary or batch of summaries. Since all of the metrics share the same interface, evaluating a summarization system with several different metrics is trivial.

In order to support older evaluation metrics written in languages such as Perl or Java, we have written Python wrappers around the original code that still implement the `Metric` interface. Internally, the wrappers serialize the input summaries to the format required by the underlying metric, a subprocess is created to run the original metric's code, and the output is then loaded from disk again in Python. This way, we do not have to port the original metric's code to Python and end-users can still use the metrics with the Python API.

SacreROUGE currently supports the following evaluation metrics:

- AutoSummENG (Giannakopoulos et al., 2008)

- BERTScore (Zhang et al., 2019)

- BEwT-E (Tratz and Hovy, 2008)

- BLEURT (Sellam et al., 2020)

- METEOR (Denkowski and Lavie, 2014)

- MeMoG (Giannakopoulos and Karkaletsis, 2010)

- MoverScore (Zhao et al., 2019)

- NPowER (Giannakopoulos and Karkaletsis, 2013)

- Pyramid Score (Nenkova and Passonneau, 2004)

- PyrEval (Gao et al., 2019)

- QAEval (Deutsch et al., 2020)

- ROUGE (Lin, 2004), including a Python-port that we wrote, which is significantly faster than the original Perl version

- SIMetrix (Louis and Nenkova, 2009)

- SumQE (Xenouleas et al., 2019)

Among these metrics, 6 have original implementations in Java, 6 in Python, 1 in Perl, and 1 with no known official implementation (Pyramid Score).

Handling Dependencies Many of the evaluation metrics rely on external resources in the form of code, models, or data files. Setting up these dependencies in the right format to use the metrics can be difficult.

The SacreROUGE library addresses this problem by providing setup scripts for each metric which download or compile any required resources. To make this process as easy as possible for the end-user, these scripts are run through a `setup-metric` command. The command takes the name of the metric to setup, then downloads the required dependencies to a common folder which is managed by SacreROUGE. Abstracting the metric setup by a simple command makes it such that the end-user can quickly and easily begin using all of the metrics within the library.

While there is nothing technically to prevent SacreROUGE from being used in a Windows environment, thus far the scripts for handling the metrics' dependencies have been written for Linux-based systems.

3 Evaluating Systems and Metrics

The two most common use cases of an evaluation metric are to evaluate a summarization system and to evaluate a metric itself by calculating its correlation to human judgments. Since all of the metrics in SacreROUGE implement a common interface, the code for these procedures is shared, so developers of new metrics do not need to rewrite the code to implement these procedures. This logic is exposed through `evaluate`, `score`, and `correlate`, which are subcommands of `sacrerouge`, the entry point for the library's command-line interface.

The `evaluate` Subcommand The purpose of the `evaluate` subcommand is to calculate a metric's score for one summarization system on one dataset, which most typically occurs when researchers compare their system's performance to others'.

The `evaluate` subcommand accepts a specific metric and an input file that contains the output of a summarization system for an input corpus. The command will load the input data, pass it to the metric, and save the metric's output at the summary-level and system-level. The summary-level output contains the metric's value for each individual summary, whereas system-level output represents the average performance across the dataset and is most often reported in papers.

The `score` Subcommand   The typical workflow for an evaluation of a metric is to first calculate the metric's score on a large number of summaries produced by multiple summarization systems on the same set of inputs. Then, a correlation coefficient is calculated between those scores and human judgments on the same set of summaries. The first step of this methodology is handled by the `score` subcommand.

The `score` subcommand is very similar to `evaluate` except for two key differences. First, the input data is not expected to be the output from a single system. Instead, it is expected to be the outputs from several summarization systems for the same sets of input documents. Providing the output from multiple systems at once allows SacreROUGE to score each of the summaries more efficiently than repeated calls to `evaluate` because it can avoid duplicate work, such as calculating reference summary-specific statistics.

Second, the `score` subcommand will run jackknifing on the input data when possible and necessary. Jackknifing is a procedure which allows the value of a metric on system-produced and human-written summaries to be fairly compared when the human-written summaries are used to assess the quality of the system summary. Briefly, if there is more than one reference summary, each reference is evaluated against all of the others. Each system summary is repeatedly evaluated against each possible subset of the reference summaries that has one reference removed. The final system summary score is an average across those evaluations. When jackknifing is performed, a `_jk` suffix is appended to the name of the metric which makes it clear that it is not comparable to the non-jackknifed version.

The `correlate` Subcommand   After all of the summaries have been scored using the `score` subcommand, the second step of the meta-evaluation of a metric is to calculate the correlation of those scores to human judgments. This step is done via the `correlate` subcommand.

SacreROUGE calculates the three correlation coefficients most commonly used in summarization: Pearson, Spearman, and Kendall. Further, these correlations are computed at three different granularities: the summary-level, the system-level, and globally. The summary-level correlation calculates the average correlation per input. The system-level calculates the correlation between average system performances for each metric. The global correlation directly calculates the correlation between all of the observed metric values. The former two granularities are most often used in the summarization literature, and we refer the reader to Deutsch et al. (2020) for a more detailed description of how to calculate each of them.

Handling Different Input Requirements   It is often the case that different metrics require different input data (e.g., some metrics use reference summaries, others need access to the input documents). Therefore, the required data must be loaded from the input file and the `evaluate` and `score` subcommands must pass the required data to the metric.

The interface for loading data from an input file in SacreROUGE is called a `DatasetReader`. For a given input file(s), a `DatasetReader` loads the `Fields` for the evaluation instances. A `Field` is a base class which contains the data for an input instance, such as a `DocumentsField` that maintains the contents of the input documents. Then, each evaluation instance contains a mapping from the name of a field to its data.

In order to pass the appropriate `Fields` to the summarization metrics, we require that every class that implements the `Metric` interface lists the names of the `Fields` that it uses. For instance, the wrapper for the document-based evaluation metric SIMetrix specifies it needs a field called `documents`, a key in the evaluation instance `Field` mapping. Then, once the input data has been loaded, the `evaluate` and `score` commands can pass the required data to a metric for evaluation.

Automatically Generated Subcommands It is desirable to have a different `evaluate` and `score` subcommand for each individual metric so that developers can easily specify different metric parameters on the command line. A naive implementation of this would require manually creating the subcommand for each metric. However, in order to eliminate as much boilerplate code as possible, SacreROUGE includes a feature to automatically generate these subcommands for any metric that implements the `Metric` interface.

Using Python's `inspect` and `typing` libraries, we are able to examine the constructor of each metric and generate a command-line argument for each parameter. For parameters with primitive types, the `argparse` library directly supports casting command line parameters to the correct types. However, some metrics may use complex types, such as a list of integers. In such situations, SacreROUGE assumes that the command line argument will be a string-serialized JSON object that can be deserialized into the required type at runtime. This allows us to automatically generate `evaluate` and `score` subcommands for every metric supported by the library.

4   A Common Dataset Format

Over the past two decades, the summarization community has collected a large number of summarization datasets and human quality annotations. However, these very useful datasets are seldom saved in a common format, forcing every researcher who wants to train a model on the datasets or use the judgments to evaluate a metric to write boilerplate code to load the data.

To mitigate this issue, SacreROUGE provides scripts that will load the datasets and their corresponding judgments, then serialize them to new files with a common format. The data is serialized in such a manner that it can be directly used in the `evaluate`, `score`, and `correlate` subcommands, thereby making it incredibly easy to run or evaluate any metric in the library on the dataset.

The preprocessing scripts will save the data in a human-readable form into three different JSONL files:[2] one for the summarization task data, one for the summaries that have been scored by the human judges, and one for the corresponding metric scores for those summaries. Each object in the task file is uniquely identified by an instance

ID and contains the input documents and ground-truth summaries for one instance. The scored summaries and metric scores files have parallel data. The objects in both files contain an instance ID that identifies the input documents that were used to generate the summary, a summarizer ID that identifies the summarization model used to produce the summary, and a string that identifies the type of summarization (either model-generated or human-written). The summaries file contains the actual summary output by the system and the references for the input instance, and the metrics file contains the corresponding metric scores for that summary. Example JSON objects from all of the files can be seen in Appendix A

The scripts to preprocess the datasets are exposed through the `setup-dataset` subcommand. The subcommand accepts the name of a dataset, an output directory, and any potential dataset-specific arguments. Then, SacreROUGE will load and preprocess the respective dataset. For datasets which are publicly available, the scripts will download the data automatically. However, many summarization datasets are licensed, so the corresponding preprocessing scripts require paths to the original data supplied to the command.

The datasets which are currently supported by SacreROUGE are the Document Understanding Conference from 2001 to 2007,[3] Text Analysis Conference from 2008 to 2011,[4] the MultiLing 2011, 2013, 2015, 2017, and 2019 Workshops,[5] and the CNN/DailyMail dataset judgments provided by Chaganty et al. (2018) and Fabbri et al. (2020). We intend to add more datasets as they become available, and other researchers can easily incorporate their own datasets to our library by serializing the data into the shared format.

5   Related Work

The idea for SacreROUGE came from the Sacre-BLEU (Post, 2018) library. SacreBLEU was developed to standardize and simplify calculating BLEU (Papineni et al., 2002) for machine translation. Like SacreROUGE, it provides a simple command-line interface to download and evaluate on common machine translation datasets. Whereas SacreBLEU is mainly for evaluating machine translation models with BLEU, our library focuses on summarization

---

[2]A JSONL file contains one serialized JSON per line.

and includes a large number of evaluation metrics. Further, SacreROUGE also provides a framework for developing and evaluating new metrics.

One goal of SacreROUGE is to standardize the implementation and meta-evaluation of metrics. The Perl-based Asiya (Giménez and Màrquez, 2010) and Python-based EASSE (Alva-Manchego et al., 2019) have been developed with similar goals for machine translation and text simplification, respectively.

Much of the design of SacreROUGE was inspired by AllenNLP (Gardner et al., 2018), a library built on PyTorch (Paszke et al., 2017) for developing deep learning models. AllenNLP provides useful abstractions over different models and neural network modules that allows for the sharing of boilerplate code so developers can quickly create and train new machine learning models. SacreROUGE provides similar abstractions for evaluation metrics.

Two concurrent works set out to achieve similar goals to SacreROUGE, the `nlp` library from Hugging Face[6] and SummEval (Fabbri et al., 2020). Both libraries provide easy-to-use interfaces for running many evaluation metrics. However, SacreROUGE provides much more functionality for developing and evaluating new metrics, including providing dataset readers for benchmark metric evaluation datasets, implementations of features such as jackknifing, and calculating common correlation coefficients.

6 Conclusion

We have presented SacreROUGE, an open-source library dedicated to the development of summarization evaluation metrics. With a unified metric interface and common data format, our library makes it very simple to use existing evaluation metrics as well as develop new ones with a minimum amount of effort. We hope that future researchers will contribute their own metrics and datasets to the library so that it is as easy as possible to run and evaluate summarization metrics.

Acknowledgments

The authors would like to thank the anonymous reviewers for their helpful suggestions and feedback.

This work was supported by Contract FA8750-19-2-1004 and Contract FA8750-19-2-0201 with the US Defense Advanced Research Projects Agency (DARPA). Approved for Public Release, Distribution Unlimited. The views expressed are those of the authors and do not reflect the official policy or position of the Department of Defense or the U.S. Government.

This research is supported by a Focused Award from Google.

References

Fernando Emilio Alva-Manchego, Louis Martin, Carolina Scarton, and Lucia Specia. 2019. EASSE: easier automatic sentence simplification evaluation. In *Proceedings of the 2019 Conference on Empirical Methods in Natural Language Processing and the 9th International Joint Conference on Natural Language Processing, EMNLP-IJCNLP 2019, Hong Kong, China, November 3-7, 2019 - System Demonstrations*, pages 49–54. Association for Computational Linguistics.

Arun Chaganty, Stephen Mussmann, and Percy Liang. 2018. The price of debiasing automatic metrics in natural language evalaution. In *Proceedings of the 56th Annual Meeting of the Association for Computational Linguistics (Volume 1: Long Papers)*, pages 643–653, Melbourne, Australia. Association for Computational Linguistics.

Michael J. Denkowski and Alon Lavie. 2014. Meteor universal: Language specific translation evaluation for any target language. In *Proceedings of the Ninth Workshop on Statistical Machine Translation, WMT@ACL 2014, June 26-27, 2014, Baltimore, Maryland, USA*, pages 376–380. The Association for Computer Linguistics.

Daniel Deutsch, Tania Bedrax-Weiss, and Dan Roth. 2020. Towards Question-Answering as an Automatic Metric for Evaluating the Content Quality of a Summary.

Alexander R Fabbri, Wojciech Kryściński, Bryan McCann, Caiming Xiong, Richard Socher, and Dragomir Radev. 2020. SummEval: Re-evaluating Summarization Evaluation. *arXiv preprint arXiv:2007.12626*.

Yanjun Gao, Chen Sun, and Rebecca J. Passonneau. 2019. Automated pyramid summarization evaluation. In *Proceedings of the 23rd Conference on Computational Natural Language Learning, CoNLL 2019, Hong Kong, China, November 3-4, 2019*, pages 404–418. Association for Computational Linguistics.

Matt Gardner, Joel Grus, Mark Neumann, Oyvind Tafjord, Pradeep Dasigi, Nelson F. Liu, Matthew Peters, Michael Schmitz, and Luke Zettlemoyer. 2018. AllenNLP: A deep semantic natural language processing platform. In *Proceedings of Workshop for*

---

[6]`https://github.com/huggingface/nlp`

NLP Open Source Software (NLP-OSS), pages 1–6, Melbourne, Australia. Association for Computational Linguistics.

George Giannakopoulos and Vangelis Karkaletsis. 2010. Summarization system evaluation variations based on n-gram graphs. In *Proceedings of the Third Text Analysis Conference, TAC 2010, Gaithersburg, Maryland, USA, November 15-16, 2010*. NIST.

George Giannakopoulos and Vangelis Karkaletsis. 2013. Summary evaluation: Together we stand npower-ed. In *Computational Linguistics and Intelligent Text Processing - 14th International Conference, CICLing 2013, Samos, Greece, March 24-30, 2013, Proceedings, Part II*, volume 7817 of *Lecture Notes in Computer Science*, pages 436–450. Springer.

George Giannakopoulos, Vangelis Karkaletsis, George A. Vouros, and Panagiotis Stamatopoulos. 2008. Summarization system evaluation revisited: N-gram graphs. *TSLP*, 5(3):5:1–5:39.

Jesús Giménez and Lluís Màrquez. 2010. Asiya: An open toolkit for automatic machine translation (meta-)evaluation. *Prague Bull. Math. Linguistics*, 94:77–86.

Guillaume Klein, Yoon Kim, Yuntian Deng, Jean Senellart, and Alexander M. Rush. 2017. Opennmt: Open-source toolkit for neural machine translation. In *Proc. ACL*.

Chin-Yew Lin. 2004. ROUGE: A package for automatic evaluation of summaries. In *Text Summarization Branches Out*, pages 74–81, Barcelona, Spain. Association for Computational Linguistics.

Annie Louis and Ani Nenkova. 2009. Automatically evaluating content selection in summarization without human models. In *Proceedings of the 2009 Conference on Empirical Methods in Natural Language Processing, EMNLP 2009, 6-7 August 2009, Singapore, A meeting of SIGDAT, a Special Interest Group of the ACL*, pages 306–314. ACL.

Ani Nenkova and Rebecca J. Passonneau. 2004. Evaluating content selection in summarization: The pyramid method. In *Human Language Technology Conference of the North American Chapter of the Association for Computational Linguistics, HLT-NAACL 2004, Boston, Massachusetts, USA, May 2-7, 2004*, pages 145–152. The Association for Computational Linguistics.

Myle Ott, Sergey Edunov, Alexei Baevski, Angela Fan, Sam Gross, Nathan Ng, David Grangier, and Michael Auli. 2019. fairseq: A fast, extensible toolkit for sequence modeling. In *Proceedings of NAACL-HLT 2019: Demonstrations*.

Kishore Papineni, Salim Roukos, Todd Ward, and Wei-Jing Zhu. 2002. Bleu: a method for automatic evaluation of machine translation. In *Proceedings of the 40th Annual Meeting of the Association for Computational Linguistics, July 6-12, 2002, Philadelphia, PA, USA*, pages 311–318. ACL.

Adam Paszke, Sam Gross, Soumith Chintala, Gregory Chanan, Edward Yang, Zachary DeVito, Zeming Lin, Alban Desmaison, Luca Antiga, and Adam Lerer. 2017. Automatic differentiation in pytorch.

Matt Post. 2018. A call for clarity in reporting BLEU scores. In *Proceedings of the Third Conference on Machine Translation: Research Papers*, pages 186–191, Belgium, Brussels. Association for Computational Linguistics.

Thibault Sellam, Dipanjan Das, and Ankur P. Parikh. 2020. BLEURT: Learning Robust Metrics for Text Generation. In *Proceedings of the 58th Annual Meeting of the Association for Computational Linguistics, ACL 2020, Online, July 5-10, 2020*, pages 7881–7892. Association for Computational Linguistics.

Stephen Tratz and Eduard H. Hovy. 2008. Summarization evaluation using transformed basic elements. In *Proceedings of the First Text Analysis Conference, TAC 2008, Gaithersburg, Maryland, USA, November 17-19, 2008*. NIST.

Stratos Xenouleas, Prodromos Malakasiotis, Marianna Apidianaki, and Ion Androutsopoulos. 2019. SUM-QE: a bert-based summary quality estimation model. In *Proceedings of the 2019 Conference on Empirical Methods in Natural Language Processing and the 9th International Joint Conference on Natural Language Processing, EMNLP-IJCNLP 2019, Hong Kong, China, November 3-7, 2019*, pages 6004–6010. Association for Computational Linguistics.

Tianyi Zhang, Varsha Kishore, Felix Wu, Kilian Q. Weinberger, and Yoav Artzi. 2019. Bertscore: Evaluating text generation with BERT. *CoRR*, abs/1904.09675.

Wei Zhao, Maxime Peyrard, Fei Liu, Yang Gao, Christian M. Meyer, and Steffen Eger. 2019. Moverscore: Text generation evaluating with contextualized embeddings and earth mover distance. In *Proceedings of the 2019 Conference on Empirical Methods in Natural Language Processing and the 9th International Joint Conference on Natural Language Processing, EMNLP-IJCNLP 2019, Hong Kong, China, November 3-7, 2019*, pages 563–578. Association for Computational Linguistics.

TextAttack: Lessons learned in designing Python frameworks for NLP

John X. Morris*   **Jin Yong Yoo***   **Yanjun Qi**
University of Virginia
{jm8wx, jy2ma, yq2h}@virginia.edu

Abstract

TextAttack is an open-source Python toolkit for adversarial attacks, adversarial training, and data augmentation in NLP. TextAttack unites 15+ papers from the NLP adversarial attack literature into a single framework, with many components reused across attacks. This framework allows both researchers and developers to test and study the weaknesses of their NLP models. To build such an open-source NLP toolkit requires solving some common problems: How do we enable users to supply models from different deep learning frameworks? How can we build tools to support as many different datasets as possible? We share our insights into developing a well-written, well-documented NLP Python framework in hope that they can aid future development of similar packages.

1 Introduction

Deep neural network (DNN) models have seen dominant use in NLP tasks such text classification, natural language inference, machine translation, and question answering. However, despite their state-of-the-art performance, NLP DNNs are still vulnerable to adversarial attacks (Zhang et al., 2020). As a result, there have been growing efforts to develop tools that can help researchers and developers better understand the capability of their NLP models. Both Wallace et al. (2019) and Tenney et al. (2020) introduced web-based visual interactive tools that enable users to see model's local explanations. Ribeiro et al. (2020) introduced a behavioral testing framework that runs a suite of tests to sanity check NLP models.

One of the challenges for building such tools is that the tool should be flexible enough to work with many different deep learning frameworks (e.g. PyTorch, Tensorflow, Scikit-learn). Also, the tool

---

*equal authorship

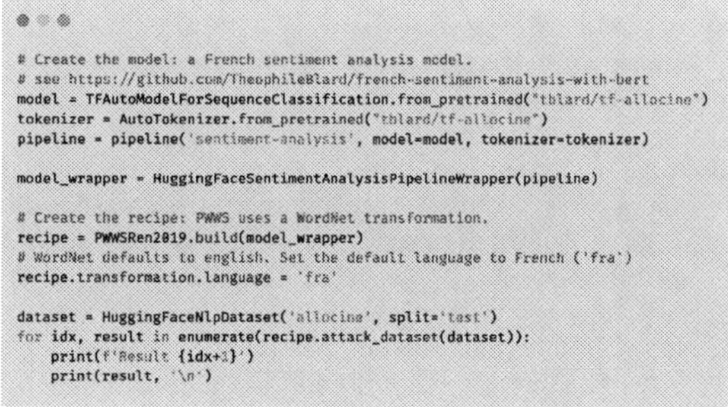

Figure 1: Example usage of the TextAttack API. CamemBERT (Martin et al., 2019) and its tokenizer are initialized using HuggingFace transformers (Wolf et al., 2019) and wrapped in TextAttack model wrappers. Adversarial attack is PWWS (Martin et al., 2019) modified to use WordNet in French (Sagot and Fiser, 2008) instead of English. TextAttack's flexible API makes these customizations possible in just a few lines of code.

should be able to work with datasets from various sources and in various formats. Lastly, the tools needs to be compatible with different hardware setups.

We developed TextAttack, an open-source Python framework for adversarial attacks, adversarial training, and data augmentation. Our modular and extendable design allows us to reuse many components to offer 15+ different adversarial attack methods proposed by literature. Our model-agnostic and dataset-agnostic design allows users to easily run adversarial attacks against their own models built using any deep learning framework.

This paper describes some lessons learned along the path to creating TextAttack. Figure 1 shows our API in action. Our advice is tailored towards researchers developing NLP libraries in Python that support a variety of models and datasets, and use them for downstream applications.

We provide the following broad advice to help other future developers create user-friendly NLP

Proceedings of Second Workshop for NLP Open Source Software (NLP-OSS), pages 126–131
Virtual Conference, November 19, 2020. ©2020 Association for Computational Linguistics

libraries in Python:

1. To become model-agnostic, implement a model wrapper class.

2. To become data-agnostic, take dataset inputs as (input, output) pairs, where each model input is represented as an `OrderedDict`.

3. Do not plan for inputs (tensors, lists, etc.) to be a certain size or shape unless explicitly necessary.

4. Centralize common text operations, like parsing and string-level operations, in one class.

5. Whenever possible, cache repeated computations, including model inferences.

6. If your program runs on a single GPU, but your system contains N GPUs, you can obtain an performance boost proportional to N through parallelism.

7. Dynamically choose between devices. (Do not require a GPU or TPU if one is not necessary.)

2　Model agnosticism

There are growing number of deep learning frameworks and different researchers and groups have preferences about which frameworks to use for different tasks. Unless the library relates to model training or development (and sometimes then), it is possible to build a library that supports deep learning models from any framework.

TextAttack supports both black-box and white-box attacks on NLP models. Black-box attacks can only access the model for inference. In essence, the attack sends lists of text to the model and receives predictions. Model predictions come as lists of floats (for classification), strings, or dictionaries. No other information about the model is required. From the start, we wanted TextAttack to work on models from any framework, without too much headache.

2.1　Original approach: "magic" (model detection logic)

Our original approach was to take a model and tokenizer as input to each attack and wrangle data into the correct format behind the scenes. This involved a complex series of decisions based by checking the format of the dataset, testing model and tokenizer superclasses, and handling errors as they arose. In the end, it worked: based on the model, tokenizer, and dataset, as well as based on errors raised by passing different data formats to the model, we could perform inference on PyTorch and TensorFlow models. It was ugly, but it worked.

This approach did not scale as there were many edge cases. For example, some TensorFlow Hub models were designed to take strings as predictions, and did not have a tokenizer at all. Some Scikit-learn models took a dataframe as input. We supported both these use cases, but edges cases requiring complex workarounds kept popping up, with no clear end in sight.

2.2　Better approach: model wrappers

Our long-term solution was to abstract away the tokenizer and require a new **model wrapper** class for each model. The idea of **model wrappers** is that each model is wrapped in a model wrapper that implements a single function, `__call__`, which takes a list of text inputs and returns a list of predictions. We designed TextAttack to interact exclusively with the model wrapper– not directly with the model, or the tokenizer.

Model wrappers allow each model to handle its own internals: including tokenization and batch size. TextAttack does not know or care about how information is tokenized before it's sent to the model. TextAttack sends the model a list of strings and receives a `list`, `numpy.ndarray`, or `torch.Tensor` of predictions.

In this way, TextAttack becomes totally model-agnostic: any user can implement a model wrapper to enable compatibility for a new model or framework. To make the process easier, TextAttack provides model wrappers for common frameworks and patterns. Currently, TextAttack provides model wrappers and example for models implemented with PyTorch (Paszke et al., 2019), HuggingFace transformers (Wolf et al., 2019), TensorFlow (Abadi et al., 2016), Scikit-learn (Pedregosa et al., 2011), and AllenNLP (Gardner et al., 2018).

3　Data agnosticism

Another goal of TextAttack was to be able to run the same attack on any dataset. This has obvious benefits: two attacks that report results on different datasets can easily be compared with TextAttack.

3.1　Text inputs as `OrderedDict` objects

We rely on other libraries for providing default datasets. We provide dataset wrappers for loading datasets from these external libraries. We also allow users to provide their own datasets– via CSV files or Python scripts that load datasets. In essence, each dataset is a list of (`input, output`) pairs. Each text input is a string (for single-input tasks) or an `OrderedDict` (for tasks that require more complex input formats).

Each input is an `OrderedDict` for two reasons: (i) to maintain column labels for display purposes and to make column-specific logic possible and (ii) to maintain ordering so that inputs can be provided to the model in the proper order. An individual text input to the model is a tuple of strings.

To create these `OrderedDict` objects from dictionaries loaded from popular dataset libraries, we maintain a tuple of input columns and a string representing the output column. Then, objects from any dataset can be mapped to a data pair for TextAttack: the input is an OrderedDict created from taking the input values in order of the input columns, and an output is the value corresponding to the dataset's output column.

4 Model output flexibility with `GoalFunction`

With the proper input and ouput columns and a corresponding model, adversarial attacks can be run on any dataset on any model. Models may have different output formats. For example, a sentiment classifier would produces a list of the probabilities of each class, while a sequence-to-sequence models produce a text output. Task-specific subclasses of the TextAttack `GoalFunction` class allow adversarial attack goal functions to be defined at a high level, such that the same goal function can be used for any model with the same output type. For example, the `MinimizeBleuScore` goal function attempts to minimize the BLEU score (Papineni et al., 2002) between the correct output and the output the model produces for a given perturbation. This goal function only assumes that the model output a prediction as a string. Given this design pattern, the `MinimizeBleuScore` goal function can be applied to attack any sequence-to-sequence model. Similar goal functions can be designed for other output formats, like classification models or sentence taggers.

5 Common functions for text inputs with `AttackedText`

Across TextAttack modules, some functionality is required over and over again. Many transformations want to split text inputs into a list of words. Many constraints require part-of-speech tagging. We want to avoid repeating code in too many places, and also to set a standard as to which tokenization, part-of-speech tagger, etc. is used.

Therefore, with the exception of models (which take string inputs), TextAttack modules operate on `AttackedText` objects – not vanilla Python strings. The AttackedText contains string functionality that performs word replacement, prepares text to input to the model, prints inputs along with their column names, and manages attack-specific context attributes.

It is relatively common for NLP libraries to provide some base class that provides additional functionality to what are essentially enhanced string objects. For example, flair (Akbik et al., 2018) performs text-level operations on a `Sentence` class. TextAttack follows a similar strategy and stores each text input as an `AttackedText` object.

5.1 Everything is a single string

A single input may consist of multiple strings. TextAttack transformations apply string-level transformations to inputs – for example, reordering words, or replacing a single word with its synonym. Most transformations are defined in the attack papers to operate on a single string-input. For multi-input classification tasks, adversarial attacks often just choose a single input on which to operate, like the hypothesis in the case of entailment (Jin et al., 2019).

TextAttack enables such single-string transformations and constraints without restricting itself to single-input tasks. Transformations and constraints assume the input is a single string. The AttackedText contains a property (`AttackedText.text`) that joins all text inputs with a space in between. This text value is passed to each transformation & constraint, and then broken up again by column.

6 Improving Performance

Model inference memoization Adversarial attacks in NLP spend most of their time on the GPU. For each text input, the attack must obtain the

Attack	Queries	Cache hits
Alzantot et al. (2018)	1029	736
Zang et al. (2020)	3745	3080

Table 1: "Queries" stands for average number of queries to victim model to attack one sample, while "cache hits" represents the average number of times a query has resulted in a hit to the model output cache. Each cache hit saves a query to the model, so more cache hits indicates a higher performance boost due to caching.

model's output, as well as the output of any models used to apply certain linguistic constraints, like a sentence encoder to ensure semantic similarity between adversarial example and the original text. Upon further examination, many of these model inferences appear over and over again during the attack process. For example, the attack needs to compute the model's score for an input that has already been seen. Some population-based stochastic search methods, like the genetic algorithm of Alzantot et al. (2018), may revisit the same input multiple times during the search process, which increases the number of redundant computations.

TextAttack caches model outputs to avoid redundant computations. This is done using a least-recently-used (LRU) function cache. Since outputs are generally small, TextAttack can maintain a very large LRU cache for each purpose without using an excessive amount of memory. In some cases, this high-level caching can cause a significant performance increase. We experimented with attacking 100 samples for `BERT-base` model (Devlin et al., 2018) trained on SST-2 dataset (Socher et al., 2013) using methods proposed by Alzantot et al. (2018) and Zang et al. (2020). Table 1 shows that in both cases, significant number of queries to the victim model result in hits to the model output cache, helping us save time by avoiding unnecessary computations.

Multiprocessing strategy Efficient use of GPUs is critical for any deep learning job. If a GPU is available, TextAttack attacks typically use it for victim model inference and for inference on any models required for constraints. These inference times are the main bottleneck for many attacks. On systems with multiple GPUs, running attacks on samples sequentially results in use of only one GPU. We provide multiprocessing feature with the `--parallel` flag to instead runs attacks in parallel.

TextAttack parallel mode works by starting a new attack worker process for each GPU. Each worker takes dataset samples off of an in-queue, runs an attack on a single sample, puts the attack result on an out-queue, and repeats, until the in-queue is empty. An additional non-GPU worker works to print attack results as they appear on the out queue.

This multiprocessing paradigm is quite simple, and works nicely with various current deep learning packages. Other libraries that face similar single-GPU-intensive workloads could employ this pattern to parallelize many GPUs. In the future, the additional help of a distributed computing interface like MPI could allow an attack to be run across multiple machines as well.

7 Enabling use across different operating systems and devices

Operating system compatibility Different operating systems follow different filesystem conventions. Specifying full file paths explicitly is almost never a good idea. Instead, prefer using absolute paths. TextAttack uses absolute paths and combines filenames using Python's `os.path.join` utility function. This enables file manipulation on any system (not just Unix).

GPU Hubris Current deep learning frameworks allow explicit device placement of tensors – choosing whether a given tensor is on CPU or a specific GPU. It is easy to design specifically for your system: putting each tensor explicitly on the GPU where it belongs. However, this hurts cross-system compatibility: the code is now only able to run on systems with GPUs. TextAttack checks to see if CUDA is available before putting tensors on the GPU, and puts them on the CPU otherwise. This allows the library to run on machines without GPUs.

8 Conclusion

Writing an excellent, well-documented library that is easy to install and run is a good way to get researchers interested in a research topic as it lowers the barriers to entry. Moreover, a well-structured, extendable design empowers newcomers to make their contributions to the field. We hope that our lessons from developing TextAttack will help others create user-friendly open-source NLP libraries.

Acknowledgments

Thanks to all the TextAttack contributors who helped us solve these tough problems– including Eli Lifland, Jake Grigsby, Di Jin, Kevin Ivey, Alan Zheng, and others. Thanks also to Robin Jia and Paul Michel who provided invaluable feedback toward the development and design of TextAttack.

References

Martin Abadi, Paul Barham, Jianmin Chen, Zhifeng Chen, Andy Davis, Jeffrey Dean, Matthieu Devin, Sanjay Ghemawat, Geoffrey Irving, Michael Isard, Manjunath Kudlur, Josh Levenberg, Rajat Monga, Sherry Moore, Derek G Murray, Benoit Steiner, Paul Tucker, Vijay Vasudevan, Pete Warden, Martin Wicke, Yuan Yu, and Xiaoqiang Zheng. 2016. TensorFlow: A system for large-scale machine learning.

Alan Akbik, Duncan Blythe, and Roland Vollgraf. 2018. Contextual string embeddings for sequence labeling. In *COLING 2018, 27th International Conference on Computational Linguistics*, pages 1638–1649.

Moustafa Alzantot, Yash Sharma, Ahmed Elgohary, Bo-Jhang Ho, Mani Srivastava, and Kai-Wei Chang. 2018. Generating natural language adversarial examples. *arXiv preprint arXiv:1804.07998*.

Jacob Devlin, Ming-Wei Chang, Kenton Lee, and Kristina Toutanova. 2018. BERT: pre-training of deep bidirectional transformers for language understanding. *CoRR*, abs/1810.04805.

Matt Gardner, Joel Grus, Mark Neumann, Oyvind Tafjord, Pradeep Dasigi, Nelson Liu, Matthew Peters, Michael Schmitz, and Luke Zettlemoyer. 2018. AllenNLP: A deep semantic natural language processing platform.

Di Jin, Zhijing Jin, Joey Tianyi Zhou, and Peter Szolovits. 2019. Is bert really robust? natural language attack on text classification and entailment. *arXiv preprint arXiv:1907. 11932*.

Louis Martin, Benjamin Muller, Pedro Javier Ortiz Suárez, Yoann Dupont, Laurent Romary, Éric Villemonte de la Clergerie, Djamé Seddah, and Benoît Sagot. 2019. CamemBERT: a tasty french language model.

Kishore Papineni, Salim Roukos, Todd Ward, and Wei-Jing Zhu. 2002. BLEU: a method for automatic evaluation of machine translation. In *Proceedings of the 40th annual meeting of the Association for Computational Linguistics*, pages 311–318.

Adam Paszke, Sam Gross, Francisco Massa, Adam Lerer, James Bradbury, Gregory Chanan, Trevor Killeen, Zeming Lin, Natalia Gimelshein, Luca Antiga, Alban Desmaison, Andreas Kopf, Edward Yang, Zachary DeVito, Martin Raison, Alykhan Tejani, Sasank Chilamkurthy, Benoit Steiner, Lu Fang, Junjie Bai, and Soumith Chintala. 2019. PyTorch: An imperative style, High-Performance deep learning library. In *Advances in Neural Information Processing Systems 32*, pages 8026–8037. Curran Associates, Inc.

Fabian Pedregosa, Gaël Varoquaux, Alexandre Gramfort, Vincent Michel, Bertrand Thirion, Olivier Grisel, Mathieu Blondel, Peter Prettenhofer, Ron Weiss, Vincent Dubourg, Jake Vanderplas, Alexandre Passos, David Cournapeau, Matthieu Brucher, Matthieu Perrot, and Édouard Duchesnay. 2011. Scikit-learn: Machine learning in python. *J. Mach. Learn. Res.*, 12(85):2825–2830.

Marco Tulio Ribeiro, Tongshuang Wu, Carlos Guestrin, and Sameer Singh. 2020. Beyond accuracy: Behavioral testing of NLP models with CheckList. In *Proceedings of the 58th Annual Meeting of the Association for Computational Linguistics*, pages 4902–4912, Online. Association for Computational Linguistics.

Benoît Sagot and Darja Fiser. 2008. Building a free french wordnet from multilingual resources.

Richard Socher, Alex Perelygin, Jean Wu, Jason Chuang, Christopher D. Manning, Andrew Ng, and Christopher Potts. 2013. Recursive deep models for semantic compositionality over a sentiment treebank. In *Proceedings of the 2013 Conference on Empirical Methods in Natural Language Processing*, pages 1631–1642, Seattle, Washington, USA. Association for Computational Linguistics.

Ian Tenney, James Wexler, Jasmijn Bastings, Tolga Bolukbasi, Andy Coenen, Sebastian Gehrmann, Ellen Jiang, Mahima Pushkarna, Carey Radebaugh, Emily Reif, and Ann Yuan. 2020. The language interpretability tool: Extensible, interactive visualizations and analysis for nlp models.

Eric Wallace, Jens Tuyls, Junlin Wang, Sanjay Subramanian, Matt Gardner, and Sameer Singh. 2019. Allennlp interpret: A framework for explaining predictions of nlp models.

Thomas Wolf, Lysandre Debut, Victor Sanh, Julien Chaumond, Clement Delangue, Anthony Moi, Pierric Cistac, Tim Rault, Rémi Louf, Morgan Funtowicz, Joe Davison, Sam Shleifer, Patrick von Platen, Clara Ma, Yacine Jernite, Julien Plu, Canwen Xu, Teven Le Scao, Sylvain Gugger, Mariama Drame, Quentin Lhoest, and Alexander M Rush. 2019. HuggingFace's transformers: State-of-the-art natural language processing.

Yuan Zang, Fanchao Qi, Chenghao Yang, Zhiyuan Liu, Meng Zhang, Qun Liu, and Maosong Sun. 2020. Word-level textual adversarial attacking as combinatorial optimization. In *Proceedings of the 58th Annual Meeting of the Association for Computational Linguistics*, pages 6066–6080, Online. Association for Computational Linguistics.

Wei Emma Zhang, Quan Z Sheng, Ahoud Alhazmi, and Chenliang Li. 2020. Adversarial attacks on deep-learning models in natural language processing: A survey. *ACM Trans. Intell. Syst. Technol.*, 11(3):1–41.

ToModAPI: A Topic Modeling API to Train, Use and Compare Topic Models

Pasquale Lisena, Ismail Harrando, Oussama Kandakji and Raphaël Troncy
EURECOM, Sophia Antipolis, France
{firstname.lastname}@eurecom.fr

Abstract

From LDA to neural models, different topic modeling approaches have been proposed in the literature. However, their suitability and performance is not easy to compare, particularly when the algorithms are being used in the wild on heterogeneous datasets. In this paper, we introduce ToModAPI (*TOpic MOdeling API*), a wrapper library to easily train, evaluate and infer using different topic modeling algorithms through a unified interface. The library is extensible and can be used in Python environments or through a Web API.

1 Introduction

The analysis of massive volumes of text is an extremely expensive activity when it relies on not-scalable manual approaches or crowdsourcing strategies. Relevant tasks typically include textual document classification, document clustering, keywords and named entities extraction, language or sequence modeling, etc. In the literature, topic modeling and topic extraction, which enable to automatically recognise the main subject (or topic) in a text, have attracted a lot of interest. The predicted topics can be used for clustering documents, for improving named entity extraction (Newman et al., 2006), and for automatic recommendation of related documents (Luostarinen and Kohonen, 2013).

Several topic modeling algorithms have been proposed. However, we argue that it is hard to compare and to choose the most appropriate one given a particular goal. Furthermore, the algorithms are often evaluated on different datasets and different scoring metrics are used. In this work, we have selected some of the most popular topic modeling algorithms from the state of the art in order to integrate them in a common platform, which homogenises the interface methods and the evaluation

metrics. The result is ToModAPI[1] which allows to dynamically train, evaluate, perform inference on different models, and extract information from these models as well, making it possible to compare them using different metrics.

The remaining of this paper is organised as follows. In Section 2, we describe some related works and we detail some state-of-the-art topic modeling techniques. In Section 3, we provide an overview of the evaluation metrics usually used. We introduce ToModAPI in Section 4. We then describe some datasets (Section 5) that are used in training to perform a comparison of the topic models (Section 6). Finally, we give some conclusions and outline future work in Section 7.

2 Related Work

Aside from a few exceptions (Blei and McAuliffe, 2007), most topic modeling works propose or apply unsupervised methods. Instead of learning the mapping to a pre-defined set of topics (or labels), the goal of these methods consists in assigning training documents to N unknown topics, where N is a required parameter. Usually, these models compute two distributions: a Document-Topic distribution which represents the probability of each document to belong to each topic, and a Topic-Word distribution which represents the probability of each topic to be represented by each word present in the documents. These distributions are used to predict (or infer) the topic of unseen documents.

Latent Dirichlet Allocation (LDA) is a unsupervised statistical modeling approach (Blei et al., 2003) that considers each document as a *bag of words* and creates a randomly assigned document-topic and word-topic distribution. Iterating over words in each document, the distributions are updated according to the probability that a document

---

[1] ToModAPI: TOpic MODeling API

Proceedings of Second Workshop for NLP Open Source Software (NLP-OSS), pages 132–140
Virtual Conference, November 19, 2020. ©2020 Association for Computational Linguistics

or a word belongs to a certain topic. The **Hierarchical Dirichlet Process (HDP)** model (Teh et al., 2006) is another statistical approach for clustering grouped data such as text documents. It considers each document as a group of words belonging with a certain probability to one or multiple components of a mixture model, i.e. the topics. Both the probability measure for each document (distribution over the topics) and the base probability measure – which allows the sharing of clusters across documents – are drawn from Dirichlet Processes (Ferguson, 1973). Differently from many other topic models, HDP infers the number of topics automatically.

Gibbs Sampling for a DMM (GSDMM) applies the Dirichlet Multinomial Mixture model for short text clustering (Yin and Wang, 2014). This algorithm works computing iteratively the probability that a document join a specific one of the N available clusters. This probability consist in two parts: 1) a part that promotes the clusters with more documents; 2) a part that advantages the movement of a document towards similar clusters, i.e. which contains a similar word-set. Those two parts are controlled by the parameters α and β. The simplicity of GSDMM provides a fast convergence after some iterations. This algorithm consider the given number of clusters given as an upper bound and it might end up with a lower number of topics. From another perspective, it is somehow able to infer the optimal number of topics, given the upper bound.

Pre-trained Word vectors such as word2vec (Mikolov et al., 2013) or GloVe (Pennington et al., 2014) can help to enhance topic-word representations, as achieved by the **Latent Feature Topic Models (LFTM)** (Nguyen et al., 2015). One of the LFTM algorithms is *Latent Feature LDA (LF-LDA)*, which extends the original LDA algorithm by enriching the topic-word distribution with a latent feature component composed of pre-trained word vectors. In the same vein, the **Paragraph Vector Topic Model (PVTM)** (Lenz and Winker, 2020) uses doc2vec (Le and Mikolov, 2014) to generate document-level representations in a common embedding space. Then, it fits a Gaussian Mixture Model to cluster all the similar documents into a predetermined number of topics – i.e. the number of GMM components.

Topic modeling can also be performed via linear-algebraic methods. Starting from the the high-dimensional term-document matrix, multiple approaches can be used to lower its dimensions. Then, we consider every dimension in the lower-rank matrix as a latent topic. A straightforward application of this principle is the **Latent Semantic Indexing model (LSI)** (Deerwester et al., 1990), which uses Singular Value Decomposition as a means to approximate the term-document matrix (potentially mediated by TF-IDF) into one with less rows – each one representing a latent semantic dimension in the data – and preserving the similarity structure among columns (terms). **Non-negative Matrix Factorisation (NMF)** (Paatero and Tapper, 1994) exploits the fact that the term-document matrix is non-negative, thus producing not only a denser representation of the term-document distribution through the matrix factorisation but guaranteeing that the membership of a document to each topic is represented by a positive coefficient.

In recent years, neural network approaches for topic modeling have gained popularity giving birth to a family of **Neural Topic Models (NTM)** (Cao et al., 2015). Among those, **doc2topic (D2T)**[2] uses a neural network which separately computes N-dimensional embedding vectors for words and documents – with N equal to the number of topics, before computing the final output using a sigmoid activation. The distributions topic-word and document-topic are obtained by getting the final weights on the two embedding layers. Another neural topic model, the **Contextualized Topic Model (CTM)** (Bianchi et al., 2020) uses Sentence-BERT (SBERT) (Reimers and Gurevych, 2019) – a neural transformer language model designed to compute sentences representations efficiently – to generate a fixed-size embedding for each document to contextualise the usual Bag of Words representation. CTM enhances the *Neural-ProdLDA* (Srivastava and Sutton, 2017) architecture with this contextual representation to significantly improve the coherence of the generated topics.

Previous works have tried to compare different topic models. A review of statistical topic modeling techniques is included in Newman et al. (2006). A comparison and evaluation of LDA and NMF using the coherence metric is proposed by O'Callaghan et al. (2015). Among the libraries for performing topic modeling, *Gensim* is undoubtedly the most known one, providing implementations of

---

[2]`https://github.com/sronnqvist/doc2topic`

several tools for the NLP field (Řehůřek and Sojka, 2010). Focusing on topic modeling for short texts, *STMM* includes 11 different topic models, which can be trained and evaluated through command line (Qiang et al., 2019). The *Topic Modelling Open Source Tool*[3] exposes a web graphical user interface for training and evaluating topic models, LDA being the only representative so far. The *Promoss Topic Modelling Toolbox*[4] provides a unified Java command line interface for computing a topic model distribution using LDA or the *Hierarchical Multi-Dirichlet Process Topic Model (HMDP)* (Kling, 2016). However, it does not allow to apply the computed model on unseen documents.

3 Metrics

The evaluation of machine learning techniques often relies on accuracy scores computed comparing predicted results against a ground truth. In the case of unsupervised techniques like topic modeling, the ground truth is not always available. For this reason, in the literature, we can find:

- metrics which enable to evaluate a topic model independently from a ground truth, among which, coherence measures are the most popular ones for topic modeling (Röder et al., 2015; O'Callaghan et al., 2015; Qiang et al., 2019);

- metrics that measure the quality of a model's predictions by comparing its resulting clusters against ground truth labels, in this case a topic label for each document.

3.1 Coherence metrics

The coherence metrics rely on the joint probability $P(w_i, w_j)$ of two words w_i and w_j that is computed by counting the number of documents in which those words occur together divided by the total number of documents in the corpus. The documents are fragmented using sliding windows of a given length, and the probability is given by the number of fragments including both w_i and w_j divided by the total number of fragments. This probability can be expressed through the *Pointwise Mutual Information (PMI)*, defined as:

$$PMI(w_i, w_j) = log\frac{P(w_i, w_j) + \epsilon}{P(w_i) \cdot P(w_j)} \quad (1)$$

A small value is chosen for ϵ, in order to avoid computing the logarithm of 0. Different metrics based on PMI have been introduced in the literature, differing in the strategies applied for token segmentation, probability estimation, confirmation measure, and aggregation. The **UCI coherence** (Röder et al., 2015) averages the PMI computed between pairs of topics, according to:

$$C_{UCI} = \frac{2}{N \cdot (N-1)} \sum_{i=1}^{N-1} \sum_{j=i+1}^{N} PMI(w_i, w_j) \quad (2)$$

The **UMASS coherence** (Röder et al., 2015) relies instead on a differently computed joint probability:

$$C_{UMASS} = \frac{2}{N \cdot (N-1)} \sum_{i=1}^{N-1} \sum_{j=i+1}^{N} log\frac{P(w_i, w_j) + \epsilon}{P(w_j)} \quad (3)$$

The **Normalized Pointwise Mutual Information (NPMI)** (Chiarcos et al., 2009) applies the PMI in a confirmation measure for defining the association between two words:

$$NPMI(w_i, w_j) = \frac{PMI(w_i, w_j)}{-log(P(w_i, w_j) + \epsilon)} \quad (4)$$

NPMI values go from -1 (never co-occurring words) to +1 (always co-occurring), while the value of 0 suggests complete independence. This measure can be applied also to word sets. This is made possible using a vector representation in which each feature consists in the NPMI computed between w_i and a word in the corpus W, according to the formula:

$$\vec{v}(w_i) = \left\{ NPMI(w_i, w_j) | w_j \in W \right\} \quad (5)$$

In ToModAPI, we include the following four metrics[5]:

- C_{NPMI} applies NPMI as in Eqn (4) to couples of words, computing their joint probabilities using sliding windows;

- C_V compute the cosine similarity of the vectors – as defined in Eqn (5) – related to each word of the topic. The NPMI is computed on sliding windows;

- C_{UCI} as in Eqn (2);

- C_{UMASS} as in Eqn (3).

---

[3] https://github.com/opeyemibami/
Topic-Modelling-Open-Source-Tool
[4] https://github.com/gesiscss/promoss

[5] We use the implementation of these metrics as provided in Gensim. The window size is kept at the default values.

Additionally, we include a **Word Embeddings-based Coherence** as introduced by Fang et al. (2016). This metric relies on pre-trained word embeddings such as GloVe or word2vec and evaluate the topic quality using a similarity metric between its top words. In other words, a high mutual embedding similarity between a model's top words reflects its underlying semantic coherence. In the context of this paper, we will use the sum of mutual cosine similarity computed on the Glove vectors[6] of the top $N = 10$ words of each topic:

$$C_{WE} = \frac{2}{N \cdot (N-1)} \sum_{i=1}^{N-1} \sum_{j=i+1}^{N} cos(v_i, v_j) \quad (6)$$

where v_i and v_j are the GloVe vectors of the words w_i and w_j.

All metrics aggregate the different values at topic level using the arithmetic mean, in order to provide a coherence value for the whole model.

3.2 Metrics which relies on a ground truth

The most used metric that relies on a ground truth is the **Purity**, defined as the fraction of documents in each cluster with a correct prediction (Hajjem and Latiri, 2017). A prediction is considered correct if the original label coincides with the original label of the majority of documents falling in the same topic prediction. Given L the set of original labels and T the set of predictions:

$$Purity(T, L) = \frac{1}{|T|} \sum_{i \in T} \max_{j \in L} |T_j \cap L_j| \quad (7)$$

In addition, we include in the API the following metrics used in the literature for evaluating the quality of classification or clustering algorithms, applied to the topic modeling task:

1. **Homogeneity**: a topic model output is considered homogeneous if all documents assigned to each topic belong to the same ground-truth label (Rosenberg and Hirschberg, 2007);

2. **Completeness**: a topic model output is considered complete if all documents from one ground-truth label fall into the same topic (Rosenberg and Hirschberg, 2007);

3. **V-Measure**: the harmonic mean of Homogeneity and Completeness. A V-Measure of

1.0 corresponds to a perfect alignment between topic model outputs and ground truth labels (Rosenberg and Hirschberg, 2007);

4. **Normalized Mutual Information (NMI)** is the ratio between the mutual information between two distributions – in our case, the prediction set and the ground truth – normalised through an aggregation of those distributions' entropies (Lancichinetti et al., 2009). The aggregation can be realised by selecting the minimum/maximum or applying the geometric/arithmetic mean. In the case of arithmetic mean, NMI is equivalent to the V-Measure.

For these metrics, we use the implementations provided by scikit-learn (Pedregosa et al., 2011).

4 ToModAPI: a Topic Modeling API

We now introduce ToModAPI, a Python library which harmonises the interfaces of topic modeling algorithms. So far, 9 topic modeling algorithms have been integrated in the library (Table 1).

For each algorithm, the following interface methods are exposed:

- `train` which requires in input the path of a dataset and an algorithm-specific set of training parameters;

- `topics` which returns the list of trained topics and, for each of them, the 10 most representative words. Where available, the weights of those words in representing the topic are given;

- `topic` which returns the information (representative words and weights) about a single topic;

- `predict` which performs the topic inference on a given (unseen) text;

- `get_training_predictions` which provides the final predictions made on the training corpus. Where possible, this method is not performing a new inference on the text, but returns the predictions obtained during the training;

- `coherence` which computes the chosen coherence metric – among the ones described in Section 3.1 – on a given dataset;

- `evaluate` which evaluate the model predictions against a given ground truth, using the metrics described in Section 3.2.

---

[6]We use a Glove model pre-trained on Wikipedia 2014 + Gigaword 5, available at `https://nlp.stanford.edu/projects/glove/`

Algorithm	Acronym	Source implementation
Latent Dirichlet Allocation	LDA	`http://mallet.cs.umass.edu/` (McCallum, 2002) (JAVA)
Latent Feature Topic Models	LFTM	`https://github.com/datquocnguyen/LFTM` (JAVA)
Doc2Topic	D2T	`https://github.com/sronnqvist/doc2topic`
Gibbs Sampling for a DMM	GSDMM	`https://github.com/rwalk/gsdmm`
Non-Negative Matrix Factorization	NMF	`https://radimrehurek.com/gensim/models/nmf.html`
Hierarchical Dirichlet Processing	HDP	`https://radimrehurek.com/gensim/models/hdpmodel.html`
Latent Semantic Indexing	LSI	`https://radimrehurek.com/gensim/models/lsimodel.html`
Paragraph Vector Topic Model	PVTM	`https://github.com/davidlenz/pvtm`
Context Topic Model	CTM	`https://github.com/MilaNLProc/contextualized-topic-models`

Table 1: Algorithms included in ToModAPI, with their source implementation. The original implementation of those model is in Python unless specified otherwise.

The structure of the library, which relies on class inheritance, is easy to extend with the addition of new models. In addition to allowing the import in any Python environment and use the library offline, it provides the possibility of automatically build a web API, in order to access to the different methods through HTTP calls. Table 2 provides a comparison between the ToModAPI, Gensim and STMM. Given that we wrap some Gensim models and methods (i.e. for coherence computation), some similarities between it and our work can be observed.

The software is distributed under an open source license[7]. A demo of the web API is available at `http://hyperted.eurecom.fr/topic`.

5 Datasets and pre-trained models

Together with the library, we provide pre-trained models trained on two different datasets having different characteristics (20NG and AFP). A common pre-processing is performed on the datasets before training, consisting of:

- Removing numbers, which, in general, do not contribute to the broad semantics;

- Removing the punctuation and lower-casing;

- Removing the standard English stop words;

- Lemmatisation using Wordnet, in order to deal with inflected forms as a single semantic item;

- Ignoring words with 2 letters or less. In facts, they are mainly residuals from removing punctuation – e.g. stripping punctuation from *people's* produces *people* and *s*.

The same pre-processing is also applied to the text before topic prediction.

5.1 20 NewsGroups

The 20 NewsGroups collection (20NG) (Lang, 1995) is a popular dataset used for text classification and clustering. It is composed of English news documents, distributed fairly equally across 20 different categories according to the subject of the text. We use a reduced version of this dataset[8], which excludes all the documents composed by the sole header while preserving an even partition over the 20 categories. This reduced dataset contains 11,314 documents. We pre-process the dataset in order to remove irrelevant metadata – consisting of email addresses and news feed identifiers – keeping just the textual content. The average number of words per document is 142.

5.2 Agence France Presse

The Agence France Presse (AFP) publishes daily up to 2000 news articles in 5 different languages[9], together with some metadata represented in the NewsML XML-based format. Each document is categorised using one or more subject codes, taken from the IPTC NewsCode Concept vocabulary[10]. In case of multiple subjects, they are ordered by relevance. In this work, we only consider the first level of the hierarchy of the IPTC subject codes. We extracted a dataset containing 125,516 news documents in English and corresponding to the production of AFP for the year 2019, with 237 words per document on average.

Table 3 summarizes the number of documents for each topic in those two datasets. In AFP, a single document can be assigned to multiple subject, so we take each assignment into account. The two

---

[7]`https://github.com/D2KLab/ToModAPI`

[8]`https://github.com/selva86/datasets/`
[9]The catalogue can be explored at `http://medialab.afp.com/afp4w/`
[10]`http://cv.iptc.org/newscodes/subjectcode/`

library	Gensim	STMM	ToModAPI
algorithms	8: LDA, LDA Sequence, LDA multicore, NMF, LSI, HDP, Author-topic model, DTM	11: LDA, LFTM, DMM, BTM, WNTM, PTM, SATM, ETM, GPU-DMM, GPU-PDMM, LF-DMM	9: LDA, LFTM, D2T, GSDMM, NMF, HDP, LSI, PVTM, CTM
language	Python	Java	Python
focus	general	short text	general
training	✓	✓	✓
inference	✓	✓	✓
corpus predictions	(by inferencing the corpus)	✓	✓
coherence metrics	c_{umass}, c_v, c_{uci}, c_{npmi}	c_{umass}	c_{umass}, c_v, c_{uci}, c_{npmi}
Evaluation with Ground Truth	-	purity, NMI	purity, homogeneity, completeness, v-measure, NMI
usage	import in script	command line	import in script, web API

Table 2: Comparison between topic modeling libraries. For details about the acronyms, refer to the documentation

datasets present multiple differences: total number of documents, distribution of documents per subject, and the fact that for AFP, one document can have multiple subjects.

20NG		AFP	
rec.sport.hockey	600	Politics	47277
soc.religion.christian	599	Sport	36901
rec.motorcycles	598	Economy, Business, Finance	31042
rec.sport.baseball	597	Unrest, Conflicts and War	21140
sci.crypt	595	Crime, Law and Justice	16977
sci.med	594	Art, Culture, Entertainment	8586
rec.autos	594	Social Issues	7609
comp.windows.x	593	Disasters and Accidents	5893
sci.space	593	Human Interest	4159
comp.os.ms-windows.misc	591	Environmental Issue	4036
sci.electronics	591	Science and Technology	3502
comp.sys.ibm.pc.hardware	590	Religion and Belief	3081
misc.forsale	585	Lifestyle and Leisure	3044
comp.graphics	584	Labour	2570
comp.sys.mac.hardware	578	Health	2535
talk.politics.mideast	564	Weather	1159
talk.politics.guns	546	Education	734
alt.atheism	480		
talk.politics.misc	465		
talk.religion.misc	377		
Total	11314	Total	125516

Table 3: Number of documents per subject in 20NG (20 topics) and AFP (17 topics)

5.3 Wikipedia Corpus

We also describe the Wikipedia corpus (Wiki)[11], which is a readily extracted and organised snapshot from 2013 that includes pages with at least 20 page views in English. This corpus has been used in other works, for example, for computing word embeddings (Leimeister and Wilson, 2018). The corpus is distributed with some pre-processing already applied, like lower-casing and punctuation

stripping. However, we performed additional operations such as lemmatisation, stop-word and small word (2 characters or less) removal. The dataset consists of around 463k documents with 498M words. This corpus will not be used for training but only for evaluating the models (trained on 20NG or AFP) in order to reflect on the generalisation of the topics models.

6 Experiment and Results

We empirically evaluate the performances of the topic modeling algorithms described in Section 2 on the two datasets presented in Section 5 using the metrics detailed in Section 3. For each algorithm, we trained two different models, respectively on 20NG and AFP corpus. The number of topics – when required by the algorithm – has been set to 20 and 7 when training on 20NG and AFP, respectively, in order to mimic the original division in class labels of the corpora (except for GSDMM and HDP which infer the optimal number of topics). Each model trained on either 20NG or AFP is tested against the same dataset and the Wikipedia dataset to compute each metric.

Table 4 shows the average coherence scores of the topics computed on the 20NG dataset, together with the standard deviation, while the results of Table 5 refer to models computed on the AFP dataset. The results differ depending on the studied metric and the evaluation dataset. LFTM generalises better when evaluated against the Wikipedia corpus, probably thanks to the usage of pre-trained word vectors on large corpora. Overall, LDA has the best results on all metrics, always being among

---

[11]https://storage.googleapis.com/lateral-datadumps/wikipedia_utf8_filtered_20pageviews.csv.gz

	C_v				C_{NPMI}				C_{UMASS}				C_{UCI}			
	20NG		wiki		20NG		wiki		20NG		wiki		20NG		wiki	
CTM	0.56	(0.15)	0.46	(0.24)	-0.04	(0.19)	-0.06	(0.16)	-5.78	(5.27)	-4.28	(3.94)	-3.09	(4.18)	-2.51	(3.95)
D2T	0.57	(0.14)	0.51	(0.10)	0.01	(0.11)	0.05	(0.05)	-2.94	(1.67)	-2.02	(0.49)	-1.56	(2.39)	0.16	(0.81)
GSDMM	0.50	(0.18)	0.41	(0.20)	0.00	(0.19)	-0.04	(0.09)	-3.86	(2.88)	-2.45	(1.04)	-2.02	(3.16)	-1.44	(2.26)
HDP	0.44	(0.21)	0.48	(0.24)	-0.09	(0.17)	-0.04	(0.10)	-5.59	(5.04)	-3.25	(3.18)	-5.59	(5.04)	-2.21	(2.64)
LDA	**0.64**	(0.14)	0.55	(0.16)	**0.10**	(0.08)	**0.07**	(0.06)	-1.98	(0.68)	-1.75	(0.45)	**0.27**	(1.30)	0.53	(0.88)
LFTM	0.53	(0.09)	**0.56**	(0.17)	-0.01	(0.10)	**0.07**	(0.06)	-2.97	(3.15)	-1.72	(0.69)	-1.47	(2.47)	**0.58**	(0.76)
LSI	0.53	(0.22)	0.41	(0.11)	0.03	(0.16)	-0.04	(0.10)	-3.25	(2.16)	-2.64	(1.08)	-1.37	(2.89)	-1.69	(2.59)
NMF	0.61	(0.19)	0.52	(0.15)	0.10	(0.15)	-0.02	(0.12)	-2.37	(1.61)	-3.08	(4.83)	-0.03	(2.24)	-1.27	(2.97)
PVTM	0.54	(0.09)	0.46	(0.11)	0.06	(0.04)	0.04	(0.06)	**-1.63**	(0.82)	**-1.52**	(0.54)	0.21	(0.92)	0.25	(0.74)

Table 4: The mean and standard deviation of different coherence metrics computed on 2 reference corpora 20NG and Wikipedia. The models have been trained on 20NG.

	C_v				C_{NPMI}				C_{UMASS}				C_{UCI}			
	AFP		wiki		AFP		wiki		AFP		wiki		AFP		wiki	
CTM	0.54	(0.15)	0.56	(0.28)	-0.05	(0.17)	-0.04	(0.09)	-6.56	(5.94)	-3.47	(2.96)	-2.75	(3.73)	-1.49	(2.17)
D2T	0.58	(0.14)	0.45	(0.10)	0.06	(0.07)	-0.01	(0.07)	-2.25	(0.49)	-2.44	(0.73)	-0.02	(0.93)	-1.07	(1.42)
GSDMM	0.51	(0.12)	0.58	(0.17)	0.09	(0.07)	0.03	(0.11)	-1.72	(0.47)	-2.73	(1.31)	0.70	(0.66)	-0.29	(1.59)
HDP	0.42	(0.10)	**0.69**	(0.22)	0.02	(0.07)	0.01	(0.16)	-2.23	(0.92)	-2.74	(2.63)	-0.20	(1.05)	-0.63	(2.86)
LDA	0.65	(0.10)	0.54	(0.11)	0.11	(0.04)	**0.06**	(0.06)	-1.40	(0.23)	-1.88	(0.48)	0.80	(0.30)	**0.25**	(0.89)
LFTM	0.59	(0.14)	0.54	(0.20)	0.06	(0.10)	**0.06**	(0.12)	-1.97	(2.40)	-1.91	(2.19)	0.11	(2.08)	0.22	(2.58)
LSI	0.58	(0.12)	0.55	(0.14)	0.07	(0.09)	0.05	(0.11)	-1.80	(0.47)	-2.59	(1.37)	0.09	(0.96)	-0.36	(1.87)
NMF	**0.67**	(0.12)	0.46	(0.12)	**0.13**	(0.06)	0.04	(0.07)	-1.27	(0.29)	-1.73	(0.69)	**0.95**	(0.42)	0.07	(1.26)
PVTM	0.52	(0.12)	0.51	(0.09)	0.07	(0.06)	0.04	(0.04)	**-1.16**	(0.34)	**-1.56**	0.86	0.49	(0.41)	0.14	(0.63)

Table 5: The mean and standard deviation of different coherence metrics computed on 2 reference corpora AFP and Wikipedia. The models have been trained on AFP.

the top ones in terms of coherence. When trained on AFP, all topic models benefit of a bigger dataset; this results in generally higher scores and in different algorithms maximising specific metrics.

We also consider the time taken by the different techniques for different tasks like training and getting prediction (Table 6). The results have been collected selecting the best of 3 different calls. The inference time has been computed using the models trained on the 20NG dataset, on a small sentence of 18 words[12]. The table shows LDA leading in training, while the longest execution time belongs to LFTM. The inference time for all models is in the order of few seconds or even less than 1 for GSDMM, HDP, LSI and PVTM. The manipulation of BERT embeddings makes CTM inference more time-consuming. The inference timing for D2T is not computed because its implementation is not available yet.

7 Conclusions and Future Work

In this paper, we introduced ToModAPI, a library and a Web API to easily train, test and evaluate topic models. 9 algorithms are already included in the library, while new ones will be added in future. Other evaluation metrics for topic modeling have been proposed (Wallach et al., 2009) and will be included in the API for enabling a complete evaluation. Among these, metrics based on word embeddings are gaining particular attention (Ding et al., 2018). For further exploiting the advantage of having a common interface, we will study ways to automatically tune each model's hyper-parameters such as the right number of topics, find an appropriate label for the computed topics, optimise and use the models in real world applications. Finally, future work includes a deeper comparison of the models trained on different datasets.

	Training		Inference
	20NG	AFP	
CTM	544	9,262	19
D2T	192	5,892	-
GSDMM	1,194	21,881	0
HDP	430	7,020	0
LDA	80	1,334	2
LFTM	3,119	15,100	1
LSI	383	6,716	0
NMF	357	6,320	5
PVTM	193	3,757	0

Table 6: Model comparison from a time (in seconds) delay standpoint for training and inference.

[12] *"Climate change is a global environmental issue that is affecting the lands, the oceans, the animals, and humans"*

Acknowledgments

This work has been partially supported by the French National Research Agency (ANR) within the ASRAEL (grant number ANR-15-CE23-0018) and ANTRACT (grant number ANR-17-CE38-0010) projects, and by the European Union's Horizon 2020 research and innovation program within the MeMAD (grant agreement No. 780069) and SILKNOW (grant agreement No. 769504) projects.

References

Federico Bianchi, Silvia Terragni, and Dirk Hovy. 2020. Pre-training is a hot topic: Contextualized document embeddings improve topic coherence. ArXiv.

David M. Blei and Jon D. McAuliffe. 2007. Supervised Topic Models. In 20th *International Conference on Neural Information Processing Systems (NIPS)*, pages 121—128.

David M. Blei, Andrew Y. Ng, and Michael I. Jordan. 2003. Latent Dirichlet Allocation. *Journal of Machine Learning Research*, 3:993—1022.

Ziqiang Cao, Sujian Li, Yang Liu, Wenjie Li, and Heng Ji. 2015. A Novel Neural Topic Model and Its Supervised Extension. In *AAAI Conference on Artificial Intelligence*.

Christian Chiarcos, Richard Eckart de Castilho, and Manfred Stede. 2009. *Von der Form zur Bedeutung: Texte automatisch verarbeiten - From Form to Meaning: Processing Texts Automatically*. Narr Francke Attempto Verlag GmbH + Co. KG.

Scott Deerwester, Susan T Dumais, George W Furnas, Thomas K Landauer, and Richard Harshman. 1990. Indexing by latent semantic analysis. *Journal of the American society for information science*, 41(6):391–407.

Ran Ding, Ramesh Nallapati, and Bing Xiang. 2018. Coherence-Aware Neural Topic Modeling. In *Conference on Empirical Methods in Natural Language Processing (EMNLP)*, pages 830–836, Brussels, Belgium.

Anjie Fang, Craig Macdonald, Iadh Ounis, and Philip Habel. 2016. Using Word Embedding to Evaluate the Coherence of Topics from Twitter Data. In 39th *International ACM SIGIR Conference on Research and Development in Information Retrieval*, pages 1057—1060.

Thomas S. Ferguson. 1973. A bayesian analysis of some nonparametric problems. *Annals of Statistics*, 1(2):209–230.

Malek Hajjem and Chiraz Latiri. 2017. Combining IR and LDA Topic Modeling for Filtering Microblogs. In 21st *International Conference on Knowledge-Based and Intelligent Information & Engineering Systems (KES)*, pages 761–770, Marseille, France.

Christoph Kling. 2016. *Probabilistic models for context in social media.* doctoral thesis, Universität Koblenz-Landau, Universitätsbibliothek.

Andrea Lancichinetti, Santo Fortunato, and János Kertész. 2009. Detecting the overlapping and hierarchical community structure in complex networks. *New Journal of Physics*, 11(3).

Ken Lang. 1995. NewsWeeder: Learning to Filter Netnews. In 20th *International Conference on Machine Learning (ICML)*, pages 331–339.

Quoc Le and Tomas Mikolov. 2014. Distributed representations of sentences and documents. In 31st *International Conference on Machine Learning (ICML)*, pages 1188–1196, Bejing, China.

Matthias Leimeister and Benjamin J. Wilson. 2018. Skip-gram word embeddings in hyperbolic space. Arxiv.

David Lenz and Peter Winker. 2020. Measuring the diffusion of innovations with paragraph vector topic models. *PLOS ONE*, 15:1–18.

Tapio Luostarinen and Oskar Kohonen. 2013. Using Topic Models in Content-Based News Recommender Systems. In 19th *Nordic Conference of Computational Linguistics (NODALIDA)*.

Andrew Kachites McCallum. 2002. MALLET: A Machine Learning for Language Toolkit.

Tomas Mikolov, Ilya Sutskever, Kai Chen, Greg Corrado, and Jeffrey Dean. 2013. Distributed Representations of Words and Phrases and Their Compositionality. In 26th *International Conference on Neural Information Processing Systems (NIPS)*, volume 2, pages 3111–3119, Lake Tahoe, NV, USA.

David Newman, Chaitanya Chemudugunta, Padhraic Smyth, and Mark Steyvers. 2006. Analyzing Entities and Topics in News Articles Using Statistical Topic Models. In *Intelligence and Security Informatics*, pages 93–104.

Dat Quoc Nguyen, Richard Billingsley, Lan Du, and Mark Johnson. 2015. Improving Topic Models with Latent Feature Word Representations. *Transactions of the Association for Computational Linguistics*, 3:299–313.

Derek O'Callaghan, Derek Greene, Joe Carthy, and Pádraig Cunningham. 2015. An analysis of the coherence of descriptors in topic modeling. *Expert Systems with Applications*, 42(13):5645–5657.

Pentti Paatero and Unto Tapper. 1994. Positive matrix factorization: A non-negative factor model with optimal utilization of error estimates of data values. *Environmetrics*, 5(2):111–126.

Fabian Pedregosa, Gaël Varoquaux, Alexandre Gramfort, Vincent Michel, Bertrand Thirion, Olivier Grisel, Mathieu Blondel, Peter Prettenhofer, Ron Weiss, Vincent Dubourg, Jake Vanderplas, Alexandre Passos, David Cournapeau, Matthieu Brucher, Matthieu Perrot, and Edouard Duchesnay. 2011. Scikit-learn: Machine Learning in Python. *Journal of Machine Learning Research*, 12:2825–2830.

Jeffrey Pennington, Richard Socher, and Christopher D. Manning. 2014. GloVe: Global Vectors for Word Representation. In *Empirical Methods in Natural Language Processing (EMNLP)*, pages 1532–1543.

Jipeng Qiang, Zhenyu Qian, Yun Li, Yunhao Yuan, and Xindong Wu. 2019. Short Text Topic Modeling Techniques, Applications, and Performance: A Survey. Arxiv.

Radim Řehůřek and Petr Sojka. 2010. Software Framework for Topic Modelling with Large Corpora. In *LREC Workshop on New Challenges for NLP Frameworks*, pages 45–50, Valletta, Malta.

Nils Reimers and Iryna Gurevych. 2019. Sentence-BERT: Sentence embeddings using Siamese BERT-networks. In *Conference on Empirical Methods in Natural Language Processing (EMNLP)*, pages 3982–3992, Hong Kong, China.

Michael Röder, Andreas Both, and Alexander Hinneburg. 2015. Exploring the space of topic coherence measures. In 8th *ACM International Conference on Web Search and Data Mining (WSDM)*, pages 399–408.

Andrew Rosenberg and Julia Hirschberg. 2007. V-Measure: A Conditional Entropy-Based External Cluster Evaluation Measure. In *Joint Conference on Empirical Methods in Natural Language Processing and Computational Natural Language Learning (EMNLP-CoNLL)*, pages 410–420, Prague, Czech Republic.

Akash Srivastava and Charles Sutton. 2017. Autoencoding variational inference for topic models. In *International Conference on Learning Representations (ICLR)*.

Yee Whye Teh, Michael I Jordan, Matthew J Beal, and David M Blei. 2006. Hierarchical dirichlet processes. *Journal of the American Statistical Association*, 101(476):1566–1581.

Hanna M. Wallach, Iain Murray, Ruslan Salakhutdinov, and David Mimno. 2009. Evaluation methods for topic models. In 26th *Annual International Conference on Machine Learning (ICML)*, pages 1105–1112.

Jianhua Yin and Jianyong Wang. 2014. A Dirichlet Multinomial Mixture Model-Based Approach for Short Text Clustering. In 20th *ACM SIGKDD International Conference on Knowledge Discovery and Data Mining (KDD)*, pages 233–242.

User-centered & Robust Open-source Software: Lessons Learned from Developing & Maintaining *RSMTool*

Nitin Madnani
Educational Testing Service
Princeton, NJ
nmadnani@ets.org

Anastassia Loukina
Educational Testing Service
Princeton, NJ
aloukina@ets.org

Abstract

For the last 5 years, we have developed and maintained *RSMTool* – an open-source tool for evaluating NLP systems that automatically score written and spoken responses. *RSMTool* is designed to be cross-disciplinary, borrowing heavily from NLP, machine learning, and educational measurement. Its cross-disciplinary nature has required us to learn a user-centered development approach in terms of both design and implementation. We share some of these lessons in this paper.

1 Motivation

Automated scoring of open-ended written and spoken responses is a fast growing field in educational NLP. Many automated scoring systems employ machine learning models to predict scores for such responses based on features extracted from the text/audio of such responses. Examples of deployed automated scoring systems include Project Essay Grade[1] for written responses and SpeechRater®[2] for spoken responses (Zechner et al., 2009; Chen et al., 2018). Automated scoring systems may offer some advantages over humans, e.g., higher score consistency (Williamson et al., 2012). Yet like any other machine learning algorithm, models used for score prediction may inadvertently encode discrimination into their decisions due to biases or other imperfections in the training data, spurious correlations, and other factors (Xi, 2010; Romei and Ruggieri, 2013; von Davier, 2016; Zieky, 2016). Given that many such systems are used to score high-stakes standardized tests, the consequences of any form of bias can have a significant effect on people's lives. Therefore, it is critical that automated scoring systems be evaluated as thoroughly as possible to detect any harmful, systematic biases in their predictions. However, this may prove difficult for an NLP or machine learning researcher since they may be unfamiliar with the required psychometric and statistical checks. *RSMTool* incorporates a large, diverse set of psychometric and statistical analyses aimed at detecting possible bias in system performance and makes them available in an easy-to-use package. *RSMTool* is open-source and non-proprietary so that the automated scoring community can not only audit the source code of the already available analyses to ensure their compliance with fairness standards but also contribute new analyses.

2 Introduction

Creating and releasing open-source software is a great way to share knowledge by making highly-specialized methods and techniques accessible to a wider community. Yet many NLP (or machine learning) tools are not designed with a user-centered focus, hindering their wider adoption. Almost a decade ago, Chapman et al. (2011) pointed out that NLP systems were seldom deployed in clinical settings because they were not well integrated into existing user workflows and required substantial input from an NLP expert. More recently, Cai and Guo (2019) found that a "steep learning curve", the need to convert raw data into algorithmic inputs and outputs, and various challenges in getting started are still the most common hurdles reported by software engineers when using open-source machine learning software.

In the subsequent sections, we share our experiences of developing and maintaining *RSMTool*, an open-source Python tool[3] which provides a framework to evaluate systems for automated scoring of

---

[1] https://www.measurementinc.com/products-services/automated-essay-scoring

[2] https://www.ets.org/accelerate/ai-portfolio/speechrater

[3] https://github.com/EducationalTestingService/rsmtool

Proceedings of Second Workshop for NLP Open Source Software (NLP-OSS), pages 141–146
Virtual Conference, November 19, 2020. ©2020 Association for Computational Linguistics

written and spoken responses (Madnani and Loukina, 2016; Madnani et al., 2017). *RSMTool* is developed as part of a close collaboration between NLP researchers and specialists in educational measurement, assessment and psychometrics. It combines the latest advances from these disciplines to provide a comprehensive evaluation of automated scoring systems, including model fairness and test-theory based measures.

RSMTool was initially developed as a monolithic command-line tool that accepted input in a single format and generated a static model evaluation report as the only output. Over time, it became clear that this one-size-fits-all approach was not ideal. Operational development of an automated scoring system requires collaboration between many stakeholders including NLP researchers, engineers, psychometricians and business units (Madnani and Cahill, 2018). The interdisciplinary nature of this community led to the emergence of several distinct *RSMTool* user groups. Each of these groups had separate requirements in terms of entry points, inputs, outputs, and documentation. Only by addressing all of these diverse requirements were we able to achieve wider adoption of *RSMTool* for model evaluation (Rupp et al., 2019; Yoon and Lee, 2019; Kwong et al., 2020).

The lessons we share are the salient ones we have learnt along the way: that different users have different needs and that going the extra mile on robustness – tests, documentation, and packaging – is essential to satisfy these needs. We believe that many of the points we discuss will be applicable to a range of NLP tools and, thus, could benefit the wider NLP OSS community.

3 RSMTool

3.1 Motivation

A single evaluation metric such as Pearson's correlation coefficient or Quadratically-weighted Kappa represents only one aspect of system performance. An automated scoring system deployed in a high-stakes application can have a significant impact on people's lives and, therefore, requires a comprehensive evaluation to ensure its accuracy, validity and fairness (Ramineni and Williamson, 2013). The goal of *RSMTool* is to encourage comprehensive reporting of model performance and to make it easier for stakeholders to compare different models along all necessary dimensions before model deployment. This includes not only standard agree-

ment metrics, but also metrics developed within the educational measurement community and not commonly found in existing Python packages, such as measures of system performance based on test theory (Haberman, 2008; Loukina et al., 2020) as well as measures to evaluate fairness of system scores (Williamson et al., 2012; Madnani et al., 2017; Loukina et al., 2019). In this respect, our approach is similar in spirit to "Model cards" proposed by Mitchell et al. (2019) or standardized data statements advocated by Bender and Friedman (2018).

3.2 Architecture

RSMTool combines multiple analyses that are commonly conducted when building and evaluating automated scoring engines in a single package. In a typical use case, a user provides a file or a data frame with numeric system scores, gold-standard (human) scores, and metadata, if applicable. The tool processes the data and generates an HTML report containing a comprehensive evaluation including descriptive statistics on the input data and multiple measures of system performance and fairness among others[4]. *RSMTool* is written entirely in Python and makes heavy use of common Python libraries such as `pandas` (McKinney, 2010) and `scikit-learn` (Pedregosa et al., 2011). Each section of the report is implemented as a separate Jupyter notebook (Kluyver et al., 2016). The user can choose which sections should be included in the final HTML report and in which order.

RSMTool is available on Github with an Apache 2.0 license and has extensive online documentation[5]. It also includes a well-documented API allowing advanced users to integrate various components of *RSMTool* into their own applications. For more details on how *RSMTool* works, see Madnani and Loukina (2016); Madnani et al. (2017).

4 Lesson 1: Users have Different Needs

Over the years, we have identified several groups of users for *RSMTool*. While the ultimate goal for each group is to conduct a comprehensive evaluation of automated scoring systems, their specific needs were very different and could not be addressed by a single one-size-fits-all approach. In what follows, we describe these users and their needs as well as how we addressed them.

---

[4]See a sample report at `https://bit.ly/fair-tool`.
[5]`https://rsmtool.readthedocs.io`

4.1 Power users: NLP researchers

NLP researchers working on automated scoring were our initial target group when developing *RSMTool*. This group of users uses *RSMTool* to evaluate how an NLP-driven change, e.g., a new scoring feature, affects various aspects of model performance, above and beyond prediction accuracy.

Entry points. We found that the users in this group feel constrained by an end-to-end pipeline. Instead, they prefer to *pick and choose* the *RSMTool* functionality to plug into *their own pipeline* for model building and evaluation while also *using other Python packages*. To achieve this, we created a comprehensive API to expose various pre- and post-processing functions as well as custom metrics contained in *RSMTool*.

Inputs and outputs. We designed the various API endpoints to accept and return standard data types such as pandas dataframes and numpy arrays. Whenever possible, we used naming and signature conventions similar to other commonly used packages such as scikit-learn and SKLL, our other open-source package for running batched machine learning experiments[6].

Documentation. Since these users rely mainly on the API, they expect standardized Python API documentation. To this end, all public functions, methods and classes in *RSMTool* code contain PEP257-compliant docstrings[7].

4.2 Minimalists: Data Analysts & Engineers

Operational scoring systems are routinely monitored by running data through the system at regular intervals to ensure that operational metrics continue to be met. The data analysts & engineers responsible for this effort may lack the statistical or programming background to interact with the API directly and generally expect an *out-of-the box pipeline*.

Entry points. A key requirement for this group is a simple way to run the evaluation pipeline in *batch mode*. To address this, we have created command-line tools as well as Python API endpoints that can run the entire evaluation pipeline that a user can easily call in wrapper shell scripts, for example.

Inputs and outputs. This group of users often need to run evaluations on data that may not have all of the information necessary for some of the evaluation notebooks. To accommodate this, we de-signed the command-line tools and API endpoints to accept custom configuration parameters via JSON files or Python dictionaries, respectively. Furthermore, we also produce the outputs of each individual evaluation as CSV/TSV/XLSX for further use in monitoring workflows.

Documentation. Minimalists need access to enough information to get started with the tool. Therefore, in addition to API doctrings, we also created plaintext documentation comprising installation instructions, how to run the full pipeline along with the available configuration options, and a detailed tutorial with a real-life example. Nonetheless, we found that such users are often reluctant to read through the (admittedly large) list of configuration options. Therefore, we built in an interactive configuration generator with autocompletion[8] that can help such users create configuration files based on their specific needs.

4.3 Decision Makers: Managers & Business Units

The final decision about the architecture of the scoring system and its deployment is made by multiple stakeholders: business units, psychometricians, assessment specialists, and senior NLP researchers not involved in hands-on development.

Inputs and outputs. The users in this group require a self-contained, concise, clear, and readable evaluation report that can be reviewed, shared or used to create a slide deck or a memo. This group remains the primary user of our HTML reports.

Documentation. A standard request from this group has been to provide a document explaining various aspects of *RSMTool* functionality, structured as a general-purpose memo rather than technical documentation. Therefore, in addition to the user manual, the *RSMTool* documentation contains a general overview of its functionality as well as the formulae used to compute all evaluation metrics.

5 Lesson 2: Go the Extra Mile

Based on our experience developing and maintaining RSMTool, we claim that one way to properly address the different needs of the different types of users is by going the extra mile to write *robust* software. We define robust software as follows: the impact of any code change on its accuracy and performance can be measured (**well-**

---

[6]https://skll.readthedocs.io
[7]https://www.python.org/dev/peps/pep-0257/

[8]https://rsmtool.readthedocs.io/en/stable/automated_configuration.html#interactive-generation

tested), its documentation is always up-to-date (**well-documented**), and it (along with its dependencies) can be **easily installed** by the users. Of course, many of us in the NLP community are not trained as software engineers and do not have much experience with these practices. We argue that it is necessary to put in the extra work to learn them in order to make a meaningful contribution to the community. Fortunately, there are several open-source and/or free-to-use tools and services that can help make adopting these practices relatively painless.

5.1 Testing & Continuous Integration

A critical component of any software is a comprehensive test suite that covers a large percentage of the overall codebase. Open-source software should be no different. As developers of the software, it is important to ensure that the code does what we (or our users) think it does. Test-driven development (Beck, 2003) is now a common development practice that is well-supported by most programming languages and frameworks. Specifically for Python, there are several open-source packages that make it easy to write tests (`unittest`; `nose`; `pytest`), generate test coverage reports (`coverage`), and reduce code duplication across tests (`parameterized`).

We also strongly recommend the use of continuous integration services like Travis CI[9] and Azure Pipelines[10]. These services are free for open-source projects and can be easily integrated with GitHub such that the entire test suite is automatically run on all major platforms (Linux, macOS, and Windows) whenever a change is proposed to the code, with the proposer of the change not allowed to merge it unless all the tests pass and there is no decrease in test coverage. This reduces the likelihood that a new change is untested or that it introduces a regression in existing functionality.

5.2 Documentation

A recent survey of open-source software users[11] reported that over 90% of them cited incomplete or outdated documentation as the most pervasive problem they encounter in open-source projects. Our experience with RSMTool echoes this: documentation is our most important resource since it helps orient users in how to navigate the project.

We have already discussed that documentation designed to accommodate different users should include the motivation for the project, installation instructions, tutorials, and a detailed user manual. 21% of respondents in the Cai and Guo (2019) survey cited lack of tutorials and examples as a significant hurdle to the adoption of machine learning packages. The respondents also noted that for users lacking conceptual understanding, a simple "hello world" tutorial makes it hard to progress beyond the initial installation. We recommend including multiple tutorials in the documentation; tutorials that not only allow the users to test that their installation works, but also walk them through using the software to solve an actual problem. Tutorials should explain the reasoning behind each step and include download links for any necessary files.

Additionally, the documentation *must* also make it easy for interested users to contribute to the project by including (a) instructions for setting up a development environment, (b) best practices for writing tests, and (c) adding to the documentation itself. Finally, we also recommend formalizing a release process consisting of specific actions that must be taken to produce a new release and including it as a part of the documentation. This makes it easy for any developer to create a new release and makes the process transparent to the users.

The documentation files must be included in version control as part of the main codebase under a separate sub-directory. To ensure that the documentation stays up-to-date, any new functionality proposed for the code *must* include a documentation component that is reviewed for accuracy as well as readability as part of the code review. Specifically for Python, we recommend using the reStructuredText format for documentation along with Sphinx[12] to build the documentation. Sphinx provides many useful functionalities such as automatic rendering of LaTeX mathematical formulae via MathJax, automatic API documentation from Python function and class docstrings, and generating documentation in multiple formats such as HTML, PDF, and ePub. Freely available services like ReadTheDocs[13] can be integrated with GitHub-based development workflows such that the documentation is automatically built and deployed to a public-facing server for specified branches.

Finally, a different but equally important part

---

[9] https://travis-ci.com
[10] https://azure.com/pipelines/
[11] https://opensourcesurvey.org/2017/#insights
[12] https://sphinx-doc.org
[13] readthedocs.org

of the documentation is the project *changelog*. Each release must be tagged in the git repository and be accompanied by a detailed changelog that clearly describes the different types of changes contained in the release: new features, bugfixes, and backwards-incompatible changes, if any. Each change in the log should ideally be linked to the corresponding issue and pull request on GitHub providing the full context and discussion for the change to the interested user.

5.3 Packages & Dependencies

Another important aspect of open-source software is its ease of installation. Using it should not require an end user to figure out how to compile and install complicated dependencies. A better solution is a self-contained package installable with a standard package management tool that can also automatically install any required dependencies. For Python, we can use either source or wheel (binary) packages that are released to the Python Package Index (PyPI) and can be installed using `pip`. An alternative is to build conda packages[14] that can be released either via the default channel[15] or via a community-managed channel[16]. New packages should be built as part of every release and deployed to the appropriate package registry: this can be done either manually or automatically using GitHub actions[17].

Most scientific open-source Python software builds on top of other packages such as `numpy`, `pandas`, `scikit-learn`, `matplotlib`, among others. An important part of building packages is to properly version such dependencies in the package manifest so that the code behaves exactly as expected when installed. The most effective way to achieve this is to *pin* every single dependency to the exact version used during development. However, such a conservative approach is likely to cause conflicts since many open-source packages frequently release minor versions. We recommend leaving most dependencies unpinned except for those where a specific or a minimum version of a dependency is required. This may cause the code to break if an unpinned package releases an incompatible update. To deal with this possibility, we recommend setting up a weekly *scheduled build* in Travis CI that will create a new test environment

– pulling in the latest versions of *all* dependencies – and run the tests in the main branch. A hotfix release can quickly be made if said weekly build starts failing. This approach works best if your test suite has high code coverage.

6 Summary

In this paper, we shared the lessons we have learned as developers and maintainers of open-source software: different groups of users tend to have different needs and to meet these needs without compromising on quality, we must spend extra time and effort on testing, documentation and packaging.

References

Kent Beck. 2003. *Test-Driven Development: By Example*. Addison-Wesley Professional.

Emily M. Bender and Batya Friedman. 2018. Data Statements for Natural Language Processing: Toward Mitigating System Bias and Enabling Better Science. *Transactions of the Association for Computational Linguistics*, 6:587–604.

Carrie J. Cai and Philip J. Guo. 2019. Software Developers Learning Machine Learning: Motivations, Hurdles, and Desires. *Proceedings of IEEE Symposium on Visual Languages and Human-Centric Computing, VL/HCC*, 2019-Octob:25–34.

Wendy W. Chapman, Prakash M. Nadkarni, Lynette Hirschman, Leonard W. D'Avolio, Guergana K. Savova, and Ozlem Uzuner. 2011. Overcoming barriers to NLP for clinical text: The role of shared tasks and the need for additional creative solutions. *Journal of the American Medical Informatics Association*, 18(5):540–543.

Lei Chen, Klaus Zechner, Su-youn Yoon, Keelan Evanini, Xinhao Wang, Anastassia Loukina, Jidong Tao, Lawrence Davis, Chong Min Lee, Min Ma, Robert Mundkowsky, Chi Lu, Chee Wee Leong, and Binod Gyawali. 2018. SpeechRater 5.0. *ETS Research Report Series*.

Alina von Davier. 2016. Fairness Concerns in Computational Psychometrics. Presented at the panel on Fairness and Machine Learning for Educational Practice, Annual Meeting of the National Council on Measurement in Education, Washington DC.

Shelby J. Haberman. 2008. When can subscores have value? *Journal of Educational and Behavioral Statistics*, 33:204–229.

Thomas Kluyver, Benjamin Ragan-Kelley, Fernando Pérez, Brian Granger, Matthias Bussonnier, Jonathan Frederic, Kyle Kelley, Jessica Hamrick, Jason Grout, Sylvain Corlay, Paul Ivanov, Damián

---

[14]`https://conda.io`
[15]`https://anaconda.org`
[16]`https://conda-forge.org`
[17]`https://github.com/features/actions`

Avila, Safia Abdalla, Carol Willing, and Jupyter Development Team. 2016. Jupyter Notebooks — A Publishing Format for Reproducible Computational Workflows. In *Proceedings of the 20th International Conference on Electronic Publishing*. IOS Press.

A. Kwong, J. H. Muzamal, P. Y. Zhang, and G. Lin. 2020. Automated chinese language proficiency scoring by utilizing siamese convolutional neural network and fusion based approach. In *2020 International Conference on Engineering and Emerging Technologies (ICEET)*, pages 1–6.

Anastassia Loukina, Nitin Madnani, Aoife Cahill, Lili Yao, Matthew S Johnson, Brian Riordan, and Daniel F McCaffrey. 2020. Using PRMSE to evaluate automated scoring systems in the presence of label noise. In *Proceedings of the Fifteenth Workshop on Innovative Use of NLP for Building Educational Applications*, pages 18–29, Seattle, WA, USA.

Anastassia Loukina, Nitin Madnani, and Klaus Zechner. 2019. The many dimensions of algorithmic fairness in educational applications. In *Proceedings of the Fourteenth Workshop on Innovative Use of NLP for Building Educational Applications*, pages 1–10, Florence, Italy.

Nitin Madnani and Aoife Cahill. 2018. Automated scoring: Beyond natural language processing. In *Proceedings of the 27th International Conference on Computational Linguistics*, pages 1099–1109, Santa Fe, New Mexico, USA. Association for Computational Linguistics.

Nitin Madnani and Anastassia Loukina. 2016. Rsmtool: collection of tools building and evaluating automated scoring models. *Journal of Open Source Software*, 1(3):33.

Nitin Madnani, Anastassia Loukina, Alina von Davier, Jill Burstein, and Aoife Cahill. 2017. Building better open-source tools to support fairness in automated scoring. In *Proceedings of the First ACL Workshop on Ethics in Natural Language Processing*, pages 41–52, Valencia, Spain. Association for Computational Linguistics.

Wes McKinney. 2010. Data Structures for Statistical Computing in Python. In *Proceedings of the 9th Python in Science Conference*, pages 56 – 61.

Margaret Mitchell, Simone Wu, Andrew Zaldivar, Parker Barnes, Lucy Vasserman, Ben Hutchinson, Elena Spitzer, Inioluwa Deborah Raji, and Timnit Gebru. 2019. Model cards for model reporting. *FAT* 2019 - Proceedings of the 2019 Conference on Fairness, Accountability, and Transparency*, (Figure 2):220–229.

Fabian Pedregosa, Gaël Varoquaux, Alexandre Gramfort, Vincent Michel, Bertrand Thirion, Olivier Grisel, Mathieu Blondel, Peter Prettenhofer, Ron Weiss, Vincent Dubourg, Jake Vanderplas, Alexandre Passos, David Cournapeau, Matthieu Brucher, Matthieu Perrot, and Édouard Duchesnay. 2011. Scikit-learn: Machine learning in Python. *Journal of Machine Learning Research*, 12:2825–2830.

Chaitanya Ramineni and David M. Williamson. 2013. Automated Essay Scoring: Psychometric Guidelines and Practices. *Assessing Writing*, 18(1):25–39.

Andrea Romei and Salvatore Ruggieri. 2013. Discrimination Data Analysis: A Multi-disciplinary Bibliography. In Bart Custers, Toon Calders, Bart Schermer, and Tal Zarsky, editors, *Discrimination and Privacy in the Information Society: Data Mining and Profiling in Large Databases*, pages 109–135. Springer Berlin Heidelberg.

André A. Rupp, Jodi M. Casabianca, Maleika Krüger, Stefan Keller, and Olaf Köller. 2019. Automated essay scoring at scale: A case study in switzerland and germany. *ETS Research Report Series*, 2019(1):1–23.

David M. Williamson, Xiaoming Xi, and F. Jay Breyer. 2012. A Framework for Evaluation and Use of Automated Scoring. *Educational Measurement: Issues and Practice*, 31(1):2–13.

Xiaoming Xi. 2010. How do we go about Investigating Test Fairness? *Language Testing*, 27(2):147–170.

Su-Youn Yoon and Chong Min Lee. 2019. Content modeling for automated oral proficiency scoring system. In *Proceedings of the Fourteenth Workshop on Innovative Use of NLP for Building Educational Applications*, pages 394–401, Florence, Italy. Association for Computational Linguistics.

Klaus Zechner, Derrick Higgins, Xiaoming Xi, and David M. Williamson. 2009. Automatic Scoring of Non-native Spontaneous Speech in Tests of Spoken English. *Speech Communication*, 51(10):883–895.

Michael J. Zieky. 2016. Fairness in Test Design and Development. In Neil J. Dorans and Linda L. Cook, editors, *Fairness in Educational Assessment and Measurement*, pages 9–32. Routledge.

WAFFLE: A Graph for WordNet
Applied to Free-Form Linguistic Exploration

Berk Ekmekci & Blake Howald

Thomson Reuters Special Services, LLC
1410 Spring Hill Road, Suite 125
Mclean, VA 221022
`[berk.ekmekci, blake.howald]@trssllc.com`

Abstract

The WordNet database of English (Fellbaum, 1998) is a key source of semantic information for research and development of natural language processing applications. As the sophistication of these applications increases with the use of large datasets, deep learning, and graph-based methods, so should the use of WordNet. To this end, we introduce WAFFLE: WordNet Applied to FreeForm Linguistic Exploration which makes WordNet available in an open source graph data structure. The WAFFLE graph relies on platform-agnostic formats for robust interrogation and flexibility. Where existing implementations of WordNet offer dictionary-like lookup, single-degree neighborhood operations, and path-based similarity-scoring, the WAFFLE graph makes all nodes (semantic relation sets) and relationships queryable at scale, enabling local and global analysis of all relationships without the need for custom code. We demonstrate WAFFLE's ease of use, visualization capabilities, and scalable efficiency with common queries, operations, and interactions. WAFFLE is available at `github.com/TRSS-NLP/WAFFLE`.

1 Introduction

WordNet (Miller, 1995; Fellbaum, 1998) is a database of English words with associated lexical properties and semantic relations. For example, WordNet includes seven semantically distinct *senses* for the noun "establishment":

[establishment.n.01/constitution.n.02] - *the act of forming or establishing something*

[establishment.n.02/institution.n.01] - *an organization founded and united for a specific purpose*

[establishment.n.03/administration.n.02] - *the persons who make up a body for the purpose of administering something*

[establishment.n.04] - *a public or private structure including buildings and equipment for business or residence*

[establishment.n.05] - *any large corporation*

[establishment.n.06] - *(ecology) the process by which a plant or animal becomes established in a new habitat*

[establishment.n.07] - *the cognitive process of establishing a valid proof*

Each of these senses are organized by individual *synsets* (synonym sets) and labeled for reference with a word.part-of-speech.number structure. Sysnsets include definitions, examples, lemmas, synonyms (e.g. establishment.n.01 is equivalent to constitution.n.02) and are organized into larger hierarchical relationships (Figure 1), which can facilitate the computation of paths between synsets to quantitatively approximate word similarity. For example, there are 2 hops (steps up or down the hierarchy) between establishment.n.02 and .05 compared to 9 hops between .02 and .06 (organized institutions being more like corporations rather than plants or animals establishing a new habitat).

Figure 1 is based on noun hypernym and hyponym relations, but WordNet includes additional parts of speech (verb, adjective, adverb) and associated relations - e.g. *entailment* between verbs, *antonyms* between adjectives, and *derivationally related forms* for all parts-of-speech. WordNet has been used for building dictionary and thesaurus applications as well as a range of natural language processing tasks such as: word sense disambiguation tasks (Patwardhan et al., 2003; Navigli, 2009; Loureiro and Jorge, 2019), document retrieval (Rada et al., 1989; Srihari et al., 2000), information extraction (Stevenson and Greenwood, 2005; Atkinson et al., 2009), and querying (Bulskov et al., 2002; Li et al., 2003) for recommender (Blanco-Fernández et al., 2008) and question-answer (Tapeh

Proceedings of Second Workshop for NLP Open Source Software (NLP-OSS), pages 147–157
Virtual Conference, November 19, 2020. ©2020 Association for Computational Linguistics

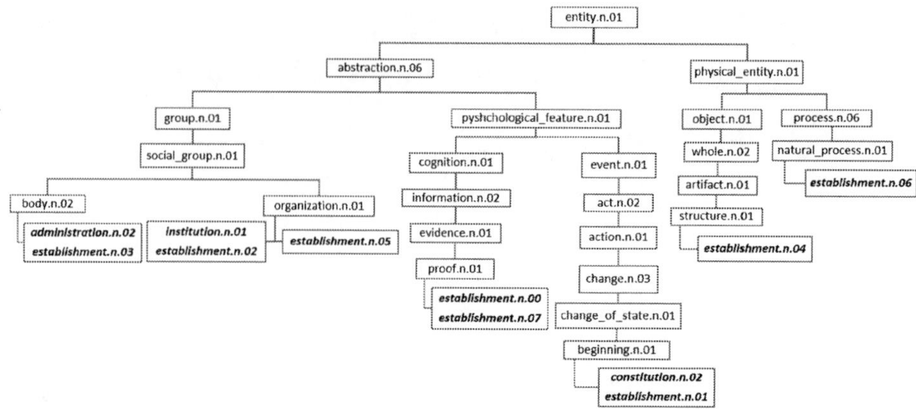

Figure 1: WordNet is-a (noun-based hypernym/hyponyms) hierarchy for *establishment*.

and Rahgozar, 2008) systems.

The current version of WordNet (117,000 synsets in version 3.1 with 27 relation types) is available through an interactive browser, APIs, and stand alone database files which can be customized.[1] However, beyond recreating common functionality, we believe there is an increasing need for the availability of WordNet in an open source graph-based data structure to support large-scale use and research (e.g. for deep learning (Yuan et al., 2016; Diao et al., 2018; Vial et al., 2019; Kobylinski and Wasiluk, 2019), hierarchical embeddings (Bernardy and Maskharashvili, 2019), and graph-based approaches generally (Naskręt et al., 2018; Pinter and Eisenstein, 2018). These use cases leverage not only the content of WordNet, but need to do so with increasing sensitivity to the *structure* of WordNet. This is not only to operate more efficiently, but to open up additional potential avenues of research. To satisfy this need, we present WAFFLE: WordNet Applied to FreeForm Linguistic Exploration as a fully-connected queryable graph representation of WordNet to provide: (1) flexibility in exploring *all* of WordNet's relations across synsets and hierarchies rather than particular part-of-speech-based subgraphs; (2) scalable processing for large datasets; and (3) support for all common operations on WordNet (look-up, similarity measures).

The remainder of this paper is structured as follows: Section 2 introduces the details of WAFFLE's graph structure, computation and descriptive statistics. Section 3 demonstrates common Word-Net operations compared to non-graph structure approaches. Section 4 discusses related methods of WordNet access. Section 5 concludes with WAFFLE's access and licensing details with plans for future versions.

2   WAFFLE Graph Overview

2.1   Data Format

Per its official description, WordNet's database is made available in:

> *... an ASCII format consisting of eight files, two for each syntactic category. Additional files are used by the WordNet search code but are not strictly part of the database.... Each index file is an alphabetized list of all the words found in WordNet in the corresponding part of speech. On each line, following the word, is a list of byte offsets (synset_offset s) in the corresponding data file, one for each synset containing the word.... Pointers are followed and hierarchies traversed by moving from one synset to another via the synset_offset s.*[2]

The two files for each syntactic category refer to a *data* and an *index* file, with the *data* file holding attributes and relationships of each word in Word-Net and *index* containing the mapping of words to synsets present in the *data* file. These relationships and indices are defined as byte offsets, which have the advantage of allowing for APIs working with the WordNet files to quickly traverse the datafile at

---

[1] `http://wordnetweb.princeton.edu/perl/webwn`

[2] `https://wordnet.princeton.edu/frequently-asked-questions`

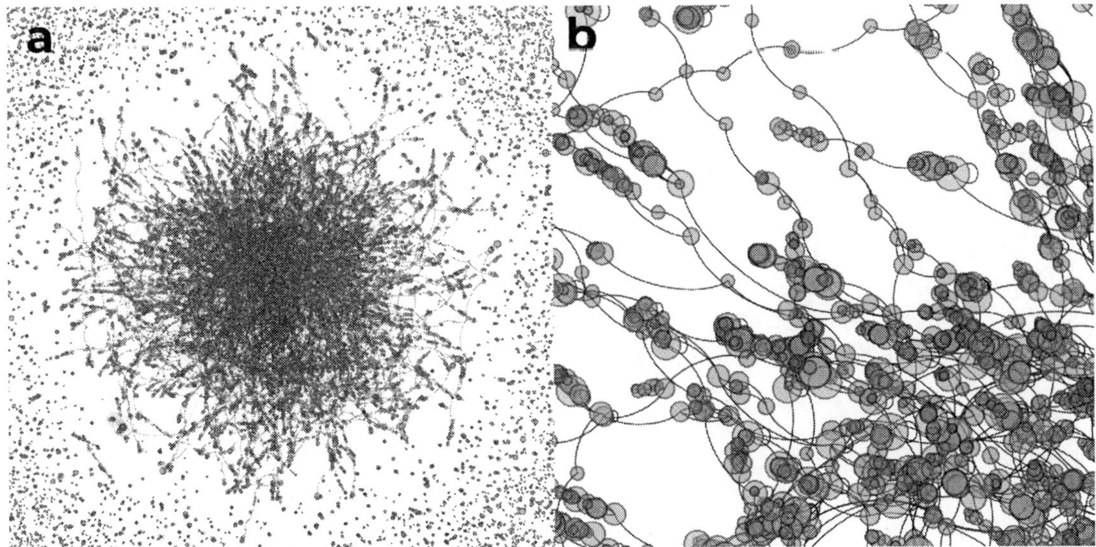

Figure 2: **(a)** The core constellation of all wordsense-wordsense relationships within WordNet, with nodes colored and scaled according to degree (darker and smaller = lower degree; brighter and larger = higher degree). In addition to the central network containing interconnected wordsenses, there exist many disconnected sub-networks that appear when synsets are not rendered. Several of these isolated networks are visible surrounding the main network. **(b)** A detailed view of the northwest corner of the graph in (a), with closely clustered neighborhoods visible as well as long chains of wordsenses that link otherwise disparate regions.

query-time, but come at the cost of being an unintuitive relationship-building and indexing scheme for humans. Further, the number of columns in each row within both *index* and *data* files are variable; for instance, a *data* entry with 3 synset-to-synset relationships will have 8 more columns than an entry with 1 such relationship, as each relationship introduces 4 new fields. This design choice makes the data terse, but increases user effort to parse the structure of and relationships within each row when loading into relational formats, graph databases, and desktop network analysis software.

WAFFLE parses the data within the *data* file and reformats the results into graph representations that trade off representation compactness (previously optimized for quick on-disk or in-memory lookup) for human-legibility and advanced graph analysis when loaded into supported tools (c.f. Section 2.2). The essential form of the transformed data format is that of a node list and edge list, output as .CSV and .JSON files. These files catalog the attributes (e.g. type, part-of-speech, definition, example sentences) and relationships (i.e. source node, type, edge attributes, and target node) of each item in WordNet, respectively. This representation is ready for import in such network analysis tools as Gephi

(Bastian et al., 2009) and Cytoscape.[3] For additional utility, WAFFLE also exports the graph as a single .graphml file, a widely-supported graph interchange format that contains both node and edge information (Brandes et al., 2002).[4] WAFFLE is designed to work with the version 3.3 data provided on GitHub under Apache 2.0 license by the maintainers of the Natural Language Tool Kit ("NLTK") (Bird et al., 2009), but is compatible with any data following the WordNet specification.[5] In the spirit of open source software and compatible with the original Wordnet 3.0 license, we present all original components of WAFFLE on GitHub under an open MIT license.[6]

2.2 Construction Methodology

WAFFLE runs in Python 3 (Van Rossum and Drake, 2009), and combines a custom parser for the WordNet format with auxiliary functions to construct an in-memory graph using the NetworkX library (Hagberg et al., 2008). The resulting graph contains

---

[3]https://cytoscape.org

[4]Specification found at https://graphml.graphdrawing.org/specification.html

[5]https://github.com/nltk/wordnet

[6]https://wordnet.princeton.edu/license-and-commercial-use, and https://opensource.org/licenses/MIT

approximately 288,000 nodes and 392,000 relationships between them, and offers a starting point for the application of any of NetworkX's network-level analysis algorithms, including clustering, centrality, link prediction, graph cutting, similarity, and shortest pathfinding families of operations.[7]

The graph construction begins with an initial parse of the *data* files, loading into memory synset and word attributes from each line sequentially through each part-of-speech's own file. For each line, a dictionary is constructed to hold the synset data with the following structure and key attributes:

- offset: byte offset for lookup of relationships
- type: part of speech type
- words: a list of word dictionaries containing
  - lemma
  - sense: the numerical representation of which use of the lemma the synset describes
- nPointers: number of outbound pointers the synset has
- pointers: a list of pointer dictionaries containing
  - symbol: the WordNet specified symbol representing relationship type (enumerated in Table 1)
  - offset: the target byte offset of the pointer
  - pos: part of speech of the pointer
  - source/target: a special 4-digit hexadecimal designation from WordNet that determines the specificity of the relationship, e.g. from a certain word-sense belonging to this synset to another word-sense, or from the synset to another synset.

This initial traversal and load from the *data* files creates a full representation of WordNet in such a way that synset, word, and lemma relationships can all be individually output and relationships traced to one another without the need for reference to the *index* file. The second pass through involves the building of a node list containing all synset and word information as well as an edge-list containing relationships by name rather than by offset. If, however, the *source/target* field of a pointer designates that the relationship is from a synset to a wordsense, wordsense to synset, or wordsense to wordsense, it is possible that the reference is to a wordsense that is known only by its offset and

not yet its identity (the synset it belongs to may be later in the file). Consequently, the synset-to-wordsense memberships are stored in a separate dictionary and relationships that belong to this category are saved. Once the synset-to-synset relationships are all constructed and the file iteration complete, the remaining relationships are traversed and edges created. This results in a complete, byte-offset-resolved data format. As synsets have no representation other than their conceptual meaning, they are identified by their offsets as primary keys in the WAFFLE graph.

At this stage, the output is in its most flexible form and users looking for maximum versatility should take the .CSV and .JSON node list and edge list outputs as starting points for their work. For users interested in analyzing WordNet within Python, WAFFLE also constructs a NetworkX graph from the in-memory representations of this data, annotating edge labels and weights that are exported into a .graphml format for graph transformations and further manipulation.

2.3 Graph Overview and Summary Statistics

The WAFFLE graph contains 117,478 nodes of type *synset*, 170,479 *wordsense*, and 391,949 edges spanning membership relations and 26 other semantic relationship symbols. Table 1 provides a breakdown of total edges in the network by relationship type, and Figure 2 illustrates a top-level look at the information content of WordNet's relationships. Figure 3 showcases the different presentations of the WordNet data that subgraph extracts and transformations on the base graph structure can provide.

2.4 Graph Transformations

The graph of synset-to-synset, wordsense-to-wordsense, and synset-to-wordsense relationships across the 27 relationships (Table 1) represents the most heterogeneous form of the WordNet graph. While this form is a good starting point for familiarizing with WordNet's structure, it can be useful to condense either multiple edge types together or represent parallel edges as one, import into a database-specific format, or study only wordsense-to-wordsense relationships wherein a common shared synset induces an edge between wordsenses. WAFFLE provides avenues for these transformations, each of which serves as a template for further user-driven customization.

---

[7]https://networkx.github.io/
documentation/stable/reference/
algorithms/index.html

Symbol	Relationship	Count
has_member	Synset Membership	208353
~	Hyponym	89174
@	Hypernym	89174
+	Derivationally Related	74591
&	Similar To	21434
#m	Member Holonym	12288
%m	Member Meronym	12288
%p	Part Meronym	9111
#p	Part Holonym	9111
@i	Instance Hypernym	8587
~i	Instance Hyponym	8587
\	Pertainym to Noun or Derived from Adjective	8054
!	Antonym	7983
-c	Domain Member Topic	6689
;c	Synset Domain Topic	6689
^	Also See	3276
$	Verb Group	1744
-r	Domain Member Region	1498
;r	Synset Domain Region	1498
-u	Domain Member Usage	1368
;u	Synset Domain Usage	1368
=	Attribute	1278
#s	Substance Holonym	797
%s	Substance Meronym	797
*	Entailment	408
>	Cause	221
<	Participle of Verb	73

Table 1: WordNet relations and counts in the WAFFLE graph. Availability of relations is keyed to part of speech (https://wordnet.princeton.edu/documentation/wninput5wn).

2.4.1 Edge Condensation and Weighting

WAFFLE provides an optional step in the graph creation process that normalizes each of the 27 semantic relationships (many are directional inverses of one another – e.g. hypernymy and hyponymy) into a single edge type of connectedness, and stores the count of relationships condensed between any two nodes in the graph as the weight between them. Although this edge condensation certainly results in a reduction of total information content, it presents the advantages of edge normalization and creation of bidirectionally-weighted edges between nodes. This makes the treatment of the graph as homogeneous in centrality and betweenness calculations more immediately accessible.

2.4.2 Graph Database Import

Although NetworkX and Python provide a powerful platform for in-memory graph creation and analysis, potential users of WordNet may be interested in loading and querying WordNet from within a user's graph database. To this end, WAFFLE produces a .graphml output that is ready for import into a graph database, and includes a Cypher query-language script for importing WordNet into Neo4j, a prominent desktop and server-deployable graph database, using its officially-supported APOC (Awesome Procedures On Cypher) plugin.[8] This enables the WAFFLE-produced graph to be readily-queryable by local and remote applications as well as data analysts issuing Cypher. Analyzing Word-Net through the use of a powerful graph query language like Cypher opens the door to direct path-based querying of the data, as illustrated in the Figure 3.

2.4.3 Expanded Graph Flexibility

For the analysis of words in specific senses and their relations to one another, users may only want to consider synsets as stepping stones to and from specific wordsenses, and in so doing analyze their relationships only by proxy. To achieve this, a transformation of the graph through the following Cypher can be conducted:

```
MATCH (w1:Wordsense)-[:has_member]-(s:
    Synset)-[:has_member]->(w2:Wordsense)

WHERE id(w1) > id(w2)
MERGE (w1)-[:shared_synset]-(w2)
```

From this point, the direct wordsense-to-wordsense relationships can be explored and sub-graphs extracted, providing an intuitive perspective towards exploring semantic relations of words and their shared meanings. This approach condenses the total number of synset-membership-based edges in half (each new edge represents two original connections), optimizing the memory footprint and query structure.

Compared to the full synset-inclusive graph, this representation is both visually-accessible and enables wordsense-to-wordsense pathfinding that neither the original graph nor references to the Word-Net *data* and *index* files provide (directly or in a specific API). A count of degrees of separation in this graph of directly-linked words translates simply to how many synsets (or other direct connections) away from one another the two words are. Similarly, by abstracting away the synset-to-synset relationships, users of this particular view do not need to resolve polarity, or semantic directionality, of the many synset-to-synset relationships and can focus on the introduced necessarily-equivalent "shared_synset" relationships. Although

---

[8]The pure Cypher (non-APOC) components of this workflow are applicable as well to any database supporting the Cypher language. See https://www.opencypher.org and https://www.neo4j.com

direct wordsense-to-wordsense relationships encoded in WordNet are retained by this example transformation, users can modify the Cypher or remove these connections before their analyses to ensure homogeneity of edge-types. As a result, node-level (e.g. degree, betweenness centrality) statistics and neighborhood (e.g. community detection) operations can be produced where each edge is directly comparable to all other edges in the network. Both this format of the WordNet graph and the synset-inclusive form are available with the WAFFLE source code (c.f. Section 5).

2.4.4 Subgraph Extraction

Subgraph extraction using WAFFLE enables focused views such as the examples in Figure 3. This process is useful not just for creating publication-ready graphics, but also for targeted exploration of specific regions of the full WordNet. A traditional example of subgraph extraction involves selecting a seed group of nodes and including nodes isometrically from that core. More creative and specialized subgraphs such as those containing all nodes and induced edges within one degree of the shortest spanning path between two wordsenses or synsets can be created as well. This flexibility in navigating and observing the WordNet graph through WAFFLE not as a tree structure but as a non-rooted graph structure offers unique opportunities. These comparisons, as well as a treatment of analogous functionality, are featured in Section 3.

3 Features, Strengths, and Comparisons

While novel in structure, WAFFLE parallels but does not present itself as a replacement to existing representations and forms of access to WordNet. For comparison, we present several canonical operations performed on WordNet through its WAFFLE-processed form and as accessed through NLTK. We break common functionality associated with WordNet into: (1) Information Retrieval; (2) Synset Relationship-finding; (3) Computation of Semantic "Distance"; and (4) Visualization. For each category, we present examples and syntax in both WAFFLE and the NLTK WordNet *wn* library.[9]

3.1 Information Retrieval

Lookup operations treat WordNet as an information repository rather than a structure or tool for

computation, and accordingly, stand to suit common methods of information retrieval just as well as graph-based approaches. Despite their simplicity, these lookups are a very natural place to begin investigation of linguistics using WordNet and offer a direct comparison between NLTK-equivalent standalone *wn* WordNet API and WAFFLE. For ease of reproduction and generalization, several WAFFLE graph examples are provided as Cypher queries.

Synset lookup by lemma in NLTK returns a list of Sysnset objects that correspond to the called lemma, in this case `wn.synsets('establishment')`, notably including synsets that do not have a wordsense corresponding to the lemma queried:

```
Synset('constitution.n.02')
Synset('institution.n.01')
Synset('administration.n.02')
Synset('establishment.n.04')
...
Synset('establishment.n.07')
```

This can be attributed to the way that *wn* identifies these synset lookups, ordering them based on frequency counts from WordNet concordance texts.[10]

By comparison, the equivalent Cypher query:

```
MATCH (w:Wordsense)-[:has_member]-(s:
    Synset) WHERE w.lemma = "
    establishment" RETURN s
```

is more verbose, but precisely describes the relationship between what's being matched (a wordsense with the exact lemma) and what's being returned (a synset with membership relation). Because of the design of the WAFFLE graph, synsets are identified not by a single exemplar usage, but by a unique identifier corresponding to the synset's original byte offset. This trade-off reduces the opportunity for synset misinterpretation, and all wordsenses belonging to a synset can be retrieved through an inversion of the original query:

```
MATCH (s:Synset {id:someID})-[:
    has_member]-(w:Wordsense) RETURN w.
    lemma
```

This operation is done in *wn* by calling the `.lemmas()` function of a Synset object.

This theme of terseness being exchanged for flexibility and explicitness in WAFFLE continues for definition and example lookups on synset objects. These operations are handled by the

---

[9]https://www.nltk.org/_modules/nltk/
corpus/reader/wordnet.html

[10]https://wordnet.princeton.edu/
documentation/wnlwn

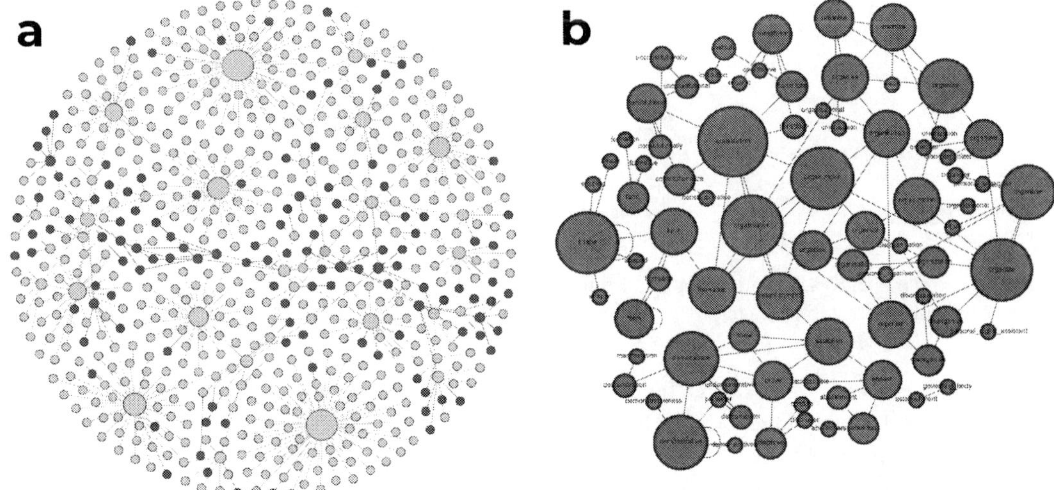

Figure 3: For the lemma *establishment*: (**a**) The uncondensed graph view of any wordsense (turquoise) with the lemma and all connections within 3 degrees of those wordsense nodes. The direct relationships of wordsenses (dark teal) to one another is not very clear, but the overall topology and role of synsets (light blue-grey) in bridging relationships is made clear. (**b**) The condensed wordsense-only graph view of wordsenses and all *shared_synset* and syntactic relationships within 4 degrees of those nodes. The connections between individual wordsenses is much more clear compared to (a), but senses that do not have any direct relationships to another wordsense or shared synsets – in this case one of the three wordsenses – are not included in this transformation. Node size is modulated by degree.

`.definition()` and `.examples()` function calls in *wn*. For WAFFLE, these values are stored as properties (attributes) of the synset object nodes in the graph and closely align to the style of retrieval in *wn*. For example, the Cypher query used to retrieve the definition of any word with its associated numerical synset identifier (n874164 - *demonstrative_0*) is:

```
MATCH (s:Synset {id:someID}) RETURN s.
    definition
```

Considering these are attribute-lookup operations rather than path-traversal operations, no graph pattern matching is required. However, in the event that *all* definitions for synsets containing a certain lemma in their word sense were to be investigated, the associated Cypher query combines two *wn* calls and organizes results into a single query. Returning to our example, in order to look up all definitions for synsets that contain words of the lemma "establishment", the Cypher would be:

```
MATCH (w:Wordsense)-[:member\of]-(s:
    Synset) WHERE w.lemma ="
    establishment" RETURN s.definition
```

As the desired lookup becomes more complex, the value of concisely stating the information retrieval task as a graph look-up begins to quickly outweigh the original advantage in terseness a traditional interface to the data offers.

3.2 Synset Relationship-finding

Relationship-finding is an operation that graphs are configured to perform, and graph-querying languages like Cypher designed to express. As a result, WAFFLE presents a method of working with familiar relationships and introduces the ability to easily specify graph traversals in WordNet that would otherwise have recalled many individually-chained or recursive function calls.

In practice, single-level depth relationship operations in *wn* are straightforward: individual functions belonging to the Synset object will return the result of the immediate neighbor lookup - e.g. Table 2. In the WAFFLE graph, the following query illustrates beginning at a target wordsense and finding synsets related to its parent synset – in this case with the @ (hypernym) relationship.

```
MATCH (w:Wordsense)-[:has_member]-(s1:
    Synset)-[:@]-(s2:Synset) RETURN s2
```

```
MATCH p=(w:Wordsense)-[:has_member]-(s1:
    Synset)-[:@]-(s2:Synset) RETURN p
```

NLTK	*return*
.hypernyms()	[body.n.02]
.hyponyms()	[county_council.n.01, curia.n.01, executive.n.02, government_officials.n.01, management.n.02, judiciary.n.01, top_brass.n.01]
.part_holonyms()	[government.n.01]
.member_meronyms()	[advisory_board.n.01]

Table 2: Example NLTK *wn* relation calls and returns for the Synset object "establishment.n.03".

Any of the relation symbols (c.f. Table 1) can be substituted in the query to replace the hypernym relationship with the semantic relation of interest. It is worth noting that two of the relationships share the \ relationship symbol, which represents either a noun pertainym or derivation from an adjective based on context and results in a total of 26 unique syntactic edge labels within the WAFFLE graph.

3.3 Computation of Semantic "Distance"

NLTK's *wn* provides a number of distance operations to quantify differences between shared synsets (common in wordsense disambiguation and document/query similarity tasks). In general, methods for computing path similarity range from simple (number of hops in a hierarchy) to complex - e.g. Leacock-Chodorow (Leacock and Chodorow, 1998) or Wu-Palmer (Wu and Palmer, 1994) similarities in Table 3.

NLTK	*return*
Lowest Common Hypernym [Subsumer] .lowest_common_hypernyms()	*entity.n.01*
Shortest Path (1/number of hops) .path_similarity()	*0.0833*
Leacock-Chodorow similarity .lch_similarity()	*1.1526*
Wu-Palmer similarity .wup_similarity()	*0.1538*

Table 3: NLTK path similarities for comparing the Synset objects wn.synset("establishment.n.03") and wn.synset("establishment.n.04").

These functionalities are unique to *wn* because of its model of WordNet as a tree structure, where traversals up and down the tree – up to and including the root nodes that bind each conceptual category (e.g. "entity") – provide markers of similarity and distance. In WAFFLE, there is no concept of moving up or down individual hierarchies; instead, these traversals in granularity and specificity represent directional edges in the graph. Distance queries, configurable to report on only one type of edge or multiple edge types, can be used to find path lengths from synsets or wordsense to one another, but these results would be incomparable to the specific calculations underlying each similarity or lowest-common ancestor lookup.

The same superimposition of multiple WordNet hierarchies that makes WAFFLE directly incomparable to existing similarity measures offers a novel approach to similarity and pathfinding in the WordNet data: the identification and exploration of cyclic structures in WordNet is now explicitly defined. Furthermore, WAFFLE's flexibility to be transformed on a graph level is unmatched by *wn*. The transformation in Section 2 is but one example of modifying the base graph structure to create a purpose-built representation.

3.4 Visualization

Building and visualizing graph structures using NetworkX and Matplotlib in *wn* is *possible*.[11] However, the nature and scope of these created graphs is tied to and limited by the funnel of the API design. For *wn*, an example of this limitation is that each graph query must involve recursive calls to the relationships branching out from a word, lemma, or synset of interest. In contrast, fluid and customizable graph visualization is one of the foremost design principles behind the structure and format of WAFFLE.

Graph data structures lend themselves naturally to network visualization, and the provision of multiple data formats in common interchange formats and specific scripts for loading and transformation in Cypher-enabled platforms creates a platform on which all users are invited to explore and expand. Figures 2 and 3 are but introductory examples of the types of visualization that WAFFLE can be used to generate in the study of linguistic relations and the structure of language in general.

4 Related Work

There are many ways of accessing the content WordNet beyond the the database files which allows for a tremendous amount of choice in developing against WordNet.[12] Further, NLTK and comparable packages from WordNet::Similarity (Pedersen et al., 2004) and spaCy, to name a few, provide

---

[11] Bird et al. (2009, 170-171) and `https://www.nltk.org/book/ch14.html`

[12] `https://wordnet.princeton.edu/related-projects`

comprehensive approaches to exploring not only the content, but also the structure of WordNet.[13] However, compared to WAFFLE, these existing offerings facilitate one-off to moderately-scalable investigations; given more to exploratory research and processing rather than use with large data sets, sophisticated applications, or classes of problems that need to leverage the structural elements of WordNet.

Some existing offerings *are* more oriented to graph-based structures. For example, the Global WordNet Association does produce formats (JSON, XML, RDF) that could be easily translated into graph data structures but introduce a number of additional relationships that reflect ongoing research and linkage to multi-lingual WordNets.[14] Similarly, FrameNet (Baker et al., 1998) is graph-based and accessible with NLTK, but provides more semantic and syntactic connections within the context of frame semantics with no direct link to WordNet. ConceptNet (Speer et al., 2017) is graph-based as well with a closer relationship to WordNet with explicit external linking, but is focused on a much broader range of information for natural language understanding, common sense reasoning, crowd sourced knowledge, etc. Future connections to these offerings will be explored, but, as is introduce a number of additional complexities that WAFFLE seeks to avoid.

5 Availability and Future Work

We have presented WAFFLE, an open source graph data structure that relies upon platform-agnostic formats to facilitate robust interrogation and flexibility when using WordNet in research or applications. WAFFLE's software, example load scripts, and the associated figures and graph files are available at `github.com/TRSS-NLP/WAFFLE`.

While we encourage users to capitalize on the advantages afforded by the design and transformations presented in Section 2 to implement the WordNet data in entirely new ways, we envisage several avenues of augmentation: (1) linking WAFFLE to corpora to perform more sophisticated path measures using information content (Jiang and Conrath, 1997; Lin, 1998; Resnik, 1995) and associated word embeddings; (2) connecting additional WordNet information such as morphosemantic links, log-

ical forms and other semantic annotations (existing as "standoff" files, and (3) multi-lingual connections through with Open Multilingual Wordnet and potentially others referenced in Section 4.[15]

Acknowledgments

Thank you to Peter Chang, Ian Coffman, Saul Dorfman, Andrew Follmann, Eleanor Hagerman, and Spencer Torene for early feedback and multiple reviews. Thank you also to three anonymous reviewers from NLP-OSS for suggested improvements and constructive comments which improved the final version of this paper.

References

John Atkinson, Anita Ferreira, and Elvis Aravena. 2009. Discovering implicit intention-level knowledge from natural-language texts. *Knowledge-Based Systems*, 22(7):502–508.

Collin F. Baker, Charles J. Fillmore, and John B. Lowe. 1998. The berkeley framenet project. In *Proceedings of COLING-ACL 98*, pages 86–90.

Mathieu Bastian, Sebastien Heymann, and Mathieu Jacomy. 2009. Gephi: An open source software for exploring and manipulating networks. In *Proceedings of the International AAAI Conference on Weblogs and Social Media*.

Jean-Philippe Bernardy and Aleksandre Maskharashvili. 2019. Two experiments for embedding wordnet hierarchy into vector spaces. In *Proceedings of the Tenth Global Wordnet Conference*, pages 78–84. Oficyna Wydawnicza Politechniki Wrocławskiej.

Steven Bird, Edward Loper, and Ewan Klein. 2009. *Natural Language Processing with Python*. O'Reilly Media Inc.

Yolanda Blanco-Fernández, José J. Pazos-Arias, Alberto Gil-Solla, Manuel Ramos-Cabrer, Martín López-Nores, Jorge García-Duque, Ana Fernández-Vilas, Rebeca P. Díaz-Redondo, and Jesús Bermejo-Muñoz. 2008. A flexible semantic inference methodology to reason about user preferences in knowledge-based recommender systems. *Knowledge-Based Systems*, 21(4):305–320.

Ulrik Brandes, Markus Eiglsperger, Ivan Herman, Michael Himsolt, and Marshall S. Marshall. 2002. Graphml progress report: Structural layer proposal. In *Proceedings of the 9th International Symposium Graph Drawing (GD2001, LNCS 2256*, pages 501–512. Springer-Verlag.

---

[13]`https://spacy.io/universe/project/spacy-wordnet`

[14]`http://globalwordnet.github.io/schemas/`

---

[15]See `https://wordnet.princeton.edu/download` and `https://compling.hss.ntu.edu.sg/omw/`

Henrik Bulskov, Rasmus Knappe, and Troels Andreasen. 2002. On measuring similarity for conceptual querying. In *Proceedings of the 5th International Conference on Flexible Query Answering Systems*, FQAS '02, page 100–111, Berlin, Heidelberg. Springer-Verlag.

Yufeng Diao, Hongfei Lin, Di Wu, Liang Yang, Kan Xu, Zhihao Yang, Jian Wang, Shaowu Zhang, Bo Xu, and Dongyu Zhang. 2018. WECA: A WordNet-encoded collocation-attention network for homographic pun recognition. In *Proceedings of the 2018 Conference on Empirical Methods in Natural Language Processing*, pages 2507–2516, Brussels, Belgium. Association for Computational Linguistics.

Christiane Fellbaum. 1998. *WordNet: An Electronic Lexical Database*. MIT Press, Cambridge, MA.

Aric A. Hagberg, Daniel A. Schult, and Pieter J. Swart. 2008. Exploring network structure, dynamics, and function using networkx. In *Proceedings of the 7th Python in Science Conference (SciPy2008)*.

Jay J. Jiang and David W. Conrath. 1997. Semantic similarity based on corpus statistics and lexical taxonomy. In *Proceedings of the 10th Research on Computational Linguistics International Conference*, pages 19–33, Taipei, Taiwan. The Association for Computational Linguistics and Chinese Language Processing (ACL-CLP).

Łukasz Kobylinski and Michał Wasiluk. 2019. Deep learning in event detection in polish. In *Proceedings of the Tenth Global Wordnet Conference*, pages 216–221. Oficyna Wydawnicza Politechniki Wrocławskiej.

Claudia Leacock and Martin Chodorow. 1998. Combining local context and wordnet similarity for word sense identification. *WordNet: An electronic lexical database*, 49(2):265–283.

Yuhua Li, Zuhair A. Bandar, and David Mclean. 2003. An approach for measuring semantic similarity between words using multiple information sources. *IEEE Transactions on Knowledge and Data Engineering*, 15(4):871–882.

Dekang Lin. 1998. An information-theoretic definition of similarity. In *Proceedings of the 15th International Conference on Machine Learning*, pages 296–304. Morgan Kaufmann.

Daniel Loureiro and Alípio Jorge. 2019. Language modelling makes sense: Propagating representations through WordNet for full-coverage word sense disambiguation. In *Proceedings of the 57th Annual Meeting of the Association for Computational Linguistics*, pages 5682–5691, Florence, Italy. Association for Computational Linguistics.

George A. Miller. 1995. Wordnet: A lexical database for english. *Communications of the ACM*, 38:39–41.

Tomasz Naskręt, Agnieszka Dziob, Maciej Piasecki, Chakaveh Saedi, and António Branco. 2018. Wordnetloom – a multilingual wordnet editing system focused on graph-based presentation. In *Proceedings of the Ninth Global Wordnet Conference*, pages 191–200. Singapore.

Roberto Navigli. 2009. Word sense disambiguation: A survey. *ACM Comput. Surv.*, 41(2).

Siddharth Patwardhan, Satanjeev Banerjee, and Ted Pedersen. 2003. Using measures of semantic relatedness for word sense disambiguation. In *Proceedings of the 4th International Conference on Computational Linguistics and Intelligent Text Processing*, CICLing'03, page 241–257, Berlin, Heidelberg. Springer-Verlag.

Ted Pedersen, Siddharth Patwardhan, and Jason Michelizzi. 2004. Wordnet::similarity - measuring the relatedness of concepts. In *Proceedings of the 3rd International Conference on Intelligent Text Processing and Computational Linguistics*, pages 136–145.

Yuval Pinter and Jacob Eisenstein. 2018. Predicting semantic relations using global graph properties. In *Proceedings of the 2018 Conference on Empirical Methods in Natural Language Processing*, pages 1741–1751, Brussels, Belgium. Association for Computational Linguistics.

Roy Rada, Hafedh Mili, Ellen Bicknell, and Maria Blettner. 1989. Development and application of a metric on semantic nets. *IEEE Transactions on Systems, Man, and Cybernetics*, 19(1):17–30.

Philip Resnik. 1995. Using information content to evaluate semantic similarity in a taxonomy. In *Proceedings of the 14th International Joint Conference on Artificial Intelligence - Volume 1*, IJCAI'95, page 448–453, San Francisco, CA, USA. Morgan Kaufmann Publishers Inc.

Robyn Speer, Joshua Chin, and Catherine Havasi. 2017. Conceptnet 5.5: An open multilingual graph of general knowledge. In *Proceedings of the 31st Association for the Advancement of Artificial Intelligence Conference (AAAI 31)*, pages 4444–4451. AAAI.

Rohini K. Srihari, Zhongfei Zhang, and Aibing Rao. 2000. Intelligent indexing and semantic retrieval of multimodal documents. *Inf. Retr.*, 2(2–3):245–275.

Mark Stevenson and Mark A. Greenwood. 2005. A semantic approach to ie pattern induction. In *Proceedings of the 43rd Annual Meeting on Association for Computational Linguistics*, ACL '05, page 379–386, USA. Association for Computational Linguistics.

Ali Ghobadi Tapeh and Maseud Rahgozar. 2008. A knowledge-based question answering system for b2c ecommerce. In *Proceedings of Fifth International Conference on Information Technology: New Generations (ITNG 2008)*, pages 321–326.

Guido Van Rossum and Fred L. Drake. 2009. *Python 3 Reference Manual*. CreateSpace, Scotts Valley, CA.

Loïc Vial, Benjamin Lecouteux, and Didier Schwab. 2019. Sense vocabulary compression through the semantic knowledge of wordnet for neural word sense disambiguation. In *Proceedings of the Tenth Global Wordnet Conference*, pages 108–117. Oficyna Wydawnicza Politechniki Wrocławskiej.

Zhibiao Wu and Martha Palmer. 1994. Verbs semantics and lexical selection. In *Proceedings of the 32nd Annual Meeting on Association for Computational Linguistics*, ACL '94, page 133–138, USA. Association for Computational Linguistics.

Dayu Yuan, Julian Richardson, Ryan Doherty, Colin Evans, and Eric Altendorf. 2016. Semi-supervised word sense disambiguation with neural models. In *Proceedings of COLING 2016, the 26th International Conference on Computational Linguistics: Technical Papers*, pages 1374–1385, Osaka, Japan. The COLING 2016 Organizing Committee.

Association for Computational Linguistics
209 N. Eighth Street
Stroudsburg, Pennsylvania 18360

ISBN 978-1-7138-2000-0